THE ANATOMY OF LIVERPOOL

THE ANATOMY OF LIVERPOOL

A History in Ten Matches

JONATHAN WILSON

WITH SCOTT MURRAY

First published in Great Britain in 2013
by Orion

1 3 5 7 9 10 8 6 4 2

A CIP catalogue record for this book is available
from the British Library.

ISBN 978 1 4091 4441 0

Typeset by Input Data Services Ltd, Bridgwater, Somerset

Printed and bound by CPI Group (UK) Ltd, Croydon, CR0 4YY

The Orion Publishing Group Ltd
Orion House
5 Upper Saint Martin's Lane
London, WC2H 9EA

The Orion Publishing Group's policy is to use papers
that are natural, renewable and recyclable products and made
from wood grown in sustainable forests. The logging and
manufacturing processes are expected to conform to the
environmental regulations of the country of origin.

www.orionbooks.co.uk

CONTENTS

ACKNOWLEDGEMENTS

A book is never just the work of the people whose names are on the cover: we both owe a huge debt of gratitude to innumerable people who gave their time and wisdom to the project.

For their knowledge and help with logistics and information, thanks to Cris Freddi, Richard Jolly, Sid Lowe, Rob Mason, Vladimir Novak and Rob Smyth.

Thanks to our agents, David Luxton and Nicola Barr, and our editor Ian Preece, as well as everybody at Orion.

Thanks to Wendy Mitchell and Margaret Murray for, well, lots, and to Kat Petersen for enormous moral support and bashing the (very) rough edges of the text into shape.

INTRODUCTION

When I sat down in the Atatürk Stadium, I was still out of breath, sweat soaking my shirt. It was about seven hours since I'd walked out of Istanbul airport and   after the experience of Celtic's Uefa Cup final in Seville two years earlier, when I'd queued for about two and a half hours for a taxi (I'd very nearly harangued a tall grey-haired man who'd jumped the queue, before, thankfully, he half-turned and I realised it was Billy McNeill) – with a sense of relief seen a long line of waiting cars. I'd even toyed with the idea of going into town and dropping my bag at the hotel before, fortunately, deciding to play it safe. With about five hours to go till kick-off, I was probably about a mile from the stadium but then we were directed into the mountains and that ludicrous loop of road that would bring me to the right side of the ground. The traffic, as everybody knows, was appalling. Eventually, about a mile and half out, I got out and ran, an overnight bag hooked over one shoulder, my laptop bag swinging from the other. There was, at least, by that time no queue in the accreditation centre. Less than a minute after easing behind a desk in the press box, the game kicked off. And less than a minute after that, Paolo Maldini put AC Milan ahead.

The adrenalin still flowing, I hammered out a paean to the greatest left-back of my lifetime, talking about a fitting end to his career (little imagining he would keep playing for a further four years, until he was forty). As Hernán Crespo added two more before half-time, my report was suddenly as good as written. After all the hassle getting there, it seemed ridiculous that I should have the whole second half to fiddle around with the final 150 words.

And then Steven Gerrard scored. Of course, under normal circumstances, I wouldn't have been thinking anything other than adding a sentence along the lines of, 'Gerrard pulled one back, but the damage had already been done ...' But those weren't normal circumstances. There was something very strange about that moment. I turned to the *Standard's* Ian Chadband, who was sitting next to me, and one of us – I don't remember which, but the other was thinking it – said, 'They're going to win this.' The six minutes that followed were simultaneously incredible and weirdly predictable. I can't really explain the sensation but I'd had something similar at the Olympiakos game, when I'd pushed away my laptop to watch the last ten minutes without distraction, partly to enjoy it (even if that meant a rush to meet my deadline) but partly because there was such a powerful sense of a twist yet to come.

I'd seen the highlights, of course, but it was only in writing this book that I watched the whole match again from start to finish. The reports the next day – and mine in the *Financial Times* was no exception – focused on the miracle, the sheer implausibility of the whole thing, on the comeback and on the tactical change that had made it possible. What I'd forgotten was that Liverpool weren't actually that bad in the first half, that Andriy Shevchenko had a goal ruled out for a questionable offside and that Sami Hyypiä probably should have been sent off for a professional foul with the score at 3–0. This, inevitably, is the nature of memory: we remember the headline but not the detail; we compress and simplify – as indeed we must if we are not to turn into Funes the Memorious, the Borges character with perfect recall for whom the recollection of a day takes twenty-four hours.

A favourite ploy of Sir Alex Ferguson when he felt journalists were getting uppity was to remind them that he still had the first editions from 27 May 1999, the morning after

Manchester United completed the Treble by winning the Champions League. In their running copy, journalists noted that Bayern Munich were much the better side, wondered why United had yet again failed to deliver in Europe and explained that the decision to move David Beckham into the middle to cover for the suspended Roy Keane and Paul Scholes had been a disastrous failure. Only in the panicky seconds that followed those two match-turning goals in injury-time did they tack on a top and a tail hurriedly describing how, despite all that, United had somehow, once again, snatched an implausible victory.

By the time of the rewrites that make up the later editions, the tone had changed to glory in United's success – but it had been the first editions that had more accurately reflected what had happened in the match, before knowledge of the outcome had coloured the perception. 'You can't validate the process through the results,' as the Spanish coach Juanma Lillo told Sid Lowe in Issue One of *The Blizzard*. 'Human beings tend to venerate what finished well, not what was done well. We attack what ended up badly, not what was done badly … Bayern Munich are a great team in the ninetieth minute when they are winning the Champions League and in the ninety-second minute they're rubbish. How can that be? … The thing is, *después del visto todo el mundo es listo*: everyone's a genius after the event. I call them prophets of the past. And yet they are wrong even to evaluate the process in the light solely of how it came out in the end.'

What is also lost in the search for an overall explicatory narrative is the nuance, the ebbs and flows a game takes on its way to an eventual result on which almost all interpretation ends up being based. A tactical tweak can change a game's percentages, a moment of brilliance can yank it one way or the other but, particularly in an even game, the outcome rests to a large degree on a side's ability to ride out its rocky patches, or to take advantage when it is in control. One moment can shape a game, and one game can shape a tournament, and one tournament can shape a career. Football is not always fair.

If we are really to understand football's past and draw meaningful lessons from it, then there is need to hack through the myths and personal recollections and go back to the sources, the games themselves, and to subject them to forensic examination. This book provides close readings of ten key games in the history of Liverpool, from a crucial defeat at the end of the 1898–99 season to that final in Istanbul in 2005. For the first two, no video footage is available and so the readings of the games themselves are taken from old match reports, which in those days tended to be relayed as the match was going on and so are less prone to be influenced by knowledge of the result. For the other eight, we've been through the DVD again and again, looking for patterns, trying to carve through the thickets of a sport that continues to confound easy analysis to find the pathways that explain the game. In Richard Ford's novel *The Sportswriter*, the main character, Frank Bascombe, whiles away the sleepless hours spent in featureless motels by watching old basketball matches on television. 'Re-runs,' he says, 'are where you learn a game inside and out. They're far superior to the actual game in the actual place where it is played, where things are usually pretty boring and you usually forget altogether about what you're there for and find yourself getting interested in other things.' Up to a point he's right, although for football writers it's usually less a case of getting bored than of having to write the match report, which means that inevitably you prioritise what happens early in the game when you have time to think and aren't just hammering away at the keyboard trying to bash out the requisite number of words – any words – by the deadline.

There must also be, though, a sense of context. Each game is also part of a sequence, whether good or bad, and it will always be influenced by personnel and the prevailing ideology. Circumstances, equally, play their part, whether sporting or to do with the wider world. The ten games discussed here have been selected not because they are necessarily the best games

Liverpool have been involved in, or even the most important in terms of happening in the latter stages of competitions, but because they highlight wider trends in Liverpool's history, or because they lie on the faultlines of history, marking the end of one era or the beginning of the next.

Some will disagree with the selection, which is only natural, and, while we hope the chapters themselves illuminate why those particular ten were chosen, there is a need to explain one omission. The most significant game in Liverpool's history was probably one that was abandoned after six minutes: the FA Cup semi-final against Nottingham Forest on 15 April 1989, the Hillsborough disaster. We left it out, frankly, because it's too big for a book of this nature. Of course we've referred to the impact, and to the consequences for the club through the 1990s, but a full discussion of that day, of the causes and the attempt by the authorities to shift the blame simply wouldn't be possible in a single chapter. There have already been many fine books about the tragedy, perhaps most notably *The Day of the Hillsborough Disaster* by Rogan Taylor, Andrew Ward and Tim Newburn, and *Hillsborough: The Truth* by Phil Scraton. As more documents are released and the cover-up is unravelled, there will almost certainly be more. But that sort of investigation requires a full volume. This is a book about specifics; to have skimped on detail in examining an event of that significance would have been wrong.

And besides, this is a book that tries to be about football as it was played on the field. It tries to re-evaluate and reassess, to go beyond the white noise of banal player quotes and instant judgements to discover why what happened happened. Of course, external events impinge, for at a certain level everything is connected, but it is, as far as possible, a football history.

JMW, London,
July 2013

CHAPTER I

Football League Division One, Villa Park, Birmingham, 29 April 1899

Aston Villa   5–0   **Liverpool**

Devey 4, 18
Crabtree 35
Garraty 34
Wheldon 44

Billy George	Bill Perkins
Howard Spencer	Archie Goldie
Albert Evans	Billy Dunlop
Tommy Bowman	Raby Howell
Jimmy Cowan	Alex Raisbeck
Jimmy Crabtree	Charlie Wilson
Charlie Athersmith	Jack Cox
Jack Devey	John Walker
Billy Garraty	George Allan
Fred Wheldon	Hugh Morgan
Steve Smith	Tom Robertson
Committee	Tom Watson

Ref: A Scragg
Bkd:
Att: 41,357

'**EARLY IN THE DAY THE** leading thoroughfares of the hardware city presented a very animated appearance, the streets being thronged with visitors from Liverpool, who could be easily singled out by reason of the red favours which they sported in their hats and buttonholes,' read the report in *Sporting Life*. 'As early as one o'clock, two and a half hours before the time fixed for the kick-off, enthusiasts began to gather at the Villa enclosure, and although the prices had been raised there was a steady flow of intending spectators. The weather was what is usually experienced in April, sunshine and shower by turn, but the rain did not seem to affect the attendance.'

Liverpool fans had descended on Villa Park in huge numbers, anticipating their first league title. Fewer than seven years had passed since the club's foundation but they went into the final game of the 1898–99 season a win away from the title – and perhaps feeling aggrieved they didn't need just a draw. Aston Villa had enjoyed suspiciously large victories over Notts County (6–1) and West Bromwich Albion (7–1) on the run-in to give them a goal average 0.02 better than Liverpool's. A travelling support of over 6,000 fans took specially discounted excursion trains to Birmingham for the game. 'They were not all afraid of showing the bent of their sympathy,' read the report in the *Manchester Evening News*, 'and nearly all of them wore flaring red ties.'

Villa were one of the two great teams of the age, having won three championships since the foundation of the Football League in 1888, a record equalled only by Sunderland. For their fans, too, this was a special occasion, a chance to become the most successful side in league history. A total of 41,357 squeezed in – generating league record receipts of £1,558.1s.6d. 'The ground was in excellent condition, but there was a strong breeze blowing straight down the field, which threatened to interfere with the game,' reported the *Sporting Life*. 'The Villa won the toss, and Liverpool opened the game with the gusty wind in their faces.' The running reports, dictated as the action unfolded, almost invariably included details of the weather and almost invariably they were irrelevant. On this occasion, though, the wind proved very significant indeed.

Liverpool started brightly, unsurprisingly for a team that had lost only once on the road since December, and, according to the *Sports Argus*, 'in the early play [Jimmy] Crabtree was twice cheered for especially good defensive work' with the away side doing much pressing and Jack Cox embarking on a speedy run before being ushered off the ball by Evans. But any early momentum was quickly lost. Charlie Athersmith misjudged a one-on-one with Bill Perkins, passing up the chance to score by blasting over the bar. Steve Smith broke through and laid off to Billy Garraty, only for Billy Dunlop to clear. And then, on three minutes, Smith picked up the ball from Fred Wheldon down the left – there were suspicions of offside – before dropping a shoulder and beating the right-back Archie Goldie. With space and time, he looped a cross into the area for the captain Jack Devey to plant a header past Perkins. Villa Park crackled in glee. The cheering was, said the report in *Sporting Life*, 'simply deafening'. It was a bad start for Liverpool and it would soon get much, much worse.

Liverpool had been formed in 1892 as the result of bitter boardroom shenanigans at Everton, the original tenants of Anfield. Ironically, given one of the reasons for Liverpool's fall from the summit of English football a century later was the club's reluctance fully to embrace the realities of a new commercial climate, their very existence was a result of one man doing exactly that a century earlier. The Everton president John

Houlding became embroiled in a rent row with his own club – he was also effectively their Anfield landlord – and began ratcheting up the fee as the team, who won their first title in 1891, enjoyed early success. A brewer by trade, he also demanded that Everton changed for their matches at his Sandon Hotel – giving his licensed premises a higher profile but leaving the players to make their way in their kit through the crowds to get to their own game – and that he should retain sole rights to sell alcohol within the ground. Truly he was a man ahead of his time.

Houlding attempted to seize complete control of Everton by registering the name Everton Football Club and Athletic Grounds Company, Limited with Companies House on 26 January 1892, but he was effectively usurped when the rest of the Everton board opted to leave Anfield and buy a new ground on Mere Green, Goodison Road. The Football League rejected Houlding's attempt to retain the club moniker, siding with the Goodison-bound splinter, and so he was left with an empty ground and a worthless sheet of paper. The solution for the brewer was simple: change the name of Everton Football Club and Athletic Grounds Company, Limited to Liverpool Football Club and Athletic Grounds Company, Limited, and form a club of his own to play at Anfield, something he did on 3 June 1892 (which is therefore officially considered the club's birthday, a view that does rather ignore the inconvenient truth that, by then, this particular concern was over five months old and had initially been named Everton).

Liverpool immediately became the victims of their own hubris. Desperate to stage money-spinning Merseyside derbies with Everton, they applied for a place in the Football League, but pitched for the top division only, scoring out the portion of the application in which clubs were asked if they were prepared to be put forward for election to the new second tier. The league blackballed Liverpool, who were forced to start life in the Lancashire League.

The creation of a new team was a more successful enterprise.

Houlding detailed his friend John McKenna – who had met the businessman in his role as vaccinations officer for the poor workers of the city – with the task of finding enough players worthy of Liverpool's blue-and-white-halved shirts. McKenna went, as anyone with an interest in progressive football did in those days, to Scotland, where players were as a general rule more skilful than in England, having avoided the public-school system south of the border which encouraged a more brutal kick-and-rush approach. In a mere three months, with cash raised from an impromptu share issue, McKenna built an impressive squad which was almost wholly Scottish. Of the nineteen players who would go on to represent Liverpool in the club's first campaign, in the Lancashire League and FA Cup, fifteen were Scots, while the four Englishmen mustered just six appearances between them.

Deliciously for Houlding, two of Liverpool's three ever-presents that season had been enticed away from Everton: the free-scoring winger Tom Wyllie and the dependable defender Duncan McLean. The other ever-present was McLean's partner at the back, the captain Andrew Hannah – another alumnus of Everton, albeit one who had played for Renton in between. In the midfield, Joe McQue was a star signing from Celtic, while up front the twenty-two-year-old John Miller arrived fresh from winning the first two Scottish League titles with Dumbarton.

Liverpool's first match, played two days before the big Lancashire League kick off, on Thursday September 1, was a friendly at Anfield against Rotherham Town, the reigning Midland League champions. Hannah won the toss and opted to defend the goal at the Walton Breck Road end of the ground. It is a tradition that is still upheld, Liverpool always keen to play towards what is now the Kop in the second half. With a ceremonial flourish, Houlding kicked off for Rotherham, and it soon became apparent that the fifty-nine-year-old brewer might as well have stayed on the pitch to give the South Yorkshire side a hand, because Rotherham were skittled 7–1, five of

Liverpool's goals coming in the first half. Liverpool's first goal was scored by Malcolm McVean, bought from Third Lanark, the strike further notable because it whistled past the famous Arthur Wharton, English football's first black superstar.

When competitive action started forty-eight hours later, Liverpool's start was hardly less emphatic as they hammered Higher Walton in front of a crowd of 300 paying customers. The day had started in high farce for Higher Walton, who arrived forty-five minutes late for kick-off having gone to Goodison Park by mistake, and it didn't get much better. Liverpool won 8–0, the opening goal coming on fifteen minutes as the winger John Smith – bought from Sunderland, who long had Scottish preferences of their own – rounded off a quick break with a daisycutter into the bottom corner. For the second game running, Liverpool went in at the break 5–0 up before completing a huge win, although they were reminded of their overall standing in the game two days later, losing 5–0 in a friendly against Ironopolis, the Middlesbrough-based behemoths of the Northern League. But the Lancashire League wasn't large enough to contain Liverpool, who won the title on goal average over Blackpool (the only team to have their number, winning both meetings, becoming the first team to beat Liverpool both in a competitive fixture – 3–0 in Blackpool – and at Anfield, where they later won 2–0). Liverpool had deservedly topped the table playing football comparable, the local newspaper the *Mercury* argued, to 'the best days of Preston North End', although they were nevertheless required to wait anxiously for a week before Blackpool contrived to lose their last game at mid-table Southport Central, a precursor of the manner in which Liverpool would be handed the 1947 league title.

But arguably the most memorable match of Liverpool's first season came in the final of the Liverpool Senior Cup, a 1–0 victory in the first Merseyside derby against Everton. It was a tetchy affair, McQue and the future manager Matt McQueen putting themselves about in a robust manner, Wyllie scoring another of his trademark low shots. Everton claimed a late penalty, arguing that the ball had been, in the words of the *Mercury*, 'fisted deliberately by one of the backs', but the referee did not agree and the cup went to Liverpool. Albeit in name only: Everton argued so vociferously after the final whistle over the 'incompetence' of the ref that the trophy was not awarded until the week after, by which time the local association had thrown out the complaint they had lodged. Liverpool had finished their first season with two titles. The momentum was with them, although the cups themselves soon were not, the pair being stolen from the shop where they were being displayed, the club forced to meet a £130 bill to replace them.

McKenna had shown considerable skill in putting together Liverpool's first side – the Team of the Macs, as they would be remembered – though arguably his greater talents lay in administration. He would eventually serve Liverpool as chairman, and was later president of the Football League for the best part of two decades; the first signs of his administrative skills came during the club's first close season, when he spotted an advertisement from the League asking for new applicants and sent a hopeful telegram off in the name of the club secretary and his fellow team-manager W. E. Barclay, stating Liverpool's case. Barclay only found out about it when the League replied and the board were initially annoyed at McKenna's impertinence, arguing that the club would be better served by consolidating their status in the Lancashire League and taking it from there. But McKenna was adamant and convinced the board to back him with a passionate speech before persuading the heads of the Football League that Liverpool should be one of two clubs admitted entry from a pool of hopefuls also containing Arsenal, Ironopolis, Doncaster Rovers and Loughborough.

Liverpool were in, alongside Arsenal and, as a result of Accrington's demise, Ironopolis. The Middlesbrough-based club had won the Northern League four times in a row, but McKenna and Barclay's side had grown up since the Teessiders had dished out that football lesson in Liverpool's third-ever fixture, and were further strengthened by signing the striker Jimmy Stott from Ironopolis's crosstown rivals Middlesbrough: he would score fourteen goals in seventeen games. Ironopolis meanwhile had stood still. The two faced each other in both teams' first Football League fixture at Ironopolis's Paradise Field, Liverpool winning 2–0, Malcolm McVean scoring the club's first league goal. Liverpool won three of their next four, drawing the other, before the two sides faced again at Anfield. Liverpool won 6–0, Stott scoring a hat-trick. Ironopolis resigned from the Football League at the end of the season, an illustration that momentum from the regional leagues was no guarantee of success on the national stage.

Liverpool, by contrast, stormed it. They went on to score five against Arsenal, Newcastle United, Crewe and Rotherham, embellishing their side with the winger Harry Bradshaw, the club's first local legend and finishing the campaign undefeated, top of the league, having won all fourteen of their home matches. It remains Liverpool's only unbeaten league campaign, although it nearly went awry in the third-last match, McQueen saving a draw at Burslem Port Vale with a fierce free-kick with two minutes left. They then required two goals in the last eight minutes at Anfield in the next match against the same opposition to turn a deficit into a scraped win. The equaliser at Anfield had come after two minutes of what was effectively a scrum on the goal-line, something that was just about legal back then, the ball eventually bundled in by Hannah, a captain's goal if ever there was one.

The club's first season in the top flight was equally messy, only just stopping short of farce. Momentum had carried Liverpool to that point; this was the year when they discovered how difficult life can be without it. According to most sources, the local hero Bradshaw had the honour of scoring their first top-flight goal, after twenty-five minutes of the season opener at Blackburn Rovers, although the *Liverpool Mercury* awarded it to John McCartney. 'The Anfield brigade rushed the leather into the net, McCartney deserving a full share of the honour in having given the final touch,' was the paper's take. But Rovers forced a draw late on. In the second match, Liverpool had what looked like a late winner chalked off at Burnley and were forced to settle for a 3–3 draw. It was hardly a disastrous start to the season, but these felt like body blows to a team competing at the highest level for the first time, and back-to-back defeats at Anfield by Aston Villa and Bolton Wanderers sapped confidence.

The little that remained was then almost totally obliterated by West Bromwich Albion, who battered Liverpool 5–0 at their Stoney Lane ground. The outside-right Patrick Gordon – who had been released by Everton and picked up on the cheap by Liverpool – limped off before the first goal was scored, but few thought the subsequent heavy defeat was a result of playing a man light. 'It was painfully evident in the last two matches that there are some of the team who do not take that care of themselves they should do,' began a report in the *Liverpool Mercury* that soon descended into rant. 'They seem to think that if they pay attention to the usual order of training once or twice a day the remaining portion of the time is to be spent as they think fit. This is altogether a mistaken notion, and is one some of the players will do well to dispel at once. By now they should have found out the truth of the old adage "it's the pace that kills," and the sustained speed at which first league games are carried out is only to be obtained by the most assiduous training, and, above all, careful and strict living. Where the team last year used to shine, in finishing so strongly, now is the weakest point of their play, and it behoves the whole team to at once bestir themselves and mend this fault, or else they will assuredly kill the goose that lays the golden eggs.'

Greater humiliation was soon to follow, as Liverpool travelled to Goodison Park for the first time, to face Everton in the league's first Merseyside derby. While Liverpool had failed to win any of their opening eight matches, Everton had won all seven of theirs and an eighth seemed inevitable from the moment Tom McInnes headed an opener on ten minutes. Liverpool never threatened and in the second half Alex Latta and Jack Bell wrapped up a comprehensive 3–0 win. Football being football, Everton lost their next fixture while Liverpool won theirs, 2–0 against Stoke. But that first top-flight win changed little. While Everton finished the season second, behind a Sunderland side managed by Tom Watson, Liverpool ended up rock bottom. Their form at Anfield was poor, but by no means the worst in the division. Away from home, though, they won only one match, scoring thirteen goals in fifteen games. Fitness and application had been an issue, but the main problem was their rickety defence, such a strong point in the lower leagues: they conceded seventy goals in total, over two a match.

Although Liverpool had gone into the campaign with hope – Houlding had told the squad that when they won the title he would be able to 'die content' – it was surely unrealistic to expect anything other than what eventually occurred. No club in the history of English football had competed in the top division when as young as Liverpool. This was just the third season of their existence. Compare that to the clubs who had made up the inaugural Football League: Derby County were only five years old at the time, but the champions Preston North End had been going for a quarter of a century when they embarked on the campaign. The clubs to win subsequent titles – Aston Villa, Everton and Sunderland – had all been founded in the 1870s. Sheffield United matched Derby's record in 1892, starting out in the First Division in their fifth season, but Liverpool were breaking new ground. The result was instant relegation.

Liverpool regrouped quickly. They shored up the defence with three more Scots: Archie Goldie, Tom Wilkie and the left-back Billy Dunlop, who would enjoy a fifteen-year career at the club, making booming clearances a trademark. If Dunlop was an atypical agricultural Scot, another signing, the twenty-year-old George Allan from Leith Athletic, was more orthodox in his excellence. Liverpool rattled in 106 goals as they bounced back up as Second Division champions again – a club-record 10–1 win over the perpetually hapless Rotherham Town and a 7–1 victory against Manchester United's precursors Newton Heath the highlights – and Allan scored twenty-six of them in twenty-four matches. Liverpool were back in the top flight. Older, wiser, and not about to make the same mistake twice.

It was all change at the start of the 1896–97 season. Liverpool were about to take their second tilt at life in the First Division, and to prove they were maturing into their identity, they ditched the blue-and-white-halved shirts that had been left at Anfield five years earlier by Everton and adopted new colours of their own. 'Liverpool's new dress of red shirts and white knickers is striking, and a contrast to Everton's blue shirts and white knickers,' ran the story in *Cricket and Football Field*.

Equally epochal was the hiring of Liverpool's first full-time manager or, to use the parlance of the day, secretary. Up to that point McKenna and his sidekick Barclay had shared the role of running the team and signing new players, but both decided to retreat into the shadows to oversee the nuts-and-bolts operation of the club and leave the football side to one man. McKenna, with assistance from Houlding, aimed high. They headhunted the first truly great manager in English football history.

Tom Watson had been twenty-nine when he became manager of Sunderland in 1889. He quickly built a side in the image of the passing game being played north of the border. Sunderland's proximity to Scotland meant he could easily plunder the hottest talent of the day: the forwards Jimmy Millar and Johnny Campbell, the midfield enforcer Hughie Wilson, the defender John Auld and the eccentric goalkeeper Ned Doig, who sported a cap secured with a chin strap to hide his thinning thatch and would later follow Watson to Anfield.

But Sunderland's geographical location also had its downside. They applied to join the nascent Football League, but were denied entry as the other teams, centred around Lancashire and the Midlands, didn't fancy the long journey north. They were certainly good enough to compete at national level: during the first Football League season, Sunderland beat the champions elect Preston North End in a friendly. That Preston side, lest it be forgotten, went down in history as the Invincibles, passing unbeaten through the league campaign. Watson's Sunderland trounced them 4–1.

His side also hammered Aston Villa, the club of the league's founder William McGregor, by the humiliating scoreline of 7–2. McGregor was stunned but to his credit did not forget his manners, cooing that Watson's side had 'talented men in every position', a quote which was soon twisted into 'they are the Team of All the Talents'. The name stuck.

Sunderland were granted league status in 1890, the first new team to be admitted, and they quickly established themselves. Watson's team won three titles in four seasons, smashing records en route: their first title saw them win all thirteen of their home matches, a campaign which also featured a thirteen-game winning run. Their second title season saw Sunderland become the first side in league history to score 100 goals; to put that feat into context, second-placed Preston managed forty-three fewer. Sunderland also reached the FA Cup semi-final twice during Watson's seven-year reign.

But money talks in football, and that is not a purely modern phenomenon. Watson asked his board for more cash, but was refused. Houlding and McKenna caught wind of the impasse and offered Watson an unprecedented yearly salary of £300 to bring his nous to Anfield. He accepted immediately, becoming the highest-paid 'secretary' in the country. Olympian, writing in the new society magazine *Sketch*, was certain that Liverpool had made an extremely shrewd signing. 'A very startling piece of news is the transference of Mr T Watson from the Sunderland to the Liverpool Club,' he wrote. 'Superficial followers of the game would not think that the success of a team would be affected by secretaryship, but I make so bold as to say that the various triumphs of the Sunderland Club have been not a little influenced by Mr Watson's personality. Mr Watson had a good eye for football talent. Big names did not move him to emotion so much as real ability and, when you come to think that Sunderland have played very few really poor players, the worth of Watson becomes more apparent.'

His worth certainly became apparent when the season began. Liverpool marked their first run-out in their new rosy garb with a 2–1 win at The Wednesday, who had just won the FA Cup. By mid-October, Liverpool were in third spot, while Watson's old side Sunderland, missing their figurehead, were rock bottom of the table.

When Watson took his new team to Wearside, Sunderland rushed into a three-goal lead and ended up winning their first game of the season, 4–3. But when the teams faced each other at Anfield three weeks later, Watson's methods were beginning to kick in. Liverpool were becoming increasingly resolute in defence, while the attack was beginning to find the net regularly. Two goals from Andrew Hannah and one from Malcolm McVean wrapped up an easy 3–0 win. 'The home forwards played a brilliant game,' reported the *Manchester Guardian*, while 'the home defence was so good that [the goalkeeper Harry] Storer had nothing to do.' Liverpool went top of the table for the first time in their history.

They were knocked off their perch the following week by Bolton Wanderers, although a feelgood atmosphere was maintained as those connected with the club began to enjoy life in the top flight for the first time. A refreshed Watson was soon to be spotted on stage at the local Roscommon Music Hall belting out a few numbers, the first in a long line of questionable musical endeavours by employees of the club that stretched as far as the 1996 effort 'Pass and Move (It's the Liverpool Groove)' and thankfully (as yet) no further. Watson's side finished in fifth place, fourteen points behind the eventual champions Aston Villa. The new parsimonious defence had come at the expense of a few goals, only forty-six being scored in thirty league matches. But a season of consolidation was seen as perfectly acceptable and in any case the gap would soon be closed.

Though not immediately. Liverpool finished the following season in ninth place, but could at least boast a league win over Everton, who, according to the *Observer*, had 'the better of the play' at Anfield but went down 3–1 in front of a 25,000-plus crowd. Joe McQue, who had scored in Liverpool's first league match back in 1893, was the hero with another landmark goal.

But Watson knew the team needed fresh blood and, as he had done at Sunderland, and mimicking the approach of his predecessor McKenna, he went to Scotland to plunder some new talent. Heart of Midlothian supplied the left-winger Tom Robertson and the inside-right John Walker; the striker Hugh Morgan came from St Mirren; the freescoring George Allan, inexplicably sold to Celtic the previous season, was enticed back; and unquestionably most importantly, the twenty-year-old Alex Raisbeck – nominally a defender but a box-to-box dynamo – came in from Hibernian. Raisbeck had already proved his abilities in England, having helped Stoke escape relegation in the 1898 Tests – the relegation play-offs – and was destined for a stellar career at Anfield, one of the five Liverpool legends categorically to define their eras (the others being Scott, Liddell, Dalglish and Gerrard).

The 1898–99 season would also be a breakthrough one for a twenty-year-old local called Jack Cox, a lightning fast winger – he won both the 120-yard sprint and the 440-yard race at the club's pre-season picnic – albeit one who according to the *Evening Post* was 'too much inclined to indulge in trickery against a weak opponent'. Watson was putting together a formidable side, one which the reporter from the *Athletic News* had decided was better than Everton's: 'With these last additions, they should go on smilingly, and I think for the first time in their history they will find themselves stronger favourites than their neighbours for the big trophies.' The *Evening Telegraph* concurred – 'There is a feeling that the team that has been got together by Tom Watson and his fellow workers is just about good enough for anything' – while the *Edinburgh Evening News* christened Liverpool 'the finest team in the world' on the back of an early-season 3–0 pasting of Rangers in a friendly.

The *Edinburgh Evening News* were certainly no strangers to hyperbole, for they had also argued that Raisbeck was 'second to none as centre-half in the country … if his practice games are a criterion of his ability'. Raisbeck was a hit from the off, the dependable star of a side about to make a serious tilt at the league and Cup Double. An honest return, some would say, seeing he was, in the words of *Cricket and Football Field*, 'having a tall wage'; the best-paid player in the league, he had cost Liverpool a £350 transfer fee and was earning £7 a week, with his earnings set to balloon to £13 by the end of the season.

Liverpool's first half of the 1898–99 season was, like the two that had preceded it, a middling affair. In the middle of November they were tenth in the table, with as many defeats (five) as wins. Arguably the most notable event of the season's first few months was the appearance at Liverpool Police Court of Allan, Walker and Morgan, the three Scots up on a charge of breach of the peace and obstructing the police. The *Dundee Courier*, in a report headed 'Prominent football in trouble', detailed the trio's drunken capers: 'They were creating a disturbance in the street, and complaint was made to a constable, who requested them to desist, but they refused, Walker saying "Let's show him some Scotch blood!" The constable took Allan into custody when the others molested him.'

But the turn of the year acted as a pivot. Liverpool enjoyed a splendid Christmas and New Year period, despite a programme of five matches, all on the road, in just ten days. They won at Blackburn and West Brom, drew at Notts County, then took a short break in Sheffield, first winning 3–0 at The Wednesday, then 2–0 at the reigning champions Sheffield United, Walker scoring in both matches. 'The Liverpool football team have paid two visits to Sheffield in rapid succession, and the city has had no reason to rejoice over their presence,' sighed the *Sheffield Independent*. 'The two matches were the last of a series of five played away from home, and out of these five matches the Liverpool men have made nine points ... they have thoroughly deserved their success. There are several stars of great lustre in the eleven – notably the two powerful full-backs and the aggressive centre-forwards; but there is not a man who is not well worthy of his place. Is it possible that the formidable Liverpool eleven may gain the Championship?'

Liverpool were up to fourth, only two points off the lead, albeit having played three games more than the leaders Villa. Then, between the middle of January and the middle of March, Watson's men won seven matches on the spin in league and Cup. They had made it to the top of the heap – a point ahead of Villa – and were about to play Sheffield United in the FA Cup semi. Having seen off United at Bramall Lane with ease three months earlier, Liverpool were expected to reach their first FA Cup final. 'The club are now fancied as the future cupholders in almost every part of the country, except, perhaps, Sheffield, and moreover have also a capital chance of bringing the League Championship to the Mersey for the second time in its history,' wrote the *Evening Express*. The team repaired to a boarding house at the fashionable seaside resort of Lytham St Annes, where they spent the week before the semi running through the following arduous daily routine: breakfast, a quick walk, baths, dinner, a sprinting exercise, tea, billiards, cards and 'other harmless amusements' before bed 'at a reasonable hour'.

A relaxed and cheery Watson was confident of victory. 'I never like to crow before the event,' he told the *Express*, 'because football is a peculiar game, and the better team does not always win. But I have no doubts whatever that we are a better team than Sheffield United, and that we ought to win. Our halves will chop up any opposing combination, our defence is splendid, and our forwards are playing a deadly, determined game ... I honestly believe they can and will win.' But Watson

– who had twice been denied in the semi-finals while in charge of Sunderland's otherwise all-conquering Team of All the Talents – was thwarted again. First-half goals from Allan and Morgan gave Liverpool a 2–1 lead, but United equalised with twenty minutes to go. A replay at Burnden Park five days later was required, a match which has serious claim to being the most farcical Liverpool performance of all time.

Liverpool built a two-goal lead by the fifty-minute mark through Walker and Allan, but were pegged back to 2–2 within fifteen minutes. The team re-established a two-goal cushion, United gifting them an own goal before Jack Cox scored with the rebound after Allan had a penalty saved by the legendary Fatty Foulkes: Liverpool were eight minutes from the final. But once again they capitulated, their captain and goalkeeper Harry Storer gifting Priest two goals in three minutes. The final whistle blew on a remarkable 4–4 draw. The *Manchester Evening News* noted that Storer had given 'a rather sorry exhibition ... almost the entire blame of the failure has been made his burden, in fact he was afterwards the object of contumely, the Liverpool partisans submitting him to a far from pleasant demonstration.' The reporter went on to argue that 'a great deal of the criticism he was subject to was not altogether too severe' and that his display had suffered due to 'an insufficiency of work'.

Storer's performance – which had been inexplicable yet also perhaps not entirely unexpected, the keeper having gone for a wander against Preston a fortnight earlier in a league game, nearly costing them a point – effectively ended his Anfield career. An incandescent Watson signed a replacement in Bill Perkins from Luton Town, although the new man could not take up his position straight away. Watson dropped Storer anyway and called up the thirty-five-year-old Matt McQueen, who had during his long career at Liverpool played in every position including goal. His last three appearances for the club would not be a roaring success. Liverpool lost every one, the first a 1–0 reverse at home to Nottingham Forest, the last a 2–1 defeat at Bolton, both in the league. But the game in the middle proved the bitterest blow: the second replay of the Cup semi-final at Derby County, a one-goal defeat, Sheffield United's winner coming five minutes from time. The result was hard to take, not least because the second replay had itself been replayed, the original match at Fallowfield in Manchester being abandoned due to a crowd invasion with Liverpool a goal up through Allan. On the final whistle of United's eventual victory, Liverpool's no-nonsense midfielder Bill Goldie, Archie's younger brother, became involved in a full and frank exchange of views with the referee, who charged him with having used 'discourteous language'. Goldie refused to tell the referee his name, Raisbeck and Walker also getting into trouble after refusing to shop their teammate by giving the official the information he had been after. Goldie was suspended for the rest of the season, while Raisbeck and Walker were 'severely censured'.

The drama, coupled with the misery of spurning the opportunity of reaching the Cup final, had taken the wind out of Liverpool's sails. Having been unbeaten since early December, a seventeen-match run, those three defeats on the bounce would prove costly. Nevertheless, hope was maintained. The arrival of Perkins coincided with an upturn in form, Liverpool winning the first four of their last five matches. That run took them to the top of the table with one game to play, at title rivals Villa. They were two points ahead of the Birmingham side and boasted a superior goal average.

But Villa had a game in hand and had just beaten Notts County 6–1 at home. Almost inconceivably, Villa then won their penultimate match of the season, against West Bromwich Albion, 7–1, their final goal, which came seven minutes from the end, edging Villa ahead of Liverpool at the top by 0.02 of a goal. That now meant that Villa only needed to hold on for a draw in the final-day decider – a league first – as Liverpool paid a visit.

Thirteen average-boosting goals in two games certainly

raised eyebrows and there were murmurings that Notts County and West Brom had thrown the matches. 'To beat Notts County by six goals to one and then to go one better and beat West Bromwich Albion by 7–1 did look as if somebody had not been trying,' said the *Sporting Life*. They were not the only ones harbouring doubts. 'How did you let Villa give you a hiding like that?' an unnamed Liverpool player is said to have asked an equally unidentified Baggies counterpart. 'Let?' came the affronted reply. 'Don't you talk about letting! Wait till you meet 'em at Aston, and you'll laugh on the other side of your face!' If that back and forth, which sounds suspiciously apocryphal, isn't quite enough to dispel the scurrilous accusations, what occurred at Villa Park when Liverpool arrived for judgement day suggested the irate West Brom player, fictional or not, had a point.

Liverpool again prepared for a big match by taking in the sea air at Lytham. Ahead of the semi-final against Sheffield United, Watson, the three-time title winner holding court, boasted that he never let his players see the ball during the week. 'Some people, he confessed, considered this injudicious,' reported the *Evening Express*, 'but his experience was quite the contrary, and in view of the fact that Mr Watson has been associated with football for twenty years, he may fairly claim to have practical knowledge on his side, particularly as Liverpool's fine performances of late have been the result of pursuing this method.' They wouldn't see much of the ball that Saturday, either.

For a while after falling behind to Devey's fourth-minute goal, Liverpool looked reasonably coherent. Walker and Allan combined well only for Howard Spencer to intercept as they approached the Villa area. Hugh Morgan and Tom Robertson also linked up for 'a couple of clever movements', according to the *Liverpool Mercury*, Spencer again putting a stop to their gallop and a Walker shot then forced Billy George into a splendid clearing punch. But Villa were not to be denied. 'The general expectation probably was that the Villa would win a hard-fought game by a goal,' suggested the *Manchester Guardian*. 'The midlanders had different views, however.' Having soaked up a little Liverpool pressure, Villa swept up the pitch after eighteen minutes, shuttling the ball along the diagonal from right to left, before the influential Smith once again set up Devey, the Villa captain 'promptly availing himself of the opportunity by sending the ball into the net at a great pace'.

Again Liverpool responded aggressively, pinning Villa back awhile. Allan sent an effort from distance straight at George, then Dunlop whistled a free-kick from the edge of the area well wide. Cox made another skittering run down the right, before being dispossessed by Evans. They certainly hadn't given up, however unpromising the circumstances; Raisbeck entertained himself by engaging in a running battle with Athersmith, the pair trading kicks at every available opportunity.

But again the resistance was brief and futile. After thirty-four minutes, Athersmith made good progress down the right and found Devey, who in turn shuttled the ball to Garraty. The striker hit a low fizzer from just outside the area, the ball sailing past Perkins and pinging in off a post. Less than a minute later, a witless scramble in the Liverpool area concluded with Crabtree guiding a header into the top corner, Perkins scrabbling for the ball, his efforts to reach it in vain.

The skies mirrored Liverpool hearts, filling with rain. A minute before the break, Wheldon bundled home from close range to make it five, the rain soon turning into a blizzard. There was still time, just before the half-time whistle, for Perkins to make an ostentatious save from Devey. The rain eased off during the interval and the wind died down, enabling the Liverpool fans to hear every note as the band played 'Say Au Revoir'.

The breeze that remained assisted Liverpool in the second half as they attempted an impossible comeback. For the third time in the match, they attacked with purpose, Robertson skimming the crossbar with a shot that George had tipped over, Cox finding the side netting after cutting in from the right, Allan doing likewise and Robertson once again going close after beating Spencer down the left. Liverpool's efforts were sustained and staunch enough for Wheldon to drop back to help his defence, which he did manfully; the visitors barely troubled George from then on, one low shot from Cox apart.

The sun came out with a quarter of an hour to go, but Liverpool's mood was darkening. 'Liverpool appeared now to be a beaten team,' noted the *Sporting Life*, 'and some of their players resorted to very shady tactics.' Villa finished strongly, befitting a team who had just scored eighteen goals in their last three games and nearly rounded the match off with a Garraty shot in the final minute, but Perkins was equal to the task.

'Villa's decisive final victory, it is not unnaturally suggested, should set the ugly rumours of collusion that have been prevalent entirely at rest,' was the *Manchester Guardian*'s clear verdict. *The Times* agreed. 'In the eleven years' existence of the league competition, this has been perhaps the most keenly contested,' it thundered. 'Playing a wonderfully fine game, Villa won easily. Their men showed superb form alike in defence and attack.' Liverpool had been considering reporting West Bromwich Albion to the Football League for their 7–1 capitulation, but quietly dropped the idea.

The *Sporting Life*'s reporter concluded that the toss had been vital. 'To a certain extent the boisterous wind prevented accurate play, and taking the elements into consideration, it must be admitted straightaway that the Aston Villa captain was decidedly fortunate in winning the toss,' he wrote. 'With the breeze in their favour during the first moiety the Villa played all over their opponents and but for the able defence of Raisbeck, Dunlop and Goldie, the lead of the home team at the interval might easily have been more pronounced.' By the second half, Liverpool's race was run. 'Whether it was that the hard work of the opening period had taken all the go out of them, or that the seasiders completely lost heart, it is difficult to state, but certain it is that they could make no impression whatever on the grand defence of the Aston Villa rear division.'

The Villa captain Devey, as he collected the trophy in front of a delirious Villa Park, announced that if his team couldn't retain the title the following year, he hoped that Liverpool would win it.

They would not. Villa managed to retain their title, winning rather less dramatically, a whole two points ahead of Sheffield United as Watson's side finished a disappointing tenth. In the wake of the Villa defeat, the *Manchester Guardian* had noted that Liverpool had 'deserved a better fate', and that 'it is not too much to say that but for the series of severe games in the semi-finals of the Cup they would not have lost to Notts [sic] Forest and Bolton Wanderers, and in that event the championship of the League would not have been in dispute.' The paper concluded by saying that 'the past cannot be undone, and Liverpool must content themselves and endeavour to atone for their disappointments next season.'

It proved beyond them. The rest of the calendar year of 1899 was nothing short of tragic. The start to their league campaign was beyond abysmal. Liverpool lost the first eight games of the season, still a top-flight record. That the team would suffer from the cruelties of the previous campaign was understandable, but this was altogether more puzzling. Suggestions grew that Watson's regime, not the strictest, might be a problem. The *Manchester Evening News*, after the denouement at Villa the previous season, offered a not particularly cryptic reason for Liverpool's capitulation: 'Since Christmas they have scarcely been away from their special training quarters and a surfeit of good things ... would appear to have wrought evils instead of the benefits sought for.' The *Sunderland Daily Echo* was even less subtle, reporting that they have been 'informed on reliable authority that drink is the cause of the poor form shown by a prominent English club this season. The players have the reputation of being "the biggest boozers going, and they seem to glory in it." Who can this mean?'

If the team were not dry, the *Liverpool Mercury* certainly was, quipping that 'whatever other failings may be placed to the account of the present Liverpool team, they cannot be charged with inconsistency.' But Watson refused to bow to criticism. He insisted that 'fortune will not smile upon us' and that Liverpool had 'played absolutely all over' most of the teams his side had gone down to. 'To be ever on the losing side is a new experience for me, as you know; and is not a happy one. But we have had days of good success, and shall, I hope, renew them.'

The manager could also point to two bitter blows faced by the club during the closing months of 1899. Their former star Harry Bradshaw, having moved to Spurs and later Thames Ironworks (the precursor of West Ham), had died of tuberculosis on Christmas Day at the age of twenty-six. That news came two months after the death of George Allan, who had fallen ill during pre-season training and also succumbed to diseased lungs, aged only twenty-four. More than most, Liverpool hoped that the turn of the year would bring them a change of luck.

Three days into a twentieth century they would dominate, Liverpool signed Sam Raybould from New Brighton Tower. The striker would become one of the club's most significant pre-war figures, scoring 128 goals in 226 matches, thirty-one of them coming in thirty-three matches in 1902–03 and his impact was immediate. In the game before his debut, Liverpool lost at Sunderland, leaving Watson's side second from bottom, propped up only by struggling Glossop North End. (To put Liverpool's plight into context, Glossop were essentially the vanity project of a Derbyshire mill owner who had seriously misjudged the ability of a town with a population of 20,000 to support a top-flight football team; even then, they only had three points fewer than Liverpool and had three games in hand.) But Raybould – relentless, robust, and always involved – galvanised his new side. He scored seven times in eleven appearances, Liverpool winning nine of their last eleven games. Liverpool ended the campaign in tenth spot, well clear of danger. Had they replicated their form of the last two months across the whole campaign, they would have won the title with four points to spare.

Notice had been served. 'One of the most remarkable and unaccountable features of last season was the failure of the Liverpool team,' noted the *Sheffield Independent*. 'Certainly on paper, Liverpool, with the famous Raisbeck as captain, seem as powerful a combination as any in the country, and on the improved form they displayed at the end of last season, they should take a prominent position during 1900–01. Their followers in the big seaport are expecting them to repeat or even improve upon the form of two seasons ago, when they were only beaten for the Cup and the league championship by the teams who ultimately carried off the honours.'

Liverpool started strongly with five wins from their first seven matches, but would soon slide into inconsistency: between the end of September and the middle of February they would lose eight times in eighteen games, but they also registered some notable victories during the sequence: a 4–3 win at Manchester City, a 1–0 win over the FA Cup holders Bury and an astonishing 5–1 trouncing of reigning champions Aston Villa. 'What a rout for the champions!' exclaimed the *Manchester Guardian*.

Still, a Liverpool title looked implausible after defeat at Bolton in mid-February left them in eighth position, nine points behind the leaders Nottingham Forest and seven adrift of second-placed Sunderland, who were up next. Watson took his team to his old home, where they ground their way to a 1–0 win, Cox scoring on the hour. The result initiated an astonishing unbeaten sequence which stretched to the end of the season, eight wins and three draws bringing an end to a nine-year quest, the league trophy going to Anfield for the first of eighteen visits.

In a pleasing symmetry, Liverpool again had to travel to the

Midlands for their final game, needing a draw to secure the title. This time they visited West Bromwich Albion, who had angered them so by capitulating 7–1 to Villa two years previously, but were now condemned to relegation. Tied on points with Sunderland, who had finished their campaign, but behind on goal average, Liverpool required a draw. They managed a win, Raybould sending in a shot on twenty minutes that the Albion keeper Joe Reader could only parry, Walker bundling home the rebound. Two seasons after suffering the harshest setback any club had been dealt in league history to that point, Liverpool had made it, the first illustration of a relentless spirit that would become part of the club's fabric.

Raybould and his fellow forwards had been the obvious heroes, the team scoring more goals (fifty-nine) than anyone else in the country, but it was Raisbeck and the defence who really mattered during the run-in, conceding only two goals in the last ten matches. It had been the kind of late-season charge which would define Liverpool during their golden era of the 1970s and early 1980s: a template had been forged. Watson would enjoy more success at Anfield: a remarkable title in 1905–06, a year after bouncing back from a shock relegation at the first attempt, and a first appearance in an FA Cup final in 1914, Liverpool losing 1–0 to Burnley. But this first title was his signature achievement; it was the one which put Liverpool on the map, their first indelible mark on English football's roll of honour. No club has ever made the journey from birth to champions as quickly, and none ever will again.

CHAPTER 2

Football League Division One, Molineux, Wolverhampton, 31 May 1947

Wolverhampton Wanderers	1–2	**Liverpool**
Dunn 65		*Balmer 21*
		Stubbins 38

Bert Williams	Cyril Sidlow
Gus McLean	Jim Harley
Billy Crook	Ray Lambert
Jim Alderton	Bill Jones
Stan Cullis	Laurie Hughes
Billy Wright	Eddie Spicer
Jim Hancocks	Billy Liddell
Jimmy Dunn	Jack Balmer
Jesse Pye	Albert Stubbins
Billy Forbes	Billy Watkinson
Jimmy Mullen	Robert Priday
Ted Vizard	George Kay

Ref: J Briggs
Bkd:
Att: 50,765

AT WHAT POINT DID LIVERPOOL secure their status as one of English football's bona fide giants? An argument can be made that they pretty much managed it from the outset: they were winning trophies from the start, landing the league title within nine years of their formation, a legendary manager in Tom Watson at the helm of a world-class team built around the rangy genius of Alex Raisbeck, the club's original star.

Others may point to 1923, when a side dominated by the no-nonsense personality of the Northern Irish goalkeeper Elisha Scott, the first heir to Raisbeck's mantle and the object of the Kop's first true infatuation, won the second of back-to-back titles. Liverpool became the first club to achieve that feat since The Wednesday during the league's infancy, nineteen years previously. At that stage, only the grandees of English football's early years, Aston Villa and Sunderland, had been champions more times than Liverpool's four. Liverpool had made room for themselves at the top table and done so despite their manager David Ashworth upping sticks for Oldham Athletic in the middle of their title defence in 1922–23, early signs that the club had already grown resilient to the whims of any one individual, no matter how seemingly integral.

The majority will, naturally, cite the moment Bill Shankly walked through the doors in 1959 as the club's true defining moment. Shankly is credited with the creation of the modern Liverpool, his success coinciding with the first television age. And yet while Shankly was an alchemist, even he could not have been expected to conjure gold out of thin air. There is one other moment in Liverpool's rich history – involving one manager, one team, and several unsung stars increasingly obscured by the mists of time – which could be pinpointed as the one which, in retrospect, ensured Liverpool had the chance to upgrade itself from the good, to the very, very great.

The 1946–47 season was one of the most important in the history of Liverpool. Without the efforts of George Kay and his team in the immediate aftermath of the Second World War, Shankly would have had precious little to build on in the first place, arriving at a club which had last won silverware thirty-six years previously, with no championship success in recent memory. Had it not been for Kay, there would have been no sleeping giant to awake.

Shades of hyperbole and melodrama? Consider the evidence, and the fate of some pre-war titans of the English game. As the Second World War began, Sunderland were one of the most successful sides in the country, having won a joint-record sixth league title in 1936 and their first FA Cup a year later. Their North East rivals Newcastle United had clocked up four titles, the last in 1927, as well as a couple of FA Cups. Sheffield Wednesday were the other big players, with four titles and three cups on their roll of honour.

All three clubs remain huge concerns, but only because of the size of their support and the fading splendour of their tradition. On the field, they have been resolutely second-rate. Wednesday never got going after the war. Things might have been different for Sunderland, had they not thrown away the 1949–50 league title along the closing stretch, or for Newcastle if parsimonious owners had built on their cup successes of the early 1950s. But it was not to be, and success has pretty much eluded them ever since.

A similar fate could quite easily have befallen Liverpool, who had been no slouches in the pre-war era, having won those four league titles, a feat bettered only by Aston Villa, Sunderland, Arsenal and Everton. But the last win had been in 1922–23, and they had still to win the FA Cup, having reached the final just once, way back in 1914.

Liverpool's successes were quickly becoming part of a distant past. In 1921–22, Watson's successor David Ashworth won
the league, Liverpool's first silverware for sixteen years, with
a team whose biggest stars were defensive heroes: the long-
serving England full-back Ephraim Longworth, the captain
and left back Donald McKinley, and Elisha Scott. Ruthlessly
dominant in his penalty box, Scott was one of the first players
to understand the worth of a powerful bond with the fans. 'I
speak to these people,' he once said gnomically, a blueprint for
Shankly to follow years later.

Despite Ashworth leaving midway through the following
season to chase a higher wage at Oldham Athletic, Liverpool
retained their title, guided home by Matt McQueen, the utility
virtuoso from their early days. The feat was almost unheard of
in topsy-turvy times; The Wednesday had been the last team
to manage it, twenty years earlier when reigns were more routine. But Liverpool could not keep it up. Everton took over as
the great force on Merseyside and, although Scott continued
to prove his star quality by keeping up a personal rivalry with
striker Dixie Dean – once famously (albeit almost certainly
apocryphally) diving at Dean's feet when the striker nodded
his greeting as the two passed in the street – Liverpool as a
team were becoming yesterday's news.

They had spent the 1930s hovering around mid-table, occasionally flirting with relegation. Their descent from the glory
of their early-twenties pomp into mid-thirties insignificance is
amply illustrated by the fate of Scott. By the end of the 1920s,
the goalkeeper was fighting for his place with the newcomer
Arthur Riley. He battled with the pretender for six campaigns,
but by the 1933–34 campaign, which saw Liverpool scrapping
to avoid the drop, the Northern Irishman's time looked up.

The pair took turns in goal for much of the season, but Scott's
final stint as number one was a disaster. In a ten-game run at
the turn of the year, Liverpool won only once with Scott in
goal, and relegation for the first time since 1904 looked likely.
The low point came on New Year's Day, when Newcastle scored

nine times past Scott. The *Manchester Guardian* did their best to absolve the goalkeeper for a 9–2 defeat – still their record top-flight loss – by commending his 'fine work', suggesting he was 'entirely blameless' and arguing that, without him, 'Newcastle's score would have run well into double figures'.

But there is a sense that the papers were just trying to show Scott some respect earned during better days. He only played six more matches for Liverpool, the last a 2–0 reverse at Chelsea, and when Riley snatched back his place, the Reds enjoyed a burst of improved form, a late-season run featuring five wins including a 6–2 thrashing of Middlesbrough and a 4–1 walloping of Birmingham City. Liverpool avoided relegation by three places and four points – their 9–2 conquerors Newcastle went down instead – while Scott left for Belfast Celtic, having joined twenty-four years earlier in 1912. He remains Liverpool's longest-serving player. 'We have always been the best of friends,' he told Anfield over the PA after the final game of the season, 'and shall always remain so. My friends of the Kop: I cannot thank them sufficiently. They have inspired me. God bless you all.'

The good times were long past. The 1930s proved an undistinguished period, leavened only by the extraordinary goalscoring feats of the South African striker Gordon Hodgson – whose record of 233 league goals in 358 games is bettered only by Roger Hunt – and the wing-play of his compatriot Berry Nieuwenhuys. Otherwise the 1930s are mainly notable for the signings of the inside-forward Willie Fagan, the future managers Phil Taylor and Bob Paisley, and Billy Liddell, a promising Scottish inside-left who joined as a sixteen-year-old in 1938 and effectively became the invaluable parting gift of Liverpool's trustworthy captain Matt Busby, who had tipped off the club's scouts, his last significant act at Anfield before moving up the East Lancs Road to Old Trafford.

The decade also saw the arrival of the manager George Kay from Southampton. A bequiffed, chain-smoking Mancunian – quiet, thoughtful and prone to nerves, probably a result of suffering shellshock during the First World War as a soldier on the western front – Kay's most significant achievement as a player had been to lead West Ham United out as captain at the famous White Horse FA Cup final of 1923. He had worked his way up through the leagues as manager at Luton Town and Southampton before taking the Anfield job at the age of forty-five. Determined and hard-working, his brooding dignity would inspire a fierce loyalty in his players which would serve them well in the years to come. He had yet to make his mark as a boss – Saints were no more than a mid-table Second Division concern – but he was well regarded in the game and, according to Gary Shaw and Mark Platt in *At The End of the Storm*, their game-by-game account of the 1946–47 season, 'renowned for his deep thinking and shrewd tactical nous' and a 'keen reader of books about psychology and a supreme motivator of men'.

War arrives at the right time for no one, but the one which raged between 1939 and 1945 did some teams fewer favours than others. Everton had won the championship in 1938–39 with a team starring Joe Mercer, a young Tommy Lawton and the great central defender T. G. Jones, but they were denied the chance to build on the success and, by the time of the big restart in 1946, Lawton had skipped off to Chelsea, while the thirty-two-year-old Mercer decided he would rather become a grocer in the Wirral than continue to play under the management of Theo Kelly, with whom he had fallen out over the gravity of an injury. (Arsenal effortlessly persuaded Mercer into a rethink, and even allowed him to stay in the north and run his shop, providing he brought a few ration-book-busting treats for his new teammates from time to time.) Robbed of quality and momentum, Everton in 1951 ended up relegated for only the second time in their history.

Stoke City – the club of Stanley Matthews, the biggest star in England – had finished the 1930s strongly, with the twenty-one-year-old winger inspiring the Potters to their best-ever league finish, fourth, in 1936, and a seventh-place spot three years later. The club were on the up, with the highly promising young centre-half Neil Franklin about to emerge, when war broke out and put a stop to their gallop. Matthews spent the war working as a physical trainer in Blackpool where, having already fallen out with the Stoke boss Bob McGrory over wages, he had his head turned by the local club. Unsettled, he bought a bed and breakfast on the coast, and though he returned to play for Stoke every Saturday when the league resumed, the situation festered.

Wolverhampton Wanderers were perhaps the unluckiest of them all. They were one win away from their first league title in 1938 but lost their last match, then the following year blew the chance to become the twentieth century's first Double winners, trotting home second in the league, four points behind Everton, whom they'd beaten 7–0 at Molineux, and losing the FA Cup final to Portsmouth. Trophies seemed only a matter of time for an impressive young side: by the end of the 1938–39 campaign, the free-scoring strikers Dicky Dorsett and Dennis Westcott were still only nineteen and twenty-one years old respectively. They also had the dubious advantage of having the idiosyncratic and scheming Major Frank Buckley as their manager. His most notorious wheeze was to claim he had injected his players with serums drawn from the glands of monkeys and oxen. 'They had glazed eyes and could have run all day,' said Lawton, years after the 7–0 thrashing. 'They were doped up to the eyes. They must have been to have licked us seven.' But by the end of the war, the Major and his box of tricks were gone, as was Dorsett, who had left for Aston Villa, while the chance to turn the promise of the late thirties into titles had been lost.

Nevertheless, all three clubs were discussed as the press previewed the big kick-off on the last day of August 1946. As reigning champions, Everton received polite mentions and, although that side was falling apart, it hadn't gone unnoticed that the club had still finished second in League North, part of a regional competition set up by the Football League to ease the game from wartime back to normality. Stoke were also much fancied, thanks to the Matthews factor, as were the 1946 FA Cup winners Derby County, built around Raich Carter and Peter Doherty, a 'team of much transferred talent' which the *Manchester Guardian* suggested could be 'the new power in the land'.

There were also hopes for Charlton Athletic, who had taken Derby to extra-time in the Cup final, the League North champions Sheffield United and Matt Busby's new club Manchester United, 'whose forwards may be devastating this year', reported *The Times*. But *The Times* believed the most likely champions were Wolves who, despite having had their momentum checked by the war, were still sprightly enough to be described as 'youthful ... with [Billy] Wright, [Stan] Cullis and [Jimmy] Alderton forming perhaps one of the strongest half-back lines in the country. Wolverhampton have acquired [Jesse] Pye, an inside-forward of great possibilities to complete the midfield link between wing-half and inside-forward from which all good sides gain rhythm and motive power.'

Nobody thought to throw Liverpool's name into the mix. Even the *Liverpool Echo* suggested that the side from Anfield would 'do nothing out of the ordinary'. In fairness, it was easy to see why Kay's side were being ignored. The club hadn't won a thing since the 1923 championship, twenty-three barren years which until recently represented the club's longest drought in the league – and at least modern fans equally starved of English titles have had a few cups to tide them over. In the final season before the war, Liverpool had been as good an example of mid-table nonentities as it was possible to get – won fourteen, drawn fourteen, lost fourteen, scored sixty-two, conceded sixty-three, eleventh out of twenty-two – and now they were all seven years further down the line. Their most consistent forward of the late thirties, the shaggy-haired right-winger Berry Nieuwenhuys, was by then nearly thirty-five; his best days as foil to his fellow South African Hodgson were long behind him. No major new signings, no recent pedigree, no hope, no chance.

Or so it seemed at first glance. Liverpool's squad did at least contain promise, in the shape of several young players who had been schooled during the wartime competitions and were itching to make their mark on the sport properly: the elegant centre-half Laurie Hughes, the balding but surprisingly young left-back Ray Lambert, the left-half Bob Paisley, noted for his long throw, and, on the left wing, the legend-in-waiting Billy Liddell. The necessary maturity was provided by the thirty-three-year-old captain Phil Taylor, who had taken over from the departed Busby at right-half; the unpopular but determined striker Jack Bulmer; and Liverpool's one notable post-war dabble in the transfer market, the Wolves reserve keeper Cyril Sidlow (who, to be fair to a Liverpool board angrily accused by supporters of tightfistedness, cost £4,000, a record fee for a goalkeeper).

The squad also enjoyed one vital advantage over the rest of the division and in some respects it can be argued that the 1946–47 league championship was decided before a single ball had been kicked. The Liverpool chairman Billy McConnell was a caterer by trade and in 1945 he had gone on a government-funded fact-finding trip to the United States to pick up tips on nutrition, cooking, industrial catering and the fancy new café and diner culture. Taking one look at the scrawny state of his players a year later, he decided to take a pre-emptive strike. 'If I could bring my team to play a few games while sampling American malted milks and ice cream, American meats and vegetables,' he had mused while in the US, 'they'd go back to Liverpool and win the First Division championship.' And so in May 1946 he sent team and manager away on an eight-week tour of the USA and Canada just days after Liverpool had finished eleventh in League North.

The trip, unprecedented at the time, was a roaring success on the field, Liverpool scoring seventy goals in ten matches, a glorious confidence booster for the upcoming season. But the main gains were made around the waist. The players, long used to rationing, feasted on steak, eggs, butter, syrup and fruit. By the end of the trip, the team had put on an average of half a stone a man. 'There was a perceptible gain in strength on the playing field,' noted the reporter from the *New York Times*, who had been following Liverpool as they travelled across North America. 'Like Jack Spratt and his wife ... they swept the platter clean.' They had also cleared a trail across the US which Hapoel Tel Aviv, Newcastle United, Internazionale and Elisha Scott's Belfast Celtic were to follow in the next few years, albeit with less subsequent success.

Only Liddell and Lambert, both still away on RAF business, had missed out on the two-month feast. Neither was available for the season's opener at Sheffield United, the winners of the previous season's League North, but their absence mattered little, Len Carney – an amateur making his full debut – glancing home a ninetieth-minute header to claim a 1–0 victory. (It would be the only goal he would ever score for the club as he made only five more appearances.) It was a classic smash and grab, Liverpool soaking up pressure, United peppering the exceptional Sidlow's goal. In fact, Liverpool's only really notable act of the opening day came ten minutes before the game had started, as they trotted out onto the pitch to warm up and tap a ball around, a curious carry-on at a time when pre-match drills were still very much a foreign concept. (Quite literally; even as late as 1953, the BBC commentator Kenneth Wolstenholme seemed astounded to see Ferenc Puskás flick a few common-or-garden keepie-uppies into the air before Hungary's famous 6–3 demolition of England at Wembley.)

Despite the fillip of two points, few thought Liverpool's opening-day performance any sort of harbinger. Wolves, for a start, had battered Arsenal 6–1, all their goals coming in a second-half shower, the new signing Pye helping himself to a debut hat-trick. In the *Manchester Guardian* there were good notices for the young Preston North End debutant Tom

Finney; Manchester United, who had narrowly but deservedly beaten Grimsby Town at Maine Road (where they played home matches while Old Trafford was repaired following bomb damage); and for the opening-day goalscorers Tommy Lawton on his league debut for Chelsea and Albert Stubbins of second-tier Newcastle United. The paper did not even mention Liverpool by name, the match only being notable as one of two 'surprising' home defeats, Sheffield United's failure matched by Everton, who had gone down at Goodison to Brentford.

Liverpool's early-season form was extremely patchy. The lucky opening-day win at Bramall Lane was swiftly followed by a lacklustre midweek defeat at Anfield to Middlesbrough, a 1–0 reverse to which Liverpool responded spectacularly, albeit not in the consistent manner that might have suggested the arrival of silverware any time soon.

Chelsea came to Anfield having spent £29,000 on new players, their side now containing not just Lawton but also the England forward Len Goulden. (Tommy Walker, who had scored 279 goals in 253 appearances for Hearts, would soon join them as well.) Lawton's return to Merseyside ensured local interest in the match – the attendance was five clicks of the turnstile short of 50,000 – although most of the excitement was generated by the news that Liddell would finally make his full debut for the home side. Paisley would also be turning out in proper competitive action for the first time, while Fagan returned to lend nous and guile to the attack.

The debutants were not slow to make their mark. In the first minute, Liddell, having played a one-two with Fagan, sent a shot screeching just wide and into the Kop. Another 120 seconds had elapsed when Paisley bustled down the left to win a corner. Liddell whipped the ball in so ferociously that the Chelsea goalkeeper Bill Robertson could only bundle it off the far post and into the net.

Liverpool, suddenly fuelled by the arrogance of youth, were rampant. The utility player Bill Jones scored twice, then Fagan made it four before half-time. Jack Balmer scored a fifth just after the restart and Liddell slalomed past several desperate Chelsea lunges to make it 6–0 on fifty minutes. A preposterous scoreline, though that was only the start of it. Len Goulden pulled a goal back on fifty-five minutes, Jimmy Argue scored Chelsea's second on sixty-four, and then Alex Machin stunned Liverpool with two goals in three minutes: with eighteen minutes remaining, Chelsea were suddenly only two adrift.

Had Liverpool squandered a six-goal lead, it's safe to assume it would have done irreparable damage to their collective confidence and would surely have snuffed out any title pretensions there and then. The smallest detail can have enormous consequences, so Liverpool owe a debt to the stand-in keeper Charlie Ashcroft, replacing the injured Sidlow, who clawed out what looked like a certain hat-trick goal from Machin after eighty minutes. A scoreline of 6–5 with ten minutes to go would have been too much for the Kop to bear. As it was, Fagan bundled in a captain's goal with three minutes remaining, taking advantage of a melee prompted by a Nieuwenhuys corner. Relief, and a famous 7–4 win. Liverpool were already ahead of hotly tipped sides such as Wolves, Derby and Stoke in the table, their season on track despite some early travails.

Or was it? The league leaders after three games – a retrospective snapshot this, seeing a league table would have never been published in 1946 until the season had been given the chance to take at least a semblance of proper shape – were Manchester United. They had won all three of their opening games, and had also outdone Chelsea, albeit in a less hysterical fashion, winning 3–0 at Stamford Bridge. Busby's managerial career started promisingly, with the team attacking all-comers from all angles, Jimmy Delaney and Stan Pearson down the right, Jack Rowley and Charlie Mitten the left. Liverpool travelled to Maine Road buoyed by the Chelsea result, but light on numbers: Liddell, yet to be demobbed by the RAF, was on duty, as was Sidlow, making his recovery from injury an irrelevance. United put on a show, Pearson helping himself to a hat-trick, Rowley and Mitten getting the others in a 5–0 humiliation.

'One cannot recall an occasion when Liverpool's play was so undistinguished,' said the report in the *Guardian*. 'They made not a single move of consequence throughout the entire match. Until the closing minutes, that is, when Paisley drove in a ball which forced Crompton, the Manchester goalkeeper, to reveal his whereabouts and prove to the crowd that he had not gone home from sheer boredom. United's apt retort to Paisley's impudence was to walk the ball upfield and invite Pearson to score the fifth.'

This was a proper skelping, and while the modern bitter dynamic had yet to take serious hold, this still hurt the visitors. United had firmly established themselves as early favourites for the championship. Liverpool went back to Anfield with their tails between their legs, while chairman McConnell appeared to be chasing his. He had nearly missed the game at Old Trafford after getting stuck in London while engaging in a futile attempt to secure an outrageous transfer: that of Lawton, who had only just moved from Everton to Chelsea. Sent back north a little abashed, McConnell sat through the misery of the United drubbing, then caught wind of a rumour that Albert Stubbins, at twenty-seven keen to experience top-flight football, had put in a transfer request at Newcastle. After a quick chat with Kay, chairman and manager drove up the A1 to see if they could do a deal that night – only to find the Everton boss Theo Kelly already at St James' Park for the same reason.

Luckily for Liverpool, Stubbins was out enjoying dinner with his wife and Kelly had not been able to engineer a meeting. The player eventually made it home, received a message that Newcastle were looking for him and immediately went to the ground, where he found both Merseyside clubs were waiting patiently. Legend has it that Stubbins tossed a coin to decide which to join, but that is not quite the case. He did toss to see which club to speak to first and Liverpool were the lucky winners, especially as Stubbins then made his mind up before giving Everton a chance to state their case. However,

even here the role of the coin, and Lady Luck, is probably over-
stated. Stubbins knew that Liverpool were planning another
trip to the US at the end of the season and, having lived there
as a child, was hoping to return. McConnell also promised the
player – who had ambitions to become a journalist later in
life and had already learned shorthand to that end – that he
would pull some strings to arrange a regular column for him
with the *Liverpool Echo*.

The arrival of Stubbins – a record £12,500 purchase – would
be the catalyst for a change in Liverpool's fortunes. The team
played poorly in their next game at Bolton Wanderers, but
won 3–1, their crucial second goal scored with eight minutes
to go by the new signing, who picked the ball up by the centre-
circle before motoring down the pitch and lashing home from
the edge of the box. 'This is the best forward line I have ever
played in,' said Stubbins after the game, having looked around
him at Liddell, Balmer, Jones and Nieuwenhuys, with Fagan on
the sidelines waiting to come back. Yet perhaps the most pleasing aspect of the Burnden Park win had been the defensive
display: after conceding nine goals in two games, Sidlow and
Lambert came in for Ashcroft and the left-back Barney Rams-
den, and the back-line managed to keep the young but already
dangerous Nat Lofthouse relatively quiet. For the remainder
of the season, one infamous aberration apart, Liverpool would
remain compact at the back.

The team embarked on a two-month unbeaten run, a sequence which culminated in one of the great individual feats
in English league history. The inside-forward Jack Balmer
had, as a youth on Everton's books, been considered the natural heir to Dixie Dean's throne. Denied chances at Goodison,
he crossed Stanley Park and became a regular goalscorer, if
not quite in Dean's class: eight goals in 1936–37, thirteen the
year after, and fourteen in the final season before the war
was a decent record for an attacker in a thoroughly average
team. However, he was not particularly popular with the Liverpool crowd, who were suspicious of Balmer's middle-class

upbringing and suave demeanour, his receding hairline and smooth pencil moustache reminiscent of David Niven, albeit a slightly craggier version. Balmer was also seen as being overly fancy, somebody who preferred to keep away from the rough-and-tumble where possible.

But fans can only remain aloof for so long in the face of sustained brilliance. Ahead of Liverpool's home game against Portsmouth in early November, Kay had decided to award Balmer the captaincy in an attempt to give a slightly diffident player some focus. It was a masterstroke. Balmer scored a hat-trick, a first-half penalty followed by two spectacular volleys from the edge of the area.

Liverpool then travelled to meet the pre-season favourites Derby County where, due to a combination of doughty defending, luck, poor finishing from the home side and adroit keeping by Sidlow, they soaked up pressure for most of the first half before Balmer took centre-stage again. Just before half-time, he curled a shot into the top corner. A minute after the restart, he swanned left to right past four defenders before caressing the ball back across the keeper Alick Grant and home, a solo goal of delicate skill. Balmer completed a six-minute hat-trick soon after, tapping in after Liddell had laid waste to Derby along the left wing. He lobbed Grant to add a fourth on the hour: four goals in seventeen minutes. Carter scored a late consolation for Derby in a 4–1 win which took Liverpool to the top of the First Division for the first time since they had won the title back in 1923.

Balmer was on a hat-trick of hat-tricks, and opened the scoring early in Liverpool's following match, at home to Arsenal, although the Gunners responded well and went into the interval leading 2–1. No matter: on sixty-one minutes Balmer battered in a loose ball after the equally in-form Liddell had caused bedlam down his wing, then seven minutes later sprang the Arsenal offside trap to score his historic third. It was the first time a player had scored three hat-tricks in a row since, of all people, Dixie Dean had managed two at the end of his sixty-goal 1927–28 season, and a third at the start of the following campaign. The feat prompted a pitch invasion, and a reception from the 51,000-plus crowd which, it was suggested in the local press, could only be compared in terms of raw emotional tumult to the hullabaloo over at Goodison nearly two decades earlier when Dean scored his famous sixtieth.

'The player that didn't get on with the crowd really was Balmer, which was a shame as he was a great player,' recalled future Liverpool winger Jimmy Payne, then yet to break through. 'He always played better away from home than he did at home. It's funny, isn't it, but the only time he was very popular with them was when he scored three hat-tricks in three games running. That made him quite popular with the crowd.'

In what was almost a footnote, Stubbins added a late fourth to seal a 4–2 win which consolidated Liverpool's lead at the top, second-placed Wolves having been held at Preston. Balmer went on to score five more goals in the next four games, completing a scoring run of fifteen goals in seven matches, one that is worth enjoying in stark numerical terms: 3–4–3–1–1–1–2.

But while Balmer continued to hit the net, Liverpool hit a wall. Having taken twenty-three years, six months and eleven days to top the table for the first time since their title win of 1923, it took them a mere twenty-one days to relinquish the position. Their two-month unbeaten run came to an end after the Arsenal game, in a 3–2 defeat at Blackpool which was more comprehensive than it sounds. Liverpool still clung to the top spot on goal average from Wolves, but the second-placed team came to Anfield the next weekend and toppled them in comprehensive style, a 5–1 victory in which Liverpool flailed and floundered, and Dennis Westcott scored four times, a feat not again achieved by a visiting player at Anfield until Arsenal's Andrei Arshavin fired the final four nails into Rafael Benítez's coffin in 2009. Westcott's feat was particularly spectacular, however, all his goals coming in a twenty-six-minute first-half flurry.

This was a full-on footballing lesson and Wolves deservedly supplanted Liverpool at the top. 'Liverpool could make nothing of Wolverhampton's fast and accurate passing,' reported the *Manchester Guardian*. 'Their forwards were in their best form … their half-backs were no less dangerous and commanded the play in attack and defence. They tackled cleanly and quickly and intercepted brilliantly. Cullis was particularly good, and Stubbins could not get past him.' Making the same point in the *Liverpool Echo*, albeit in a more light-hearted style, the cartoonist George Green pictured Stubbins peering myopically into the distance – and in the wrong direction – as Cullis swanned off in possession. 'It was not fair,' the caption ran. 'Liverpool supplied the ball and Cullis would not let Stubbins look at it.'

Liverpool bounced back with a pair of 4–1 wins against Sunderland and Aston Villa, keeping them two points off the top with a game in hand, but that offered a deceptive sense that all was well. It was shattered by a miserable sequence of five defeats in six games in the league. Kay's side fell to sixth, seven points behind the leaders Wolves. The young defender Hughes had lost confidence before succumbing to injury, while Balmer's boots had cooled considerably. However, there had been good performances throughout the bleak run from Paisley, Taylor, Liddell and Stubbins. And it was Stubbins who, at the beginning of February, struck a dramatic goal that turned Liverpool's season around.

Although his side was outplayed at Leeds, Stubbins popped up with an eighty-fifth-minute winner. That much-needed victory was followed by a fifth-round FA Cup win over the holders Derby County that was as comprehensive as the Leeds result before it had been fortunate. Liverpool won 1–0 thanks to a late Balmer goal, but had dominated the game almost in its entirety, even though Balmer himself had been injured early on and forced to limp along the right as a passenger. The early rounds of the Cup had given Liverpool succour through their barren run in the new year – to the point at which some fans had given up on the championship in the hope of a first FA Cup – but now the competition was kickstarting their league campaign too.

The win at Leeds and the Derby cup victory were the first and second of seven games won on the bounce, four more league victories following, plus a 4–1 victory over Birmingham City in a freezing FA Cup quarter-final, Stubbins scoring a hat-trick which included the most famous goal of his career, as he converted a powerful Liddell free-kick at the far post with a diving header two feet from the ground. 'With the force and velocity of the ball coming over and me heading it, the ball went past Gil Merrick like a rocket,' said Stubbins of an effort which would go down in legend as the Goal in the Snow. 'But with the pitch being so icy I skidded along the top of the ice and as I picked myself up my knees were all bloodied. Although at the time I didn't mind in the slightest.'

The season was suddenly full of promise again for Liverpool, who were back up to second in the league, albeit four points behind Wolves having played a game more, and with a semi-final against second-division Burnley to come. Sure enough, given the increasingly topsy-turvy nature of the season, they embarked on another nightmare sequence, one which looked to have completely scuppered any chance of glory whatsoever. A late equaliser denied them a win at Anfield over Derby and Liverpool then played out two turgid goalless draws, first in the FA Cup semi-final against Burnley at Ewood Park, then away at Preston on Good Friday, the first of three fixtures in four days over the Easter weekend.

The second game nearly did for their championship challenge. Two goals up at home to Blackpool with twenty-one minutes to go, the Reds shipped three in eleven minutes, Stan Mortensen scoring twice. That dropped Liverpool to third as Blackpool went top, although they'd played thirty-eight games compared to Wolves's thirty-three and Liverpool's thirty-four – the awful winter, as evidenced by Stubbins's Goal in the Snow coming in March, had wreaked havoc with the fixture list.

A week later, Burnley reached the FA Cup final at Liverpool's expense, Ray Harrison sweeping home a loose ball after Sidlow had flapped at a corner with eleven minutes to go. 'It was a bitter disappointment,' recalled Stubbins in *Three Sides of the Mersey*. 'Right through our cup run we thought we were good enough to get to Wembley and win the cup.' The team were not quite so self-assured when it came to the league run-in. Between the Blackpool debacle and the Burnley blow, Liverpool had beaten Preston North End 3–0 at Anfield in the final Easter fixture – the game mainly noteworthy these days because the Preston number four Bill Shankly missed a penalty – but that result was beginning to look like something of an irrelevance. 'We had seven games left,' recalled Liddell, 'only two of them at home, and the championship seemed out of reach. But we were not a team to give up on anything and everybody was determined to have a go of it.'

The seven-game run-in of 1946–47 stands – with all due respect to the team which charged from mid-table at Christmas to claim the title in 1981–82, and the class of '86 which reeled in Everton to win the Double – as the most spectacular, impressive and dramatic denouement to any of Liverpool's eighteen championship victories. It began quietly enough, with a workaday 1–0 win over Sunderland at Anfield. But from then on, as the realisation slowly mounted that the unlikely was becoming increasingly possible, and each match took on greater and greater significance, all that was left were mini epics.

Liverpool's next game was at Aston Villa, where they had not won since 1929. In the match against Sunderland, Balmer hobbling had rekindled old suspicions from the crowd. He received so much criticism for his inability to contribute meaningfully that the correspondent from the *Daily Post* wrote that 'they levelled their laughter at Balmer and I hate them for it ... barracking home players has become a disgrace, and perhaps the Anfield enthusiast is never so happy as when he is miserable.' How quickly they had forgotten the fifteen goals in seven games. For the Villa game, the injured striker was replaced by the debutant Billy Watkinson, who scored after nine minutes, as Liverpool chalked up another hard-fought two points with a 2–1 win.

Two down, five to go, and the next was a big one: Manchester United in the final home game of the season. Liverpool avenged the 5–0 embarrassment at Old Trafford with a 1–0 victory, Stubbins sticking a foot out to score in a penalty-box scramble instigated by lightning work from Liddell after twelve minutes, the home side digging in for the remainder. 'United's inability to produce a shot in keeping with their excellent midfield and approach play cost them dear,' reported the *Guardian*. 'Again and again over-elaboration when a first-time shot was called for allowed the Liverpool defence to cover and preserve the lead ... United did their best work in the second half [but] Liverpool's defenders did well, particularly Hughes, Jones, Lambert and [Eddie] Spicer.'

Liverpool's resilience had clearly been key, although despite United's dominance in attack, the paper was quick to point out nevertheless that 'Liddell was the best forward on view, and was always the master of [Johnny] Carey.' Liverpool's only real outlet, Liddell was rewarded for his bothersomeness by being cleaned out by the United keeper Jack Crompton. 'As Liddell got to his feet,' Crompton said in *Red and Raw*, 'I heard a voice not far behind me shout something like "Hey Crompton, we'll fucking get you after the match." I just grinned and put it out of my mind, because if you worried every time someone swore at you, you'd never walk onto a football field again. But after the game I was walking outside the ground with Johnny Carey when we were approached by four big fellows. Suddenly I remembered the voice in the crowd and wondered what we were in for. Then one of them said to me, "It's OK, Jack, there's no one here. We heard what those silly buggers shouted at you and we thought we'd come along to make sure the sides were equal." And the best part of it was, these four men were scousers ... That sort of generous feeling was typical of the way the

Liverpool and United camps behaved towards one another at that time. Somewhat healthier than modern developments, wouldn't you say?'

Liverpool had responded to the pressure applied by history better than United – who, it should be remembered, had won nothing of note themselves, a Second Division title apart, since 1911 – and were only three points off the leaders Wolves, in fourth place. Next up was a visit to Charlton Athletic, who had beaten Burnley in the FA Cup final when the Reds were scraping past Villa a fortnight earlier. It was Charlton's first match at the Valley since winning the Cup, and they showed it off before the game. Perhaps relieved that they were able to do so – the Charlton manager Jimmy Seed had managed to break the top off the lid and was forced to get a local garage owner to solder it back on as best he could – the relaxed home side offered little resistance to Liverpool, for whom Stubbins scored a hat-trick – although Bill Robinson showed some fight, scoring a late consolation in their 3–1 defeat and also breaking a post with a shot. (Charlton were quickly getting used to gear disintegrating around them. The shenanigans with goal-frames and cup lids came soon after a hat-trick of burst balls: in the Cup final they had just won, the Cup final they had lost against Derby the previous year and, weirdly, the league match against the same opposition a week before that 1946 final defeat.)

The main dramas of the day were occurring elsewhere. Everton, of all sides, condemned Wolves to their first home defeat in five months. Stoke were busy spectacularly shooting themselves in the foot, selling Stanley Matthews to Blackpool for £12,000, the winger having fallen out once and for all with Bob McGrory. And at Hampden Park in Glasgow, Billy Liddell, who had been selected for Great Britain in a representative exhibition against the Rest of the World, and therefore could not be at Charlton with his Liverpool teammates, pulled a muscle which would keep him out of the next two games. Still, on balance, it was a day Liverpool ended in credit as, all of a sudden, one point separated the top four teams: Wolves had fifty-three points, Stoke, United and Liverpool one fewer, United having played a game more than everyone else.

Time, then, as this season's preposterous narrative surely demanded, for Liverpool to lose ground at exactly the wrong moment. In the match they probably expected the least trouble in, too: a trip to Brentford, who were on their way to relegation. Liverpool huffed, puffed, and looked to have scraped a win when Liddell's replacement, the young South African winger Robert Priday, scored on seventy-two minutes, but George Stewart pulled Brentford level with seven minutes left. The draw should have buried Liverpool's title pretensions – but Wolves and Stoke were both also held, and Kay's side remained one point off the pace set by Wolves and United, the latter having won.

With two matches remaining, Liverpool were not in control of their own destiny. They sat in fourth, on the same points as Stoke City but with a worse goal average, and a point behind Manchester United, the only one of the four potential champions with just a single game remaining, and Wolverhampton Wanderers. Liverpool could overhaul United, then, and Wolves, who they visited in their final game. But even if they managed that, two wins for Stoke – now, absurdly, without Matthews – would send the title to the Potteries.

But first, Liverpool had to see off Arsenal at Highbury. Neither team fielded a full-strength line-up. Arsenal were without Leslie Compton, who was keeping wicket for Middlesex, while Bryn Jones was injured, although the Hoylake grocer Joe Mercer – who had an agreement to train at Anfield during the week – would make the team. Liverpool, meanwhile, had to make do without the injured Liddell and Paisley, who had limped off during the Brentford shambles.

Priday, however, did a magnificent job of standing in for Liddell down the left, causing Arsenal plenty of bother during an otherwise uneventful first half. But it was Arsenal who gained the upper hand during the early exchanges after the break and on the hour took the lead through Ian McPherson. Liverpool failed to respond immediately, and with time running out and the win a necessity, the game looked up for Kay's side.

Kay, however, was not in attendance himself. Astonishingly, he was away on unspecified transfer business, and left the running of the team pretty much to itself. The tactical change which followed, then, has to go down as one of the strangest and yet most effective switches in the history of English football, with the Liverpool directors taking a panicked vote and getting a message down to the touchline for the versatile Bill Jones – standing in for Paisley at left-half – to stay forward.

The added pressure paid off. With fourteen minutes to go, Liverpool won a corner from which the much-maligned Balmer ghosted beside Mercer to place a header past Arsenal's keeper, George Swindin. Three minutes later, Priday hit what might have been a cross, or might have been a shot, from the left. Balmer, busy making a nuisance of himself in the middle, enticed Swindin and the full-back Walley Barnes into a messy tangle, Barnes accidentally guiding the ball into the net (though the goal would, despite additional suggestions that Balmer may have got a touch himself, be credited to Priday).

Somehow, an under-strength and under-performing Liverpool had turned it round, and made it to the top of the table for the first time since November, although none of the other three challengers had played. Two days after the Arsenal win, on the Whitsun bank holiday Monday, all three of Liverpool's rivals won, although Manchester United, despite thrashing Sheffield United 6–2 in their final game of the season, could no longer win the league as they had inferior goal average to Wolves (which meant that either Wolves or Liverpool, playing each other on the final day, were certain to finish above them). Liverpool were back down to fourth, two spots behind United, but could still win the title if they beat Wolves and Stoke failed to win their final game at Sheffield United. Confused? You wouldn't have been alone: the *Sunday Times*, for example, in the wake of Liverpool's victory at Highbury, had called either the Reds or Wolves as champions – 'Last Match Soccer Decider!' – totally ignoring the claims of the other two hopefuls.

But the equation for Liverpool was simple: win or bust at Molineux, and then wait to see whether Stoke City could respond.

Wolves, for their part, could have secured the title for themselves with a victory, whatever Stoke did later on. They were strong favourites to do so. Liverpool were admittedly the form side, having won six and drawn one of their previous seven, while Wolves had stumbled on the run-in, drawing at Portsmouth, then following up a home loss to Everton with a careless 3–3 draw against Blackburn at Molineux. But they had dug in for a 1–0 win at Huddersfield in their penultimate game and in any case had looked the team most likely all season: apart from a short period when they had been deposed by a Blackpool side that had played several games more, Wolves had been the leaders of the division since reaching the summit in early December. Which, it was not forgotten, they did by leapfrogging Liverpool with that 5–1 thrashing at Anfield. 'Wolves should make sure today,' trumpeted the *Sporting Chronicle* on the morning of the match. Billy Wright was back for the home side after England games in Switzerland and Portugal, and the paper's correspondent suggested that 'the return of Wright, who was at his best in the Lisbon international will, I feel certain, turn the scales in favour of Wolverhampton.'

But neither side went into the game at full strength. Crucially, Wolves were missing the league's leading goalscorer Dennis Westcott, who had added thirty-four goals to the four he had scored at Anfield. They were also collectively reeling from the news that their thirty-one-year-old captain and defensive pivot Stan Cullis was retiring after the game, a fact announced to a shocked Molineux crowd over the PA system sixty minutes before kick-off. He had been suffering from frequent and severe concussions and was told by doctors that repeated heading of the heavy old-style balls could prove fatal. This match, then, would serve as his last chance to win a medal, Wolves having come home second in the 1937–38 and 1938–39 league championships and surprisingly lost that FA Cup final in 1939.

Liverpool, meanwhile, were still without Paisley and Taylor, and Fagan had picked up a knock, so despite Liddell's return, Priday kept his place. 'We had to make a switch,' explained Stubbins, 'with Liddell playing in the unusual position for him of inside-left, even though he wore number seven. Bob Priday came in at outside-left. I said to him before the game, if you lie deep and pick up the ball, just hit a long pass, not to my feet but past me and past Stan Cullis. I'll see what I can do with it.'

It was a baking hot day. 'There was about 50,000 there and there were men with handkerchiefs tied around their heads,' said Sidlow, who as a former Wolves charge 'got a grand rally' from both sets of supporters as he took to the pitch. 'They were carrying some of the girls out of the terraces because it was too hot. When I took off my sweater after the game, you'd have thought I'd taken my undershirt out of the bath.' With the conditions blistering, the teams were unable to go at it full pelt, but Liverpool's renowned stamina – the last beneficial drops of the McConnell-inspired pre-season trip to the States being almost literally wrung out – eventually gave them the upper hand in a coruscating first half.

Wolves won the toss and kicked off, and were immediately on the attack, but a header from Jimmy Mullen flew behind. Mullen proved a thorn in Liverpool's side during the opening exchanges. He was denied twice when lurking in the area, both times by Jim Harley, who first cleared with a spectacular overhead kick, then by nipping in at an opportune moment to intercept the ball. Mullen miskicked when looking to shoot on the turn, then fired a free-kick straight at Sidlow after a clever dummy from Wright. 'Considering the conditions, the first ten minutes had produced fine fast football,' reported the *Echo*, 'but the testing time would come later when the pace had taken toll of stamina.'

Liddell made a couple of abortive sorties upfield, but was initially spending most of his time helping out at the back, Wolves having started the stronger. 'Although Wolves so far had done nearly all the attacking, the visiting goal had never been in danger,' added the *Echo*. 'The Wolves were not producing shots commensurate with their territorial advantage.'

A costly mistake, as Liverpool were to stun the hosts on twenty-one minutes with a 'beautiful copy-book move' involving five men. From a throw down the left, Liddell raked a pass forward to Balmer, the captain since that fateful match against Portsmouth back in November – who exchanged passes with Watkinson and Priday, then clipped a left-footed shot into the right-hand corner of the net. 'This was forward teamwork at its best,' noted Ranger from the *Echo*. 'Though it was against the run of play, Liverpool deserved reward for the sheer brilliance of the move.'

The home side came back at Liverpool, increasing the pace, but 'still Sidlow had nothing to do but watch shots go over his bar or wide of the post', one promising triangular interchange between Wright, Pye and Mullen fizzling out with no end product, Johnny Hancocks firing wide from close range and Jimmy Alderson coming closest with a rising effort that only just cleared the bar. But Sidlow, when required to step into action, was in determined form. On thirty-seven minutes, he made a point-blank, strong-handed save from Jimmy Dunn. From the resulting Wolves corner, Liverpool broke on the counter, whereupon the decisive act of the season took place.

Cullis had dominated Stubbins in Liverpool's humiliation at the hands of Wolves back in December. On that day, the Wolves defence and midfield intercepted almost everything, Liverpool attempting to carve open their opponents with short passing manoeuvres in the middle and failing. But Stubbins had been thinking long and hard about going more direct and the instructions he had issued to Priday before the game were about to be carried out to the letter.

'The first opportunity Priday got, he knocked it straight down the middle for me to chase,' recalled Stubbins. 'It took the Wolves defence completely by surprise. Anticipating what he was going to do, I had already set off ... Without wasting any time, I was ready for it ... Bob hit a long pass over the head of Stan Cullis, who went after it. So did Billy Wright, while the two full-backs tried to close the gap. I got the ball, accelerated, and took it past them. As I closed in on goal, the keeper Bert Williams came rushing off his line but I just managed to get my toe on the ball and rolled it past him into the corner of the net.' It was catharsis for Stubbins and effectively the moment the title was decided.

The modest Stubbins underplayed what had been a spectacular effort. 'The flame-headed centre-forward took the blind side of Cullis – caught on the wrong foot – and in a twinkling was in full cry for goal,' reported David Williams in the *Herald*. 'A deft right-foot flick and an elated Golden Miller leap over the prone Williams crowned a 70-yard solo run. Even at 85 shade degrees one sensed the chilly shock of this setback for Wolves.'

Two down at half-time despite the lion's share, Wolves were sorely missing Westcott and, with Mullen and Pye out of sorts, threw Wright into the forward line after the break. Their desperation should have cost them when, having loaded the Liverpool box for a corner, Balmer broke upfield and fed Stubbins, who found himself one on one with Bert Williams only to clank the ball off the keeper's knee and away to safety.

Liverpool did find the net for a third time when Liddell's free-kick ballooned in off Cullis, but the referee whistled for offside. The escape gave Wolves succour, and after a period of pressure which saw Mullen force Sidlow into an instinctive save with a snap shot and Pye slice a golden opportunity wide from close range, the Liverpool dam eventually broke. Chasing after a corner on sixty-five minutes, Sidlow could only send a weak punch out to Jimmy Dunn, who lobbed the keeper. But despite a barrage of pressure – 'We hammered them after we scored,' recalled Dunn, a boyhood fan of the Reds – the Liverpool back-line held firm, Wolves unable to manufacture any other notable opportunities. 'The Liverpool defence remained too solid and surprisingly quick to recover despite the blistering heat,' reported the *Herald*. The full-time whistle went, Cullis shaking Stubbins's hand with tears rolling down his cheeks, his last chance of a medal gone. 'That goal I scored plagued him,' the striker said years later. 'Wherever he went, people asked him about it and why he hadn't tugged my shirt. I think he deserves a lot of credit for the fact that he didn't, because he might have got away with it.' Cullis himself reflected that 'I suppose I could have done, but I didn't want to go down in history as the man who decided the destiny of a championship with a professional foul.' An outstanding sporting gesture from the Wolves captain, the sort to be expected from a man Bill Shankly would, in his dotage, describe as 'soft as mash ... he would give you his last penny.'

For Wolves, and Cullis, whose heart had already been broken once at the 1939 Cup final, the dream was over. 'We were on top too long,' reflected their broken captain. 'It was as though [the British middle-distance runner] Sydney Wooderson had tried to win a race by leading all the way, instead of keeping handy in second or third place. It's been the hardest season I've known, and has ended in the second great disappointment of my career.'

But Liverpool still harboured hope. The Liverpool players chaired their captain Balmer – Liverpool's other scorer that day, their leading marksman of the season and the man who had shrugged off so much stick from his own fans – off the pitch although they knew the title was not yet theirs. A fortnight later, Stoke City would travel to Sheffield United, where a win would see them leapfrog Liverpool at the top on goal average.

Once again, Liverpool were priced as second favourites in a two-horse race, because Stoke were expected to prevail against a side with nothing to play for, even without the departed Matthews. In the *Telegraph*, squirrelled away under a lengthy report on the victory of Willie Turner of New York over Richard Chapman of Pinehurst in the final of the British Amateur golf championship at Carnoustie, was a small titbit headlined 'Stoke City may win title'. The possibility of Liverpool doing so seems not to have occurred.

Stoke's form on the run-in had been even better than Liverpool's – unbeaten in eleven, having won eight of their previous nine. But Stoke went down 2–1. United's veteran inside-left Jack Pickering – a thirty-eight-year-old making his only appearance of the campaign, his first competitive game in eight years – was the star of the show. He opened the scoring after three minutes, and then, Alec Ormston having equalised not long after, set up Walter Rickett for the winner just after the restart. A message detailing Stoke's failure was relayed to Anfield, where Liverpool were playing Everton in the final of the Liverpool Senior Cup. 'Midway through the second half we heard a hubbub amongst the crowd,' said Stubbins. 'We knew something was happening. Then we heard cheers and the news was brought to us in the centre of the pitch that we were champions. The Everton players immediately shook our hands to congratulate us on the pitch.'

Cyril Sidlow put it more succinctly: 'Everyone went mad.'

Everyone went mad on Merseyside, anyway. Liverpool's success was curiously underplayed in the national media. The headline news on the sports pages the following day concerned the England squad which had been selected for the upcoming first Test against South Africa, although this said more about the respective value of cricket and football at the time rather than being any slight on Liverpool.

The *Sporting Chronicle*'s analyst suggested that 'teamwork rather than individual brilliance has been responsible for

Liverpool's championship success' although he did go on to isolate two players for particular praise. 'Stubbins has proved to be worth every penny of the £13,000 spent in securing him. His interchanging of position with Jackie Balmer has been one of the features of Liverpool's play.'

Meanwhile Ranger, in the *Liverpool Echo*, acclaimed the 'balanced teamwork, good managerial direction and training and harmony between the boardroom and the dressing-room … Taylor has reached the highest pinnacle as a right-half, and further honours are almost certainly in store for him … There has been the general utility work of Bill Jones, who has acquitted himself well wherever he has played; the ability to occupy any position is the hallmark of the born footballer, though few can fill so many niches with such brilliance as Jones has done … Ray Lambert has had a great season. Today he is one of the deadliest tacklers in the game, with exceptional powers of recovery … Like Taylor, Bob Paisley has had spells in the past in the forward line but the left-half berth is undoubtedly his forte. What a terrier-like type he is, and what a terrific worker.'

But Liverpool failed to build on the success of 1947. Having come close to the Double in the first post-war season, they came close again three years later, in what is probably the club's great forgotten campaign. The spine of the team was pretty much the same – Sidlow, Lambert, Spicer, Taylor, Hughes, Jones, Stubbins, Fagan and Liddell were all still there – and having suffered two distinctly average, mid-table seasons since their title win, Kay's side found their form again in 1949–50. They made a then-record unbeaten start to their league campaign, going nineteen games without defeat until the middle of December. They lost back-to-back games against Huddersfield and Sunderland, though the wheels took a while properly to work themselves off the axle. When they won 2–0 at Burnley on Good Friday, they were still top of the table, and had already reached the FA Cup final, Bob Paisley famously scoring with a speculative lob in the Maine Road semi-final against Everton. But the day after, Stubbins was helped from the field with concussion at Newcastle, and the Reds crashed to a 5–1 defeat.

Their season never recovered. Liverpool lost three of their remaining four league matches, drawing the other, and limped home in eighth spot, five points behind the eventual winners Portsmouth. In fairness, they weren't the only team to usher Pompey through; Sunderland lost three of their last five, missing out by a point, while Manchester United were three points adrift at the end, having won only one of their last ten matches – and that when it was too late for them. (Dramatic as the denouement was, it wasn't unprecedented: league campaigns of yore, children of the Premier League may be surprised to note, often held the interest of several clubs right up until the final matches, teams taking huge leaps and suffering large falls as the table reshaped itself dramatically over the closing stretch as fatigue and panic or inspiration set in.) But Liverpool's misery was completed at Wembley when Arsenal, decked out in golden shirts, tarnished their gentle-manly image by unleashing the half-back Alex Forbes on his compatriot Liddell, kicking Liverpool's star player out of a wretched match the Gunners won 2–0. Their old friend Joe Mercer – still welcome to train at Anfield during the run-up to the final, the world being a thoroughly more sporting place back then, the Reds even detailing a young Jimmy Melia to work with the Arsenal captain – lifted the Cup.

The final had been a painful experience from start to finish for Liverpool. Paisley had been controversially left out, de-spite his semi-final goal against Everton and having his name printed in the final programme. The young striker Kevin Baron had been forced to spend the night before the game on a bunk bed in the ballroom of the team hotel, the result of a mix-up with the booking. And Kay looked pale and drawn as he sat on the bench, suffering from the stress and nerv-ous exhaustion that would force him to retire a year later and contribute to his premature demise in 1954. ('He smoked himself to death,' noted Cyril Done. A strapping six-footer, Kay weighed less than seven stone when he died aged sixty-two.)

There was one consolation for the players: the support. Liverpool still hadn't broken their FA Cup duck – they were by far the biggest club in the country not to have won the trophy and the only team to have won the league but not football's oldest and grandest tournament – but their fans made sure the team knew their efforts had been appreciated. When Liverpool arrived back in the city after their Wembley disappointment to an empty Lime Street station, they had glumly assumed nobody had bothered to come along to commiserate with the losers. In fact, the crowds had simply not been let into the station. 'When we got out it was fantastic,' said Maisie Taylor, the captain's wife. 'I've never seen so many people on Lime Street. Even when they won the Cup for the first time it wasn't as good as that.' The team went to the Town Hall, standing awhile on the balcony, then travelled all the way to Anfield, which was packed to its rickety roof-beams. 'There were men and women shedding tears,' recalled Stubbins. 'If we had won the Cup we couldn't have had a better occasion. That was typical of the Anfield crowd, and I remember Phil Taylor had to say a few words as captain, and it was a very emotive thing, and I think Phil had a few tears.'

The bittersweet conclusion to the 1949–50 season was the last time for over a decade Liverpool flirted with glory. Kay resigned through ill health in 1951 and was replaced by Don Welsh, who had captained Charlton to the FA Cup four years earlier. 'I don't think he took to the responsibility of the job that he was doing,' suggested Ray Lambert. The winger Jimmy Payne offered an illustration that suggested Lambert had not required the benefits of hindsight to arrive at his conclusion. 'He [Welsh] used to walk around the boardroom on his hands when we'd won a match. Do you know the steps at Anfield where you come off the ground? I don't think they're there now. He'd walk down them steps on his hands.'

It would be nice to think Welsh at least had cheap metaphors in mind, because under his management Liverpool embarked on an inelegant descent into the Second Division, suffering relegation for the first time in half a century in 1954. He was replaced by Phil Taylor, but the legendary captain could never quite guide his sides into the top two promotion places. Perhaps the only high point left in the entire decade for Liverpool was a 4–0 win over Everton at Goodison in the FA Cup in January 1955, during which Liddell – who had been offered an escape route upon the club's relegation via a transfer to Aston Villa, but turned it down as both club and city meant too much to him – scored what he considered the best goal of his career. Taking delivery of a distinctly average cross from the right, ten yards out, he dinked it over Everton defender Tommy Jones's head, dropped a shoulder to glide past him on the left, then whipped a shot into the bottom right. 'I cannot recall a goal which gave me a greater thrill,' Liddell said.

Liverpool would tread water under Taylor, the immediate post-war era over. It is one in danger of being neglected, especially as there are so few yards of film capturing the side of the late forties in action and those who remember it pass on. And yet, pound for pound, George Kay's great side contained as many bona fide Liverpool legends as any other: Phil Taylor; Bob Paisley; Cyril Sidlow; the versatile and invaluable Bill Jones, a class act in several positions; Jack Balmer, unloved then, but surely begging to be reclaimed as a cult hero, Liverpool's support owing him a great karmic debt.

And then there were the side's two big names: Albert Stubbins, a gentle giant who quietly went about repaying his record transfer fee with immediate effect, though not so gentle that he wouldn't later belligerently, and rather marvellously, go on strike when he felt the mandarins on the Anfield board had reneged on his contract stipulations – also later destined to find everlasting fame as a member of Sgt Pepper's Lonely Hearts Club Band; and, of course, the winger Billy Liddell, to a certain generation of Liverpool supporter still the greatest player ever to pull on a red shirt.

And finally there was the chairman Bill McConnell, the caterer who quite literally fed Liverpool the fuel that would propel them to the 1946–47 title, then used up his own last precious drops of energy to ensure the capture of Stubbins. Despite being struck down with what proved to be a fatal illness during the run-in, McConnell survived long enough to see the club he ran so inspirationally collect the league trophy and be awarded the match ball from Stoke's ill-fated game at Sheffield United as a souvenir. A photo exists of McConnell, propped up by pillows in his hospital bed, receiving the tatty old orange ball that had seen his club crowned champions of England for the first time in twenty-three years. As he reaches out to take it from the nurse, he is smiling. It is not the weak, struggling, thin-lipped smile of a dying man. It is the broad, toothy, sunny grin of a child, enlivened by the innocent joy football can bring, wondering what, of the game's infinite world of possibilities, awaited his beloved Liverpool next.

CHAPTER 3

FA Cup final, Wembley, London, 1 May 1965

Liverpool   **2–1**   **Leeds United**
Hunt 93   *Bremner 100*
St John 113

(after extra-time)

Tommy Lawrence	Gary Sprake
Chris Lawler	Paul Reaney
Gerry Byrne	Willie Bell
Geoff Strong	Billy Bremner
Ron Yeats	Jack Charlton
Willie Stevenson	Norman Hunter
Ian Callaghan	John Giles
Roger Hunt	Jim Storrie
Ian St John	Alan Peacock
Tommy Smith	Bobby Collins
Peter Thompson	Albert Johanneson

Bill Shankly   Don Revie

Ref: W. Clements
Bkd:
Att: **c.** 100,000

LIVERPOOL'S PLAYERS WOKE AT 11 A.M. in the Oatlands Hotel in Weybridge. It was a grey, wet May morning but, as far as Bill Shankly was concerned, it was the most important day in the club's history. His revolution had taken the club to promotion in 1962 and to the league title two years later but, for him, there was still something missing. 'Liverpool had never won the FA Cup,' he said, 'and that was a terrible thing.'

So focused was Shankly on winning the Cup that he'd rested seven players for the final league game of the season. Liverpool won 3–1 away at Wolves, but the FA still reprimanded Shankly. He had reason to be cautious, though: in a 4–0 defeat at Chelsea ten days earlier, on Good Friday, Ian St John, Ian Callaghan and Gordon Milne had all been injured. Callaghan was in such pain from an ankle injury that his parents, with whom he was still living at the time, had to call out a doctor that night. He and St John recovered to play in the final; Milne, having damaged his knee, did not. His father, a teammate of Shankly's at Preston, had similarly missed the 1938 FA Cup final through injury.

Thirteen years earlier, Liverpool had stayed in the same hotel before a Cup final. Then too they'd been recent winners of the league and had been desperate to underline the club's status as one of the elite. On that occasion two goals from Reg Lewis had undone them as they'd lost 2–0 to Arsenal. This time it was the Leeds United of Don Revie who opposed them, a side who seemed to be following a similar trajectory. They'd been promoted a year after Liverpool and had finished second in the league that season, behind Manchester United on goal average having stumbled on the run-in when faced with a final schedule of five matches in ten days. Liverpool themselves – as defending champions – had finished only seventh. 'Our opponents, Leeds United, have proved themselves beyond doubt to be a great team,' Shankly acknowledged. 'Clearly the whole set up at Leeds is one of the finest. But the better the opposition, the better we play.'

He knew the significance of the occasion, but he was determined the players should be as relaxed as possible for it. The night before the final, Shankly took his team to the London Palladium to see the Liverpudlian comedian Ken Dodd. They went backstage with him and were given tickling sticks as a souvenir before taking the coach back to Weybridge. Having had their lie-in, the players took a walk around the grounds, returning to the hotel for a pre-match meal of beef, fish or eggs at noon. They boarded the coach at the riskily late time of 12.30 – Shankly hated his players hanging around at stadiums before games, feeling it made them anxious – and, after a brief delay as they waited for a promised police escort that failed to show up, set off, an empty coach tailing them in case the first bus broke down. On the way, the players listened to a recording of Shankly on *Desert Island Discs*, the programme having originally been broadcast the previous Monday.

That Shankly's selections should have leaned to Celtic nostalgia – Kenneth McKellar singing 'My Love is like a Red, Red Rose' and 'The Last Rose of Summer' performed by Sydney MacEwan and Robinson Cleaver – was perhaps predictable but his choice seemed to go beyond a yearning for the old country and the simple values of home to something quite maudlin. His list also included 'Because You're Mine', sung by Mario Lanza, who had died from a pulmonary embolism six years earlier at the age of thirty-eight, and 'Danny Boy', sung by Jim Reeves, killed aged forty in a plane crash less than a year before. It's almost as though he were drawn to tragedy; certainly, for all he liked to play the Jimmy Cagney-style hard man, there was also a broad streak of sentimentality about

Shankly. And that, of course, was part of what made him so popular in a city not averse to a bit of Celtic sentimentality itself: beneath the tough exterior lay a raw and beating heart. 'They say he's tough, he's hard, he's ruthless,' said Joe Mercer. 'Rubbish, he's got a heart of gold, he loves the game, he loves his fans, he loves his players. He's like an old collie dog; he doesn't like hurting his sheep. He'll drive them, certainly, but bite them never.'

Shankly's chosen book was a biography of Robert Burns; his luxury item, predictably enough, was a football; while there were also songs favoured by the Kop: Danny Kaye and Louis Armstrong performing 'When the Saints Go Marching In' and, of course, the Gerry and the Pacemakers version of 'You'll Never Walk Alone'. The way that song was adopted and became the anthem of Liverpool, Shankly insisted, was emblematic of how central the club was in the great cultural boom the city enjoyed in the early sixties. 'The whole of Liverpool came alive … with the Beatles and Cilla Black and comedians like Ken Dodd and Jimmy Tarbuck …' he wrote in his autobiography. 'The whole thing was boiling and bubbling and this is what I'd been looking for from the start.'

Liverpool, suddenly, was fashionable. Between April 1963 and May 1964, there was always a Liverpool act at number one in the charts. Shankly's side was part of that phenomenon and it also benefited from it, lifted by the general sense of optimism. Bill Harry, who was one of John Lennon's classmates at Liverpool Art College and founded the magazine *Mersey Beat*, insisted that 'Liverpool is like New Orleans at the turn of the century, but with rock 'n' roll instead of jazz.' The city, wrote Paul Du Noyer in *Liverpool: Wondrous Place, Music from the Cavern to the Coral* became 'the pride of Great Britain and – increasingly – a source of wonder to the world. The media was infatuated. Everyone was talking about this damp, grubby town that nobody had thought twice about for fifty years … Liverpool, so often out of step with the national mood was now its very model: cheeky and young, un-posh, un-stuffy, democratic to the boot heels.' The result was a sense of un-stoppable momentum, football and music going hand in hand to create the sense of a city on the up.

Perhaps Shankly was fortunate to catch the wave but few other managers would have been as adept as he was at riding it and benefiting from the cultural uplift. To say he was an arch-manipulator makes the process sound cold, contrived, when it was almost certainly heartfelt, but there was no man-ager better at the time – and there may not have been any since – at whipping a crowd into a fervour. He felt for the fans and understood the fans, because he had been a fan; he knew what it was to have worked at a hard manual job and how foot-ball could provide a release. 'I came to Liverpool because of the people,' he later claimed. 'They have a fighting spirit with fighting blood in the veins but mixed with it is a tremendous kindness.'

There is a famous shot of Shankly walking round a trium-phant Anfield taken by the noted Liverpool photographer Steve Hale. He is wearing a jacket and a bright Jimmy Cagney-style tie, while round his neck is knotted a scarf tossed by a fan. It is his eyes that stand out, though: they have a mysti-cal quality, as though he sees more than anyone else there, knows the tribulation and the trauma that lie before and beyond any triumph. Shankly, far more than Paisley or any of his other successors, was a utopian. He wasn't just building a great football club, he was building a socialistic paradise, a movement of the workers and the people of Liverpool. He was always available for photographs, autographs and kickabouts; knock on his door – he lived by Everton's training-ground at Bellefield in West Derby, only a mile or so from Liverpool's base at Melwood – and the chances were you'd be asked in for a cup of tea. There are countless stories of him procuring tick-ets for fans or reaching into his own pocket to help fans get home from away games. As he told Harold Wilson when the prime minister appeared on the radio show Shankly hosted after retiring as manager, he was a socialist in the simplest, most instinctive sense in that he had read no books of theory but believed in equality and building networks of mutual support. He saw football as a means for changing the world, largely because he knew nothing else but football. (Shankly's obsession with football meant that, at times, he could seem startlingly unworldly. On one trip to the US, for instance, he saw a fleet of VW vans and reflected on how astonishingly broad the reach of Woolworth's was, refusing to accept that it wasn't their logo he was seeing.) Paisley was in some ways – although only some – a gentler, more approachable figure, less abrasive and more worldly wise, but he lacked Shankly's idealism: football management for him was not about building a community but about winning matches and trophies.

As the bus neared Wembley that afternoon, Shankly stood at the window, waving to fans while telling the players they couldn't let the support down. 'I knew we were going to win the Cup and the thought of getting beat didn't enter my head,' said Ron Yeats, Liverpool's captain and, to use Shankly's term, their colossus. 'We were a better team than Leeds and were better organised. I actually spent more time worrying about what I was going to say to the Queen than about the match itself. That may sound big-headed but it's the truth. I didn't suffer from pre-match nerves, I was looking forward to the game and couldn't wait to get started. Leeds had a hard reputation but we had done well against them in the league that season. The best team in the league we all felt was Chelsea and we had beaten them in the semi-final.' In the league, Liverpool had beaten Leeds 2–1 at Anfield but had been beaten 4–2 in the return; although as both games were played in the first fortnight of the season, their worth as a guide to how the game might go was limited.

As they approached Wembley, the bus was caught in heavy traffic and there were genuine concerns that kick-off might have to be delayed – as it had been before the fourth-round game against West Bromwich Albion – but a lone police motorcycle was spotted and Bob Paisley dispatched to arrange an impromptu escort. The traffic itself was an indication of how the club had captured the imagination of the city. So dense was it that many fans didn't get in to Wembley until half an hour of the final had been played, while the trains south had been rammed. 'By 5am Euston station had been transformed into a seething mass of red and white as nearly 1500 supporters from the first three specials milled around in the station entrance ...' reported the *Liverpool Echo*. '"Lime Street station was crammed to the brim when our train left. They were singing and dancing in the streets and playing guitars," said one fan.'

Aside from concerns they might be late, the build-up was all about relaxation. Jimmy Tarbuck and Frankie Vaughan were invited into the dressing-room before kick-off, while Shankly made a point of leaving the door open; Leeds's remained defiantly locked – an indication, he insisted, of how terrified they were. It was typical of Shankly's approach to psychology. 'You're going to win because you're the best team,' he told his side. 'Leeds are honoured to be on the same field as you. And you're not going to disappoint the greatest supporters in the world. If necessary – and it won't be – you should be prepared to die for them.'

Shankly's story at Liverpool began in a sense with an FA Cup tie, specifically the 2–1 defeat to Worcester City of the Southern League in January 1959. Although that embarrassment came in the midst of a run of eight straight league wins that lifted Liverpool to second in the Second Division, it crystallised frustration. When Liverpool's form faltered and they missed out on promotion, there was a sense that the manager Phil Taylor couldn't afford a poor start to the following season – but that was precisely what he suffered. Liverpool lost five of their first eleven games and when they could only draw against Portsmouth, who had been promoted from the Third Division the previous season, the crowd responded with a slow handclap. A 4 2 defeat at Lincoln City on 14 November that left Liverpool eleventh in the table proved the final straw and Taylor, who had won the championship as a player and captained the side in an FA Cup final, resigned – twenty-four years after he'd joined Liverpool.

A fortnight later, Liverpool lost 1–0 at Huddersfield Town, who climbed to fifth as a result. Two days after that, Liverpool confirmed the appointment of the Huddersfield manager Bill Shankly as Taylor's replacement. T. V. Williams, the Liverpool chairman, had reputedly approached him and asked him if he'd like to manage the best club in the country. 'Why, is Matt Busby packing up?' he replied.

That Liverpool's potential was greater than Huddersfield's was clear, though, which explains why Shankly made the move. Why Liverpool went for him is less obvious. Williams had been at Huddersfield's league game against Cardiff on 17 October and, although his side had lost 1–0, Shankly had impressed the chairman both with his constant shouting and with the players' response to his instructions. Other directors seemed swayed as much by Liverpool's 5–0 defeat to Huddersfield a year earlier as by anything else in Shankly's career.

Shankly had been born in the Ayrshire mining village of Glenbuck in 1913, the son of a postman who became a tailor. He was one of ten children, five girls and five boys; all the brothers ended up as professional footballers, most notably his elder brother Bob, who went on to manage Dundee to the Scottish title in 1962. Having left school at fourteen, Shankly worked as a miner for two years until the local pit closed, leaving him unemployed. He later admitted that even when he was working, he'd effectively been killing time until he was offered professional terms by a football club.

Contrary to popular myth, Shankly seems never to have played for Glenbuck Cherrypickers, the local side with a proud history of producing professionals. He had a trial there but they folded a year later and he ended up playing his first organised football twelve miles from Glenbuck at Cronberry. It was there that he was spotted by scouts from Carlisle United and invited for a month's trial. They signed him after just one game, even though Carlisle reserves lost 6–0 to Middlesbrough reserves. Shankly spent a single season at Brunton Park, helping the reserves to the North Eastern League Cup and making sixteen appearances for the senior side. In 1933 he moved to Preston and soon became a regular, playing as a tough right-half in the side that lost to Sunderland in the 1937 FA Cup final and then won the competition the following year, beating Huddersfield Town in the final.

He served in the RAF during the Second World War, turning out occasionally for Partick Thistle in wartime friendlies. His new wife Ness – a member of the Women's Auxiliary Air Force – came to see him play at Celtic Park but left before the end of the game because Shankly, by his own admission, was 'having a bit of rough-house on the floor'. After the war, he resumed his playing career with Preston and became club captain. He missed most of the 1948–49 season through injury and, realising his time as a player was coming to an end, began looking for an exit. He applied for every coaching job he saw in the small ads in sporting papers and magazines and even completed a physiotherapy course, reasoning he may have to work as a trainer before getting a coaching job (a route followed by Paisley). When Ivor Broadis, Carlisle's player-manager, sold himself to Sunderland, the club were left looking for a replacement. Shankly applied for the job and, after retiring as a player in March 1949, was appointed as manager, taking charge of his first game the following month, the Cumberland Cup final in which Carlisle beat Workington 2–1.

Preston were furious, realising suddenly how valuable Shankly could have been in a fight against relegation they ultimately lost. They tried to entice him to stay by pointing out he was due a benefit at the end of the season; Shankly pointed out he didn't need to be at the club to receive it. Needless to say, it was never arranged, contributing to the distrust of directors that characterised his dealings with them throughout his career.

Carlisle, impoverished and geographically remote, was not an easy place to start. While Shankly clearly learned about the role and its responsibilities – and more about the untrustworthiness of directors – he was in a sense simply putting into practice there the principles he had carried throughout his life. As Dave Bowler wrote in his authorised biography of Shankly:

The domestic stability offered by his wife and children were crucial to his success, his home offering a haven where he could forget the pressures of club football and recharge his batteries prior to the battles that lay ahead. That family ideal was perhaps the central tenet of Shanklyism. As a boy he was one of a large family and a member of an even greater community in the mining village of Glenbuck. His political ideas grew from that time, leaving him a lifelong socialist who played like a socialist and managed like a socialist. Everything about Shankly was geared to fostering a community, a powerful team spirit that acknowledged the fact that no individual component was more important than the greater good.

When Shankly arrived at Carlisle it was in a mess, run down and with directors, players and fans all seemingly convinced things could never improve. They were right to the extent that the possibilities for growth were restricted, but Shankly set about raising morale and raising the club's profile. He bought new kit, organised the purchase of a club house for players to lodge in and began broadcasting to the crowd over the Tannoy before games. Fans, it was said, would turn up a couple of hours before kick-off just to hear him speak. Very quickly, he instilled a sense of purpose, smartness and dedication. 'In Glenbuck,' Bowler wrote, 'life was lived within a moral framework of helping your neighbour, looking after one another, taking an interest in your locale. Carlisle United would become a village where all those virtues were practised. The club would become the focus of the city, bringing it to life, giving it a source of pride, a virtuous spiral that would benefit club and city.'

He changed training, bringing in methods that would become familiar at Liverpool, getting rid of much of the running on roads that had dominated sessions previously, insisting on practices on grass and increasing the use of the ball to develop technique. Five-a-sides became a regular feature for their value in enhancing special awareness, first touch and team spirit. 'Results,' Shankly said, 'will come from organised football. I don't want any haphazard football at all.'

He told the players they were the best side in the division and treated them as though they were even better than that. He would arrange for plumbers or electricians to visit if they were having problems, believing players should be left free to concentrate on their football. He himself took defeats badly, typically responding to setbacks by going home and scrubbing the cooker from top to bottom.

Carlisle finished ninth in 1949–50, his first full season in charge. So effectively had he caught the imagination of the local public that the club sold a record number of season-tickets for the following year. Shankly seemed aware, though, that there was a limit on what could be achieved at Carlisle and, the following season, he was dissuaded from accepting a coaching job at Grimsby Town only by the promise of a bonus if his side finished in the top three in the division. Despite that, he applied for the Liverpool job the following February after the retirement of George Kay. The eccentric Don Welsh was preferred – seemingly in part because in his interview Shankly had been so adamant that he, rather than the directors, should have the final say over team selection – and Shankly returned to Carlisle, leading them to third in the table. The board, though, cavilled over the bonus – at which Shankly walked. He'd initially applied for the position of coach at Grimsby but when it became apparent that the manager, Charlie Spencer, was ill and was unlikely to recover quickly, the board asked if he would be his successor.

A First Division side before the war, Grimsby had been relegated in 1948 and had just slipped into Division Three North when Shankly arrived. His first task, he realised, was to lift the club out of the despondency into which it had sunk, something he achieved with his usual mix of positivity and industry. He didn't concern himself overly with tactics but did develop one trick: if they won a throw in midfield on the left, Paddy Johnston would take it. Everybody else would run away with Jimmy Hernon, the inside-left, turning sharply as the throw was taken to head it back to Johnston, who would then be in space to try to work a simple pass to the inside-right.

As Grimsby's reputation for fine football grew, so did crowds, with attendances regularly topping 20,000. They missed out on promotion by three points, though, finishing second behind Lincoln City at a time when only the top team went up. With his wife Nessie finding it difficult to settle by the Humber, Shankly applied for the Middlesbrough job that summer but failed to get it and subsequently blamed Grimsby's directors for having turned their counterparts at Boro against him. An ageing Grimsby side struggled for consistency the following season and, with no more investment forthcoming, Shankly resigned in December 1953. Again he blamed the board for not having paid a bonus he was due for having elevated Grimsby into the top three in his first season: directors, he concluded, were not men to be trusted.

Grimsby fans may have loved Shankly and appreciated the improvements he had brought to the club – and it says much for what his personality had achieved despite difficult circumstances that they had to apply for re-election eighteen months after his departure – but he was a manager of no great reputation. He was also somebody who needed a job: from his days in Glenbuck, he knew the damage unemployment could do and money wasn't plentiful. He needed an offer and the club who made it were Workington, elected to the league just two years before and bottom of the Third Division North when he took over in January 1954. Conveniently, it allowed the Shanklys to move closer to Scotland.

Not only was the population of Workington just 30,000, the majority of them preferred rugby league to football and, although Borough Park, the town's stadium, was owned by the football club, the rugby team had won the Double the previous season and were influential tenants. The ground-share caused repeated rows. Shankly felt the way rugby churned up the pitch worked against the passing approach he wanted to instil, while there was a protracted argument about where the touchlines should be: Shankly wanted the pitch as wide as possible, but the rugby team were concerned about the danger of a tackle sending them flying onto the surrounding track if the touchline was too close to the edge of the grass.

Again Shankly's passion was key in raising morale – even if fans of opposing teams didn't always like it. On one occasion, as he ranted on the touchline at an A-team game at Cleator Moor, he was attacked by an old woman wielding a walking stick. Workington finished that first season twentieth, six points clear of having to apply for re-election. 'As a motivator, I've never met anyone like him,' said the wing-half Jackie Bertolini. 'If he'd been a general, he'd never have lost a war.'

The following season, 1954–55, was even more impressive as Workington finished fifth, but that November Shankly moved to Huddersfield to work under his former Preston teammate Andy Beattie. Less than a month older than Shankly, Beattie had had a promising start to his managerial career, taking the club to what remains their post-war best finish of third in the First Division, and leading Scotland at the 1954 World Cup, where he was stymied by his own FA, who restricted him – ludicrously – to a thirteen-man squad. Huddersfield were struggling in the First Division and Beattie had wanted to resign a year earlier but the board persuaded him to stay on. When Shankly arrived, Huddersfield had eight points from sixteen games and were bottom of the table. He had hoped to work as first-team coach but Beattie instead put him in charge of the reserve team, wanting him to nurture talent for when the ageing players in the first team were moved on. If that suggested a confidence that Huddersfield would get out of danger, it was misplaced: they were relegated amid seeming friction between Beattie and Shankly, the former coming to believe the latter ran the reserve team as his own fiefdom, at the expense of the club.

With Ray Wilson and Denis Law emerging from Shankly's reserve side, hopes were high of an immediate return to the top flight, but Huddersfield began inconsistently and, after three straight defeats had left them tenth, Beattie resigned in the November – although it was never clear to what extent he'd been coerced. Wilson even suggested that the first team had threatened to go on strike because they found training so boring and wanted to experience the sort of practice sessions Shankly was putting on with the reserves. Shankly agreed to replace Beattie, although he later admitted regretting not having asked Beattie if he really wanted to leave before accepting the job. After he'd been appointed, Shankly went to Beattie's house to tell him, driving round the block six times before summoning the nerve to knock on the door, not realising that Beattie had been watching his circuits with increasing amusement. There was, as Shankly's biographer Stephen Kelly put it, 'a mutual embarrassment' between them, but they later patched up whatever differences there had been, with Beattie working as a scout for Shankly at Liverpool and unearthing Kevin Keegan.

Shankly was far from an unqualified success at Huddersfield, who finished twelfth in that first year, eighth a year later and then fourteenth in 1959. They had a young side with a handful of gifted players but Shankly knew real progress was impossible without further investment. Liverpool, he recognised, were a team of far greater potential.

The rain eased off before the players came out to be presented to Prince Philip. 'There is no way anyone can prepare you for that moment when you first walk out in a Cup final at Wembley,' said Tommy Smith, the youngest player on either side. 'I had played at Wembley before, in an England youth international but the ground wasn't even half full then. I walked out and everything just seemed to explode. It felt like my ears were going to burst and that the whole atmosphere was going to suck me in. For a minute I felt like I wanted to lie down and fall asleep, and I thought to myself, "I can't do this."'

Unusually, the president of the FA, the Earl of Harewood, was not part of the presentation party, as he was also president of Leeds. As the prince walked down the line of Leeds players, he realised Bobby Collins, the Leeds captain who had been voted Footballer of the Year a few days before, was wearing different socks to his teammates and pointed out the discrepancy. 'I preferred woollen to nylon because I felt more comfortable,' Collins explained. 'The only trouble was that with constant washing they turned yellow. Throughout the campaign I'd worn my yellowing socks and for the final we had bright new white ones, which I was not happy about. After explaining this to Don [Revie], being incredibly superstitious himself, he insisted I wear my old discoloured socks that had served me so well during the season.'

Collins, at 5ft 3ins, was the shortest man on the field. His opposite number was the tallest. Not only did Yeats have a full foot on Collins, he also won the toss and opted to kick off. For all the talk of Liverpool as a passing team, they began in age-old British fashion: tap, tap, knock it back and then belt it into the corner for the winger to chase. As so often, the pass was overhit and Peter Thompson chased it fruitlessly. That set the tone for the opening minutes: there were a lot of long balls – goalkeepers in particular seemed keen to belt the ball forward – and a lot of anxiety. 'It was a very heavy ground, the first time Wembley had been that heavy,' Tommy Lawrence explained.

It was all quite scrappy, something not helped by a number of stoppages for injury. As early as the third minute, Norman

Hunter went down after challenging for a long clearance from Lawrence and he was still down when Collins, as feisty as he was gifted, dispossessed Roger Hunt and then, in chasing the loose ball, clattered into Gerry Byrne, his foot raised and his shoulder thumping into the left-back's torso. It was a challenge that in the modern age would almost certainly have brought a red card, but back then it merited only a stern word from the referee.

Byrne and Hunter received treatment and both seemed to have recovered; only later did it transpire that Byrne had broken his collarbone. In the days before substitutes, it was common for injured players to hobble around on the wing but Shankly, recalling a game he'd played in for Preston at Blackpool in which Andy Beattie had strained a muscle but had managed to play on behind him at full-back, keeping his movement to a minimum, decided to keep Byrne where he was; to have shifted him to the wing, he reasoned, would not only have caused disruption to the rest of the side but would have advertised that he was a weak link.

'I'd never broken a collarbone before so I wasn't aware of what damage had been done straight away,' said Byrne. 'I just felt a sharp jagged bone moving about. It wasn't until Bob Paisley came on to treat my injury that I was aware what I'd done. It didn't cross my mind to leave the field and I played on with my arm dangling almost motionless by my side. I could move it slightly but the pain when I did was terrible. I remember accidentally taking a throw in, I could hardly lift my arm above my head and I never took another one during the match.'

Willie Stevenson floated the free-kick deep into the box. It should have been easy enough to deal with but Gary Sprake and Jack Charlton both went for it, the ball skimming off the defender's head and going out for a corner – an early indication of the uncharacteristic skittishness that would afflict Charlton for much of the afternoon. Leeds were a physical side and he was a key part of it but Charlton never dominated in the air as he often could. Yeats, significantly, won the header as the corner was slung to the edge of the area and St John wasn't far from taking advantage as it dropped on the edge of the six-yard box. Yeats was commanding at the other end as well, having much the better of his individual battle with the angular centre-forward Alan Peacock.

Even on the odd occasion when Yeats was beaten, he had Smith alongside him to mop up. This was a key part of the Shankly revolution – and gives the lie to any suggestion he was somebody who dealt only in motivation and lacked tactical acumen, even if he was scathing of the abstract theorists he believed overcomplicated the game. He, Bob Paisley, Joe Fagan, Reuben Bennett and Ronnie Moran once attended a coaching course at Lilleshall, reporting on a Saturday evening. Shankly wanted to leave the following day and lasted until the Tuesday before returning to Merseyside. 'He didn't like Lilleshall, he didn't like boards with diagrams on them or somebody talking posh about football,' said Tommy Lawrence. Moran and Fagan, though, found meeting with other coaches useful and went back to Lilleshall in each of the next five years.

Shankly's disdain for Lilleshall was part of a more general struggle between what Stephen Wagg characterises in *The Football World* as the 'muddy boots' approach of former pros and the 'chalky fingers' of a new breed of technocrats. A scepticism about theory, though, doesn't mean a manager eschews tactics entirely and Tommy Docherty ridicules the idea that Shankly didn't bother with tactics. 'He knew the game inside out,' he said. 'He was clever enough to know what it was that each of his players was good at and play to that.'

Liverpool won the championship in 1963–64 playing with a modified W-M, the system Shankly had been familiar with as a player and a style that had dominated the British game from the late twenties. Rather than operating with three backs, two wing-halves, two inside-forwards, two wingers and a centre-forward, Shankly advanced one of the inside-forwards to create a strike pairing (Ian St John and Roger Hunt), balancing that by pulling the inside-forward (Jimmy Melia and then Alf Arrowsmith) deeper to become an additional midfielder.

Brazil's success with a back four at the 1958 World Cup had begun to change attitudes, but it was after seeing Belgium outplay England at Wembley that Shankly had his moment of revelation. The game had finished 2–2, but the result, he thought, was 'a farce' and he was troubled by the knowledge that many of the Belgians would be in the Anderlecht side Liverpool faced in the second round of the European Cup. Paul Van Himst had had the better of Maurice Norman in the international, so Shankly devised a specific plan for him. 'I said I would play Tommy with ten on his back, defensively, and I would give Gordon Milne the specific job of marking Van Himst when they had the ball. "When we have the ball, come out and play it, Gordon, then pick him up wherever he goes," I said. They had a defender to mark Tommy, who was sweeping up with Ronnie Yeats. Milne revelled in the job.'

It was Shankly's decision to switch to red shorts for the game – the first time Liverpool had worn all red – that caught most of the attention, but the switch to a back four was at least as significant. It was a system that, inevitably, removed a little pizzazz from Liverpool but it also meant they could control games better, building slowly from the back in the confidence they had sufficient numbers behind the ball. It also meant that Hunt, who wore the number 8 shirt that would usually be taken by the inside-right, operated further forward: he and St John interchanged regularly and were much more akin to modern notions of a strike partnership than was usual at the time.

Leeds, by contrast, still played a modified W-M, with Norman Hunter dropping back from left-half to help Charlton in the centre of defence. John Giles, the right-winger, was unusually mobile, regularly drifting infield to link with Jim Storrie and Billy Bremner, while Hunter's depth meant Collins playing deeper on the left, at times leaving the left-winger Albert Johanneson, the first black player to play in a Wembley final, isolated. Chris Lawler, playing two days before his wedding, was relatively comfortable in dealing with the South African, meaning Smith essentially had a free role, regularly striding forward to link with the midfield. Again and again as Leeds sought to spread the play to Johanneson, Smith intercepted, as he did after seven minutes, cutting out a Giles pass and helping the ball on to Callaghan. The winger advanced, then checked infield, giving the ball square to Stevenson, who played it right to Smith, by then ten yards inside the Leeds half. With Leeds sitting off, letting Liverpool have the ball, Smith returned it to Stevenson, who played it to Callaghan, cutting in off the flank. His shot was half-blocked and was gathered comfortably for Sprake, but the template had been set. Callaghan was vital to Liverpool's style of play. 'Ian made a 4-2-4 into 4-3-3 because he had so much industry,' Shankly said. 'He covered the back and if we played against someone like Bobby Charlton he would drop back and cut his service a bit.'

Liverpool were methodical, passing in front of Leeds – even if Lawrence did regularly kick long – while Revie's side was more direct. 'We thought we were a better team than Leeds, much better, and we could have gone out and tried to go after them,' said Shankly. 'But Leeds were cagey and we took our time.' Conditions, specifically the 'wet, thick' grass, convinced him how to approach the game: '[We] would play the ball and be patient. We were not going to be erratic. We wanted to win that Cup. Whether we entertained people or not didn't make any difference.'

Shankly had formally taken charge of Liverpool on 14 December 1959. Oddly, given the apparent reasons for him not having got the job eight years previously, he allowed the board to select the team for the first game and began with a 4-0 defeat at home to Cardiff. Liverpool then lost 3-0 at Charlton Athletic but, according to Roger Hunt, who had begun to establish himself as the first-choice centre-forward that season, there was no sense of panic; on the contrary, 'everyone seemed to be walking about with a new sense of purpose'.

The existing coaching structure, which already included Bob Paisley and Joe Fagan, the two men who would succeed him, and Reuben Bennett, a key member of what would become known as the Boot Room, was retained. Shankly's philosophy, as laid out by a piece in the *Liverpool Echo*, was clear. 'Shankly,' it said, 'is a disciple of the game as it is played by the continentals. The man out of possession, he believes, is just as important as the man with the ball at his feet. Continental football is not the lazy man's way of playing soccer. Shankly will aim at incisive forward moves by which continentals streak through a defence when it is "closed up" by British standards. He will make his players learn to kill a ball and move it all in the same action ... he will make them practise complete mastery of the ball.'

He took time to implement his vision, though; his was not a sudden or violent revolution. Gradually he began to make his players practise more with the ball than they had, making training as much like a match as possible. Passing was the priority and games of three , four- and five-a-side became the focus. There was also the so-called 'sweat box', four boards forming a square of about twenty yards in which players would spend a minute receiving and laying off passes from teammates stationed at the four corners, improving their fitness and concentration under pressure. 'He made so few changes initially that it was at least a year before anyone outside Anfield began to realise that things had really changed,' said the forward Alan A'Court.

Shankly, though, was plotting the future. Within a few weeks, he said, he had drawn up a list of twenty-four players he deemed surplus. All of them left the club in the following year. He also took Gerry Byrne off the transfer list, a decision that would be emphatically vindicated even if the full-back had to be banned from tackling in five-a-sides because he was so brutal. Twelfth on Boxing Day, Liverpool improved radically in the second half of the season, ending up in third, just a point off promotion. Shankly wasn't just changing things on the field, though. He had described Melwood, the training ground, as 'a shambles' when he arrived, joking that the grass was long enough for the diminutive Jimmy Melia 'to hide in standing up', and set about improving facilities. He, the other coaches and the young players literally built the club: Paisley's training as a bricklayer was a major boon, while the ground-staff painted the barriers and swept the terrace. Shankly also began to overhaul the wage structure at the club, lowering the basic salary while raising bonuses so that every point brought a financial reward.

There was similar disappointment the following season as Liverpool again finished third. Gates fell, dipping below an average of 30,000 for the first time since the Second World War – something that was in part down to the worsening economic situation. As trade with Europe became increasingly important, Liverpool began to lose out to ports on the east coast, while airfreight and containerisation meant there were alternatives to transporting everything through the docks – something that came as a particular blow to a city, which, whether fairly or not, had gained a reputation for inefficiency, with old-fashioned equipment and a militant workforce. The heyday of the Liverpool docks had passed and unemployment stood at 4 per cent – a long way from the peak it was to reach in the 1980s but worrying enough in context, particularly given the rising jobless levels among young people.

The frustration of Liverpool fans was magnified by the free spending of Everton under their chairman John Moores, one of the founders of Littlewoods Pools. While the Toffees became the latest club to be nicknamed 'the Bank of England', Liverpool's record signing when Shankly took over remained Albert Stubbins, bought from Newcastle United for £12,500 in 1946. Moores was an Everton fan – and had given up his chairmanship of the pools company to become a director at the club – but he also owned shares in Liverpool and regularly played bridge with their chairman, T. V. Williams, and recognised the commercial advantages of a city having two successful clubs, the rivalry generating interest and thus revenue. The accountant Eric Sawyer was elected to the Liverpool board on Moores's recommendation and, as he backed Shankly's vision, money began slowly to be released for transfers. In that 1960–61 season, £13,000 was spent to bring the winger Kevin Lewis from Sheffield United – the winger would go on to score the goals that secured promotion for Liverpool in 1962, as well as their first back in the First Division the following season – and £16,000 to sign the half-back Gordon Milne from Preston. Shankly had tried to make his first signing the gangling centre-back Jack Charlton, but his £18,000 bid fell short of Leeds's valuation. He later claimed that if Liverpool had signed him Leeds would never have gone on to have the success they did because 'half their strength would have gone with Jack'.

That was only the beginning. In the summer of 1961 Shankly completed his clear-out while signing St John from Motherwell for £37,500 to partner Hunt. With his swagger, confidence and irreverence, St John, as John Williams wrote in *Red Men*, 'symbolised the arrival of the 1960s at Anfield'. A further £30,000 went on the defender Ron Yeats from Dundee United. So impressed was Shankly by his physique that he described him as 'a mountain' and urged journalists 'to go into the dressing-room and walk round him'. Shankly told the director Sidney Reakes that the pair would win Liverpool the league and Cup.

Training had become more sophisticated: there was no slogging on roads or over dunes in pre-season, rather an emphasis on peaking physically at the right time and on ball work. 'Above all,' Shankly said, 'the main aim is that everyone can control a ball and do the basic things in football. It's control and pass ... control and pass ... all the time. At the back you're looking for someone who can control the ball instantly and give a forward pass. It gives them more space and time to breathe. If you delay, the opposition have all run back behind the ball. It's a very simplified affair and, of course, very economical. At Liverpool we don't have anyone running into no man's land, running from their own half with the ball into the opposition half. That's not encouraged at all. That's nonsense. If you get a ball in the Liverpool team you want options, you want choices ... you want at least two people to pass to, maybe three, maybe more ... Get the ball, give an early pass, then it goes from me to someone else and it switches around again. You might not be getting very far, but the pattern of the opposition is changing. Finally, somebody will sneak in.'

Most training was led by Fagan and Bennett, with Fagan noting everything down in A4 notebooks that became a vital log to refer to in rare times of crisis. After Liverpool had beaten Bristol Rovers 2–0 at the start of the 1961–62 season, Melia commented that it was the first time he'd played the opening game of the season and felt he could play another match straight after. Liverpool went on to win ten and draw one of their opening eleven games of the season, establishing a lead that never looked like being overhauled. A 2–0 win over Southampton at a rain-soaked Anfield, Lewis getting both goals, confirmed promotion with five games of the season still to play – although celebrations were soured when safe-blowers stole £4,000 from the club secretary's office five days later. Elsewhere, the trend of falling crowds continued but at Liverpool, with fans excited by a return to the top-flight after eight seasons in the Second Division and inspired by Shankly's confidence and rhetoric, attendances were at their highest for thirteen years. Increased revenue led to investment at Anfield and at Melwood, everything carefully planned by Shankly, who had essentially taken sole control of the club after threatening to quit when the winger Johnny Morrissey was sold to Everton for £10,000 without his knowledge.

There had been a feeling, a hope at least, that a game between the reigning league champions and a side as clearly on the up as Leeds would be a classic, although the preview in *The Times* was less sanguine. 'It promises to be a taut, shrewd struggle of tactics between two "method" teams,' it noted, presciently as it turned out. Even in those scrappy early minutes, though, there was a sense that Liverpool had a touch more poise. St John gathered a Lawrence clearance on halfway and knocked it back to Byrne, his broken collarbone far from obvious. He helped it on to Stevenson who went forward and played in left to Strong. He was half-tackled but Liverpool retained possession through Stevenson, who sent it right to Strong. He shot from range and the ball deflected for a corner off Charlton. Neither side was making much progress but when Liverpool won possession they at least retained it for a while.

Byrne may have suffered the worst injury but Leeds had problems themselves. Bremner, Storrie and Charlton all required treatment in the opening sixteen minutes, which perhaps goes someway to explaining why they were quite as patchy as they were. Or perhaps the injuries were part of a deliberate plan, breaking up the game while Leeds found their feet. Twice around the quarter-hour mark Liverpool threatened to break through. First a flowing passing move initiated by Callaghan and passing through Smith, Strong and Byrne reached Thompson, who cleverly worked the ball to Hunt with the outside of his right foot. He played it to St John on the edge of the box and moved for the return but his strike partner tried a strange flick and Collins was able to steal in and chip the ball back to Sprake. Peacock fouled Smith in leaping for the goalkeeper's clearance and, inexorably, Liverpool built again: Byrne to Stevenson, inside to Strong and square again for Byrne, who played it forward for Hunt. He cut infield past Giles, slipped a pass to St John and this time did receive the return, only to strike his shot well wide.

Leeds at that stage were awful. Storrie, in particular, seemed nervous, misplacing pass after pass even before suffering a muscular injury just before half-time that left him effectively a passenger (this being the last competitive game in English football before substitutions were permitted), while Charlton swung one free-kick straight out of play. Not until the eighteenth minute did they pose anything resembling a threat, Johanneson and Collins creating space for Giles, who turned the ball infield for Bremner, whose attempted chip over the defensive line for the onrushing Paul Reaney was over-hit, allowing Lawrence, always quick off his line, to gather.

That at least seemed to give Leeds some confidence. Collins thrashed a thirty-five-yard drive wide moments later and for a couple of minutes they began to look like the side they really were. Reaney advanced from full-back and that in turn freed Giles for his incursions infield. Johanneson skipped by Strong, his first real chance to run at Liverpool, and as Smith closed him down he laid the ball wide for Willie Bell, overlapping. A tussle with Callaghan resulted in a corner, from which Peacock won the header but placed it wide. As Hunter then won Lawrence's long clearance and Peacock knocked down his long pass for Collins, the Leeds fans, many of them wearing circular white paper hats, at last began to be heard, even if Bremner's eventual chipped cross was too long.

Liverpool's first season back in the top flight began anxiously. Over 50,000 turned up for the first match, at home to Blackpool, but Liverpool lost 2–1. Although they beat Manchester City 4–1 in their next home game and Sheffield United 2–0 in the one after that, by November they lay twentieth, having collected just eleven points from their first fifteen matches. Things, though, were stirring: the Beatles' first single, 'Love Me Do', was released that October and, after a draw at Old Trafford on 10 November, Liverpool clicked.

Shankly promoted Tommy Lawrence, the 'Flying Pig' as he was nicknamed, to take the place of Jim Furnell in goal and, although he might not have had the most athletic physique, his ability to leave his box and sweep up behind his defence would gradually become a key element in Liverpool's emerging style. There was also need for greater guile in midfield. Tommy Leishman was popular with the fans, but the pace and physicality that had allowed him to dominate in the Second Division made less difference in the top flight. Shankly found his replacement in Willie Stevenson, then in the reserves at Rangers, having been displaced by the arrival of Jim Baxter and seemingly set to move to Australia. He was slower than Leishman but more thoughtful, a better distributor of the ball, and that made him better suited to the patient style Shankly was creating.

Liverpool won nine games in a row and at one point in February they had climbed as high as fifth. Their form fell apart in the final weeks of the season but they finished eighth and lost to Leicester City in the Cup semi-final, a respectable and encouraging start to life back at the top. That summer, Shankly signed the winger Peter Thompson from Preston for £37,000 – 'daylight robbery', according to Shankly – and so added to his side the sort of intelligent, skilful player he had had in Billy Hogan at Carlisle, Jimmy Hernon at Grimsby and Ernie Whittle at Workington. Shankly had always opposed 'haphazard' football but that didn't mean there was no place in his system for a player with imagination. Thompson flourished while the emergence of Alf Arrowsmith, who scored fifteen goals in twenty games, gave Shankly the option of dropping St John deeper.

Liverpool lost their first three home games of 1963–64, but won their first three away. Reasoning the pressure of performing in front of an expectant home crowd was unsettling his team, Shankly spoke to each individually before the fourth home match, against Wolves, reminding them of their ability. They won 6–0. They then lost at Sheffield United, though, meaning that after nine games Liverpool lay tenth. A 2–1 home win over the champions Everton began a run of ten wins in eleven games that lifted them to the top of the table. 'We were the fittest team in the country,' said Hunt. 'In game after game, we took control because even if our opponents could match us for skill, they could not match us at producing it right at the end.' Although Liverpool faltered in the new year, a run of seven straight victories from the middle of March saw them seal the title with a 5–0 win over Arsenal. So many turned up to watch that game that the gates had to be closed an hour before kick-off.

That was the season when singing on the terraces took off, a phenomenon considered so noteworthy that the BBC sent their *Panorama* cameras to record the Kop in full voice (even if the older members of the crowd clearly knew few of the words to 'She Loves You' or 'Anyone Who Had A Heart', miming unconvincingly. According to Stephen F. Kelly in *Shankly: It's Much More Important than That*, the first chant simply replaced the words 'Let's Go!' in the Routers' hit of the same name with 'St John!' Terrace anthems would soon become far more complex and sophisticated, the city's footballing and musical cultures feeding off each other to produce an intoxicating sense of optimism.

Rain began again to fall midway through the first half, while the game followed its scrappy pattern. As Peacock started to win the occasional long ball, Leeds posed more of a threat than they had but it was still Liverpool who looked the more dangerous, St John having a shot blocked by Charlton after he'd seized on a Hunt knockdown. Leeds seemed oddly obsessed by playing straight balls over the top, which was perhaps an attempt to use the pace of Johanneson but seemed to speak of their frustration at the diligence of Liverpool's defending.

And every now and again, Liverpool would string together a few passes that offered a reminder of their quality. Yeats collected a long clearance after twenty-five minutes and played it to Byrne – still more than willing to offer himself for a pass despite his injury – and he looped it down the line to St John. Collins hooked the ball clear as St John flicked it on but Stevenson headed it down for Strong who knocked it back to the centre-forward. He slid a pass inside Johanneson, covering deep, for Callaghan who crossed. Sprake, whose reputation for haplessness would be cemented when he threw the ball into his own net at Anfield two years later, missed the cross but Hunt couldn't quite get there and Giles cleared.

By the half-hour, Leeds seemed finally to have settled but if anything that just reduced goalmouth incident further as they began, if not to match Liverpool's passing game, then at least to hold the ball themselves for periods. With ten minutes left before the break, the patience of the commentator Kenneth Wolstenholme had gone and he wondered whether because both teams were so organised 'they're organising each other out of business'. As Smith made a well-timed challenge on Peacock in the box, he reflected on 'the inside-right as sweeper-up', an indication of how prevalent belief in the W-M as the default formation was in Britain at the time: who cared if he was playing at the back, demonstrably behind the right-half? For Wolstenholme, if Smith wore the number 10 shirt he had to be an inside-forward. 'It's almost impossible for anyone to get through,' he went on, sounding thoroughly fed up.

If anything the game became even more scrappy. Leeds were thwarted repeatedly by Yeats's domination of Peacock while Liverpool, perhaps feeling the pressure of an opponent beginning to stir, began to misplace passes. The capacity for flowing football never entirely left them, though. Three minutes before the break, Collins gathered after Charlton had headed out a Lawler cross and switched the ball out to Johanneson, who beat Strong only for Smith to cover. He hit it forward for Callaghan who went left to Thompson. He darted infield again and laid the ball right for Strong who touched it inside for Smith, rumbling forward from the back. The ball popped up from his first touch, offering the opportunity of a shot as the ball dropped. His effort was too high but the passage of play illustrated Liverpool's strength: they were always capable of holding the ball for long spells and always capable of breaking quickly. Their facility in possession in itself pressured the opponent if only because it could take so long to win the ball back if they gave it away.

Finally, in the last minute of the half, there came a save, the first meaningful one of the game. Smith intercepted a poor pass from Peacock to Johanneson and sent the ball wide left for St John. He played it infield to Thompson who returned it to the advancing Smith. He went back to Thompson and Hunt, gathering his pass, slid by Hunter, only for Bell to nip in. Johanneson dallied, Hunt regained possession and shot from twenty-five yards, forcing Sprake to tip over. Had it not been for the final, the keeper would have been in Florence with the Wales squad preparing for a friendly against Italy the following day; without him, Wales lost 4–1.

Briefly, the game was alive. Collins went wide for Johanneson, who knocked the ball infield for Hunter. With his strangely hunched gracefulness, he sent a long diagonal to Peacock, who won the header in the box but could not get the power on it that might have troubled Lawrence. For once the keeper threw his clearance, finding Smith, who went long for Hunt, a flurry of passes eventually forcing Bell to concede a corner. It was headed clear but, as Johanneson helped it away, Stevenson collected and helped the ball on to Strong, whose shot was deflected wide.

Hindsight has a habit of seeing patterns where none exist, of ascribing causality where there is merely coincidence, but there does seem to have been a sense in the summer of 1964 that, having won the league, the next target had to be the FA Cup. 'The desire to win the Cup for the first time ran right through the club,' Yeats insisted.

Europe perhaps also was a distraction and Liverpool began the season poorly – although Shankly blamed a summer tour to the USA on which they'd played a number of exhibition games and appeared on the *Ed Sullivan Show* with Gerry and the Pacemakers, saying his players hadn't had time to rest and that had led to injuries. Liverpool had flown over on two planes, with Shankly on the second one. Paisley met him at the airport and suggested going to see Jack Dempsey's bar. 'At this time of night?' Shankly asked. Paisley pointed out that he needed to turn his watch back six hours and that it was only 7 p.m. 'No Yank's going to tell me what time it is,' Shankly responded and went to bed.

Liverpool shared the Charity Shield in a 2–2 draw with West Ham at Anfield, then faced Arsenal on the opening day of the league season in the first game ever shown on *Match of the Day*. 'Phew, well, I'd call it the match of the century, I don't know about Match of the Day,' Wolstenholme enthused after the game, which had been decided in Liverpool's favour by a late Gordon Wallace goal. The former Arsenal and Wales full-back Walley Barnes shuffled awkwardly into the frame and, perhaps feeling coerced by the main presenter's hyperbole, added that 'match of the century is probably very right'. Few would disagree: the programme went out on the new BBC2, which couldn't even be received on Merseyside, and therefore went unseen by all 47,620 who'd actually been at the match.

Liverpool, though, lost eight of their next fourteen matches to lie nineteenth in the table by the end of October. Injuries – whatever their underlying cause – had been partly to blame and, with Arrowsmith and Wallace both out and St John suffering appendicitis, Shankly bought Geoff Strong from Arsenal for £40,000. 'We didn't buy him as an attacker or anything specific at all,' said Shankly. 'We signed him as a footballer, like they used to do in the old days. If we'd signed him five years earlier he'd have been an even greater player. He could have become one of the finest sweepers of all time. He was cool as a cucumber with a brilliant football brain.'

Liverpool had lost to West Brom in the October but by the time they faced them in the FA Cup third round, they'd gone ten games without defeat, the last of them a 3–2 win in Blackpool. Shankly took advantage of the fixture list and gave his players a three-day break at the seaside so they could wind down after the Christmas programme. That hinted at the importance of the Cup to Liverpool, a point hammered home by an editorial in the *Liverpool Echo*: 'Already people are beginning to whisper the resurgent Liverpool side as "for the Cup" – something which always vexes their following since whenever they have been tipped for the trophy, they have always come unstuck.'

Things almost came unstuck even before they'd begun as the team coach was held up in traffic in the Wolverhampton area. The players changed on the bus and, after a police escort was arranged, eventually arrived at the Hawthorns to kick off twenty minutes late. The disruption didn't seem to unsettle Liverpool, though, and they took the lead just before half-time as Milne laid in Hunt to score. As West Brom pushed forward in the second half, Liverpool countered, a long pass from Thompson finding Hunt who squared for St John to crash in off the underside of the crossbar.

The game seemed safe but then came a bizarre lapse from Yeats. Thinking the referee had blown for a free-kick in his favour, he picked the ball up only to realise that the whistle had come from the crowd, leaving the referee, Kevin Howley, no option but to award a penalty. Bobby Cram, whose nephew Steve would win a World Championship gold medal in the 1500m in 1983, put the penalty yards wide. 'It was the worst penalty I have ever seen in my life,' said Smith. Jeff Astle did pull one back with ten minutes to go but Liverpool survived a late onslaught.

Liverpool drew Stockport County, struggling in the Fourth Division, in the next round. Shankly, for the only time in his Liverpool career, didn't attend the match, instead travelling to Germany to watch 1. FC Köln, Liverpool's quarter-final opponents in the European Cup, play Werder Bremen in the Bundesliga. It says much for the hold of the Cup and the rising sense that Liverpool could at last win it that over 51,000 packed into Anfield, despite Winston Churchill's funeral, one of the first big state occasions to be televised live and trans-mitted to a mass TV audience, being broadcast the same day. Shankly, returning from Cologne, bumped into a former Rangers player, a friend of Willie Stevenson's, at the airport on his return. 'Any Cup shocks?' he asked. 'Arsenal lost at Peter-borough,' the player replied, at which Shankly picked up an evening sports edition of the paper. 'Liverpool 1 Stockport 1,' he read out incredulously. 'Is that not a shock to you?'

Stockport, playing surprisingly open football, had taken an eighteenth-minute lead through Len White, who forced the ball in despite being knocked unconscious as he and Lawrence collided in challenging for a John Watt cross. Milne, swivel-ling just inside the box six minutes into the second half, kept Liverpool in the competition, but Shankly was furious.

For the replay, Liverpool played in red shorts, the first time they'd worn all red for a domestic game. It was a raw night, the pitch bumpy and uneven, although Paisley later suggested Stockport had erred in sanding it; had they left it rutted, he said, Liverpool would have found the conditions much harder. Hunt opened the scoring from a St John cross six minutes before half-time and then latched onto a misplaced back-pass from Ean Cuthbert to make it 2–0 five minutes from time.

The enthusiasm for the Cup was extraordinary. Liverpool were given an allocation of 20,000 for the fifth-round tie away to Bolton Wanderers, relegated the previous season but fourth in the Second Division at the time. After season-ticket hold-ers had taken their allocation, other fans queued for hours for the 7,000 that remained. In Bolton's side was the inside-forward Freddie Hill, who had won two England caps and whom Shankly rated as one of the best players in his position in the country. He had even tried to sign him the previous season only for the deal to fall through when one of Liver-pool's notoriously stringent medicals showed he suffered high blood pressure.

With Milne injured, Arrowsmith came in at centre-forward, St John dropping back to right-half. Liverpool were typically patient in their approach and the game seemed to be heading for a replay when, with five minutes remaining, Thompson gathered the ball on the left, switched onto his right foot and floated it to the back post where Callaghan nodded in. 'For Cally to score with his head was an unusual way for us to win a match and it got the lads talking afterwards that anything was possible now,' St John said. 'I don't think he ever scored another headed goal throughout his career.' Liverpool were through to the last eight for the third successive season.

Victory over Birmingham the following Wednesday was Liverpool's fifth in a row in the league and lifted them to sixth, but any lingering thought that they might still be in the title race disappeared with defeat to West Ham. That increased the pressure on the Cup quarter-final, against Leicester City, a team Smith described as Liverpool's 'bogey side'. The Foxes had overcome them in the semi-final in 1963 and Liverpool had beaten them only once in six league meetings since Leicester's return to the top flight. On a poor surface at Filbert Street, frozen solid in the shade and greasy where the sun had melted the ice, Smith and Lawrence were excellent as Liverpool drew 0–0. The crowd at Anfield for the replay was the biggest in two years; Lawrence described it as the best atmosphere he'd ever experienced. Leicester held out until eighteen minutes from time, when a Lawler free-kick was headed down by Yeats for Hunt to sweep in the winner.

The semi-final against Chelsea at Villa Park came three days after a play-off against Köln, required after both legs of their European Cup quarter-final had finished goalless. Liverpool squandered a two-goal lead in the play-off, held in neutral Rotterdam, but won through on the toss of a coin. Against Tommy Docherty's young Chelsea side, who were joint top of the table and had reached the League Cup final, there was a serious danger Liverpool's jadedness would be exposed. 'Normally,' Hunt said, 'we tried to beat teams by incessant attacking, but this time they advised us to conserve our energy by letting the ball do the work. We played some lovely football that day, the sort of fluid passing game that the club became famous for later, and it paid off.'

An edge was added by the fact Docherty and Shankly were

good friends, Docherty having been signed by Preston from Celtic for £4,000 to replace Shankly when it became apparent the club couldn't cope without him. Shankly had got in touch with Docherty to congratulate him, telling him to 'just put the shirt on and let it run around. It knows where to go.' Docherty had tested the friendship to the limits in Rotterdam, heading over to the Netherlands to invite his countrymen Yeats and St John out for 'a few beers' to celebrate Liverpool's progress in Europe, hoping that a couple of looseners might encourage the pair to let slip a few tactical plans. Unfortunately for Docherty, Shankly had been keeping tabs on his stars and turned up at the bar to march the pair home, pausing only to discuss the matter with the Chelsea manager with a familiar forthrightness.

Shankly had also got his hands on a cheeky Cup final 'programme' produced by the young Chelsea midfielder Terry Venables for the amusement of his teammates, detailing the London side's proposed appearance at Wembley. Shankly showed it to his players ahead of the Villa Park showdown by way of motivation, telling them to 'stuff those wee cocky southern buggers'. The gambit worked.

With sixty-three minutes played, St John found Thompson wide on the left. He cut inside, swerving by Marvin Hinton before thrashing the ball into the roof of the net. Fifteen minutes later, Ron Harris fouled St John in the box. With Ronnie Moran, the usual penalty taker, having lost his place in the side, Stevenson converted, despite losing his footing as he struck the ball. It was the only penalty he ever took for the club. Liverpool were in only their third FA Cup final, and their first since 1950.

Hunt won a throw off Reaney by the corner flag. It was worked neatly to Thompson who played it to Strong, surrounded by a phalanx of white shirts. He managed to get the ball through to St John but Bell nipped in to concede another throw. Callaghan took it to Lawler and he crossed for Hunt, who beat

Charlton again but sent his header across the face of goal and just wide.

The rain fell increasingly heavily, forcing the backroom staff from both teams off the exposed benches to shelter in the tunnel under the royal box. Liverpool pressed harder. Strong won a challenge in centre-field and went left for Byrne. Hunt knocked his long pass down the line wide to Thompson. St John took the ball on his inside and slipped a pass through for Hunt who, as Sprake came wide to meet him, played it back to Thompson. With the goalkeeper struggling to get back, the winger crossed low towards Stevenson but Bremner slid in to intercept, turning the ball behind for a corner. Thompson took it, an inswinger. St John flicked on and Sprake just got there ahead of Hunt. Collins cleared but only as far as Thompson, who swooped infield and shot, the ball hitting Charlton and falling to Callaghan, whose strike on goal was deflected wide by Hunter. Suddenly there was urgency in the game and although Giles got a free-kick on target – struck well but comfortably held by Lawrence – two misplaced passes in quick succession from Collins suggested how rattled Leeds were.

Callaghan began to find more space and exert more of an influence. St John had a shot blocked by Bremner and then, taking over possession after a Callaghan surge, played a one-two with Hunt before rolling the ball back for Strong, whose shot wasn't too far off target. The move was typical of the relationship between the strike pairing: St John dropping just a little deeper than Hunt, operating as the creator of the pair. 'He was very unselfish and we understood each other,' said Hunt. 'He was very astute, a brainy player; he could read situations and pretty soon we knew exactly what each other was going to do.' St John then headed a Lawler cross wide. None of it was especially thrilling and there were long scratchy periods but it was clear that Liverpool were in control, holding possession, trying to draw Leeds out, every now and again working space for a shot.

Callaghan took a throw to Strong inside his own half. He played it to Stevenson who exchanged passes with St John and spread the ball to Thompson. He darted inside Bremner and hit a low shot that required a touch from Sprake to divert it wide. The keeper then did well to bend and gather a Hunt cross under pressure. By the midway point of the half, though, the game had slipped back into torpor. The memory now, on Merseyside at least, is of raucous support – and Horace Yates suggested in the *Liverpool Post* at the time that Wembley had never known such a noisy atmosphere – but while that may have been true of the beginning and end of the game, by the midpoint of the second half, Wolstenholme was commenting on how quiet it was.

Not that that did much for Leeds. Charlton, chasing an over-hit St John pass to Stevenson, clattered into one of the photographers sitting to one side of the goal and required further treatment from Les Cocker. Storrie, given the ball wide on the right by Bremner, sliced his cross dreadfully behind the goal. Charlton, after blocking a cross from Stevenson, went down again. As Leeds's play became increasingly frantic, a Liverpool goal began to seem inevitable.

And yet still it wouldn't arrive. St John slipped at the back post as a Callaghan cross was deflected to him, then Sprake made another fine save, pushing wide a Thompson shot after Smith had dispossessed Storrie. Leeds, in desperation, changed shape, with Bremner advanced from right-half to centre-forward alongside Peacock, Giles pulled back into his position and Johanneson switched to the right as Storrie was hidden on the left wing. 'Leeds's vaunted wing strength had been negligible ... the ... wingers were having an extraordinarily thin time against the excellent defence of Byrne and Lawler,' Leslie Edwards reported in the *Liverpool Football Echo*. Hunt couldn't quite get over a cross from Stevenson after he'd beaten Johanneson, a Thompson shot was blocked and Strong's follow-up hit straight at Sprake after a brave forward burst from Byrne, his arm clearly hanging limp. Liverpool finished much the stronger, as they had in the first half, their superior fitness clearly evident.

As the game entered its final minute Stevenson played a ball forward for St John and he lofted it square for Strong who helped it on to Callaghan. Stevenson headed his chip across goal for Hunt but Sprake, easily Leeds's key performer, got bravely down to save, taking a kick to the shoulder as he did so. There was still time for a St John drive from eighteen yards that Sprake saved, but it ended goalless. Leeds, somehow, had forced the game into extra-time – although Collins had forgotten the game would go to extra-time and tried to leave the field when the whistle went. 'It was incredible that Liverpool could have the game so much in their grasp without being in the lead,' wrote Edwards, 'yet their propensity for too many crossfield passes left many of their moves without much penetration and that was … the reason why they were still goalless.'

Liverpool's domination continued in extra-time. Stevenson dispossessed Hunter and, although he was forced wide, slipped the ball back to Strong, whose shot was blocked. Chances were arriving more frequently as the attritional value of Liverpool's passing approach began to be seen. Giles, who had won the FA Cup with Manchester United in 1963, went down with cramp, prompting Wolstenholme to note acerbically that Cocker had 'played a blinder'.

When Giles had recovered, the game restarted with a throw on the Liverpool right, taken by Callaghan back to Smith. He sent it infield to Strong who was forced back to Lawler. He knocked it forward for Hunt, who headed back to Stevenson twenty yards inside the Leeds half. 'Leeds, I think,' Yates wrote, 'underrated Stevenson, just as the Scottish selectors have done for years.' For once, he ran with it rather than passing, dribbling by Collins and Hunter and then, as Charlton came to meet him, sliding a pass between him and Reaney for Byrne advancing from the left-back. He crossed and, with

Sprake drawn to his near post, Hunt could head into an empty net.

As Liverpool fans celebrated, one staged a lonely pitch invasion. Two policemen held him and another cuffed his backside, but he seemed undeterred, waving his rattle defiantly even as two more policemen arrived to carry him off. 'I've never seen such sights,' said Wolstenholme. 'The crowd have gone mad.' As a brusque challenge from Charlton denied St John at the end of another fine passing move, 'Oh when the Reds go marching in …', the terrace variant of one of Shankly's *Desert Island Discs* selections, could clearly be heard.

The game seemed won. Liverpool controlled possession, linking passing move to passing move. Sprake cut out a Stevenson cross as Hunt loitered menacingly. As Stevenson went down with cramp, Liverpool fans struck up a very slow version of 'You'll Never Walk Alone', the hymnal style and tempo of which would be reprised during half-time at another major final, forty years later, in a rather more desperate situation. Wolstenholme was prone to misreading situations and simplistic overstatement, but few can have disagreed when he said, 'One gets the feeling that Leeds just haven't got the steam for this game now.' As though to prove his point, Storrie pulled up with cramp after Collins had spread the ball to him on the left. He kept the ball in play, though, and Bell sent it infield to Peacock. He knocked it back to Hunter who, with that strange hunched gait, lofted the ball forward to Charlton, by then playing as an emergency centre-forward. Yeats and Smith both went to him but he won the knockdown and Bremner, who had scored in the semi-final win over Manchester United, lashed a first-time shot into the top corner. It was a stunning goal, both in terms of execution and context. 'That Leeds should have scored off this one difficult chance was incredible,' wrote Edwards. 'This must have been one of the most shaking goals Liverpool have endured. It meant that they had got to start out all over again to do what it had taken them more than a complete ninety minutes to achieve.'

A Leeds goal simply hadn't seemed a plausible turn of events until that moment. 'When Leeds equalised I felt sick,' said Hunt, 'dead sick.' Byrne had shown great physical bravery but Shankly also defined courage in mental and emotional terms. It was, he said, 'the ability to get up when things are getting you down … to get up and fight back. Never to know defeat, let along accept it. To have principles – be they of fitness or morality – and stick by them. To do what you feel you must do, not because it's the most popular thing to do but because it's the right thing to do. Courage is skill, plus dedication, plus fitness, plus honesty, plus fearlessness. It is a big word, but it is one which should hang above your bed if you really want to be a footballer – and to be one that is a credit to the game and yourself.'

Liverpool had that. They kept going and, even before half-time in extra-time, it had taken a superb sliding challenge from Charlton to prevent St John bursting onto a Thompson pass. Shankly always said that Thompson did a lot of indirect damage as teams were afraid to play offside against somebody with his pace: this was a perfect example, Leeds sitting deeper than they might have done and so giving St John the opportunity to make the run.

For all Shankly's talk of patience, Liverpool were desperate to avoid a replay that would have meant playing Internazionale in the European Cup semi-final on the Tuesday before taking on Leeds again on the Thursday. With Leeds increasingly showing signs of weariness, Liverpool's superior fitness meant they just kept coming. Bremner, in the first action of the second period, turned onto a Reaney pass and, seemingly exhausted, miscued his cross straight to Lawrence. Moments later, Strong moved smoothly onto Thompson's pass and unleashed a twenty-five-yard drive that Sprake saved up and to his left. The contrast was clear. Yeats got to Callaghan's corner first, his looping header falling to St John, who lobbed over.

Liverpool were relentless. Hunter cleared a St John cross awkwardly. Byrne scudded a low ball across the box that missed everybody. And then, at last, it came. Peacock got a flick on a Sprake goal-kick but Yeats headed clear, the ball falling for Stevenson. The familiar pattern was set in motion again. Stevenson to Hunt, back for Thompson, infield to Smith and on to Callaghan. 'The team that panics now will lose this Cup final,' said Wolstenholme gravely. Callaghan ran at Bell and seemed to have lost control when he hooked a foot around the ball and crossed. Sprake was again caught at his near post and St John nodded it in. There was another one-man pitch invasion, this time from a fan with a knotted handkerchief on his head and this time, with just seven minutes left, the goal was decisive.

Leeds, shattered, couldn't raise themselves and Liverpool could easily have extended their advantage. Charlton, trying to carry the ball out from the back, was dispossessed by Thompson who jinked by Giles and then smashed a shot towards the top left-corner that Sprake saved well. Strong, running on to the resulting corner at the top of the box, thumped a shot into the side-netting and another fluid passing move ended with Lawler crossing for Hunt who headed wide. It didn't matter. Leeds were spent and the Cup was Liverpool's – and deservedly so. 'They played almost all the football that was played – sometimes almost too much of it,' Edwards wrote. 'They made practically all the shots; they outgeneralled and outmanoeuvred Leeds with such nonchalance there were times when it looked almost like an exhibition.'

Yeats led his team up the thirty-nine steps to collect the Cup from the Queen, who was – appropriately if slightly insensitively – dressed all in red. 'It seemed to me to be a hard game,' she said. 'Yes, Ma'am,' Yeats replied. 'So hard that I can scarcely lift this trophy.'

Compared to Byrne, though, he'd had it easy. 'Walking up the steps to collect the trophy was worse than actually playing in the match,' the full-back said. 'People were slapping me on the back and every time the pain seemed to become more and more unbearable. I was trying to avoid them all in the end.' Whether a manager other than Shankly could have inspired such courage is debatable. Certainly he was aware of the magnitude of Byrne's sacrifice. 'At half-time, the doctor tried to freeze it but he couldn't, so we left him,' he said. 'The bones were grinding together but Leeds United didn't know he was injured. That was the main thing … He was the hero; he should have got all the medals.'

Shankly was also, as ever, aware of his audience, and at the final whistle strode across the pitch to salute the Liverpool fans. 'My shoes and pants were covered in white from the chalk off the pitch as I walked up to the end where our supporters were massed,' he said. But his reception made it worthwhile. 'To think a team like Liverpool had never won the FA Cup was unbelievable,' he said. 'So many had prayed for it to happen over all the years but it had never come to pass. So when we beat Leeds, the emotion was unforgettable. Grown men were crying and it was the greatest feeling any human could have to see what we had done. There have been many proud moments. Wonderful, fantastic moments. But that was the greatest day.' It was also the first Liverpool game Ness Shankly had ever attended; so taken was she by the spectacle that she went to watch her husband's side play Inter the following week.

Shankly put Smith in charge of the Cup as the squad left the ground and he managed to lose the base before the dinner at the Grosvenor Hotel in Park Lane. A panicked phone call to the coach company, though, revealed he'd left it on the bus. Milne, despite missing the game, played a full part in the dinner and Strong offered him the shirt he'd worn in the final, saying he'd earned it over the previous rounds. Milne refused it but the gesture suggests the team spirit and sense of mutual respect in the team.

It was only on the return to Liverpool, though, that it really dawned on the players what the win meant. From miles outside the city, houses were draped in red banners and scarves, while over a quarter of a million people came out in celebration. 'It seemed the entire city of Liverpool had turned out to greet them,' said the report in the *Liverpool Daily Post*. 'It made the recent Beatles reception look like a vicarage tea party.' In some places two-inch-thick barriers buckled under the weight of people. Hospitals reported 604 casualties – mainly people who had fainted in the crush or fallen from roofs trying to get a better view. 'The scenes were so fantastic as to be almost un-believable,' said Herbert Balmer, the acting chief constable. 'The crowd seemed to be electrified by emotional fervour. While 99.9 per cent were good-humoured throughout it all there was just a small element of hooligans who seized their opportunity to cause trouble.'

Shankly, as ever, was keen to milk the occasion for all it was worth. 'There has never been a reception like this in the whole history of the game,' he told fans who greeted them back in Liverpool. 'This has been fantastic; there is no other word for it. I have been in football all my life and had my ups and downs and played in Cup finals, both losing and winning. Without doubt this has been the happiest day of my life.'

Yeats was stunned by the depth of the reaction. 'As captain, I received a tremendous amount of mail after the final, con-gratulating me on our victory,' he said. 'Some letters were from older supporters who actually wrote that they could now die in peace after Liverpool had won the FA Cup.'

Not all were so enthused. The *Mirror*, in particular, was critical of both teams after what it saw as a tedious match redeemed only by the stretched nature of the game in extra-time. 'Dis-cipline was destroyed by tiredness, determination blunted by the pain of having to run some more,' wrote Ken Jones. 'A dour, defiant and dull struggle was suddenly transformed. It became a match that swung excitingly one way and then an-other … it was tiredness and not talent that saved the Final. Men and not method that so nearly wrecked it. Behind the boredom was the failure of individuals like Leeds left winger Albert Johanneson and Liverpool left winger Peter Thompson, men who could and should have lifted the game with their talent. But because this was the Final, the spectacle showpiece of the season channelled out to millions of TV viewers all over Europe the biggest problem in the game has at last been spot-lighted …'

This, Jones believed, was the curse of modern football, as in-dividuality gave way to team structures. 'More and more clubs are turning to method and discipline, sick of being sacrifices every season to the teams with talent and the money to buy it …' he wrote. 'Leeds, short of quality forwards and not yet the team they soon may be, were not capable of injecting ex-citement into Wembley. Liverpool, too, must share the blame because their quality forwards lacked the purpose to pierce Leeds's line of defenders.'

For the columnist Peter Wilson, it was all too much. If this was modern football – and it was – he wanted no part of it. 'I am told that if we are to survive the rigours of the World Cup, we must forget individualism, the brilliant flashes of in-spiration which transform a treadmill into a flying machine … which transmutes a muddied oaf into a booted genius,' he wrote. And, of course, there was some accuracy to this. The widespread shift from a back three to a back four that had followed the 1958 World Cup had changed the game; indeed, it was probably the biggest jolt in the tactical evolution of the game since the 1925 change in the offside law. Liverpool had fully embraced that approach and Leeds were still moving towards it but, for both, team play and a patient build-up through midfield had come to replace the old method of shov-elling the ball to the winger as quickly as possible and hoping he could turn an effective trick. And that, in turn, meant those watching had to adjust their expectations, something acknowledged in *The Times*. 'In spite of much lateral "method" play it was a tense battle of human qualities,' its report said. 'The opening half, in particular, was a quiet prelude. This was the careful shadow boxing that led up to a pulsating finish. Indeed, there was a certain hypnotic element about the whole thing. The fascination lay in trying to assess which side would first break the stalemate.'

And that is the unspoken truth of Shankly's sides. They were neat and effective and played a precise, modern style of football but, to many contemporary observers, adjusting to the changing style of the game, they were boring.

For all the jubilation, Liverpool still had the chance of winning another competition that season: on the Wednesday after their Wembley triumph they faced Inter in the home leg of the European Cup semi-final. Shankly announced that the FA Cup would be paraded before kick-off and it was that as much as the prospect of the Italians that had fans gathering at Anfield as early as 9 a.m. for an evening kick-off. So many were there that the gates were opened at three and areas of terrace were full by six.

Shankly had Milne and Byrne, both injured and so unable to play, parade the Cup before kick-off, beginning at the Anfield Road end and progressing to the Kop, so the noise gradually built to a ferocious climax. An eleven-year-old Phil Thompson was there and he always said it was the atmosphere that night that made him a devout Liverpool fan. The initial roar had barely settled when Hunt gave Liverpool a fourth-minute lead, scooping in Callaghan's cross from the right first time – a goal from the training-boards, as Shankly later described it. 'We were on a high from winning the Cup and it was one of those nights where the atmosphere made a real difference to the result,' Hunt said.

A Yeats error allowed Mazzola in to equalise six minutes later. Callaghan restored Liverpool's lead, dummying a free-kick, carrying on his run and receiving the ball from Hunt, standing a yard or so from the end of the wall, before finishing calmly – a move, it turned out, they had never practised but were replicating from a film of Brazilians Shankly had shown them earlier that day. St John added a third after Hunt's shot had been parried but it could easily have been more: Lawler had a goal ruled out and they twice hit the woodwork. 'We have been beaten before, but tonight we were defeated,' said the Inter coach Helenio Herrera. 'The enthusiasm of the Liverpool fans stunned my players. They are a great team.' As it turned out, though, 3–1 was not quite enough.

Amid the satisfaction at a job well done, there was tragedy. The following day, the body of the club secretary, Jimmy McInnes, was found dangling beneath the Kop. Quite why he had hanged himself, nobody knew, but Kelly suggests Shankly feared the pressure of the extra games Liverpool had played that season, the need to arrange additional travel for players and ticketing for fans, had been a contributory factor and that that unsettled him in the days before the second leg.

In terms of significance it hardly compares, but if Shankly is to be believed, there was one other sour note as an Italian journalist approached him and told him, 'You will never be allowed to win.' They weren't. There were the familiar complaints about noisy fans outside the hotel who kept them awake the night before the match but what happened once the game had started was far more serious. Corso struck an indirect free-kick straight past Lawrence after eight minutes and José María Ortiz de Mendíbil, the Spanish referee, allowed the goal to stand (or that, at least, was Shankly's version of events; looking at the video, it's far from clear that Ortiz de Mendíbil's arm is raised). Two minutes later Joaquín Peiró nicked the ball from Lawrence as he bounced it in preparation for a kick downfield, and again Ortiz de Mendíbil gave the goal. The third with which Giacinto Facchetti sealed the game was brilliant, but that was hardly the point.

Although nothing was ever proven about that night, Ortiz de Mendíbil was later implicated in the match-fixing scandal uncovered by Brian Glanville and reported in the *Sunday Times* in 1974, in which Dezső Solti, a Hungarian fixer, was proven to have offered $5,000 and a car to the Portuguese referee Francisco Lobo to help Juventus through the second leg of their European Cup semi-final against Derby County in 1973.

Lobo refused the bribe and reported the matter to Uefa but Glanville's research suggested other referees were less honest when it came to gifts from Italian clubs.

A sense that they had been cheated, the feeling that they deserved recognition not just on a national but a European scale, fired a yearning in Liverpool and in Shankly for continental success. Winning the FA Cup had ensured Liverpool could – perhaps for the first time, despite all their successes in the league since 1901 – be considered a big club, but to be a great club they needed more. Satisfaction would take longer than anybody imagined.

CHAPTER 4

European Cup, second round, second leg, Anfield, Liverpool, 6 November 1973

Liverpool   1–2   **Crvena Zvezda**
Lawler 84   *Lazarević 60*
                                   Janković 90

(Zvezda won 4–2 on aggregate)

Ray Clemence   Ognjen Petrović
Chris Lawler   Nikola Jovanović
Alec Lindsay   Vladislav Bogićević
Phil Thompson   Miroslav Pavlović
Larry Lloyd   Kiril Dojčinovski
Emlyn Hughes   Petar Baralić
Kevin Keegan   Slobodan Janković
John McLaughlin (Brian Hall 63)   Stanislav Karasi
Steve Heighway (Phil Boersma 72) Vojin Lazarević
John Toshack   Jovan Aćimović
Ian Callaghan   Vladimir Petrović

Bill Shankly   Milan Miljanić

Ref: Rudi Glöckner (GDR)
Bkd:
Att: 41, 774

SHANKLY HAD BEGUN THE REVOLUTION but before Liverpool could dominate Europe, it had one further stage to pass through. That final phase was plotted on 7 November 1973, in a shabby, windowless room off the corridor to the dressing-room at Anfield, as the coaching staff contemplated the previous night's European Cup defeat to Crvena Zvezda. The previous year, Liverpool had won the Uefa Cup, their first European honour, but that wasn't enough. Losing to the Yugo-slav side was part of a pattern: Liverpool kept on falling short against continental opposition – and often not even against what might have been considered the continent's best sides. Something, clearly, had to be done.

'Liverpool's inquest on their European Cup exit last night will inevitably include a parade of all the dreary familiar claims and excuses,' wrote Frank McGhee in the *Mirror*. 'It is true they did most of the attacking, had more of the pos-session, created more chances. They also ran faster, worked harder, fought more ferociously. But the name of the game is not running or working or fighting. It is football – and the Yugoslav champions had a virtual monopoly of that priceless commodity.'

The shift in emphasis from eight years earlier, when the *Mirror* had lamented Liverpool's methodical approach in winning the FA Cup, is striking. What England's World Cup win in 1966 had hammered home was the primacy of team play in the modern game, the lessons of Austria in the 1930s, the Dinamo Moscow tourists of 1945 and Hungary in 1953 at last being absorbed. Perhaps conditioned by the memory of West Germany hammering England 3–1 at Wembley in the quarter-final of the European Nations Cup the previous year – crushing confirmation that England's model had been surpassed by a more technical variant – the complaint now, remarkably given how Liverpool tried to approach the game, was that their style wasn't sufficiently based on team play, that there was need for yet greater control and inter-passing.

It was a conclusion reached also by Shankly, Paisley, Fagan, Moran and Bennett: Liverpool, they decided, had to go even further down the patient road they had taken. This was the Boot Room revolution, the meeting that secured the position of the cramped cubby hole in the legend of the club. It was, as the name suggested, primarily the store-room for the players' boots, which hung from hooks along one wall, the other three sides being decorated with team photos and topless calendars. From Shankly's earliest days it had become the tradition for the coaching staff to meet there after games, carrying out a relaxed debrief over bottles of beer provided by the chairman of Guinness Exports, whose Runcorn works team often used Liverpool's facilities. 'You got a more wide-ranging discussion in the boot-room than the boardroom,' Paisley said. 'What went on was kept within those four walls. There was a certain mystique about the place.' Managers, coaches and directors of opposing teams would pop in and were pumped for information. Anfield legend has it that when Elton John visited in his time as Watford chairman and was offered a drink, he asked for a pink gin. He was given a beer. Fagan began to store his notebooks detailing training there and so it became a repository of Liverpool's expertise. In *Winners and Losers: The Business Strategy of Football*, the economist Stefan Szymanski and the business consultant Tim Kuypers claimed Liverpool's success in the seventies and eighties was a result of their organisational structure, of which the Boot Room was a key part. 'The boot-room,' they wrote, 'appears to have been some kind of database for the club, not merely of facts and figures, but a record of the club's spirit, its attitudes and its philosophy.'

BIRMINGHAM 1899 The young Jack Cox and Alex Raisbeck, two players who brought fresh talent to the game (both Popperfoto/Getty Images).

Tom Watson, who applied his brilliance with Sunderland to create a formidable side, seen here on the right end of the middle row with the 1905–06 team (Popperfoto/Getty).

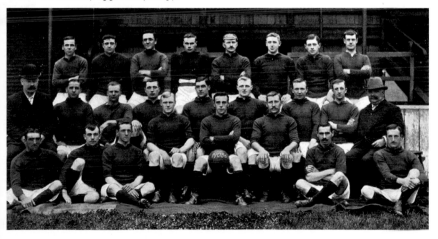

WOLVERHAMPTON 1947 *Above* Billy Liddell (Getty) and *below* Jack Balmer (Colorsport).

WOLVERHAMPTON 1947: *continued.* Albert Stubbins (Getty).

LONDON 1965 Roger Hunt takes a shot at goal (Mirrorpix).

LONDON 1965: *continued.* Bill Shankly and Ron Yeats celebrate after their win (Mirrorpix).

Ian St John scores the winning goal with a diving header past Paul Reaney (Colorsport).

LONDON 1965: *continued.* Ron Yeats is hoisted aloft by his jubilant teammates (PA).

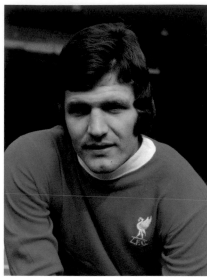

LIVERPOOL 1973 *Clockwise from top left* Chris Lawler (Colorsport), John Toshack (Getty), Emlyn Hughes (Getty), Phil Thompson (Action Images).

ROME 1977 *Above* Terry McDermott scores the first goal as Borussia's Berti Vogts and Wolfgang Kneib look on (Getty).

Left Tommy Smith heads the second goal (Colorsport/ Stewart Fraser).

Below Phil Neal scores goal three from the penalty spot (Colorsport/ Stewart Fraser).

ROME 1977: *continued. Above* Bob Paisley embraces Ian Callaghan, and *below* Kevin Keegan and Ray Clemence celebrate (both Getty).

The Boot Room, a think tank on which Shankly, who rarely attended meetings there, could always draw, had presided over Liverpool's rise. Defeat to Zvezda made its members realise that if Liverpool were to rise further, there needed to be further evolution, that for all the progress that had been made since Shankly had first instituted an approach the *Echo* had described as 'continental', there was more work still to be done. The reaction to that defeat was what defined the Liverpool philosophy for the next decade and a half, developing the Shankly model into a style that would dominate Europe.

Having won the FA Cup, and removed that great absence from Liverpool's roll of honour, Shankly's focus had turned back to the league for 1965–66. After the experience of the previous summer and the trials of the US tour, he insisted the players should rest during the close season. The injuries the club had suffered the previous year may have hampered the league campaign but they had given experience to Chris Lawler, Tommy Smith and Geoff Strong and Shankly envisaged that the side that had won the Cup final, with Milne restored, would be his first choice, with the versatile Strong as the regular substitute, in the first season substitutes were permitted in the league. A run of four successive wins beginning at the end of October took Liverpool to the top of the table, a position they never surrendered as they won the title by six points. Remarkably, they used just twelve players regularly, with two others sharing four games towards the end of the season, vindication of Shankly's methods of preparation.

Liverpool went out of the Cup in the third round to Docherty's Chelsea, some payback for the previous season's semi-final, but the Cup-Winners' Cup offered another opportunity of silverware and kindled the desire for continental success that had been ignited the previous season. Liverpool beat Juventus, Standard Liège, Honvéd and Celtic on a tough route to the final but against Borussia Dortmund at Hampden Park, they never got going. 'It was one of our few poor displays that year,' said Hunt. 'It was just an off night ... It was probably the most disappointing defeat over the years because we just didn't play.' Borussia Dortmund won 2–1 after extra-time, the ill-fated winger Reinhard 'Stan' Libuda scoring a freakish, looping, deflected extra-time winner from long distance over Lawrence and in off a post via Yeats. If Liverpool in truth weren't quite battle-hardened enough to win a European trophy yet, they were also not getting any of the breaks required by even the best teams to reach the top.

Shankly, for once, decided not to add to his squad, reasoning that a physically fit side in its prime needed no bolstering. They were never quite as effective again, though, and never played with the same level of consistency. After a hesitant start to the next league season – three defeats and five draws in the opening thirteen games – Liverpool hit a run of form that had them in the top three by the beginning of December. They'd beaten Petrolul Ploieşti of Romania after a replay in the first round of the European Cup and faced Ajax in the second.

English teams at the time often had the sense of forces conspiring against them when they played in Europe: on this occasion it was fog, so thick it reduced visibility to around fifty yards. Shankly was adamant the match should never have gone ahead but it did, and by half-time a side inspired by the youthful genius of Johan Cruyff led 4–0. Shankly was able to staunch the bleeding but Liverpool lost 5–1. They had shown a surprising lack of discipline, perhaps provoked by frustrations at the conditions. 'Willie Stevenson and Geoff Strong started raiding,' Shankly said. 'They were stung and went mad and tried to retrieve the game.' With the score at 2–0, Shankly had gone onto the pitch in the fog, unseen by the referee, and reminded them there was still a second leg to come. It was too late: the pattern of the game had been set.

Yet Shankly didn't give up hope. He dismissed the first leg as 'ridiculous' and criticised Ajax for 'playing defensive football on their own ground' – although he may not have been entirely serious (as Bill Nicholson once commented, Shankly never lost, not even in defeat). It says much for how infectious his enthusiasm could be that others clearly bought into the idea that the tie was salvageable. When Cruyff scored early in the second half at Anfield to make it 1–0, Gerry Loftus, commentating on ITV, noted 'And that's it!' and added, 'That must be the end of Liverpool's hopes,' as though he had really thought a comeback possible. Even more absurdly, after Hunt had made it 2–2 on the night with four minutes remaining, Loftus said, 'Well, wonders never cease, miracles constantly happen in football, could it possibly be that Liverpool could pull four back in just over four minutes?' Even the on-screen caption seemed to believe, the numbered wheel next to the word 'Liverpool' having been wound on too far past the '2' so part of the '3' was showing, as though its operator was primed to spin through the goals.

Liverpool ended the season fifth, winning only two of their last eleven games of the season. They had drawn seven times at home, suggesting an inability to break down teams who came to defend against them. Other lessons, meanwhile, were being learned. The process of regenerating a side is a fraught one, requiring a team to be broken up almost as soon as it begins to be successful and Shankly perhaps had too much faith that his champions could keep on winning. When Emlyn Hughes was bought from Blackpool in March 1967, he was the first signing in almost two years (Shankly, having lost a rear light in a bump, was stopped by police as he drove him to Anfield. 'Don't you know who I've got in this car?' he demanded of the officer. 'The captain of England.' The policeman replied that he didn't recognise him, to which Shankly said, 'No, but you will.') As Hunt reflected, measuring the cycle of a team isn't as simple as looking at their age. 'Perhaps a team has a certain lifespan …' he said. 'Maybe you're not quite as hungry if you've won things. You still want to win, you hate to lose but it's not the first thing any more and perhaps subconsciously you aren't so desperate for it.'

The 1967–68 season followed a similar pattern to the

previous one. Liverpool entered the League Cup for the first time since 1960–61 but lost to Bolton in the second round. West Brom beat them in the sixth round of the FA Cup. They were league leaders through much of September, October and November, but fell away to finish third and so complete a second year without a trophy. In the European Fairs Cup, they beat Malmö comfortably enough and hammered 1860 Munich only to be beaten 1–0 in both legs by Ferencváros in the third round. Snow affected both games and to an extent Liverpool were unlucky, but it was a first home defeat in Europe and another season without continental success.

With Alf Arrowsmith regularly succumbing to injury, Shankly wanted another centre-forward, preferably somebody with the aerial ability to make the most of the service from the flanks provided by Callaghan and Thompson. He signed Tony Hateley from Chelsea for £96,000 in the summer of 1967, but although he contributed sixteen goals in his first season, he too proved injury-prone and never played consistently again. So the next summer saw another forward arrive, Alun Evans from Wolves, the first £100,000 teenager. He started well enough, scoring five goals in his first seven games, but the pressure of the price tag seemed to weigh on him and he faded.

Liverpool collected sixty-one points the following season, which would often have been enough to win the title. That year, though, it left them second, six points behind Revie's Leeds. Again fortune was against them in Europe, the toss of a coin eliminating them after a 2–1 win and a 2–1 defeat against Athletic Bilbao in the Fairs Cup.

It's easy in retrospect to say that Shankly should have broken up the team sooner, but they were never far from success and it's easy to see why he felt such loyalty to the players who had won promotion – much, indeed, as Revie did at Leeds; the chaos of Brian Clough's forty-four days at Elland Road in 1974 was at least partly brought about by his attempt radically to rejuvenate a squad that had grown old together.

Shankly argued that his own best years as a player came between the ages of twenty-eight and thirty-three, but then he had lost part of his career to the war. The intensity of regular league competition perhaps more quickly sapped the energy of players who had played straight through from their late teens. By the end of the 1968–69 season, Yeats and St John were thirty-one and Hunt and Byrne thirty. The longevity of Shankly's first great team, and his initial reluctance to break it up, snaps into focus when juxtaposed with the progression of the Beatles, who had soundtracked the squad's first joyous foray back into the top flight: John Lennon, for example, was no longer playing jaunty harmonica licks and singing the innocent greetings-card lyrics to an imaginary sweetheart on 'Love Me Do', but was about to release 'Cold Turkey', a harrowing paean to heroin addiction.

That season, Liverpool lost 1–0 at home to Leicester City in an FA Cup fifth-round replay, a game that suggested Shankly was beginning to lose patience with his regulars. Previously he had never substituted a player for any reason other than injury; on this occasion he took off Hunt to introduce Bobby Graham. Hunt stood for a moment, disbelieving, before eventually jogging off, ripping off his shirt and throwing it down. For Shankly's first great Liverpool side, it was the beginning of the end.

The next year, St John was dropped for the first time, left on the bench for a game against Newcastle, a decision he found out about only when Jackie Milburn, to whom he was chatting in a corridor at St James', was handed a team-sheet. When St John demanded an explanation as to why he hadn't been given prior warning, Shankly blamed him for not being in the dressing-room when the team was revealed; it was as though he couldn't bear to tell him to his face that his time was almost over. And there again, as in his *Desert Island Discs* selection, is revealed the sentimentality beneath the hard-man exterior. 'If Bill had one failing, it was that he did not like to upset players that had done well for him,' said Paisley. 'He was a softie at heart.' If St John hadn't realised the writing was on the wall, the message was hammered home that Christmas. The club gave every player a turkey and when St John queried why he'd been given a particularly scrawny bird, the club secretary Bill Barlow told him that the plump ones were for first-teamers.

The end came in February 1970. Liverpool had begun the season well, winning seven and drawing two of their first nine games, but they won just three of the thirteen that followed. Their Fairs Cup campaign ended in the second round with an away goals defeat to Vitória de Setúbal. Liverpool had lost 1-0 in Portugal and, thanks to a penalty and a Strong own goal, found themselves 2-0 down with half an hour of the second leg remaining. They roared back with three goals and perhaps might have pushed harder in injury-time had they fully understood the away goals rule: they had believed it was applied only after extra-time. Again there was an excuse but the pattern of underachievement in Europe was becoming established.

The third Liverpool goal was the last Hunt scored for the club before he was sold to Bolton. By mid-February, Liverpool were sixth in the league with only the FA Cup offering hope of salvation. In the sixth round they faced Watford, then struggling near the bottom of the Second Division. They lost, 1-0, Barry Endean scoring a goal that would have just as much resonance as the Dick White own goal which sealed Worcester City's epochal win over Liverpool in 1959. Shankly described Watford as 'the worst team that ever beat us' and he knew enough was enough. 'I knew I had to do my job and change my team,' he said. 'It had to be done and if I didn't do it I was shirking my obligations.'

Shankly raged in the Vicarage Road dressing-room, telling a number of players they were finished – although, for all his loyalty, he must have known what was coming. Indeed, the replacements to a large extent had already been lined up in the reserves; all the Watford defeat did was persuade Shankly to use them. Over the following weeks, Lawrence, St John,

Yeats and Strong were all discarded and replaced by younger models: Ray Clemence, Larry Lloyd, Steve Heighway, Alec Lindsay, John McLaughlin and Brian Hall. 'It was sad to see the sixties side go, but it was inevitable,' said Hughes. 'They just couldn't compete with the kids any more.' Peter Thompson, struggling with cartilage problems, departed a few months later.

Not that it was just the old guard who were being replaced. Evans never settled into a sustained run of form, to the clear exasperation of Paisley, and an incident in a nightclub that left the forward with facial injuries came as the final straw. Shankly bought John Toshack from Cardiff City for £110,000. By December 1970, Clemence was the regular keeper, with Lloyd partnering Smith in the centre of defence, Lawler and Lindsay at full-back, Hughes and McLaughlin in central midfield, Callaghan and Hall wide, with Heighway partnering Toshack up front. The revolution, once begun, happened quickly.

The players may have changed, but the method didn't. 'The policy of the new team was the same as that of the old,' Shankly explained. 'We played to our strengths. We pressurised everybody and made them run. We didn't concede many goals and perhaps didn't score as many goals as we should have done, because we had the opposition back and defending their own goal ... We had devised a system of play which minimised the risk of injuries. The team played in sections of the field, like a relay. We didn't want players running the length of the field, stretching themselves unnecessarily, so our back men played in one area, and then passed on to the midfield men, in their area, and so on to the front men. So, whilst there was always room for individuals within our system, the work was shared out.'

As he explained to Harold Wilson, this was not merely a footballing strategy but also part of the political lesson he had absorbed in Glenbuck. 'Our football was a form of socialism,' he said. 'Liverpool have character, they're never beaten, they can last the pace because we share the work. You don't have to do any more work than me if we're in the same side.'

That Shankly's theory on keeping players fit was effective was demonstrated by the fact that five of his players – Callaghan, Lawler, Hunt, Thompson, Lawrence – played more than 300 league games under him. It helped too that he was so picky over medicals: moves for both Freddie Hill and the notoriously hedonistic Frank Worthington fell through when they were found to have high blood pressure. There was no room for weak links in his side, for players who didn't pull their weight, whether for reasons of attitude or of health.

Yet Shankly himself changed. He became more distant, with Paisley acting as liaison between players and manager. In the sixties he'd rarely shouted at his team but with the new side, according to Brian Hall, it was '90 per cent rollickings'. 'We were all frightened,' Heighway said. 'A lot of people see Shanks as being amusing and warm, and he was all those things, but I guarantee that 99 per cent of all the players were frightened to death of him because he had that very abrasive, aggressive side to him as well.'

The transition was rapid, but teams take time to mature. Liverpool went unbeaten at home through 1970–71, but drew ten matches at Anfield, lacking the guile consistently to break down blanket defences. They finished fourth that season but enjoyed good runs in both the FA Cup and Fairs Cup. In Europe, Liverpool saw off Ferencváros by a 2–1 aggregate before eliminating Dinamo Bucharest and Hibernian to set up a quarter-final against a Bayern Munich side featuring Franz Beckenbauer, Gerd Müller and Paul Breitner. Alun Evans, in what turned out to be his final fling, was superb, scoring a hat-trick at Anfield as Liverpool overpowered the Germans 3–0. A draw in Munich completed a 4–1 aggregate victory. In the semi-final, though, Liverpool met Leeds and were beaten by a single Billy Bremner goal over two legs. The FA Cup final against Arsenal was even more frustrating: it was a nervous, uneventful affair in which Liverpool took the lead in extra-time through Steve Heighway but conceded a scrappy equaliser to Eddie Kelly before Charlie George's crisply struck winner. Clemence admitted he froze to the extent that he couldn't remember any of the day. He wasn't the only one, although Hughes remained convinced that Liverpool only lost under the blazing Wembley sun because of their heavy cotton shirts, which absorbed too much sweat; he never wore a long-sleeved shirt again. Nonetheless, hundreds of thousands turned out for a parade through the city the following day, acknowledging this was a young team that was still growing.

The tally of forty-two goals in forty-two games made clear where Liverpool's problems lay; the answer had been signed from Scunthorpe a few months earlier. Shankly had initially seen Kevin Keegan as a long-term replacement on the right for Callaghan but such was his intensity in training that he had forced himself into the first team by the start of the 1971–72 season. He scored twelve minutes into his debut, against Nottingham Forest, and went on to form a fruitful partnership with Toshack.

Liverpool went out of the League Cup and the FA Cup early and stuttered in the league. By mid-January they were tenth, but a run of thirteen wins and a draw from fourteen games took them to the brink of the title. They lost 1–0 at Brian Clough's Derby County in their penultimate game, though, which meant they needed to beat Arsenal on the final day of the season. They drew 0–0, having had a goal controversially ruled out with five minutes remaining. As a result, Derby, their players already in Mallorca having completed their games, took the title, while Shankly's run without a trophy stretched to six years.

As the football club stagnated, Liverpool's economy fared even worse. The era of the Beatles had passed, Harold Wilson was voted out of office in 1970 and, although he returned in 1974, he seemed diminished. The docks were in decline and the Cammell Laird shipyard in Birkenhead was struggling. Unemployment was rising to levels not seen since the depression of the thirties. Football would become a great comfort in difficult times but in the early seventies it was one source of frustration among many.

The next season the rebuilding work came to fruition. 'Every player in my team has to play for the team,' Shankly said. 'Not himself. We do things collectively. Specialist players in specialist positions. We didn't complicate them, they had a simple job to do. Teams need a system, they should be able to play, know what should be done. Players should be on speaking terms, not strangers. When they can do that, they have freedom to play.' Liverpool were remorseless. They went top of the table with a 5–0 win over Sheffield United in September and, although successive defeats in February meant they briefly surrendered that position, they clinched the title on the final day of the season with a goalless draw at home to Leicester as Arsenal were hammered 6–1 by Leeds. 'We were playing the European way,' said Keegan. 'We didn't have to change too much and the players were good enough to just change the pace. Shanks always wanted us to quieten the crowd away from home and then he felt we'd have a chance.'

That European style – characterised by a patient, methodical build-up, a willingness to run down the clock – carried Liverpool past Eintracht Frankfurt, AEK Athens, Dynamo Berlin, Dynamo Dresden and Tottenham to the Uefa Cup final, where they met Borussia Mönchengladbach, whose talisman, Günter Netzer, had orchestrated West Germany's 3–1 demolition of England at Wembley the previous year.

Gladbach breezed in to Liverpool vowing to play attacking football – as was their natural mode. Shankly, for once, was taken in and set up Liverpool in a defensive formation. Borussia, though, played within themselves, deploying Netzer as a sweeper, and seemed in control when torrential rain forced the game to be abandoned after half an hour. In his autobiography, Shankly described how he had pretended to the referee he didn't think it was too bad ('I knew these continentals') so that he wouldn't realise he wanted the game called off.

The next morning an irritated Toshack accused Shankly of allowing Paisley and Fagan to pick the side. He went home and when Shankly rang him he admitted he feared he was going to be told he was being sold. As it was, Shankly told him to rest because he was playing in the rescheduled final that evening. Gladbach, he had realised, defended deep and lacked height at the back; tactically they were exactly the sort of side likely to be vulnerable to a player of Toshack's physique and aerial strength.

Brian Hall missed out – and Shankly, as he had with St John, failed to tell him until an hour before kick off. Fired up for the game, Hall was furious. Perhaps Shankly would argue he had more to worry about than an individual player's feelings, but not letting him know seemed a strange omission – particularly given the obvious tactical sense the switch made, the obvious explanation that was there – and hints at his dislike of confrontation, or at least of confrontation that involved him telling a regular he wasn't playing. As it was, the decision was thoroughly vindicated, Toshack setting up two for Keegan in a 3–0 win.

The return leg wasn't quite the formality many had expected. Gladbach scored twice in the first half but Shankly persuaded Liverpool at half-time that the West Germans were spent – and after another twenty minutes or so in which Liverpool barely got out of their own half, he was proved right, and by a 3–2 aggregate, Liverpool had – at last – their first European trophy. Although Shankly did everything he could to keep his players grounded, his young side were established as the best side in England – and one of the best in Europe. But they weren't quite the best – as the Zvezda game proved.

Liverpool had struggled by Jeunesse d'Esch of Luxembourg in the first round of the European Cup, winning only 3–1 on aggregate after two sluggish performances. The general assumption, though, was that they would find their edge against the Yugoslav champions. The first leg seemed to have gone well enough, even if, as David Lacey wrote in the *Guardian*, 'much of Liverpool's play was depressingly unimaginative, especially when compared to the shrewd, intuitive skills of the opposition.' Janković gave Zvezda a half-time lead, crashing in an angled drive from the edge of the box to complete a stunning move, begun by the young winger Vladimir Petrović's dummy and sprint and carried on by a backheel from Vojin Lazarević before a deft one-two between Nikola Jovanović and Stanislav Karasi. Three minutes after half-time, Vladislav Bogićević volleyed a second as Liverpool timed their offside trap poorly in attempting to deal with a short corner. Hope, though, arrived in the form of a scuffed Lawler shot that bobbled into the bottom corner after a Heighway corner had been half-cleared.

Shankly clearly expected Liverpool to progress – although given he had expected them to overturn that 5–1 first leg deficit against Ajax in 1966 that perhaps isn't saying too much. 'They are a good side, even though our fans would not pay to watch the football they play,' he said, an admission that hinted at the lack of patience in England for possession-based football. Zvezda's coach Miljan Miljanić, though, decided to focus even more on ball-retention in the second leg.

The irony is that Miljanić had been heavily influenced by England's success at the 1966 World Cup, a tournament he'd driven himself around in his year as coach of Yugoslavia, sleeping in a van and eating tins of food he'd brought from home to cut costs. 'Miljanić had an unbelievable desire for knowledge and love for football,' said the Zvezda midfielder Jovan Aćimović. 'He worked twenty hours a day for football. Teaching himself, he taught also us because we were kids. He was excellent and methodical. Later he developed as a very good tactician, but what was decisive was his hunger for innovation and knowledge.' He had taken over as Zvezda coach in 1966, and won four Yugoslav league titles. So great was his international reputation that he was appointed at Real Madrid in 1974.

The match at Anfield was a high point for him. 'That was

one of the rare games in which the head coach gets every-thing right,' said Aćimović. 'The tactics were perfect. It was clear that if we'd played an open game, our chances of beating Liverpool would not have been great. We were trained to avoid that, to go for a safety-first approach. In the home leg we played as we usually play. Our system was a 4–4–2: we were like the England team that won the World Cup in '66. We had a withdrawn right-winger like Ball which was Slobodan Jank-ović and a strong forward player on the left wing, who was Vladimir Petrović and a classic centre-forward in Lazarević who was a giant in the air. Our plan was that during the game there would come an opportunity for Petrović that he would get himself into positions where he might put in crosses for Lazarević who was an exceptional player in the air and that would create goalscoring opportunities. And we knew we had to close down so as not to allow John Toshack command in the air.'

Zvezda had played Tottenham in the Uefa Cup the previous season, losing 2–0 at White Hart Lane and being unable to overturn that deficit in Belgrade. 'We weren't so inferior to them,' said Aćimović, 'but we learned from that game. In the history of Yugoslav football it was always regarded as a big event when we played against English teams. English football was always something that we as players looked up to. Liverpool in our eyes with the players they had was something big. We were young in age but we had experience so we knew about hard away games. Of course we knew about Anfield and the Kop. And we were prepared. One of our main goals was to survive the first 10–15 minutes. We knew that because of the fans there would be huge pressure on the opening period.'

Vladislav Bogićević, usually a deep-lying midfielder, was deployed deeper to deal with the aerial threat of Toshack, while Kiril Dojčinovski went man-to-man on Keegan. Zvezda were without their most celebrated player, Dragan Džajić, the left-winger who had scored the only goal when Yugosla-via had beaten England in the semi-final of the European

Championship in 1968, who was away performing his military service. Had he been there, Petrović would presumably have switched to the right. Nicknamed '*Pižon*' (a Serbian variant of the French for 'pigeon'), Petrović was only eighteen but had made his debut two years earlier and was prodigiously gifted. He would go on to play for Arsenal and would be named, along with Džajić, as one of the *Zvezdine zvezde*, the 'stars of the Star', a title given to only five individuals. 'Usually we played a style like Brazil – people recognised this as the style not only of Zvezda but of Yugoslavia,' Petrović said. 'We had a lot of short-passing, dribbling … Even the smaller clubs played like that. That was our tradition, our school of football. In the second game, we couldn't play that open, but we defended very well.

It didn't take long for the pattern of the game to unfold. Callaghan, receiving the ball on the right, took on the left-back, Petar Baralić, but he used his strength to nudge Callaghan off balance and then timed his tackle superbly to put the ball out for a throw in. Zvezda may have been a neat passing side but they also knew how to defend. As soon as they got the ball, they showed how technically adept and fluid they could be. A neat move involving Aćimović and a preposterously audacious backheel from Lazarević led to a corner on the right as Lindsay blocked a Janković cross. Janković, the right-winger, took the corner short to Bogićević, who rolled it back to him. He hit a low cross and Hughes, seemingly in two minds as to whether to boot it out for another corner or try to turn, did neither, the ball ricocheting off him to Aćimović who, a little off balance and presumably startled to have been presented with the ball eight yards out, snatched at his shot, allowing Clemence, quick off his line as ever, to block and smother.

Shankly may have said Liverpool fans wouldn't want to watch a side like Zvezda, and from the time of the defeat against Ajax in 1966 it had been apparent that, for all his advocacy of possession football, he had little truck with teams who, to use the expression popularised by José Mourinho,

rested with the ball. Zvezda, though, were not just about keeping the ball; they may not have looked to get it forward as
quickly as Liverpool but there was a purposefulness to their
approach play, always the threat of a sudden change of tempo
to release Slobodan Janković on the right or the exciting Petrović on the left. The tendency for Lloyd and Lindsay simply
to hit the ball forward wasn't particularly unusual by English
standards but by contrast with Zvezda it seemed extraordinarily wasteful.

'Our basic idea,' Aćimović explained, 'was to keep them
from the ball, to have as much possession as possible and to
keep it out of our danger zone, so we would not come into a
situation where we were under pressure. We trained to make
triangles and offer square options in lateral positions, and
maybe it baffled them a bit, because we did not respond to
their active play with active play. We played reserved football,
often going back, a lot of passes, very calm. I think it was the
first time we went for this obstructive approach. There were
other away games when opponents made us defend, but that
was not our main characteristic. As far as I can see, now it's
the dominant approach. Today it's a normal part of tactics, but
at that time, when you passed the ball back the whole stadium
booed and hissed.'

With around half the first half played, a Heighway pass was
intercepted by Miroslav Pavlović. The break, suddenly, was on.
Pavlović found Petrović who helped it on to the busy Karasi.
He switched the angle of attack right for Aćimović and he
went outside for Janković. The winger crossed deep; Lazarević,
backpedalling at the back post did well to guide a header back
and into the centre of the box, where Thompson blocked off
Karasi. Lawler cleared down the line to Toshack under pressure and when he was half-tackled, Petrović stole in, laying
the ball inside for Bogićević, who operated as the great con-
ductor, always looking to step up from his defensive role to
orchestrate attacks. Another move slowly swelled, only cut off
when Petrović's cross was headed clear.

At the back, meanwhile, Dojčinovski was doing a fine job on Keegan, while helping out elsewhere as required. When Thompson threatened to reach a Callaghan cross, for instance, Dojčinovski eased him away from the ball superbly, leaving the midfielder appealing vainly for obstruction. Most of Thompson's work, though, was done at the other end, mopping up as Zvezda countered as they did with increasing danger. Aćimović played a one-two with Karasi and then weaved between two Liverpool challenges before laying the ball outside to Lazarević; Thompson read his ball back and intercepted, but Liverpool were wobbling.

Liverpool threatened only occasionally but they did create the best chance of the first half. A Thompson cross was headed clear and fell for Lawler who knocked it back to Thompson. He sent it out to the right to Heighway, who had briefly switched flanks with Callaghan. He came infield, beating Baralić, but was tackled by Dojčinovski, the ball rolling back to Hughes. He advanced, turning inside Karasi's challenge and then slid the ball vertically for Keegan, making an angled run in the box to a position just to the right of goal. Keegan – whether shooting or crossing it wasn't clear – turned the ball across the face of goal, beating the goalkeeper Ognjen Petrović. Toshack, no more than three yards out, slid in, but Janković made a superb challenge somehow to keep the ball out. Toshack looked hopefully at the referee Rudi Glöckner, but he saw nothing amiss.

From then on, the first half was all about Zvezda possession. They won a throw on the left, deep in the Liverpool half, after Lawler had glanced a cross away from Lazarević. It was taken back to Aćimović who was dispossessed by Callaghan. The loose ball broke for Baralić, who slipped it inside to Bogićević. His attempt to release Lazarević was misplaced but Heighway, under little real pressure, hoofed the ball forward, returning possession to Zvezda. Pavlović gathered and spread the ball to Janković on the right. He chipped it infield to Karasi who touched it off to Bogićević, stepping up to provide the extra man as ever. Bogićević lobbed it to Aćimović, then took a return pass before playing it square to his right to Pavlović. Suddenly there came an injection of pace and a straight ball forward to Janković moving into the box. He took on Thompson and seemed to have got by him when Lindsay intervened to help the ball back to Clemence.

But by then Zvezda had found their rhythm and their passing was relentless. There was a remarkable calm about them, a sense that they had such faith in their technical ability that the possibility of a miscontrol never occurred to them. Dojčinovski serenely headed down a Lindsay cross at the edge of his own box for Bogićević. He sent the ball forward for Lazarević on halfway, just to the left of centre. The forward knocked it back to Karasi who went square for Bogićević as he moved into the centre-circle. He went forward and right to Janković who knocked it back to Pavlović, inside for Bogićević, forward to Janković, back to Bogićević, the move mesmerising in the simplicity and angles of the passing. He went forward again for Lazarević, who laid it back to Janković and he at last picked up the pace, accelerating by Thompson and then laying a pass left to Aćimović who had found space outside Lawler. From just inside the box the playmaker hit his shot first time with the outside of his left foot, the ball arcing just wide of the top left-hand corner of the net as Clemence leapt hopefully across goal.

At times it felt as though Liverpool would never get the ball back. One Zvezda move, that went forward, across the pitch about twenty-five yards out and then back across the pitch on halfway, totalled twenty-seven passes. Gerald Sinstadt, commentating for Granada, spoke of the 'ominous silence' that had fallen over Anfield, the realisation that, even though they needed only one goal, this was a Zvezda side who were more than capable of holding out and more.

Bogićević, who went on to have a successful career at New York Cosmos, had an outstanding game. He was, McGhee wrote, 'tall, straight-backed and ... nonchalantly certain of his own skill, does nothing by chance or accident. When he operated in defence, he was ice-cool, commanding. When he dominated the midfield – as he mostly did – he displayed the asset that proclaims world class, an aura of calm amid the rush.'

Ognjen Petrović, the goalkeeper, took a free-kick awarded for offside, rolling the ball short for Bogićević. And so the pattern began again. To Vladimir Petrović, back to Aćimović, square for Bogićević, forward for Petrović, those eternal triangles confounding Liverpool. Petrović went back to Bogićević who went wide right to Pavlović, now well inside the Liverpool half. He played an angled pass back inside for Karasi, who dummied cleverly and the ball ran on for Petrović. He advanced to the edge of the box and knocked the ball right for Karasi, who played a return. The ball slightly got stuck between his feet and when he extricated it, he could only scoop his shot wide of the left-hand post. It resulted in a goal-kick, but the move had been sensational.

Only right on the stroke of half-time did a glimmer of hope present itself, after Janković had chopped down Heighway on the left as he chased a Lindsay ball. Glöckner warned the defender, pointing repeatedly to the badge on his breast pocket as the defender, in a demonstration of contrition, bowed his head solemnly. Lindsay delivered the free-kick and Toshack, for once, got away from his marker but couldn't get sufficient purchase on the header to trouble Petrović. There were a few jeers as the teams walked off at half-time and, as Sinstadt said, even though a 1–0 win would have been enough for Liverpool, that looked 'a mammoth task'.

The second half started promisingly, though, Callaghan running onto Lawler's pass down the right and being bundled off the ball by Bogićević. He took the free-kick himself. Toshack challenged with the goalkeeper, the ball looping up to Lawler who, under pressure from Aćimović, nodded the ball towards the empty net. There was little power on it and Bogićević was able to hack the ball clear. The keeper looked a little shaky then but any thought he was vulnerable to crosses was dispelled a few minutes later as with almost impudent casualness he claimed a cross from Toshack under pressure from McLaughlin. But that was a sign of renewed attacking vigour from Liverpool and Toshack headed just over from a Heighway free-kick wide on the left – won after an incisive move that began with Lawler and passed through McLaughlin and Keegan that offered promise of a way through Zvezda.

A Lindsay free-kick from inside his own half was pumped into the box and headed clear. Petrović won it but was dispossessed by Thompson, who laid the ball wide for Heighway. His cross was deep and directed towards Keegan but Jovanović got enough of a touch to send it out for a corner, Liverpool's sixth of the game. Callaghan swung it out to the edge of the box where Lloyd headed down. Dojčinovski, a little panic beginning to show, skewed the ball into the air. Toshack leapt with Bogićević and helped the ball on for Keegan who was denied from point-blank range by Ognjen Petrović. The ball spun back to Toshack who, with the keeper grounded, had most of the goal to aim at from no more than eight yards out. He got the ball over Petrović, but dragged his effort just wide of the left-hand post.

The pressure, though, was building; the intensity of Liverpool's approach unsettling Zvezda. No longer were they effortlessly putting together the long chains of passes. Petrović took the goal-kick long but it was taken down by Thompson in the centre-circle. He sent it wide to the right for Callaghan, who crossed from deep. Toshack won the header and Dojčinovski cleared as far as Heighway, a couple of yards outside the box. He worked the ball onto his right foot and shot low where Petrović saved to his left.

In the first half, Liverpool hadn't been able to get the ball; in the second Zvezda couldn't get it clear. Again and again it came back – and yet it was Zvezda who took the lead. Lloyd won the ball in the air and rolled it to Hughes who sent it out to the right-back Lawler. As Keegan came off Dojčinovski, he laid the ball down the line, but the defender recovered to win the ball back and slipped a pass inside to Bogićević in the Zvezda box. He moved the ball forward to Petrović and when he helped it on to Aćimović, Lawler fouled just inside the Zvezda half.

Dojčinovski took the free-kick short to Barasi, got it back and played it again to Barasi, who then sent it left to Baralić crossing halfway. He came in to Aćimović and continued his run, receiving the ball back. His cross was headed out by Lloyd but Pavlović regained possession in a challenge with Heighway, working it to Janković. He touched the ball on for Lazarević and the centre-forward, from twenty-two yards, crashed an angled shot with the outside of his right foot that had just enough shape on it to arc round Clemence and pick out the top corner. 'Lazarević's goal was untypical because he got ninety per cent of his goals with headers, and here he scored a great long-ranger,' said Aćimović. 'We got a lot of luck.'

That's as may be, but it was a magnificent strike and, after the initial silence that greeted the goal, Anfield broke into a smattering of applause. Shankly's reaction was rather more practical and he withdrew the ineffective McLaughlin for Brian Hall. Quickly, Liverpool picked up the pace again. A Heighway throw was headed out for a corner by Bogićević. Heighway took the corner, Ognjen Petrović came for it and then seemingly decided to let it go. It probably would have drifted out for a goal-kick but Baralić at the back post wasn't as confident as his keeper and swung a foot at the ball. It looped up and across goal. Lloyd, surrounded by three Zvezda players, leapt superbly to win the knockdown and Keegan, six yards out, pivoted, hitting the ball on the turn. It went through the legs of Petrović, but on the line behind him Dojčinovski thrust out his left foot. The ball struck him near the ankle and spun along the line. Falling, he almost sat on the ball, stopping its forward progress with his right thigh and allowing Petrović, throwing himself backwards, to smother. Keegan and Toshack appealed for the goal and Sinstadt commentating was convinced. 'That really must have been over the line,' he squawked but, while replays were inconclusive, it appeared Dojčinovski had indeed stopped it in time.

With a quarter of the game still remaining, though, that was a sign of Zvezda's vulnerability: crosses and high balls troubled them and that gave Liverpool hope. Yet Zvezda still posed a threat and as Liverpool became increasingly agitated, their aptitude for drawing fouls became increasingly evident. Lloyd climbed on Lazarević to concede a free-kick thirty-five yards out. It was taken short and Hughes, clumsily swiping at Aćimović, conceded another free-kick a little to the right and about five yards further forward. Petrović took it, crashing the ball right-footed round the wall. Clemence, springing to his left, not merely saved it at almost full stretch but held the ball too.

Shankly played his final card, taking off Heighway for Phil Boersma, while Hughes began to advance. Hughes took a free-kick short to Lindsay after Bogićević had fouled Keegan and when the left-back crossed, Zvezda again stuttered. Dojčinovski headed the ball straight up and Lawler, running in, nodded just wide. The sense was that if Liverpool could get one, they might easily get a second to take the game into extra-time.

Boersma surged through the middle, knocked the ball to Hughes and carried on his run. Hughes's attempted return was a little heavy but Boersma, with a stretch and slide, managed to turn it back to Keegan on the left. He drifted infield and played a ball forward for Hughes on the left side of the box. His first attempt at a cross was headed straight back to him; his second found Toshack at the back post. He met the ball with a firm downward header but Petrović, diving to his left, saved the ball and held it.

Still the Liverpool wave kept coming. Lawler hoisted a ball in from the right. Keegan challenged Petrović, who spilled the cross to Toshack. He rolled it goalwards but Bogićević got back to clear off the line again and put the ball out for a corner. Hall took it, Lloyd won the header and Keegan's effort was blocked, Jovanović hacking away, the attempts at controlled, possession football abandoned.

Liverpool won a free-kick for handball in the centre-circle. Lloyd played it to Thompson who spread it to Callaghan on the right. He knocked it back to Thompson, who sent an up-and-under into the heart of the Zvezda box. Toshack again won the knockdown, Lawler chested down and lashed the ball goalwards. Petrović got a hand to it but could only turn the ball against the underside of the bar from where it bounced down and into the net. There were still six minutes remaining; given the way Liverpool's physicality was troubling them, that must have seemed an eternity to Zvezda.

Yet Liverpool never really exploited that. There was one Lindsay cross that Toshack headed back into a crowded goal-mouth only for Petrović bravely to claim but the one last chance they must have hoped for never came. And then, in the final seconds, Thompson fouled Aćimović just outside the box. Janković struck the free-kick right-footed round the end of the wall and it curved back at high speed into the top corner – another superb strike that gave Clemence no chance. And that was that. The goals may have been almost freak-ish – two powerfully struck drives from well outside the box that flashed inches inside the post – and they came, oddly, not when Zvezda were dominant but during the spell when Liverpool seemed to have the edge, but the overall quality of Zvezda's play, the way they had almost mocked Liverpool with their possession in the first half, couldn't be doubted. The better side had won, something acknowledged by the applause of the Anfield crowd at the final whistle and by the tone of the meeting in the Boot Room the following day. That Shankly was there suggested its importance. The realisation was stark: although Zvezda were not as fit as Liverpool, although they had struggled at times to deal with Liverpool's crossing, their control of possession had enabled them to control the game.

'They showed themselves the artists who deserved their prize richly,' wrote Geoffrey Green in *The Times*. 'It was the night when the lid was held down on a steaming kettle. So much happened – or nearly happened – that the thoughts ran around the head like coloured beads in a box … here, basically, was a contest between the bull (Liverpool) and the matador … a match full of everything, artistry, drama and courage which kept us on the edge of our seats to the last moment, when Red Star, with a final dazzling shot by Janković, settled the affair.'

The applause at the end suggested that, for once, Shankly had misjudged his audience; this was a crowd that fully appreciated what Lacey termed 'football of a profound quality and ingenuity'. Had it been a one-off, the significance of the game could perhaps have been overlooked, but it was part of a more general trend: Ajax, Ferencváros, Athletic Bilbao and Vitória de Setúbal had all frustrated Liverpool, while Bayern Munich had produced a consummate display of containing football to draw 0–0 at Anfield in 1971 before winning the return. A week before the tie in Belgrade, England had drawn with Poland at Wembley, so failing to qualify for the World Cup for the first time; although Liverpool were far more patient than most, the traditional English virtues of pace and power had begun to look inadequate. That was why the debate in the Boot Room the day after the Zvezda defeat was so fevered; that was why, for once, Shankly joined his staff. 'We realised it was no use winning the ball if you finished up on your backside,' said Paisley. 'The top Europeans showed us how to break out of defence effectively. The pace of their movement was dictated by their first pass. We had to learn how to be patient like that and think about the next two or three moves when we had the ball.'

That meant everybody had to be able to pass the ball; there was no room for the old-fashioned stopper centre-half. Larry Lloyd, exactly the kind of central defender they had declared extinct (although he would later enjoy an unlikely renaissance at Nottingham Forest), then ruptured a hamstring, and Phil Thompson, originally a midfielder, was pushed back to partner Emlyn Hughes at the heart of the defence. 'It was a clever decision by the boss and his staff,' said Thompson. 'They were ahead of the time. All of a sudden we were looking to play from the back. If it took fifty passes to score we didn't care.'

For Shankly, it was simply a question of taking his basic philosophy and extending it. He had always believed in passing, in not giving the ball away, in control; what Zvezda had shown was that Liverpool had to carry those principles even further. 'The Europeans showed that building from the back is the only way to play,' Shankly explained. 'It started in Europe and we adapted it into our game at Liverpool where our system had always been a collective one. But when Phil Thompson came in to partner Hughes it became more fluid and perhaps not as easy to identify. This set the pattern which was followed by Thompson and [Alan] Hansen in later years. We realised at Liverpool that you can't score a goal every time you get the ball. And we learned this from Europe.'

Liverpool had begun the season as league champions and Uefa Cup winners and yet, perversely, 1973–74 became a season of transition. Revie's Leeds were ageing and supposedly in need of the sort of reform Shankly had overseen, but they began the season with a record twenty-nine games unbeaten. Liverpool stayed in touch and, by the beginning of April, they were just four points behind with three games in hand. But with the title seemingly in reach, fatigue set in and Liverpool won only one of their eight remaining matches.

The FA Cup, though, offered what would turn out to be a glorious finale – not that anybody realised that was what it was at the time. Liverpool beat Doncaster, Carlisle, Ipswich and Bristol City before a meeting with Leicester City, their old bogey side, in the semi-final. It took a replay, but they won through for a final against Newcastle United, whose centre-forward Malcolm Macdonald filled the back pages in the week before the game with confident predictions of what he would do at Wembley. 'Let him talk,' said Shankly, 'and on Saturday we'll play.'

Liverpool's demolition of Newcastle was masterful, not the greatest game Shankly's side ever played but arguably their best performance. It was an afternoon that began with another consummate performance. There were jeers when Bruce Forsyth, wearing a navy blazer and maroon slacks, walked out to lead the community singing but, as the band of the Royal Marines struck up with the theme tune to *The Generation Game*, he charged half the length of the pitch with a ball at his feet, mugging furiously, and swept the ball into the net, transforming the boos into cheers. By the time he had mounted a podium in the centre-circle, the crowd were eating out of his hand, happily joining in with his 'nice to see you, to see you …' catchphrase.

It took Liverpool fifty-eight minutes to open the scoring – Lindsay's earlier rampage down the left and strike from a narrow angle having been questionably disallowed for an offside against Keegan, even though the ball had come back off the Newcastle prodigy Alan Kennedy, later an Anfield hero himself – but Newcastle, who had won only three league games since Boxing Day and had only beaten Nottingham Forest in the quarter-final after a pitch invasion when they were 3–1 down shifted the momentum (they came back to win 4–3 but the FA ordered the game to be replayed), rarely threatened. It was Keegan who got the opener, flicking up Hall's cross and lashing in from the edge of the box, setting David Coleman babbling: 'Goals pay the rent and Keegan does his share.'

'Newcastle's frail, fumbling challenge hardly amounted to a challenge at all,' reported David Lacey in the *Guardian*. 'It was always going to be the Kop's Cup, with Kevin Keegan no more obvious an executioner had he worn a black mask.' Steve Heighway added a second, then just before the end, came a moment of transcendence as Newcastle, in Coleman's words, 'were undressed'.

'Liverpool's third goal will never be bettered as an example of their style,' wrote Lacey. 'Seven of the team were involved and there were 11 passes in the movement. The ball went from Ian Callaghan to Brian Hall to John Toshack and then to Tommy Smith on the right; Smith passed across the field to Lindsay, who found Keegan near the left-hand touchline; Keegan dodged away from two opponents and sent a high ball back to Smith who exchanged passes with Hall, then Heighway and finally sent a low ball back from the goal-line to the far post for Keegan to touch it over the line. Possession, positioning, accuracy of passing and finishing, they were all there. It was a most satisfying end to a largely predictable afternoon.'

So predictable, in fact, that the astrologer from the *TV Times* magazine had got it almost spot on a week before the game. 'Jupiter is going into Pisces so I can assure you that Malcolm Macdonald will be terribly depressed and will be overwhelmed afterwards with a desire to recount his troubles,' he wrote. '[The Newcastle manager] Joe Harvey is in for emotional upsets, but Bill Shankly's Jupiter aspects look marvellous and Keegan's restless creative activity is just bursting to get loose.'

Late in the second half, television cameras showed Shankly on the bench, in grey suit and bright pink shirt, hands fashioning shapes in front of him, left then right then back again, like a master puppetmaster. Perhaps Shankly recognised that in that third goal his side had reached some sort of culmination and perhaps he recognised that it is precisely at the moment of its fullest bloom that the flower begins to wither. Two months later, on 12 July 1974, Liverpool's chairman John Smith addressed a packed press conference at Anfield. Nobody knew what it had been called for and his words came as a total shock. 'It is with great regret,' he announced, 'as chairman of the board I have to inform you that Mr Shankly has intimated to us that he wishes to retire from League football.' At the press conference that followed, Shankly admitted his only regret was not winning the European Cup.

It was a decision that stunned journalists, fans and others at the club. His resignation was announced over the Tannoy at St John's Market in the centre of the city. The journalist Hugh McIlvanney was covering the Open golf when the news broke. The story, he said, 'passed round Royal Lytham like a rumour of death ... when the word that he had abdicated (no other term can cover such a dismounting from a throne) percolated through the press tent, even the most insular golf writers permitted themselves to look slightly aghast.' Tommy Smith initially refused to believe the news. Clemence admitted he couldn't take it in until he'd heard it from 'two or three people and then on the radio'. Even Paisley, who as his number two might have been expected to have an inkling, was flabbergasted. 'Every year, virtually, he'd say he was going to pack in,' he said. 'You didn't take him seriously. When he finally did I was lost for words, shocked. It was the day I got back from holiday and it was like a bomb being dropped.'

In his autobiography, Shankly insisted that the realisation of how 'tired' he was had come to him immediately after the Cup final, as he ate a pie and drank a cup of tea in the dressing-room. 'I had been around a long time and I thought I would like to have a rest, spend more time with my family and maybe get a bit more fun out of life,' he wrote. 'Whilst you love football, it is a hard, relentless task that goes on and on like a river. There is no time for stopping and resting. So I had to say I was retiring. That's the only word for it, although I believe you only retire when you are in your coffin and the lid is nailed down and your name is on it.'

There had been suggestions that Shankly was becoming disillusioned with the growing commercialisation of the game. 'There are men with tennis courts and swimming pools who haven't even won a championship medal,' he had commented, while he admitted alarm at the prospect of freedom of contract.

And there were persistent rumours of friction with the board. 'He was bitter about the meagre financial rewards his accomplishments have brought him,' McIlvanney wrote in the *Observer* the week after Shankly's resignation. Shankly had spoken to him about setting up his two daughters in 'nice homes', saying 'and we did it without any help from those people. I don't need those people.' 'You fight on the field to win,' he said for the 'Shankly Speaks' record, 'but you've other battles to fight inside the club too, political battles. Candidly it was a shambles here when I came, not good enough for the people here. I'd fought the battles inside and outside and I was only in it to win games for the people. I left because I was the manager when I left and that was satisfaction.' As Dave Bowler pointed out, there's a clear implication that soon he might not have been the manager.

Shankly described the feeling of telling the chairman as being 'like walking to the electric chair' but his mind was made up, even if he clearly soon came to regret it. 'Managing a football club is like drowning,' Shankly told Tommy Smith: 'supremely peaceful once the struggle is over.'

From a football point of view, it was a logical time to go. He'd thought of going after the league and Uefa Cup Double, but decided against it, perhaps looking to scale that one last peak, the European Cup, to reprise the success of Stein and Busby. Zvezda ended that dream and, with Leeds winning the league, that meant he would have to win the championship again before having another crack at the greatest prize: he would be committing to at least two more years. And by 1976, the squad would be ageing and would be getting to the stage of needing to go through the process of renewal that had proved so painful three years earlier. He wouldn't be able to leave that to somebody else; his sense of duty to Liverpool was too strong. The FA Cup final, and the magnificence of Liverpool's display, provided Shankly with the perfect exit: not merely in the performance but also in the sense of handing on a side in fully working order that wouldn't need major work for another couple of seasons.

But while it was an exit with honour and glory – and, as it turned out, no little regret and bitterness – it was also an exit made with one more land left to conquer. For his successor, the European Cup remained the final challenge.

CHAPTER 5

European Cup final, Stadio Olimpico, Rome, 25 May 1977

Liverpool   3–1   **Borussia Mönchengladbach**
McDermott 28   *Simonsen 52*
Smith 64
Neal 82 (pen)

Ray Clemence   Wolfgang Kneib
Phil Neal   Berti Vogts
Joey Jones   Hans Klinkhammer
Tommy Smith   Hans-Jürgen Wittkamp
Ray Kennedy   Rainer Bonhof
Emlyn Hughes   Horst Wohlers ('Wilfried Hannes 79)
Kevin Keegan   Allan Simonsen
Jimmy Case   Herbert Wimmer (Christian Kulik 24)
Steve Heighway   Uli Stielike
Ian Callaghan   Winfried Schäfer
Terry McDermott   Jupp Heynckes

Bob Paisley   Udo Lattek

Ref: Robert Wurtz (FRA)
Bkd: Stielike
Att: c. 57,000

HOW DID YOU REPLACE SHANKLY? It seemed a ridiculous task. It wasn't just that his charisma and motivational abilities would be lost; for a generation of fans, he simply was Liverpool. In fifteen years he had built the club, taking the ruins of the side of the late forties and fashioning a proud new edifice in his image. His ideas were Liverpool's ideas. His personality was Liverpool's personality. Little wonder that when a *Granada Reports* television crew toured Liverpool informing people that Shankly had resigned and filming their reaction, the majority either refused to believe the news or reacted as though they had been informed of a death. One boy of perhaps ten gave the most memorable reaction, his jaw visibly dropping, eyes beginning to fill with tears even as he uttered a horrified denial, unwilling to accept that Shankly could have gone. Liverpool without Shankly was inconceivable.

The reporter for Granada that day was Tony Wilson, who would later discover Joy Division and launch Factory Records. Although a professional Mancunian and Old Trafford regular since the late 1950s, Wilson considered Shankly to be the 'greatest football manager ever ... equal charisma, equal strength, equal power'. Years later, in an interview in *Jack* magazine, Wilson recalled the vox pops, but misremembered one crucial detail: 'I was actually filming in Liverpool when the awful news came through that he'd died.' That it was possible to misfile a resignation in the memory as a death perhaps goes some way to illustrating the shocking impact of Shankly's retirement at the time.

The club secretary Peter Robinson considered looking

outside the club for a replacement – Jack Charlton, at the time beginning to establish a reputation at Middlesbrough, was one of the names Shankly had suggested as a potential successor – but instead turned to the Boot Room and promoted Bob Paisley. If there was no Shankly, the logic seemed to be, then somebody who had served under him and contributed to the success was the next best thing.

It was not such an obvious or popular choice as hindsight might make it seem. 'Most of the players at that time,' said Kevin Keegan, 'if they are honest, would admit they were not sure that Bob could do the job. Bob was a good number two, but he wasn't very good communication-wise.'

Paisley himself was a little overawed at first. 'I knew, taking over from him, there would be difficulties to combat because of the type of extrovert personality Bill was and the fantastic record he had,' he said. 'I knew comparisons would be made.' At first, as Shankly continued training at Melwood where the players, by instinct, still called him 'Boss', the comparisons were a little too direct and Paisley, regretfully, had to ask him to stay away – at least while the players were there.

Paisley had already begun to assert himself. Three weeks after he took over, Larry Lloyd was sold to Coventry for £240,000 – he wanted to go having realised he wasn't first choice with Liverpool having moved to a system that required passing centre-backs. When John Smith then spoke about possible future signings in a local newspaper interview, Paisley upbraided him, insisting that was his domain; he was not a man to be pushed around. As Matt Busby said of him on *This is Your Life*, 'He is a very quiet person ... but he has this inner steel to motivate his players to great heights.'

Shankly took badly the suggestion he should train at Melwood only in the evenings, seeing it as part of a wider rejection of him by the club, although according to John Keith it was a piece in a Sunday newspaper after a defeat to Ipswich at the beginning of November in which Paisley was (mis-)quoted as saying he'd run things even in his predecessor's day that led to

Shankly deciding not to come back to Melwood. Whether he was ever offered any sort of directorial or ambassadorial role is a matter of some debate; it seems probable he was initially offered a post as some kind of director of football, seemingly with an office at Anfield and a brief to come and go as he pleased, but turned it down and was then too stubborn to ask if the offer could be resurrected when he realised he missed the day-to-day involvement with the club – a yearning that worsened when he led pre-season training as the board considered who should replace him.

In an interview with Stephen Kelly, Smith suggested Shankly had even asked to be restored as manager two months after retiring, only to be told it was too late and his opportunity to change his mind had gone, although Ness Shankly was sceptical. It all contributed to Shankly's bitterness, which spilled out in his 1976 autobiography in which he said he'd been made more welcome at Goodison Park after his retirement than he ever had been at Anfield. He hated that no role had been found for him and was too proud ever to ask for tickets. Even worse, he told the journalist Ian Hargreaves, he resented the fact that the board hadn't offered to pay the tax on the bonuses he won for winning the league championship and the FA Cup.

Banning Shankly from the training-ground also emphasised the hardness of Paisley; he didn't shirk, as Shankly had, from telling somebody he respected that they weren't welcome. In terms of image, Shankly was the hard man, Paisley more avuncular, but it was Paisley who was the more ruthless. As Patrick Barclay put it, 'It takes more than a cardigan to make an uncle.' He mixed up words and regularly forgot players' names but nobody doubted the sharpness of Paisley's football brain. 'I think Bob just got wiser and wiser and wiser,' said Keith Burkinshaw, who played under Paisley in Liverpool's reserve side. 'There was absolutely nothing fancy about Bob. He just got right to the meat of the problem immediately. There were no fancy words with him and he stripped everything to the bone. The players knew this and they responded and reacted to the honesty that shone through and the plain way he said things. Liverpool had tremendously good habits. I think that Bob Paisley was responsible for that as much if not more than anybody else at Anfield.'

Paisley had been born in the Durham pit village of Hetton-le-Hole in 1919. His father was a miner and his uncle was a slaughterman for the Co-op, a job that meant he could provide pigs' bladders for kickabouts in the street. Football stood alongside horse-racing and pigeons as one of the village's three main leisure pursuits and Paisley was only four when his father, who later suffered horrific arm injuries in a mining accident, gave him his first pair of boots.

His father had been desperate for Paisley to avoid the pit and he escaped it by a stroke of good fortune that hinted at his abilities as a coach. Paisley's friend Geordie Oxley, who played for Hartlepools United, would run in the handicap foot races that were popular across the North East and carried cash prizes. Paisley began training him and when a group of builders won a significant amount betting on Oxley to win a race, they expressed their gratitude by offering him an apprenticeship as a bricklayer.

Paisley impressed enough playing amateur football for Bishop Auckland to turn professional at the age of twenty, joining Liverpool in May 1939. He had played just two reserve games when football was halted after the declaration of the Second World War. That October, Paisley joined the 73rd regiment of the Royal Artillery. His battery was sent to the Far East but he was redeployed because he was the regimental football captain. It was a fortunate escape: his unit was soon captured and spent the majority of the war in a prison camp. Paisley was deployed overseas in August 1941, travelling via South Africa to take up a posting in Cairo. In total, he spent four years and two months overseas, serving with Montgomery's Eighth Army at the relief of Tobruk, the victory at El Alamein and then in the campaign through Sicily and Italy until Rome was finally liberated in June 1944.

Paisley returned to Britain in 1945 and initially had to be given leave each weekend to go and play for Liverpool. On one of his train journeys home, he entered the compartment and threw down his greatcoat on the seat realising too late that a young woman had left her sandwiches there. He apologised to Jessie, as he found out she was called, they got talking, and a year later they married at St Peter's in Woolton. Eleven years later, it was at the same church that John Lennon and Paul McCartney met each other at a fête.

An aggressive left-half who became noted for his hard tackling and his long throw, Paisley soon became a regular. 'Bob was a very underrated player,' said the centre-half Laurie Hughes. 'He never looked classy but he was brilliant defensively and read the game so well.' Even as he relished his first full season as a player, Paisley's analytical mind was preparing for what would come later. 'I got to know the routine,' he told John Keith, 'and I think the game's one of understanding, both from a player's and a manager's point of view. The perfect man has never been born and players, like everyone else, have their weaknesses. It was on this theme, later, that I tried to select sides and pick players. I think foremost in my mind when I went to the coaching side was to consider what I couldn't do as a player ... I won the ball as much as anyone but I didn't always distribute it correctly. It was something I tried to instil into other people.'

Paisley was in the side that won the league title in 1947 and then scored the winner in the semi-final in 1950. An injury kept him out for the final four league games of the season but he was fit for the final and, when he was left out, he considered leaving the club. He stayed, but when Liverpool were relegated in 1954, he knew his time as a player had come to an end. He considered a return to bricklaying in the North East and toyed with the idea of selling fruit and vegetables or opening a newsagents. He'd done a correspondence course in physiotherapy and was offered a job on Liverpool's backroom staff by T. V. Williams, a board member who had been a shareholder since 1918 and would go on to become chairman.

Initially Paisley took charge of the reserve side. He was an instant success, finishing second, first and second in the Central League in his three seasons in the role before being promoted to work as a trainer for the first team. He had a gift for that as well, often being able to work out what was wrong with a player – or a horse – just by watching the way they walked. Paisley was convinced footballers were similar to racehorses: some older ones were bored by training but still thrived on the big occasion, some needed a loud voice and some a soft one, some couldn't cut it on heavy ground. Edginess, he believed, could be transferred from coach to players just as surely as from trainer to horse. And he was sure, John Keith wrote, that 'a real thoroughbred will often want a donkey or a goat to travel with it in its box. In the same way, the great players need lesser lights to support and bolster them.' The animal comparisons only went so far, though, and when a friend of Shankly's brought him an injured greyhound to be treated, Paisley had to remind him he wasn't a vet.

Promoting Paisley ensured continuity; he had, after all, been with Shankly from the start. Fagan took Paisley's old job as chief coach, Moran became first-team coach while Roy Evans, at twenty-five, became reserve-team coach, preferring to join the backroom staff than to continue his playing career away from Liverpool. Vitally, Paisley was secure enough in his own position to be neither a revolutionary nor a disciple. He didn't follow Shankly's methods slavishly but neither did he feel any need to stamp his authority by changing them. He added to the squad, but in the familiar, incremental Liverpool way, bringing in the right-back Phil Neal from Northampton Town and the midfielder Terry McDermott from Newcastle. Neal, in particular, would become a stalwart. Between August 1975 and May 1985, he missed just one of 420 league matches.

The year 1974 had been one of change for a number of clubs. Manchester United had been relegated, Revie had left an ageing Leeds in need of rejuvenation, while Derby were in flux after the departure of Clough late in 1973. Clough, of course, added to the turmoil by succeeding Revie but lasting just forty-four days. Paisley, by contrast, had inherited a settled side that already knew how it needed to play. Yet that first season ended in disappointment as Liverpool finished runners-up in the league behind Dave Mackay's Derby.

The gloom went far beyond football. Although the port of Liverpool had been in decline since the end of the First World War (in 1914, it accounted for 31 per cent of the UK's visible imports and exports, a figure that had fallen to 21 per cent by 1938), it was in the early seventies that the real impact of the downturn began to be felt. After Shankly's departure, there was a genuine possibility the football club could also have sunk into decline.

The one thing Liverpool did win in 1974–75 was the Fair Play trophy, which some saw as indicative of a softening of attitude. An end of season trip to Benidorm proved they still had their ruthlessness, though; with the players taking it easy in a friendly against a local amateur side, Fagan told Smith to start a fight. He lunged into a challenge and as tempers flared, Liverpool began to play properly, winning comfortably. Beneath the neat passing, there was always a toughness about Liverpool and that stemmed from Paisley.

He was, Souness said, 'a football intellectual. Had he been more articulate he would have been hailed as one of the greatest thinkers and managers on the game ... He may have been regarded as a fatherly figure by the supporters ... let me tell you he ruled Anfield with a rod of iron ... he was a commanding man and there were few who dared mess around with him. If we looked as though we were becoming a little complacent ... Bob would say, "If you have all had enough of winning, come and see me and I will sell the lot of you and buy eleven new players."'

Paisley's philosophy – and to an extent it had been he who had determined the team's playing style even under Shankly

– was rooted in the lessons of 1973. It was summed up by Neal as '"If the ball's controlled, keep it controlled." By this he meant that, if you received a controlled pass on the ground, give a controlled pass on the ground … Another saying of the boss is the longer you keep the ball the less time the next man to receive it has. This has become known as the "early ball" game.' Paisley's other priority was that his players should stay on their feet; tackling, he felt, was to be avoided if at all possible. 'If you can win the ball by interception, it not only cuts down on injuries … it also means you can use the ball better because you've got it cleanly, you're not at full stretch, you're in space.'

With Fagan still leading training, nothing much changed – in part because there wasn't much to change. Neal, for instance, was initially 'exhilarated' on arriving at the club in 1974 that so much training was based around sessions with the ball rather than the stamina work he'd been used to at Northampton, but he was soon struck by the fact that training 'never varies, week-in week-out the routine is exactly the same … as long as the side keeps winning all the powerful voices in the boot-room will be able to claim without fear of contradiction that the results on the field fully justify the system. I'd go even further and suggest that something as simple as superstition could be at the heart of the matter.'

But it did work, and this was part of the genius of the Liverpool method. There may have been minor tactical tweaks for individual games but essentially tactics were done on a macro level: players were accumulated whose skills were complementary, who fitted, without great modification, into the overall strategy. 'When Liverpool bought me and the other players, we were told to play our natural game,' Neal explained. 'Playing with the lads and training with them week after week made modifications to their game and to ours. The newcomers and the old hands learn to work together by combining their skills, not by playing to a set, mechanical pattern.'

Still, there was a certain anxiety about the start of the

1975–76 season. After the apotheosis of the 1974 Cup final there had been an expectation that further silverware would follow and that Liverpool hadn't won anything led to doubts – insubstantial and only half-voiced, perhaps – about Paisley's suitability. That summer he made only one signing, bringing in the left-back Joey Jones, who had been a regular on the Kop as a boy, from Wrexham for £110,000. Liverpool began the season uncertainly, winning only three of their opening seven games, but they then lost just one of their next twenty-four, a run at least partly prompted by switching Ray Kennedy – who had arrived as a forward from Arsenal the morning Shankly had left – into midfield. They were as low as eighth by the end of September but went top in February, only to suffer a stutter as they lost at Arsenal, drew at Derby and then lost at home to Middlesbrough in successive games. By the end of March, Liverpool lay fourth, only two points off the top but behind Queens Park Rangers, Manchester United and Derby.

They were also making progress in the Uefa Cup. After beating Hibernian, Real Sociedad and Śląsk Wrocław, Liverpool faced Dynamo Dresden in the quarter-final. Clemence, having been told which way to dive by Tom Saunders, a former headteacher who became part of the Boot Room set-up and the club's chief scout, saved a penalty from Peter Kotte as Liverpool battled to a 0–0 draw in East Germany and a 2–1 win at home set up a semi-final against Barcelona. The presence of Johan Cruyff in their line-up might have awakened memories of 1966 at Ajax, but this was a smarter, better Liverpool. Toshack got the only goal in the first leg in the Camp Nou after Keegan had flicked on a Clemence clearance and when Phil Thompson turned in a Toshack shot after fifty minutes of the return at Anfield, Liverpool looked safe. Charly Rexach did pull one back but Barça couldn't find the second away goal that would have taken them through. That set up a final against Club Brugge, who had beaten Hamburg by a 2–1 aggregate.

The Saturday after overcoming Barcelona, Easter Saturday, Liverpool returned to the top of the table with a 5–3 win over

Stoke City in their third-last league game of the season. They followed that up with a 3–0 win over Manchester City on Easter Monday, which left them a point clear of QPR and four ahead of United, who had two games in hand. With Wales's European Championship qualifier against Yugoslavia meaning Toshack and Jones were unavailable for the scheduled final game of the season, away to Wolves, Liverpool were granted a postponement until Tuesday 4 May – after the first leg of the final against Brugge.

It was a game that went badly wrong from the off, with Brugge controlling midfield at Anfield and going 2–0 up before half-time. Paisley withdrew Toshack for Jimmy Case, who scored one of the goals – Alan Kennedy and Keegan with a penalty got the others – as Liverpool came back to win 3–2. That left them with two games remaining, each of them potentially bringing a trophy.

QPR had beaten Leeds in their final game to take them a point clear at the top, which meant Liverpool needed either to win at Molineux or, thanks to the vagaries of goal-average, to draw 0–0, 1–1 or 2–2 (but not 3–3 or higher) to take the title. It became one of the iconic nights in the club's history, far more than the official 48,000 packing in as Paisley sought his first trophy. When Steve Kindon put Wolves ahead early on, there were serious jitters, but Keegan levelled with fourteen minutes remaining. That was enough for the title, but further goals from Toshack and Kennedy rounded off the league season in style as Liverpool became champions for the ninth time, making them the most successful team in league history, moving one title ahead of Arsenal. The group at the top of English football's roll of honour was beginning to get strung out: a mere six seasons previously, Everton had won their seventh title to join Arsenal, Liverpool and Manchester United at the top of the list of high achievers, with Aston Villa and Sunderland one behind on six. Liverpool, then Manchester United and to a lesser extent Arsenal, were about to charge away from the pack.

The league was one trophy – the second followed fifteen days later. Eleven minutes in to the second leg of the Uefa Cup final, Hughes handled in the box and Raoul Lambert converted the penalty, giving Brugge the advantage on away goals. But four minutes later, Hughes laid off a free-kick for Keegan, who blasted home to make it 1–1 on the night and restore Liverpool's aggregate lead. They held out to win the competition for the second time in four seasons.

Liverpool had won everything – or nearly everything. That they were the best team in England could hardly be disputed but there was one further stage to go. 'There's a tremendous ambition among all the lads to win the European Cup,' Keegan said in the summer of 1976. 'We've won everything else in the last five years and there's a feeling that the European Cup is going to be next.'

As ever, Paisley looked to strengthen the squad: there was no room to relax, never any scope for settling for what Liverpool had: under his leadership, they were always looking to improve, always looking to develop further. He considered moving for Ray Wilkins, Chelsea's nineteen-year-old captain, but the form of Terry McDermott in pre-season persuaded him to stick with what he had in midfield. In the week of the Charity Shield, though, he moved for David Johnson, spending a club record £200,000 to bring the former Everton striker from Ipswich.

John Toshack scored the only goal as Liverpool beat Southampton to win the Charity Shield but the day was overshadowed by the announcement that Keegan would be leaving at the end of the season; as he pointed out, with income tax at 83 per cent for the top earners, he would be financially far better off abroad.

Liverpool began the season uncertainly, going out of the League Cup at West Bromwich Albion and losing to Birmingham in the league but, by mid-September, they were level at the top with Middlesbrough. The European Cup first-round tie against the Northern Irish side Crusaders was expected to be a formality and when Joey Jones hit the bar and Phil Neal put Liverpool ahead at Anfield with an eighteenth-minute penalty, controversially awarded for a supposed push on Toshack by the Crusaders captain Walter McFarland, there was every expectation of a crushing victory. Despite sustained pressure, the anticipated avalanche of goals failed to materialise and there was a level of anxiety before Toshack finally headed a second twenty minutes into the second half. Paisley later described the game as the most one-sided he could remember and when it emerged one of the Crusaders players had lost a contact lens during the game, he noted drily that 'he'll find it in one penalty area or the other.'

Uefa regulations demanded that teams arrive for matches the day before a match but because of the political situation in Northern Ireland and the threat of violence, Liverpool were given dispensation to arrive on the day of the game. Fog delayed their departure, though, and for a brief time there was a serious danger that they might be expelled from the competition for failing to fulfil a fixture. They eventually arrived at Aldergrove Airport in Belfast two hours before the scheduled 4 p.m. kick-off and made their way straight to the ground, which was rammed to its 10,000 capacity. Determined to be welcoming, Crusaders allowed Liverpool to use the home dressing-room but then had the better of the opening half hour, Ron McAteer twice striking the woodwork. Liverpool recovered, though, and took the lead after thirty-four minutes, Keegan volleying in a Johnson cross. The arrival of Terry McDermott after an hour for his European debut added impetus to Liverpool's play and four goals in the final ten minutes – two for Johnson and one each for McDermott and Heighway – finally gave a true measure of Liverpool's superiority over the tie.

Although it became awkward, Liverpool could hardly have had less distance to travel for their first-round game. The second-round game against the Turkish side Trabzonspor, though, entailed the longest flight they had ever undertaken, and involved hiring a different plane as the one they usually flew in was too large for the runway. They landed first in Ankara, trained at the national stadium and then flew on to Trabzon, sharing their flight with the reigning Miss Turkey. Unsettled by the poverty they witnessed on the bus ride from the airport Liverpool were further upset by the realisation that they'd been switched from the hotel they'd booked to one so bad that Paisley said he hadn't slept anywhere worse since he'd served with the Desert Rats in the Second World War.

The stadium wasn't much better: the grass was long, there were only two showers and two seats in the changing room and the ball was heavy and bounced strangely – 'worse than a pig's bladder at a Durham miners' gala', Paisley said. Liverpool seemed to be holding out when the Romanian referee Nicolae Rainea made what Emlyn Hughes described as 'the most ridiculous decision I've ever seen', giving a penalty after Necmi had fallen over his challenge. Cemil converted the penalty off the inside of the post. Liverpool's players were glad enough to get away with only a one-goal defeat and retired to a local bar to ease their last night in town. They found it full of transvestites.

Around 3,000 Trabzon fans poured into Liverpool for the second leg – the most an away side had brought to Anfield for a European fixture since Ajax in 1966. It took just nineteen minutes to settle the tie. Heighway scored the first after Keegan had headed a McDermott cross into his path, Johnson dispossessed Cemil to put Liverpool ahead on aggregate just over a minute later and a close-range Keegan header from a Callaghan cross wrapped up the victory with over three-quarters of the second leg still to play. An ill-tempered second half in which the substitute Milemic Cemil was sent off did little to alter the perception of serene progress.

In the league, though, Liverpool's progress was anything but serene. They started well enough, losing only two of their opening sixteen games and going top of the table, but a 1–0 defeat to Ipswich in December – the game after which Shankly was asked to stay away from training sessions – rattled them. Liverpool beat QPR 3–1 at home but then went to Aston Villa where they suffered an unthinkable 5–1 defeat, all the Villa goals coming in the first half – an absurd reminder of the events of seventy-seven years before. It was Liverpool's biggest defeat since losing to Ajax in 1966 and, while there was something freakish about it – a sense that everything Villa had tried had flown in – there was no doubting the unease it provoked, especially when it was followed by a 2–0 reverse at West Ham.

Liverpool had for a long time been a club that looked to the long term. There was no panic and that same month Bob Paisley and Peter Robinson agreed seven-year contracts. At the press conference that announced the deals, it was revealed that a drive was being launched to market the club and sell merchandise overseas with some matches being sponsored. Astonishingly, up to that point, there hadn't even been perimeter advertising round the pitch at Anfield. That sounds absurd now but at the time, Liverpool's reluctance to flex their corporate muscle while the going was good, eventually a major factor in their downfall during the 1990s, was worn as a badge of honour by fans. In an interview with *When Saturday Comes* in 1987, for instance, the Radio 1 DJ John Peel, arguably Liverpool's most credible celebrity supporter of the era, bemoaned the club's capitulation to market forces. 'I wish they hadn't had advertising in the ground, you know,' he said. 'I wish they'd just kept themselves above all that.'

Five points from a possible six over Christmas and New Year steadied the nerves and restored Liverpool to the top of the table and, by the time European competition was rejoined at the beginning of March, Liverpool were not merely two points clear of Manchester United at the top of the table with a game in hand but had reached the sixth round of the FA Cup.

*

Talk of the great European nights at Anfield, and one game rises inevitably above the rest: the second leg of the quarter-final tie against St Etienne, an epic battle of two of the best sides in Europe at the time, a fraught, brilliant affair that wasn't settled until its final moments. St Etienne's yearning for European glory was similar to Liverpool's own: they knew they were a top side but they needed that final validation of European success. Ten months earlier, they'd been unfortunate to lose to Bayern Munich in the European Cup final, and forever blamed 'les poteaux carrés' of Hampden Park. Had the goalframe been round in cross section, as was common in France, rather than square as it was in Glasgow, Jacques Santini's thirty-ninth-minute header would – St Etienne insisted – have cannoned in rather than out and they would have taken the lead. Les Verts' domestic form was indifferent but they were the French champions and had conceded just once in their previous nine European games.

Keegan missed the away leg with a knee injury but Liverpool, calm and patient as ever, seemed to have stifled St Etienne when, with ten minutes remaining, Gérard Janvion's mishit shot from a corner fell for Domenique Bathenay, who had also hit the woodwork in the final at Hampden, to score the only goal of the game. Keegan returned for the second leg, but Liverpool were without Phil Thompson, who had sustained cartilage damage in a collision with Newcastle's Alan Gowling in a league game. He was replaced by Tommy Smith who, on the plane back from St Etienne, had decided he would leave Liverpool and take up a player-manager's role at Wigan.

St Etienne, meanwhile, were without the Brazilian centre-back Osvaldo Piazza, suspended after picking up a yellow card in the first leg. What they did have was the support of around 6,000 fans, many of whom ended up sleeping on the streets as hotels were full. Home fans began queuing in the afternoon, desperate to secure their place. Turnstiles were closed half an hour before the 7.30 kick off, locking out around 5,000 fans, but a gate was broken down on the Kemlyn Road side of the

ground allowing many more than the official 55,000 attendance to squeeze in.

The game started two minutes early, meaning many fans
had not taken their seats when Keegan put Liverpool ahead
after forty-two seconds, latching onto a short corner and
beating Ivan Ćurković from an acute angle with something
between a cross and a shot. 'I just drove the ball across to the
far post,' said Keegan, 'and the wind did the rest.'

The noise was extraordinary. 'The atmosphere got better
and better as the game wore on,' Neal told Mark Platt for his
book *Cup Kings*. 'It was the only game in which I found it difficult to concentrate solely on the football. When the ball was
up the other end of the pitch, I couldn't help but look up in
amazement at the crowd. The whole stadium seemed to be
moving, even the people in the stands. They were bobbing up
and down, swaying and bouncing. You couldn't better that
night.'

St Etienne defended high, their offside trap repeatedly
thwarting Liverpool. They also posed an attacking threat –
far more than in the first leg – and they broke through six
minutes into the second half. When Heighway lost possession,
Bathenay picked up the loose ball and struck a dipping, swerving shot past Clemence from thirty yards – a goal of quite
stunning quality.

Paisley responded by leaving his seat in the directors' box
and heading down to the dug-out. He sent the twenty-year-
old David Fairclough, already renowned for his ability to turn
games from the bench, to warm up. Christian Lopez almost
scored an own goal and then, just before the hour, Ray Kennedy gave Liverpool hope, his low shot beating Ćurković from
the edge of the box. 'The ball came to me off Toshack's shin,'
he said. 'I didn't hit it that hard but I hit it true.'

With Toshack, who had been booked for dissent, suffering
a blow to his heel, Paisley took him off for Fairclough after
seventy-four minutes. St Etienne could have had a penalty as
Clemence seemed to foul Domenique Rocheteau but the Dutch

referee, Charles Corver, was charitable. And then, with six minutes left, Kennedy flicked the ball beyond the St Etienne defence. Fairclough ran on, chested the ball down, held off Lopez and, as Ćurković advanced, decided to hit it close to him, realising he would struggle to get down quickly enough to get his body behind it. Anfield held its breath and then, as the ball passed the goalkeeper and struck the back of the net, erupted in a roar that, it's said, could be heard three miles away. 'I was really up,' said Fairclough. 'I remember Jimmy Case being the first one to catch me, and we're spinning around, and we've fallen down to the ground, and then everyone's come on top. I remember Kevin Keegan getting in on it, and he's got his arm around me, and he's saying, "Stay down, stay down, let's waste some seconds."'

'Supersub does it again,' roared Gerald Sinstadt, commentating for ITV, a nickname – and a role – that irritated Fairclough, for all his aptitude at it, 'I hated sitting on that bench, despite what people might think,' Fairclough said. 'It was frustrating, horrible at times. At the start of my career, I was just grateful to be involved. But that changed, of course.' Although he spent nine years at Liverpool, he never quite became a regular, but as a boyhood fan of the club, he at least had the thrill of scoring what remains one of Anfield's most memorable goals.

Not that he celebrated particularly vigorously that night, as he recalled in an interview with lfchistory.net. 'After the game, by the time I had done one or two interviews I met up with my parents and when we decided to leave the stadium it must have been quarter past ten,' he said. 'In those days pubs closed at half past ten and we were just going to have a pint at the pub we used to go to. I looked over and it was jam packed with people. It was nearly half past ten so probably we wouldn't get a drink there so I just went home.'

The injury to Thompson meant Tommy Smith becoming a regular again, despite his plans to retire at the end of the season.

'It's a blow to lose Phil,' said Paisley, 'but Tommy knows his way round all right. He's got the nous to sort out situations less experienced players may lack. He can read things and react to them.'

It was a typical response. There was no fuss, no histrionics, just a pragmatic determination to make the best of it. 'Whatever Bob said was plain, straightforward stuff,' said Fagan. 'He wasn't a flamboyant man ... The extraordinary thing about him was his ordinariness. There were no gimmicks with Bob.'

After the drama of St Etienne, the European Cup semi-final was anticlimactically straightforward. Zurich had knocked Rangers out in the first round so Paisley rang their manager, Jock Wallace, for a scouting report and was told of how good Zurich's defensive control had been. So Liverpool must have feared the worst when, in the first leg in Switzerland, Peter Risi put Zurich ahead from an eighth-minute penalty. Neal, though, levelled seven minutes later, drifting in at the back post to convert a Kennedy free-kick having made a show of not being interested in the set play – a rare rehearsed move that he would reprise in the final.

Liverpool's second arrived two minutes into the second half, McDermott finding Heighway who held off a couple of challenges and finished neatly. A Neal penalty midway through the second half as good as settled the tie. They got another three in the home leg to reach their first final. Jimmy Case capitalised on a slip by Pierre Chapuisat to get the first and added the second with a free-kick before Keegan, with his last goal at Anfield, completed a 3–0 win, nudging in the rebound after Alan Waddle's header had come back off the bar. As Tommy Smith pulled off a backheel, the game ended with a sense of carnival amid chants of 'It-tal-lee, It-tal-lee, we're the greatest team in Europe and we're going to Italy.'

In the other semi, Borussia Mönchengladbach overcame a 1–0 first-leg deficit to beat Dynamo Kyiv 2–1. The Dynamo forward Oleh Blokhin, never one to let tact get in the way of an opinion, thought Liverpool were clear favourites.

'Liverpool will win the final,' he said. 'Despite the win, Borussia Mönchengladbach disappointed me. They only won with a great deal of luck.'

Tom Saunders, who had watched Gladbach in the second leg against Dynamo and then on three further occasions, was rather more complimentary. 'I rated them as one of the best teams I'd seen,' he said. 'I thought St Etienne were top class but this side were a lot stronger on team cohesion. They were well organised, moved back and forward together as a unit and, if an attack broke down, they'd all race back to get behind the ball. It was an impressive sight. Another thing was that they played for each other and, in that respect, they reminded me a lot of Liverpool. They could boast outstanding individuals, as Liverpool could, but I'd say that their great strength was their overall teamwork.' He was right. The final may not have had quite the sense of drama of the St Etienne game but it was a match full of intelligent football, both teams fluent and prepared to interchange positions, both relying on careful probing rather than firing the ball into dangerous areas and hoping for the best.

Three days after seeing off Zurich, Liverpool faced another semi-final, against Everton in the FA Cup. Everton's manager Gordon Lee seemed almost to idolise Paisley, and had written a piece for the National Coal Board magazine saying Paisley should be England manager (a weirdly prescient recommendation, given Don Revie would quit as national boss to take up a lucrative role in the UAE a little under two months later). That was typical of an intense but respectful rivalry between the Merseyside clubs, although that semi-final would place a severe strain on the relationship.

A neat clip from Terry McDermott gave Liverpool the lead but a Hughes slip allowed Duncan McKenzie to level before half-time. Case headed Liverpool back in front but with six minutes remaining, McKenzie laid on another equaliser for Bruce Rioch. Then came the moment of controversy. Ronny

Goodlass crossed and McKenzie helped the ball on to the substitute Bryan Hamilton, who beat Clemence. With the goalkeeper distraught and Everton celebrating, though, the referee Clive Thomas ruled the goal out. Immediately after the game he said only 'an infringement of the rules of the Football Association [had] occurred.' The following day he revealed the goal had been ruled out for offside, even though the linesman didn't flag. In his autobiography he went further, saying Hamilton had been offside and had then handled the ball. Evertonians, needless to say, weren't convinced. Hamilton, who had had an effort ruled out by Thomas in similarly mystifying circumstances in a semi-final two years previously playing for Ipswich against West Ham, insisted he was onside and that the ball had struck his hip.

Either way, Liverpool escaped to a replay. 'Henry Cooper had Ali down for eight but he couldn't finish him off,' noted Toshack, who had watched from the bench with injury. 'Everton have had the same experience. They won't get a second chance.' They didn't, Liverpool winning the replay 3–0.

By the time of their next league game, at Anfield against Ipswich, Liverpool were level on points at the top of the table with Manchester City, but had played a game fewer. Ipswich themselves were a point behind, but had played two games more than Liverpool. A 2–1 home win was a major step towards a tenth league title but it came amid unpleasantness, with the game having to be stopped while an announcement was made asking the Kop, angered by the officiousness of the referee Peter Willis, to stop throwing objects into the goalmouth. (In 1985 Willis would become the first man to send a player off in an FA Cup final, dismissing Kevin Moran of Manchester United, who still went on to beat Everton 1–0.)

After away draws against QPR and Coventry, Liverpool sealed the title with a goalless draw against West Ham. It was Kevin Keegan's last game at Anfield and the success meant Ian Callaghan, who was playing for the reserves at Burnley at the time, equalled the Arsenal forward Cliff Bastin's record of five championship medals, but even those two milestones couldn't disguise the contrast with the euphoria of the previous season. If anything the feeling was one of relief, one of the three legs of a possible Treble complete, with two cup finals still to come.

The FA Cup final against Manchester United proved an immense frustration. The FA had decided that if the game were drawn, because of the Home Internationals, England and Scotland's tours of South America and, as their statement had it, 'important meetings', the replay wouldn't take place until 27 June. Having planned to start pre-season on 12 July, Paisley was appalled. 'I'm not intellectual enough to find words to express my disgust at this stupidity,' he said. 'It's cruelty. The FA are taking blood from the fans and the players, though obviously we in football don't matter to them.' With Tommy Docherty, the United manager, also appalled by the plan, Liverpool even suggested settling the match on the day, by penalties if necessary.

The FA vetoed that proposal and Paisley, desperate to avoid a replay so deep in the summer, let it affect his team selection. He went with a front three, using David Johnson rather than Ian Callaghan, something he later admitted he regretted. How much bearing his selection had on the final is difficult to say, but Paisley felt it cost Liverpool control of midfield. Fagan had, irrespective of tactics, been concerned about the players' attitude, fearing they were distracted by the excitement and the clamour for tickets. He had laid into them on the Monday before the FA Cup final. 'Training was bloody awful,' he wrote in his diary. 'The lads had two meetings about arrangements for Wembley then came out expecting an easy-osey time. They didn't get it. I bollocked them and told them it is the football that counts, not bloody tickets.'

Liverpool still almost took the lead when Ray Kennedy headed Case's cross against the post but, although Case cancelled out Pearson's opener, United found a winner as Lou Macari's shot cannoned in off Jimmy Greenhoff's chest. 'It was as I feared,' Fagan wrote. 'The adrenalin didn't seem to be flowing as it should have been. Too many players did not play well enough on the day. They did try, though, so hard luck.'

Afterwards the players sat gloomily around the dressing-room, until Ray Clemence threw his boots in the bath, jumped in after them, and shouted, 'I don't know about you lot, but I'm getting pissed tonight!' The train back to Liverpool was delayed by two hours but a sugar fight instigated by Heighway raised spirits and, by the time they arrived back at Lime Street, the players were lustily singing their Cup final song, 'We Can Do It'.

There were minor distractions to preparations for the European Cup final. Kennedy had a thigh problem and Jones had a cut above the knee, while Keegan had stayed in London after the Wembley defeat to sort out a £500,000 move to Hamburg. Toshack, though, was able to resume full training on the Monday after the final and Udo Lattek, the Mönchengladbach manager, as good as admitted he was concerned about a repeat of the 1973 Uefa Cup final when Toshack had been such an influential figure. 'English players are famous for their strength in the air and Liverpool are particularly dangerous in this aspect,' he said. Borussia's main injury doubts had been Uli Stielike and Jupp Heynckes but both had returned with goals the previous weekend as Borussia had retained the Bundesliga title, their third championship in a row.

Jones was never really a doubt and Kennedy, to Paisley's great relief, also recovered. He was, Paisley said, 'one of Liverpool's greatest players and probably the most underrated ... his contribution to Liverpool's achievements was enormous and his consistency remarkable ... [he had the] ability to open up a game and give you the width of the park ... He had so much control and was such a good shielder of the ball that an opponent virtually had to knock him over to take the ball off him.' He was, in other words, the ideal player for the possession-based game Paisley favoured.

Before the Liverpool players boarded the plane at Speke

Airport, Paisley told them that the side that had finished the FA Cup final would start in Rome. On the flight over, Paisley revealed his team to journalists and told them that if he'd started with that eleven in the FA Cup final, Liverpool would have won.

On the morning of the game, with the sun shining brightly, Paisley took his players through a gentle final training session on an all-weather pitch offered by a semi-professional club. There came a further setback as Toshack's Achilles broke down again. Paisley considered giving him a place on the bench so he would win a medal but realised that would be unfair on Phil Thompson who was in a similar position. In Toshack's place, Alan Waddle, whose only first-team experience had been against Zurich, was named among the substitutes.

Liverpool fans had begun queuing at travel agents before they opened the day after the semi-final and over 30,000 made the trip to Rome. As the players performed their walkabout in the stadium before kick-off, Smith said he couldn't see a single German. Liverpool fans outnumbered those from Gladbach by a factor of around four to one. Among the many flags was the famous banner that read, 'Joey ate the frog's legs, made the Swiss roll and now he's Munching-Gladbach.' Yet for all the excitement, it turned out that Liverpool were on a much lower win-bonus than the Germans: £1,600 a man as opposed to £3,750. Not that money was uppermost on the minds of Smith and Callaghan, the only two survivors from Liverpool's ill-fated European Cup venture in 1965, and hoping their return to Italy would, as Smith put it, 'make up for things that had happened twelve years previously ... we did mention it: "Here's hoping the referee hasn't been got at tonight."'

It was appallingly hot, the bright sunshine of the morning developing into a sultry evening. 'It seems absurd to me,' Michael Charters wrote in the *Liverpool Echo*, 'that Uefa should pick Rome in late May for the final of the most important inter-club competition in the world.' Perhaps conditions did seem ludicrous, but after a World Cup in the heat of Mexico and European Cup finals in Madrid and Lisbon, it surely didn't seem that outrageous, while Charters's comment seemed to tap into a strand prevalent in English football writing throughout the century that used to excuse English defeats by blaming conditions, as though football were only football when played on a damp pitch in a November drizzle.

In the dressing-room before the game, Paisley started telling anecdotes about how the last time he'd been in Rome had been in a tank during the war, having fought his way up from Africa. Whether it was deliberate policy or not, the effect was to relax the players.

There is perhaps nothing in football so conservative as the kick-off. For decades, it seems, English teams, irrespective of the type of football they favoured, belted the ball long at the opposing full-back and hoped their wide midfielder could get forward to put pressure on – as Liverpool themselves had done in the 1965 FA Cup final. English tradition said the other team should either let the ball run out of play or should whack it back, but Hans-Jürgen Wittkamp headed the ball out to Hans Klinkhammer who, with remarkable chutzpah given the circumstances, skittered off diagonally across the field, before allowing Allan Simonsen to take over. Simonsen, a slight, impish presence who would be named European Footballer of the Year a few months later, chipped the ball forward, trying to land it in the path of Klinkhammer, who had continued his forward run. He couldn't quite get there, but as an illustration of Borussia's attacking intent and the willingness of their full-backs not merely to get forward but also to switch wings, it could hardly have been bettered.

It wasn't just the full-backs. Rainer Bonhof, the libero, also strode forward from the back, his head-up style and graceful gait reminiscent of Franz Beckenbauer. When Callaghan's pass was intercepted by Uli Stielike, a roving centre-forward who often dropped back into his own half, it was Bonhof who showed for the pass. He gave a return, Stielike jinked and played the ball on to Herbert Wimmer, 'Iron Lung' as he was nicknamed, a defensive midfielder whose ability to cover for Günter Netzer had been such a key part of West Germany's demolition of England at Wembley five years earlier. Wimmer beat Kennedy but turned back and laid the ball off to Wittkamp, who struck a long pass for Schäfer to contest. The ball dropped for Stielike and his shot from thirty yards wasn't too far over. It was a mightily impressive first minute from the Germans.

Liverpool, for once, looked a little rattled and Neal hit a long ball towards Keegan. He won the flick, but his header went out of play. It seemed insignificant but it was the beginning of a trend. Keegan had the game of his life, despite the man-marking of Berti Vogts, dragging him this way and that and winning header after header. Keegan repeatedly pulled left and Heighway right, a ploy to haul the defence apart and give the midfielders space to break into.

It was Gladbach who looked the more settled in those opening minutes, though, the rhythm of their passing, the long spells of possession, working the ball in triangles across the pitch, reminiscent of that West Germany game at Wembley. As the ball moved from Vogts to Stielike to Wimmer to Heynckes to Simonsen, forward, back, forward, back, forward across the pitch tracing the shape of a W, it was easy to imagine how the 'pattern-weaving' approach of the great Scottish sides around the First World War would have looked; the difference was that they had done it along a fixed forward line, whereas Borussia's players were constantly on the move, forming the triangles for a second or two and then moving on. This was the best of the German version of Total Football, a style of play that, by eschewing the hard pressing favoured by the Dutch, was possibly even more fluid.

As Hughes inadvertently flicked on a free-kick for Heynckes, Neal had to block and in those early stages it seemed Keegan was the only hope. He got his chest to a Callaghan cross but couldn't quite control it and, a minute later, flicked the ball over Vogts in the box having seized on a Heighway pass, only for Wittkamp to get across to block. It wasn't long before Vogts, some two inches shorter than Keegan, began resorting to a physical approach to try to quell him. 'I found myself, not unexpectedly, man-marked by Berti Vogts,' Keegan said. 'I loved that challenge because I knew I would have to be at my very best to get the better of him. He gave me a lot of respect and followed me everywhere. In an odd way, that built up my confidence. He stuck so close to me that, after some pretty serious shirt-pulling from him, I told him I'd be happy to change shirts with him after the game but it wasn't usual to swap them during it.' Their battle would become central to the flow of the game as Liverpool began to realise that Keegan had the beating of Vogts, that a fifty-fifty between them was actually weighted in Liverpool's favour. Jones, with ten minutes played, knocked a pass in to Keegan and, as Vogts challenged, the ball spun loose to McDermott, whose shot was blocked. Suddenly it was Liverpool who seemed to have the momentum and almost everything they did from an attacking point of view went through Keegan. That night, Vogts came to the Liverpool hotel and sought Keegan out. He had never been given a run around like that, he said, and bought the forward a drink.

Hughes played a long ball to Keegan, who dropped off Vogts and flicked a pass to Heighway. He crossed towards Case and Bonhof only just got in front of him to head the ball away for a corner. Wolfgang Kneib punched away but McDermott gathered, played it to Case and took a return. His cross was cleared by Klinkhammer but there was that familiar sense of mounting pressure, of pass after pass coalescing into relentless waves.

Wimmer was dispossessed by Callaghan. Forward to Kennedy, out to Jones, back to McDermott, on to Callaghan and then to Neal on the right. He sent the ball long to Keegan who flicked it on to McDermott. He checked back inside and laid a pass to Kennedy arriving at the top of the box. He hit his shot first time, clipping the ball with the outside of his left foot and forcing Kneib into a diving tip-over. Borussia weren't cowed, but it was clear that Liverpool's skeins of passes were both longer and more purposeful.

Wittkamp and Bonhof headed dangerous crosses clear in quick succession, then Heighway blasted wide after a Case shot had been half-blocked. A swift passing move from Borussia worked Simonsen into a dangerous position on the right. His cross was just too high for Stielike and Neal came away with it, surging down the line and winning a corner as Wittkamp headed his cross behind. Case took it but Bonhof, elegant as ever, cleared to Stielike. The centre-forward carried the ball as far as Heynckes who laid it inside to the advancing Bonhof. As Hughes moved to close him down, he struck an unexpected shot from thirty yards. It passed between Hughes's legs, bounced once and, with Clemence scrambling, struck the post – a warning to Liverpool that however dominant they seemed, Gladbach had the attacking wit to cause them problems.

Almost immediately, though, Wimmer was forced off by injury and replaced by Christian Kulik. Without his energy and ability to cover, Borussia lost a key element of their fluid approach. Perhaps the timing was just coincidence but it seemed significant that three minutes later, Liverpool took the lead. Vogts possibly fouled Keegan but the referee, Robert Wurtz of France, allowed play to continue and as the ball broke for Simonsen, the Dane drifted infield to link with Stielike. He tried to play the ball left to Bonhof, but Callaghan, anticipating superbly, intercepted and played the ball forward to Heighway in space. He came inside, taking Klinkhammer and Horst Wohlers with him. Klinkhammer, drawn by Neal's overlapping run, checked left and, as Heighway kept coming infield, space opened between Wohlers and Wittkamp. Heighway slid a pass through the space and McDermott, running on, let the ball run across his body, took the ball in his stride and lifted it over the dive of Kneib to nestle, spinning, in the loose netting just inside the post.

Keegan played a key part in the goal, even without getting

near to the ball. As Paisley put it, he had Vogts 'selling pro-grammes to the crowd … so far had he pulled him away from where the build-up was taking place. He was a key defender and he didn't realise what was happening until it was too late. Borussia were spread-eagled and Ian Callaghan, fully recovered from injury and restored to the team at thirty-five, won the ball in midfield and pushed it out to Steve Heighway on the right. Cally followed on down the flank, pulling the Germans even wider and allowing Steve to cut inside and play the ball in to Terry McDermott's path. It was a perfect example of Terry's awareness, anticipation and running and he scored magnificently.'

As Gladbach kicked off again, Barry Davies, commentating for the BBC, noted that when he'd asked fans before the game what the score was likely to be, the most common reply had been 3–1. For a time Liverpool seemed content to kill the game, looking to draw Borussia out, something that invited pressure. Stielike fired a bouncing ball over the bar after Liverpool had half-cleared a free-kick, and then Clemence claimed a Kulik cross superbly as Stielike threatened to get on the end of it. The Keegan outlet, though, was always there and, when a Vogts foul led to a free-kick on the left, Neal, arriving late and unmarked as he had against Zurich, saw his volley from Kennedy's delivery blocked. Then Smith, advancing from the back as he had a dozen years previously, forced Kneib into a comfortable diving save. At half-time, it was 1–0 and Liverpool seemed in control.

There had been a moment towards the end of the first half when he'd been drawn too far upfield and had been fortunate: McDermott had got back to cover but Hughes, whose personality and occasional wildness could obscure his defensive qualities, made a superb challenge to dispossess Bonhof in the opening minute of the second half. The match soon settled into the pattern of the first, both sides building patiently, Liverpool looking marginally the more threatening. But then, after fifty-one minutes, Case was caught offside. Borussia, as was their way, took the kick short. Bonhof exchanged passes with Wohlers and then got lucky as a misplaced pass cannoned back to him off Keegan's shins. He laid the ball out to Klinkhammer on the right. The full-back played it to Heynckes who moved it on to Kulik, who sent it out to Simonsen on the right wing. He came infield to Stielike, who worked it to Kulik. He found Klinkhammer in space and he crossed. It was headed out and Callaghan had a swing at it, sending the ball high into the air. Stielike gathered it and returned the ball to Klinkhammer, who turned inside Keegan and sent the ball square to Bonhof. The libero tried to squeeze a ball through the defensive line but Case blocked and moved the ball to Callaghan, who aimed a pass towards Neal on the right. Simonsen, though, intercepted twenty-five yards out on the left, accelerated into the box and lashed a ferocious shot past Clemence and into the top corner. After all the painstaking team play, the scores had been levelled by a moment of breathtaking individual brilliance.

'Every team,' said Hughes, 'no matter who you are playing, get at least a couple of chances in a match. Borussia were no different. They had a five-minute spell where they were on top and they took full advantage by grabbing an equaliser.' They stayed on top for a while longer. Again what was impressive was the rhythm of their play, the way that, as Liverpool had in the first half, they passed and advanced with an almost hypnotic relentlessness. Kneib, wearing tracksuit bottoms despite the warm evening, rolled the ball out to Klinkhammer. On it was moved, to Bonhof, to Kulik, to Schäfer. He played it down the line to Heynckes and took the return, then beat Jones, playing the ball one side of him and running round the other before crossing. Simonsen, the shortest man on the pitch, was at full stretch, and couldn't guide his header on target.

Kulik then played the ball down the left for Heynckes who, remarkably, had never lost a game in which he'd started for Gladbach. He crossed and Clemence, having looked so secure until then, came to catch and missed the ball completely. Jones, fortunately, was there to clear up. Liverpool needed something to tip the momentum back their way and it came, unsurprisingly, from Keegan. With just under an hour played, Callaghan clipped a ball from the right into the box. Keegan gathered four or five yards from the goalline with the goal behind him and to his right. His first touch took him away from goal, at which Vogts slid in: he did reach the ball eventually, but seemed to go through Keegan to get there. In the modern age it would certainly have been a penalty and probably should have been then. The Liverpool fans behind that goal, who had been in fine voice anyway, were enraged and their fury seemed to lift the tempo of the game again.

Heighway, having taken a throw-in by the left corner flag, received the ball back from Keegan. As he moved onto his right foot, perhaps looking to open an angle for a shot, Klinkhammer challenged. The ball broke towards Jones who jabbed it unconvincingly goalwards. Bonhof came away with it and the break was on. The libero played it right to Simonsen, who swept a ball crossfield to Stielike, breaking through the inside-left channel. His first touch was excellent and as he approached the box, a goal felt inevitable. Clemence, though, was out quickly and threw himself towards the forward, arms spread to make himself as big as possible. Stielike's stabbed shot cannoned off the keeper's right shin to safety. 'People,' Clemence said, 'often ask me, "What was my greatest ever save?" I judge great saves not necessarily in terms of how spectacular they were, but how important they are in terms of having an influence on the game. On this occasion I just spread myself and luckily the ball hit me. But if Stielike had scored, I'm not sure we'd have gone on to win the European Cup.'

The two incidents, less than four minutes apart, changed the tone. 'It was the turning point of the game,' said Paisley of Clemence's save. 'The Germans never recovered.' At the same time, it galvanised Liverpool. 'At Wembley, Ray Kennedy did everything right with that header, but the keeper scrambled it round the post with his legs,' said Smith. 'We had played all the football but they were winning and it was obvious the Cup didn't have our name on it. This time it was different. They gave us a fright when they hit the post, and later Ray Clemence saved with his legs. I knew it was our night then.'

Hughes, storming forwards, hit a low drive that took a deflection off Keegan and passed no more than a foot wide of the post. Kneib took the goal-kick long for once and McDermott, running backwards, was in enough space to control it as it dropped just inside the Gladbach half. He sent a long ball forward towards Keegan, not dissimilar to the Callaghan pass that had led to the penalty shout six minutes earlier. This time, though, Vogts got in front of Keegan to win the header. It came to Case, who shaped to shoot but, under pressure, turned and looked to knock the ball wide for Callaghan. Vogts, though, nipped in and slid the ball out for a throw-in by a sign advertising 'FET Bearings from Poland'.

Callaghan took it, back to Smith in space. He laid it to Neal, whose run had created the room for him. Neal turned and crossed and Klinkhammer turned it behind for a corner. Heighway took it and Smith, making his 600th and last appearance for the club, ran from the penalty spot on an angle to the near post. Vogts and Schäfer came to close him down, but Smith met the cross with a thumping header. Kneib didn't even have time to raise an arm as the ball flashed past him. 'I always evaluate it to a hole-in-one in golf,' said Smith. 'It was sent over at the right height and right speed, it was met at the right height, for a change, and it went into the net like a bullet. If someone had written a script, you'd have said: this is not true.'

It was a goal that deflated Borussia and Liverpool should have had a penalty three minutes later. Keegan, yet again, won the header and as Heighway got behind the defensive line, Wohlers slid in to challenge. From the referee's angle it probably looked as though he got the ball but the replay from behind the goal was definitive: Wohlers hadn't touched the ball and had felled Heighway with his thigh. A low Case free-kick was struck straight at Kneib, then the goalkeeper was forced to beat a Heighway cross behind as the forward, coming into his own, beat Klinkhammer.

It took ten minutes or so for Gladbach to recover but finally, with a quarter of an hour to play, they came again. Smith stopped a promising break by clipping Stielike's heel. A Simonsen dart and attempted one-two was interrupted by McDermott. Clemence, earlier wobble forgotten, confidently punched out a Klinkhammer cross.

Liverpool settled back, dropped their two banks of four deep and set about frustrating Gladbach. After Heighway had been fouled deep in his own half, Hughes knocked the free-kick back to Clemence. He rolled the ball to Neal who gave it back to him. It was all slow, all deliberate, a conscious effort to run down the clock. After Heighway had won a corner off Klinkhammer, he dawdled in going to take it. Possession was used to take up time rather than with any attacking intent.

And then, unexpectedly, there came an error. Wittkamp dispossessed Case and played the ball to Simonsen who released Stielike. Hughes, charging to his left to cover, couldn't get across to cover as the centre-forward slung the ball left – a move very similar to the one that had created the great opportunity for him a quarter of an hour earlier. Heynckes, though, was a fraction behind where Stielike had been and Clemence, charging off his line, got there first. He couldn't gather cleanly, but had the wherewithal to kick clear as Simonsen closed in.

That seemed to prompt Liverpool to seek a third and, as Case headed down a Heighway cross, Vogts blocked a McDermott shot. Finally, with nine minutes left, came the goal that settled the game. Liverpool won a free-kick by their own box. Neal played it to Smith. On the bench, Paisley shuffled his feet. Did he sense something was coming? Or was he frustrated at Smith for not just returning the ball to Clemence? Smith played it down the line where Keegan won it and worked the ball back to Case. He moved it forward to Callaghan, who knocked it inside to Keegan. He accelerated by Vogts who made a desperate, lunging challenge. He took man and ball and this time, although it seemed a less obvious penalty than the two previous shouts, Wurtz pointed to the spot.

As Callaghan, his hands pressed together, visibly prayed on the edge of the box, Neal sent Kneib the wrong way, sidefooting neatly inside the left-hand post – the eleventh penalty he had converted that season. 'Mönchengladbach had a massive keeper,' he explained. 'I remember walking out and thinking, "Christ, if you get a penalty tonight, Nealy, you'll have to keep it low."' He put his plan into action. 'I assumed my previous penalties would have been shown around Europe and that their keeper would have done his homework,' he explained. 'So I decided to put my kick in the opposite corner to where I put it against Zurich in the semi-final.'

Even Paisley, the least demonstrative of men, was moved to manic celebration. 'I remember seeing him jump off the bench waving his arms in the air when the penalty went in,' said his wife, Jessie. 'He rarely did things like that because he wasn't an outwardly emotional person, but, deep down, he was very, very proud to be the first English-born manager to win the European Cup.'

From there on it was a procession. Bonhof headed one cross over and Clemence did well to claim another but the game was won and the final minutes were a long serenade from the Liverpool fans massed on the terrace behind Kneib's goal. Few doubted Liverpool had been deserved victors. 'The victory of the English was based on a constantly aggressive game, always on the attack, powerfully pressed by Kennedy, Callaghan and Case and made dangerous by a great showing by Kevin Keegan,' said the report in *Corriere della Sera*. Liverpool, *Il Messagero* noted, were 'better organised, knew how to deal with their adversaries and used a strategy to block and disorient them'.

Lattek noted that he had been forced to field players who weren't fully fit, but Paisley was scathing. 'We did not allow them to play and German teams usually complain when that happens,' he said. 'We planned to pace the game in the heat, which did not seem as intense as it had been at Wembley, to be patient, play the ball around and to challenge the Germans in their own half before they could build up their breakaway attacks. It worked. It was our greatest display in Europe. Everyone played their part and it was a magnificent performance. If we had been as patient at Wembley instead of going hell for leather, we'd have won that Cup as well, but this more than makes up for that disappointment. We have achieved our greatest ambition.'

Almost as importantly, they had achieved vindication for the stylistic changes made in the wake of the Zvezda defeat in 1973, something noted by Ron Greenwood, who would succeed Revie as England manager later in the year. 'There was no swank or side at all and I felt that if they were typical of England's footballing people then there wasn't much wrong with our game,' he said. 'The measured rhythm of the Liverpool team comes from understanding the good technique. They vary their pace and point of attack. They build from the back and they use the whole width of the field. One moment they are playing within themselves, creating space and passing beautifully, the next they put their foot down and go looking for a kill.'

Paisley didn't touch a drop of alcohol at the celebratory banquet after the game, preferring to stay sober so he could savour the moment. Fagan, Moran, Smith and Callaghan sat together with their partners and as more and more fans sneaked in, Fagan told Smith to grab one bottle of everything from behind the bar. They hid them in a corner and then, as the party began to get rowdier, retired to a hotel room where they drank with various Gladbach players, including Vogts.

As players surfaced the next morning they and journalists

were thrown in the hotel pool. Keegan emerged with a black eye – it was rumoured he'd ended up fighting with Case or Smith but it was actually Neal who had inflicted the damage, desperately trying to take off a pair of expensive leather shoes before being thrown in the pool.

The usual tens of thousands welcomed Liverpool home, packing the city centre. Again, players and staff gathered on the balcony of St George's Hall. Three years earlier, after Liverpool had won the FA Cup, Shankly had taken the microphone and asserted, to rapturous cheers, that 'Chairman Mao has never seen a greater show of red strength than today.' He was there again this time, but noticeably on the periphery, looking, as Bowler put it, 'like the father of the bride, pleased to see his child grown up and happy, but sad to see her go, realising that his role as the centre of his daughter's universe is over and that he is now merely a well-loved but ultimately irrelevant observer'. When he was, at last, passed the microphone, his words were tinged with regret. 'If you think I'm jealous,' he said, 'then you're bloody well right.' Liverpool had moved on, had, in a way unthinkable when Shankly had retired, reached new heights.

CHAPTER 6

European Cup final, Stadio Olimpico, Rome, 30 May 1984

Liverpool	1–1	**Roma**
Neal 13		Pruzzo 42

(Liverpool won 4–2 on penalties)

Nicol missed	Di Bartolomei scored
Neal scored	Conti missed
Souness scored	Righetti scored
Rush scored	Graziani missed
Kennedy scored	

Bruce Grobbelaar	Franco Tancredi
Phil Neal	Michele Nappi
Alan Kennedy	Sebastiano Nela
Mark Lawrenson	Ubaldo Righetti
Ronnie Whelan	Falcão
Alan Hansen	Dario Bonetti
Kenny Dalglish	Bruno Conti
(Michael Robinson 94)	
Sammy Lee	Toninho Cerezo
	(Mark Tullio Strukelj 115)
Ian Rush	Roberto Pruzzo
	(Odoacre Chierico 64)
Craig Johnston (Steve Nicol 72)	Agostino Di Bartolomei
Graeme Souness	Francesco Graziani
Joe Fagan	Nils Liedholm

Ref: Erik Fredriksson (SWE)
Bkd: Neal; Conti
Att: 69,693

NO GROUND THAT IS NOT their own stands so important in the history of Liverpool as the Stadio Olimpico in Rome. It was there, in 1977, that they had secured their place in the elite and it would be there, in 2001, that, with a victory in the Uefa Cup quarter-final, Liverpool brought an end to the years of exile after Heysel and proved they could, once again, compete with the best in Europe. And it was there, in 1984, that Liverpool's years of dominance in Europe reached a pinnacle as they lifted their fourth European Cup in the most difficult of circumstances, beating Roma in their own stadium. 'No English soccer team,' Frank McGhee wrote in the *Mirror*, 'will ever match what Liverpool achieved in the Olympic Stadium.'

Liverpool had happy memories of Rome from seven years earlier, when 30,000 fans had made the trip from Merseyside; this time only half that number could go and they found the Italian capital far less welcoming. Rome itself was festooned with yellow-and-red bunting, dotted with signs that prematurely declared AS Roma '*Campeone 84*'. English supporters told of locals shouting abuse at them in the street or pelting them with fruit as they walked through a market. Riot police herded fans onto buses at the airport and, as they drove into town, fans with scarves over their faces rode alongside the buses on Vespas, brandishing knives and making slitting gestures across their throats. By the time the final was over, forty fans required hospital treatment, five after being stabbed. The long-term consequences would prove even more serious.

There'd been fears that street parties would keep Liverpool awake but the only players who suffered any loss of sleep were

Kenny Dalglish and Graeme Souness, who roomed together. They'd been kept awake by the noise of a radio playing in the next room and, when banging on the wall failed to make a difference, they called reception to complain. Within a couple of minutes the radio had been turned off – presumably as the result of a call from the front desk. It was only the next morning that Souness and Dalglish realised the next room was occupied by the Liverpool manager Joe Fagan.

A pitch had been arranged on the edge of the city for Liverpool to conduct one last light training session on the morning of the final. When the players got there, though, it was quickly apparent it was wholly unsuitable, the surface badly rutted, something that was taken as yet another example of Italian gamesmanship; Alan Kennedy's memoir *Kennedy's Way* is strikingly paranoid, even suggesting that the coin toss to decide who took the first penalty was fixed. Fagan took his players for a walk instead, after which they returned to the hotel for a nap. Five hours before kick-off, Alan Hansen turned his television on and saw the stadium already two-thirds full. It was, he said, the most intimidating thing he'd seen in his life. 'It was frightening how much those fans wanted Roma to win that match,' he said. 'It put fear into me.'

At the pre-match meal, Fagan had to read out a Uefa directive warning players not to run towards the crowd if they scored. Fagan changed the wording to 'when', then told his players to obey the rules for the first two goals and to do what they liked for any goals thereafter. Although he was clearly joking, he saw it as vital that confidence should be maintained. After the meal, Fagan sent the waiters out because he wanted to speak to his players in private. He gave no great rousing speech, though, merely mumbling about what a good team Roma were before concluding that Liverpool were better and telling his players what time the bus was going to leave the hotel.

Rocks and other missiles were hurled at the Liverpool coach as it approached the stadium and as the players wandered out onto the pitch to get a feel of the atmosphere, Souness insisted the team should demonstrate how unafraid they were by strolling around the perimeter of the pitch, ignoring the cacophony of jeers. As they walked back into the tunnel, Dave Hodgson struck up with the opening verse of the Chris Rea song 'I Don't Know What It Is (But I Love It)', a favourite of Craig Johnston's who had played it so often all the players knew the words. A different player would sing each verse with the whole squad joining in the chorus. The Roma coach Nils Liedholm later said that he'd heard the singing as he was trying to conduct his team-talk and that his players had become noticeably more nervous from that moment. It was the sign of a team with a profound self-belief, but it would be sorely tested in the two hours that followed.

The Paisley years were a time of extraordinary achievement, unprecedented in English football at the time. Once unleashed, the wave of success never stopped. The key to the summer of 1977 was Keegan's departure and finding a replacement: having received £500,000 for Keegan from Hamburg, Liverpool paid £440,000 to land Kenny Dalglish from Celtic, a less energetic option, but one whose intelligence and imagination led him to surpass the man he succeeded. 'Let's get out of here before they realise what we've done,' Paisley said to John Smith, after concluding the deal with Jock Stein during a late-night meeting in a Glasgow hotel. Alan Hansen had already arrived, signed from Partick Thistle for £100,000 in May. He had been rejected by Liverpool as a fifteen year old, when he played in midfield but had developed rapidly after being converted into a defender by the Partick manager Bertie Auld. Graeme Souness would complete a trio of Scots in the squad when he arrived from Middlesbrough in January 1978.

Dalglish settled immediately, scoring on his league debut, a 1–1 draw against Middlesbrough, and adding another five in his next six games. But Liverpool missed out on a hat-trick of titles, pipped by Brian Clough's Nottingham Forest having only once topped the table in 1977–78. Forest, promoted only the previous season, became a persistent irritation and also beat Liverpool in a League Cup final that left Paisley fuming. Terry McDermott had a goal ruled out for offside and no penalty was given when Kenny Burns appeared to trip Dalglish in the box in a goalless draw at Wembley. In the replay, Forest got the only goal from a John Robertson penalty awarded after a foul by Phil Thompson on John O'Hare that, while cynical, had clearly been committed a couple of feet outside the box – it's hard, in the modern context, not to be amused by the post-match interview in which Thompson is outraged, insisting he had perfectly timed what even he called 'a professional foul' (Forest's assistant manager, Peter Taylor, made an equally hilarious defence of the referee: 'Obvious penalty,' he said, eyes flicking away from the interviewer, Gerald Sinstadt. 'I think John would have stuck it in. No one's doubting it, surely? ... Your cameras will catch it, surely?' When Sinstadt said the cameras caught it being outside, Taylor stared resolutely at the floor, somehow both affronted and shifty, before continuing defiantly, 'As long as they show we've got the Cup, that's the main thing.') To aggravate Liverpool further, McDermott then had another strike ruled out, this time for handball. 'I'd swear on the Bible there was no way the ball hit my hand or my arm,' he said. To cap it all, the referee Pat Partridge booked Callaghan for a shoulder charge on Peter Withe, his only booking in his 849 domestic games for the club.

Forest, though, couldn't stop Liverpool in Europe – at least not that season. Disciplinary sanctions imposed on Albania meant there were only thirty-one entrants in the European Cup, granting Liverpool a bye through the first round. They then faced Dynamo Dresden – their third meeting in European competition in five seasons and an auspicious one given that the previous two occasions they'd beaten them they'd gone on to win the trophy. Liverpool won the first leg 5–1 at Anfield, Alan Hansen scoring on his European debut. Dynamo pulled two back in the second leg but a Steve Heighway goal midway through the second half sealed a 6–3 aggregate victory.

Liverpool returned home to lose to Aston Villa, a first home defeat in forty-six games and the first time they had so much as conceded at home in seven months. Given they'd lost at Manchester City before the game in Dresden, that was three defeats in a row and it became four when they then lost at Queens Park Rangers.

That dropped Liverpool to sixth and their title campaign never recovered, though before the year was out they had thrashed Keegan's new side Hamburg 6–0 at Anfield on their way to a 7–1 aggregate victory in the Super Cup. 'I'd heard Liverpool hadn't been doing too well but from where I was stood watching there didn't seem to be much wrong with them,' said Keegan. 'There were no cracks and they look as strong, if not stronger, than they ever were.'

But there were cracks and Paisley was not about to paper over them. When they crashed 4–2 to Chelsea in the FA Cup – 'bloody pathetic we were, their heads were full of sawdust,' he said – Liverpool had only the European Cup left to fight for. That defeat prompted Paisley to pursue his interest in Souness and sign him from Middlesbrough. First impressions weren't great as Souness ran up a £200 bar bill in his first fortnight at the hotel where he was staying but once he'd settled – and his first goal for the club, a screaming volley into the top corner against Manchester United, hastened the process – his combination of grace and graft made him a key presence in the Liverpool midfield. 'Souness was a real Jekyll and Hyde character,' said Paisley. 'He's one of the most fearsome players I've ever seen but he can also create poetry with one of his perfectly timed passes. He has a brilliant vision for space and an instinct for passing that few players possess. It was the way he disguised his intentions that gave Liverpool so much advantage.'

Souness was not eligible, though, for the European Cup quarter-final against Benfica. The first leg, in Lisbon, was played in torrential rain. 'All the umbrellas made it look as if there were thousands of black beetles watching the match,' said Paisley. Liverpool fell behind to Nené, but a Case free-kick and a rare strike from Hughes gave Liverpool a 2–1 advantage. The tie was over within twenty minutes of the start of the second leg, Callaghan scoring the only goal of his final season at Liverpool and Dalglish making it 4–1 on aggregate. In the end, Liverpool cruised to a 6–2 aggregate win. 'It was the same old story,' said Paisley. 'They can only play as well as you let them.'

That set up a semi-final against familiar opponents: Borussia Mönchengladbach. Souness made his European debut coming off the bench in Germany with nineteen minutes remaining and Liverpool trailing to a Wilfried Hannes goal. The other substitute, David Johnson, levelled with two minutes to go, but a swerving Bonhof free-kick gave Gladbach a 2–1 win. Liverpool, though, proved far too good back at Anfield. Ray Kennedy equalised early in the return before goals from Dalglish and Case sealed Liverpool's progress.

And there was another meeting with an old rival in the final at Wembley as Liverpool faced Club Brugge, the side they'd beaten two years earlier in the Uefa Cup final. Smith was ruled out, missing the final few weeks of the season after a pick-axe had fallen on his foot in his garage, handing a start to Hansen. The game was a negative, cagey affair, settled after sixty-four minutes as Dalglish ran onto Souness's clipped pass, waited for Birger Jensen, Brugge's Danish keeper, to commit himself and then dinked the ball over him into the net. Dalglish cleared the advertising hoardings in elation, circumventing them gingerly on the way back to the pitch for the restart, later noting that 'the emotion made my legs weak'. It was a fitting end to a hugely impressive debut season. 'Kenny can make a team spark collectively with his gifted ability to read situations and offer other players so many options with his wide-ranging distribution and vision,' said Paisley. 'Of all the players I have played alongside, managed and coached ...

he is the most talented. When Kenny shines, the whole team is illuminated.'

Hansen, who always insisted he was far more nervous than his serene appearance suggested, almost gifted Brugge a late equaliser, his weak backpass letting in Jan Simoen, but after he had rounded Clemence, Thompson got back to make a stretching clearance on the line, and Liverpool were European champions again.

Not that Paisley was content with that. The evolution continued. Callaghan, Smith, Lindsay and Waddle all left that summer as Paisley maintained the policy of building from a position of strength not weakness, and in came the left-back Alan Kennedy from Newcastle for £330,000. When he'd worked as a bricklayer, Paisley often went to the cinema in Houghton-le-Spring on a Friday night. On his way home, he'd pop into the chip shop for his supper and flirt with the women who worked there; one of them was Kennedy's mother. Kennedy effectively replaced Joey Jones, who was sold back to Wrexham the following October.

Kennedy's no-nonsense approach earned him the nickname 'Barney Rubble' and he was an example of Paisley's belief that technically gifted players had to be balanced by those whose greatest assets were their energy and determination – and as such, he was a replacement for Jones in more ways than merely operating in the same position. Kennedy had a shocking debut away at QPR, although the tale that he knocked off a policeman's helmet with one sliced clearance may be apocryphal. 'I think they shot the wrong bloody Kennedy,' said Paisley as the players returned to the dressing-room at half-time. He would soon establish himself, though, as a crowd favourite.

Forest remained Liverpool's main rivals and put the defending champions out in the first round of the European Cup, following up a 2–0 win at the City Ground – when Liverpool conceded a late second as they chased an equaliser – with a goalless draw at Anfield, but domestically Liverpool were imperious. They suffered a shock defeat to Sheffield United in the League Cup and were beaten by Manchester United in the FA Cup semi-final – they didn't beat them in the competition between 1921 and 2006 – but they won the league by eight points, even though Forest hit the target Brian Clough had set for them at the start of the season. Hansen said that was the best side he played in, and the stats bear that out. Liverpool amassed sixty-eight points, a record under the two points for a win format, scored eighty-five goals and conceded just sixteen, only four of them at home. No side had ever had such a goal average (5.31 as opposed to the previous record of 2.88 set by Forest a year earlier) while they equalled the goal-difference record of sixty-nine set by Arsenal in 1934–35. The signature performance came in a 7–0 demolition of Tottenham, featuring the World Cup-winners Ossie Ardiles and Ricky Villa, the week after Paisley had berated his players for giving possession away too easily in a 4–1 win at Manchester City. One goal of the seven stood out, as Kennedy headed on a Clemence clearance for Dalglish, who played it left to Johnson. He clipped it left again for Heighway and when he crossed, McDermott, having charged sixty yards, headed in a goal Paisley described as 'probably the finest ever seen on this ground'.

A similar pattern developed in 1979–80, the league providing comfort for disappointment in the cups. Forest beat them in the League Cup semi, while Arsenal eventually overcame them in a third replay in the FA Cup – the tournament's longest semi-final. In Europe, Liverpool again went out in the first round, beaten by an extremely talented Dinamo Tbilisi that used home advantage to the maximum. Liverpool started slowly in the league, winning only two of their first seven, prompting Paisley to demand they be more ruthless. 'Great teams score goals,' he said. 'It's no use looking impressive and then not producing the goods at the end. We're making six or seven moves in build-ups but then we get carried away with the music of them. The music soothes us when we should be exploding.' Paisley spoke of it as a great test of character – Liverpool passed it. A 2–0 win over Manchester United on Boxing

Day took them clear at the top of the table and they never relinquished the lead.

Liverpool that season also broke new ground by becoming the first British league club to wear the name of a sponsor, Hitachi, on their shirts, a continuation of the broadening commercial outlook signalled by the press conference at which Paisley had been given his six-year contract. 'The days are gone when a club like ours can control its destiny on the money coming through the turnstiles,' said John Smith. It's telling that in 1978–79, Liverpool's turnover was £2.4m but their profit only £71,000. 'While we are very successful in football terms, in economic terms we are broke,' Smith said. 'Costs are going up all the time. Wages are high – and rightly so – and we have to use every avenue to increase our income.' Liverpool would go just about anywhere at any time to play a money-raising friendly, an early indication of the financial limitations that would constrain the club in the 1990s and beyond. Even in the mid eighties, as Simon Inglis wrote in *Football Grounds of Britain*, it was apparent that 'Anfield was still lagging behind other leading clubs in terms of executive boxes and was still often too small to cope with demand.'

Hopes of becoming only the third side to complete a hat-trick of league titles were dashed by an uncharacteristic run of injuries and by too many drawn games in 1980–81: seventeen in all. Liverpool finished the season fifth but this time there was glory in Europe. They beat the Finnish side Oulon Palloseura in the first round, then Alex Ferguson's Aberdeen in the second. In the quarter-final Liverpool met CSKA Sofia, who had eliminated the reigning champions Nottingham Forest. Souness hit a hat-trick in a 5–1 win at Anfield and Johnson's goal settled the away leg.

The semi-final was one of the classic Liverpool European ties. They faced Bayern Munich, whose general manager Uli Hoeness, noting Liverpool's shift to a more 'continental' approach since the sides had met in 1971, insisted the two sides were the best in Europe. Bayern, defending superbly, forced

a goalless draw at Anfield. By the time of the return, Liverpool had failed to score in four successive games and were
struggling for form. Bayern, though, ended up being undermined by their own arrogance. Comments from Paul Breitner
suggesting Liverpool had lacked intelligence in the first leg
and the discovery that leaflets had been distributed advising
Bayern fans how best to get to Paris for the final combined to
rile Liverpool.

Thompson and Kennedy were both injured and, after five
minutes, Dalglish was forced off after damaging his ankle in
a challenge with Calle Del'Haye. The obvious thing for Paisley
to have done would have been to bring on Ian Rush, whom
he had signed from Chester City for £330,000 the previous
summer. Based on nothing more than an intuition that, he
admitted, may have sprung from an Austrian Uefa delegate
asking him before the game for more details on a little-known
twenty-two-year-old who had been included in the squad, he
sent on Howard Gayle for only his second senior appearance.
His pace terrified Bayern and he probably should have had a
penalty when he was sent sprawling by Wolfgang Dremmler.
Bayern responded by trying physically to intimidate him and,
when Gayle was booked for reacting to a challenge midway
through the second half, Paisley took him off for Case. His job,
though, had been done: he'd stretched Bayern, forcing them
to leave men back and, with Lee man-marking Breitner, they
were far from their fluid best. 'Howard's performance was outstanding,' said David Johnson. 'It was gritty, it was hard, and
it was courageous.' For Paisley, it was a tactical triumph. 'He
loved that game,' Souness said.

Still, using both substitutes left Liverpool with a problem
if they suffered another injury and they did when Johnson's
hamstring went. Paisley, legend has it, asked one of the armed
police patrolling the stadium if he could borrow his gun to put
the forward down. He hobbled on, and it was his touch from
Ray Clemence's long clearance that played in Ray Kennedy to
score after eighty-two minutes. Karl-Heinz Rummenigge did

equalise five minutes later, but Liverpool advanced on the away-goals rule.

Kennedy had the cast taken off his broken wrist for the final, against Real Madrid in Paris, and for the first time in months Paisley was able to field what he felt was his strongest team – the side that had played in the second leg against Aberdeen. With eight minutes to go, Ray Kennedy took a throw for Alan Kennedy, who ran on, shrugged off Rafael García and lashed the winner in at the near post.

Despite the success, that was not an easy summer. Rush was furious at not even making the bench for the final, being overlooked for Gayle, and confronted Paisley about it. Paisley told him that he didn't score enough and that he had to be more selfish. It was advice that, once heeded, made Rush into one of the most potent forwards in Europe. 'We complemented each other well,' said Dalglish 'He was easily the best partner I had at Liverpool. We also had another role which people often don't give us credit for. Bob Paisley told us that we were his first line of defence. When the opposition had the ball, Rushie and I worked hard to allow our midfield or defence to regroup.'

Towards the end of 1980–81, Paisley had signed the Australian forward Craig Johnston and the Zimbabwean goalkeeper Bruce Grobbelaar, the intention with both being slowly to acclimatise them to the Liverpool way of doing things. Clemence, though, asked for a move that summer, saying that he'd felt flat in Paris and needed a new challenge. Appreciative of his service, Paisley allowed him to move to Tottenham for £300,000, significantly less than he was probably worth. Paisley also broke Liverpool's transfer record, spending £900,000 to sign Mark Lawrenson from Brighton, driving the defender to Anfield in cardigan and carpet slippers.

Liverpool began the season slowly and after seventeen games lay twelfth in the table, nine points behind the leaders Swansea, who were managed by the former Liverpool forward John Toshack. Paisley took decisive action, stripping

Thompson of the captaincy and giving it to Souness. The effect was immediate. Liverpool won eighteen of their next twenty league matches, a run that carried them to the title. It was arguably the most spectacular of all Liverpool's championship wins, yet it is mainly remembered for the season's nadir, Grobbelaar fumbling a Kevin Reeves header into his own net in a 3–1 home defeat against Manchester City on Boxing Day. 'Grobbelaar's misery is complete,' said the BBC commentator Alan Parry as the keeper rocked on his haunches. 'Reeves gets the goal, but really it was almost an own goal by this sad figure.' The clip would repeatedly be shown in club videos down the years, emphasising as it did the subsequent turnaround in Liverpool's form.

They also won the League Cup for the first time, beating Spurs in the final. Only the European Cup proved a disappointment, as Liverpool lost to CSKA Sofia in the quarter-final, thanks in part to another Grobbelaar error that gifted Stoichko Mladenov an equaliser and in part to the red card Lawrenson was shown in extra-time for retaliation against Tzvetan Yonchev.

Paisley announced in the summer of 1982 that the following season would be his last at the club, retiring aged sixty-four. 'We have been among the very best for nearly twenty consecutive years now,' he said. 'Teamwork is key to that success. When I was a professional footballer it was barely a team game. It was essentially about individuals. At Liverpool we look for born winners and we show them how to win as a team.' Another league title followed, won rather more easily than the previous season as Liverpool went top at the end of October and never relinquished their lead, so far clear that they could take just two points from their final seven games and still finish eleven clear of Watford in second. Although yet another Grobbelaar mistake cost them in another European Cup quarter-final, this time against Widzew Łódź, and Brighton put them out of the FA Cup in the fifth round, Liverpool retained the League Cup, Ronnie Whelan's curler sealing an extra-time victory over Manchester United. That meant that in the nine years since replacing Shankly, Paisley had amassed three European Cups, a Uefa Cup, six league titles and three League Cups, a quite staggering haul. When Shankly had resigned, it had seemed inconceivable anybody could surpass him, yet Paisley perhaps did. At the very least, it's hard to imagine how anybody could have better developed his legacy.

Unlike Shankly, Paisley had at least given the club warning he was going. The response of the board was no different, though, and they turned again to the Boot Room, determined to maintain continuity. Joe Fagan was sixty-two but he was an obvious choice as an interim solution for two or three years until Kenny Dalglish or Phil Neal came to the end of their playing careers. Fagan took some persuading but, as far as it's possible to tell, he seems to have agreed sometime in December 1982 to take over at the end of the season, although the appointment was only confirmed in May 1983. Even the fact that it was so difficult to tell says much about how the club was run. 'We're a very, very modest club,' said the chairman, John Smith. 'We don't talk, we don't boast, but we're very professional.'

There was a calm efficiency to Liverpool, something emphasised that summer with two typical signings: the bustling centre-forward Michael Robinson arrived from Brighton and the composed defender Gary Gillespie from Coventry, good players to be moulded to the Liverpool way rather than stellar names. The biggest concern was attendance figures, which by 1982–83 had dipped under 35,000, the lowest since promotion in 1962 and more than 13,000 down on a decade earlier, a reflection less of the club than of the impact of the recession. By the summer of 1983, one in five people of working age on Merseyside was unemployed, the bleakness of the economic situation captured by Alan Bleasdale's 1982 television drama *Boys from the Black Stuff* in which Sammy Lee and Graeme Souness both had cameo roles. His series *Scully*, which was broadcast two years later, emphasised the importance of the club in providing hope: it featured a teenager who dreamed of playing for Liverpool and hallucinated players in everyday situations. Dalglish, Grobbelaar and Paisley all appeared in the drama as themselves.

'The usual rule, that footballing success and economic development and growth move in step, was turned over,' David Goldblatt wrote in *The Ball is Round*.

While Bill Shankly's first side had flourished in an age of working-class confidence, full employment and social mobility, the Liverpool FC he bequeathed to the city blossomed under conditions of urban decay, deindustrialisation, mass unemployment and widespread disorder, most notably the Toxteth riots of 1981. Liverpool was also the stronghold of Militant, the entryist Trotskyites devoted to penetrating and radicalising the lumbering wreck of the Labour Party. Their control over Liverpool City Council and their protracted head-on conflicts with the government in Westminster saw the city demonised on the political right as the last redoubt of a lumpenproletariat that prospered on social security fraud and voted for a lunatic municipal socialism. In a city cast as an outsider in its own land, battered by the deliberately engineered economic downturns and clear-outs of the early 1980s, Liverpool Football Club was an enduring source of pride, a magnet for the energies and emotions of a public hungry for success.

Fagan began his managerial career with a 2–0 defeat to Manchester United in the Charity Shield, a game that seemed to highlight both the rise of United under Ron Atkinson and Liverpool's potential problems after Paisley. They took fourteen points from their first six league games but scored only eight goals as they did so: results, it seemed, weren't quite living up to performances. Their European campaign got under way in Denmark, against Odense. Dalglish scored the only goal in the away leg and then hit two of Liverpool's five in the return to go past Denis Law's British record of fourteen European Cup goals.

With Dalglish playing behind Rush and Robinson, and Johnston holding his position more in a three-man midfield, Fagan said his side were 'playing so well it's almost frightening'. His one concern was that they were overly patient in the build-up and that, Odense aside, they weren't scoring the goals their dominance merited. Between the two legs of that tie they'd lost 1–0 in the league to Manchester United and when they then lost 1–0 at Sunderland there seemed cause for genuine concern.

Robinson was struggling and Fagan worried he may be too slow both physically and mentally. He persuaded him to take out the metal supports he'd worn throughout his career to correct fallen arches to see if that would sharpen his reactions. The result was two goals at Anfield against Odense and he then hit a hat trick in a 3–1 win at West Ham, but that was a brief respite and the goals never came in great quantities. Fortunately for Liverpool, as Dalglish's goals dried up, Rush hit rich form. When he scored five in a 6–0 win over Luton on the final Saturday of October, Liverpool went top of the table for the first time under Fagan.

That game came at just the right time, providing a boost to morale before the second leg of the European Cup second-round tie away to Athletic of Bilbao. Liverpool, frustrated by the aggressive approach of Javier Clemente's side and their willingness to break up the game, were held to a 0–0 draw at Anfield. It had been, Stuart Jones wrote in The Times, 'as though Liverpool were lying in the arms of Morpheus. No one could recall a more subdued performance at Anfield, usually a noisy arena that became as quiet as the city streets at dawn.' But at San Mames, Liverpool produced one of their great European away performances. Souness was superb as Liverpool withstood Athletic's early assault and Rush headed in an Alan Kennedy cross to settle the tie midway through the second half.

In the second round of the Milk Cup, Liverpool played Fulham, then on the rise in Division Two under Malcolm Macdonald. They drew 1–1 at Craven Cottage with Rush nicking a late equaliser and then could only draw 1–1 after extra-time back at Anfield. For Fagan this encapsulated an irritatingly persistent failing: an inability to finish opponents off. Liverpool remained top, but a 1–0 win over the bottom side Stoke City confirmed the extent of the problem. Fagan was critical even of Dalglish, saying he was being caught in possession too often. Ultimately, though, he came to the conclusion that the 4–3–3 was to blame. 'Our three-man midfield is being overrun by teams with four in the middle,' he wrote in his diary. 'The strain is telling on Sammy, Graeme and Steve Nicol.' For the trip to Ipswich on 26 November, he brought in Ronnie Whelan for his first game of the season, leaving out Robinson and switching to 4–4–2. Although they drew 1–1, Fagan saw a marked improvement.

A Souness goal four minutes from the end of the Milk Cup second replay at Fulham finally ended that tie. That meant that at the beginning of December, Liverpool were top of the league by a point from United, in the quarter-finals of the European Cup and the last sixteen of the Milk Cup. All seemed set for another season of glory, particularly given how good Liverpool traditionally were in the second half of the season. But then, on 10 December, Liverpool crashed 4–0 to Coventry, their worst defeat in eight years, in a mystifyingly bad performance. Fagan was furious and laid into the team, something that had a profound impact given how rarely he lost his temper. He accused them of complacency; Notts County were the unfortunate recipients of the backlash and were beaten 5–0 but, still, all was not well.

By the time United arrived at Anfield for the first game of 1984, Liverpool's lead was three points. Liverpool were significantly the better side and took a deserved lead through Craig Johnston. But then Dalglish challenged for a high ball with Kevin Moran and took a blow in the face from the cast

Moran was wearing over a wrist injury, suffering a depressed fracture of the cheekbone and, with five minutes remaining, Norman Whiteside equalised.

A furious Souness had had to be restrained by Liverpool staff as he tried to confront Moran as the players left the field at half-time and his anger continued to burn long after the game. 'For the first time as captain I had words with Joe,' he told Andrew Fagan and Mark Platt in their biography of the manager. 'They were loud words as well as I rather forcefully put over my opinion that Liverpool had gone soft. After going a goal up we were not professional enough to see it through and I told him, Ronnie Moran and Roy Evans in no uncertain terms that I thought Manchester United would win the league and not us.' Softness was never something likely to set in under Fagan; it had, after all, been he who in 1975 instructed Tommy Smith to start the fight to ensure there was some edge to a friendly on a post-season trip to Benidorm.

The injury kept Dalglish out for a little over a month but even without his creativity, Rush kept on scoring. He ended up with forty-seven goals in all competitions that season and was widely hailed as the most natural British finisher since Jimmy Greaves. Although Liverpool then lost 1–0 to Wolves, a Rush hat-trick at Villa Park as Liverpool came from behind to win 3–1 maintained some momentum. 'Without even a glance, he seems to detect when a goalkeeper is off balance or out of position and therefore vulnerable to an immediate early strike,' said Paisley. 'You can't teach players that.' The injury situation, though, continued to worsen. Souness damaged a hamstring in a fourth-round FA Cup defeat to Brighton. He was replaced by Whelan, whose season had been disrupted by a pelvic injury, for a league match against Watford which Liverpool won 3–0. There were only 20,746 there, though, Liverpool's lowest league crowd since 1961, evidence of the economic climate but also, perhaps, frustration at the club's comparatively indifferent form.

The Milk Cup, meanwhile, had become exhaustingly

protracted. Liverpool needed replays to see off Birmingham City and Sheffield Wednesday and when they could only draw 2–2 at Anfield against Walsall in the first leg of the semi-final, Fagan reflected that without Souness, Dalglish and Lawrenson, who also missed the game through injury, Liverpool were 'an ordinary side'. Souness returned for the second leg and underlined his importance as Liverpool won 2–0, a thirteenth-minute strike from Ian Rush easing nerves before Whelan sealed the win. As Liverpool fans surged forward in celebration of his goal, the wall at the front of the away terrace at Fellows Park collapsed and the game was held up for several minutes as players helped rescue supporters from the rubble. In itself, it was a minor incident but it was yet another indication of the deplorable state of English stadiums in the 1980s and, of course, it presaged far worse crushes to come.

In the quarter-final of the European Cup, Liverpool faced a Benfica side managed by Sven-Göran Eriksson, who had visited Melwood in the 1970s as he studied English coaching methods. Benfica, as Athletic had, looked to keep things tight and were largely successful in a goalless first half. Fagan turned to Dalglish, bringing him on for his first appearance in two months. His guile helped unlock Benfica, Rush heading the only goal of the game midway through the second half. Other sides might have sat back in the second leg and looked to absorb pressure, playing for a goalless draw, but Fagan was determined Liverpool should operate at a high tempo and prevent the game becoming one of Benfica attack and Liverpool defence. Benfica were nonplussed and, with their goalkeeper Bento having a difficult night, Liverpool scored twice in each half to win by an emphatic 4–1.

In the league, meanwhile, Liverpool were unconvincing but clinging on. They'd drawn 0–0 against Sunderland and Watford and had United been able to find any consistency they would surely have fulfilled Souness's prediction and overhauled them. As it was, Liverpool maintained their advantage. After a draw at Everton at the beginning of March,

Fagan wrote in his diary that 'sheer guts' was the only thing preventing collapse. Although Liverpool beat Spurs 3–1, Fagan was concerned Lee, Nicol and Whelan were too 'easy-osey' and his fears were realised in a 2–0 defeat at Southampton – with Souness absent following the death of his mother – that allowed United to regain top spot. Drastic action, he decided, was needed to stiffen the midfield: Liverpool spent £450,000 to land John Wark from Ipswich.

The Milk Cup final against Everton, the first all-Merseyside cup final, predictably, went to a replay, meaning Liverpool had failed to negotiate a single round in one game, playing a total of thirteen matches in the competition that season. Hansen got away with a handball on the line after Adrian Heath had dinked the ball over Grobbelaar and Rush somehow fluffed a shot over the bar from six yards but it finished goalless at Wembley. The replay at Maine Road was settled by a fierce low volley from Souness after twenty-one minutes; it meant a fourth straight League Cup for Liverpool but, perhaps more importantly, also meant Fagan would not be the first Liverpool manager since Phil Taylor in the 1950s to fail to win a trophy, that, whatever else happened, he had at least won something. Grobbelaar said you could almost see the weight lifting off him.

Wark made his debut at Watford, coming in for Johnston, who had fumed after being taken off at Wembley and had then submitted a transfer request after being left out at Coventry, and scored the opening goal. Liverpool won 2–0 while United lost 2–0 at West Brom, allowing Liverpool to return to the top of the table. They celebrated by demolishing West Ham 6–0.

Liverpool faced Dinamo Bucharest in the European Cup semi-final, stirring uneasy memories of recent defeats to Dinamo Tbilisi, CSKA Sofia and Widzew Łódź; Liverpool, more than most sides, knew how difficult games behind the Iron Curtain could be. The first leg at Anfield was scrappy and unpleasant as Dinamo set out to spoil. One player in particular,

Lică Movilă, drew the ire of Souness. 'Movilă was the worst of the lot,' he wrote in his autobiography. 'He was a disgrace. He kicked everything that moved and three times caught me with punches off the ball. I went completely crazy when he came in late and high yet again and as he half turned I let loose the best punch I have delivered in my life.' The Swiss referee, André Daina, saw nothing, but Movilă's jaw was broken in two places. Sammy Lee headed the only goal from a Kennedy free-kick.

In Bucharest, Souness was an obvious target, of fans, security men and players. His every touch was booed, even in the warm-up, but he seemed to relish the challenge of European away trips and remained calm, producing a performance of implacable authority in teeming rain. Rush gave Liverpool the lead with his hundredth goal for the club, a superbly deft finish having found space on the left side of the box, and, although Costel Orac levelled with a neat free-kick, Rush's second, capitalising on defensive chaos with typical precision six minutes from time, secured Liverpool's place in the final. 'I don't think the lads could believe we'd won,' said Hansen, 'because Bucharest had looked so good at Anfield. I remember when Joe came in the dressing room. He said, "Right everybody, sit down. It's a time for reflection. You don't want to be going overboard about this. What I want you to do is follow my example." He went "Yaaaaaaaa beeeeeeeeauty!!!" and punched the air. We'd never ever seen Joe like this in our lives before.'

Between the two legs, Liverpool stuttered domestically, losing 2–0 to the bottom side, Stoke. Fagan described Dalglish's performance as 'his worst game in years', saying he looked 'thoroughly bored and out of touch'. Souness, in frustration, smashed his hand through a pane of glass in the dressing-room door – but Manchester United missed their chance to regain the lead in the title race, losing to Notts County the same afternoon.

With five games to go, Liverpool led United by two points. Liverpool drew with Ipswich but United drew with West Ham.

Liverpool drew with Birmingham, United drew with Everton. Atkinson's side, faltering badly, won only one of their final ten games of the season so although Liverpool took just eleven points from their last nine games, they finished six clear of United, who ended up fourth with QPR third and Southampton second, three points adrift. Having avenged the defeat at Highfield Road earlier in the season with a 5–0 home win over Coventry, Liverpool became only the third side to claim three successive titles with a goalless draw at Meadow Lane. Fagan, as though to make a point of the humility and practicality of Liverpool's approach, celebrated by sweeping out the chang ing room.

It may have been a struggle that ended anticlimactically but John Smith rated the title as Liverpool's greatest achievement. Fagan singled out the pairings of Rush and Dalglish and Hansen and Lawrenson and, especially, Souness for praise. Remarkably, the goalkeeper and back four had played together in every game but one when Neal sat out with an injury.

Roma prepared for the European Cup final with a typical *retiro*, in a camp surrounded by trees, cut off from the outside world. Liverpool lay on a beach in Israel, relaxing and drinking. 'It was a trip that summed up how much he treated us like the adults we were,' said Souness. 'He [Fagan] imposed no curfews or restrictions on us out there. We were allowed to relax, enjoy the sun and have a few drinks.' Italian journalists were staggered by what they saw as a lack of professionalism but a similar approach had served Nottingham Forest well before they'd faced Hamburg in the 1980 final.

With temperatures in Tel Aviv in the eighties, the trip was seen as a useful acclimatisation exercise for the game in Rome and, after a tough season towards the end of which Liverpool had looked weary, it seemed a logical thing for the players to wind down and relax. 'It was a long time to dwell on things and be at home,' said Gillespie. 'All you do is monotonous day-to-day training. So it was suggested that we went to Israel for the week, and it was a real blow-out, a real blast. It was all about camaraderie.' Whelan described it as 'relaxation, a good laugh', while Lawrenson spoke of 'drinking twenty beers a night'.

Liverpool did train as well, of course, and, in their final warm-up game, despite being without Rush, who was on international duty with Wales, and Hansen, who had a thigh strain, Liverpool beat the Israel national team 4–1. Before heading to Rome, the squad returned to Liverpool and had one final gentle training session at Melwood. After a little jogging, they took on the youth team in a penalty shoot-out – and lost. Nobody seems quite able to agree on an actual score but nobody doubts the result.

Roma had finished runners-up to Juventus in Serie A that season and in getting past IFK Göteborg, CSKA Sofia, Dynamo Berlin and Dundee United to reach the final they hadn't conceded a goal at home. That may have emphasised what a huge advantage it was to play the final in their own stadium but, as Fagan pointed out, Liverpool had won every away game they'd played in the European Cup that season. 'Our chaps grow bigger when the atmosphere is there,' he said.

And, as Dundee United had found, the atmosphere in Rome could be ferocious. Jim McClean's side – the great team of Paul Sturrock, Maurice Malpas and Eamonn Bannan – had won the first leg 2–0 at Tannadice thanks to second-half goals from Davie Dodds and Derek Stark, but almost as soon as the final whistle had blown the gamesmanship began. Several Roma players accused McLean of having called them 'Italian bastards' while some flippant comments about hoping his players would keep taking whatever pills they were on were wilfully misconstrued and spun into accusations that they were systematically doping. The effect was to whip Roma fans into an even greater fervour than usual.

The Olimpico was almost full ninety minutes before kick-off and when Dundee United's players wandered onto the pitch before the game, they were pelted with fruit. Banners were brandished bearing messages in English: 'God curse Dundee United', 'McLean fuck off' and 'Roma hates McLean, he's a cunt.' It later emerged that Roma had attempted to bribe the French referee Michel Vautrot. After a nervous United had been beaten 3–0, Roma's players responded disgracefully, spitting at their opponents and taunting McLean and his assistant, Walter Smith, both verbally and with raised middle fingers.

Fagan watched videos of Roma but was very much of the British school of playing your own game. 'If I go through all this I will feel like we can't play,' he said. 'Too much can bog your own team down and make you forget to let them worry about you.' He went to see Roma's league game against Fiorentina, played the weekend after they'd beaten Dundee United and, although they tired towards full-time and were without Falcão, he was impressed by Roberto Pruzzo and Bruno Conti. Tom Saunders, meanwhile, was sent to scout them three times. 'Bob Paisley considered they were the best team he had seen in the competition so far and we shall need to be at our best to deal with them,' he reported. 'My own view is that if Falcão and [Agostino] Di Bartolomei perform as they can do, the battle will need to be won in midfield.'

Fagan, determined not to overcomplicate preparations, showed his players no videos, didn't even tell them what formation Roma played and said nothing at all about set-play routines. In fact, the main thing he seemed to have learned was not to make the mistake McLean had of antagonising Roma or their fans, making a point of being diplomatic.

In the final pre-match press conference, he said that 'our team-talk will be a bit longer than usual – about five minutes.' Italian journalists desperate for a line took that as a sign of complacency and eagerly wrote up the story that way. It was, though, what Paisley would have called 'a bit of toffee' – a sweet but essentially insignificant morsel offered up to satisfy the press while distracting them from potentially more serious issues.

*

As Roma kicked off, a mass of flares were ignited among their fans at the end they were defending. Liverpool's fans, penned in at the opposite end of the ground and surrounded by riot police and an extraordinary number of dogs, responded by waving their flags, the terrace a mass of red-and-white checks. Falcão, Roma's *regista*, launched the ball long, aiming at Pruzzo. His pass was too long, though, and Grobbelaar – who recalls the atmosphere as 'particularly warm for myself, frightening in the beginning' – was quickly out to gather. Grobbelaar's speed off his line was to become a regular feature, evidence of his value as a sweeper-keeper. Since Tommy Lawrence, Liverpool had required their goalkeeper to be able to leave his line to allow the back four to push high and play the offside trap but Grobbelaar took it to extremes. When his sorties from goal went wrong he was derided for his adventurousness; the benefits were often overlooked but they were clear enough in Rome. 'He's a keeper of exceptional ability: athletic, agile and brilliant at coming to claim crosses,' said Clemence. 'He is also a born entertainer and that is the side of his game that attracts the publicity and gets him into trouble. With a team like Liverpool the goalkeeper can often be out of action for long periods. When this happens to Bruce he seems to feel like he has to do something out of the ordinary to justify his existence but there's no need for it.'

Grobbelaar rolled the ball out short and Liverpool embarked on one of the long, slow passing movements that characterised their play in Europe, particularly away from home: control the ball, control the pace of the game and try to dull the fervour of the crowd by denying their side any sniff of an opportunity. A heavy third-minute challenge on Souness by Toninho Cerezo, who had played alongside Falcão in the centre of the Brazil midfield at the 1982 World Cup, and another long ball, played this time by Di Bartolomei, hinted at Roma's frustration. With Souness beginning to dominate in midfield, knocking long diagonals into the corner for Rush, who pulled to either flank from his centre-forward's position, it was Liverpool who had much the better of the opening eight minutes.

But then, almost from nothing, came a reminder of Roma's quality and the threat they posed. Falcão, on the left flank by the halfway line, played a one-two with Francesco Graziani, turned infield to Di Bartolomei, a languidly graceful figure at the back of midfield. The Brazilian spread the ball right for Michele Nappi, who came inside to Cerezo. He played the ball outside again to Bruno Conti, the winger who had been such a key part of Italy's World Cup-winning side two years earlier. He ran at Whelan and shaped a pass towards Pruzzo. As the forward and Lawrenson challenged for it about five yards outside the box, both missed it and the ball ran on behind Neal. For a moment it looked as though Graziani, darting in from the left as ever, might be through, but Grobbelaar was quick off his line and smothered Roma, though, were encouraged. Then a superb – if it were intentional, which it may not have been – touch from the left-back Dario Bonetti hooked Di Bartolomei's long pass into the path of Graziani. The forward took the ball almost to the line and chipped the ball across goal as Pruzzo closed in but Grobbelaar claimed with the sort of ease that can only inspire confidence.

Three minutes later, Franco Tancredi's failure to gather a cross gifted Liverpool the lead. Sebastiano Nela's headed clearance fell to Whelan on the Liverpool left and he swept forward into the Roma half, before turning the ball inside to Dalglish. He knocked it back for Kennedy and the full-back rolled it inside for Hansen. Always happy to advance, he strode over halfway and played the ball to Dalglish, who advanced, checked and went square for Souness. He had space and, as he had already done a number of times, he spread the play, sending the ball right for Lee. He slid the ball down the line for Johnston, who sent a cross deep beyond the far post. Tancredi went for it, backpedalling and, at full stretch, seemed to have caught it when he collided with Whelan. There was no deliberate foul but it's hard to imagine in the modern game that the contact would not have brought a free-kick. The Swedish referee Erik Fredriksson, though, saw nothing amiss as Tancredi dropped the ball and play continued as it fell to Sebastiano Nela in front of his own goal. Under pressure from Rush, he looked to belt it out for a throw-in, but his clearance struck Tancredi on the head and ricocheted back into the centre of the goalmouth where Neal jabbed the ball over the line with the outside of his right foot. Roma clearly felt it was a foul but the goal stood.

Liverpool had the ball in the net again two minutes later, but this time, it was ruled out. Souness ran over a free-kick on the left and Kennedy delivered to the back post. Neal headed the ball back across goal and Johnston glanced the ball past Tancredi only for Rush to be penalised for offside. The decision was correct but the incident highlighted Roma's vulnerability to the crossed ball.

Grobbelaar, by contrast, couldn't have looked more secure even as Roma, five minutes or so after the goal, began finally to exert some pressure. Di Bartolomei, the origin of so many of Roma's attacks, sent the ball wide for Conti, who played a first-time pass to Cerezo then took the return before crossing high. Grobbelaar came through a copse of players, leapt, and with arms fully extended, took the cross, a moment of supreme judgement and athleticism. Two minutes later, Nappi intercepted a Johnston pass and, as Roma broke, Falcão tried to weight a through-ball for Pruzzo. Grobbelaar, though, immaculate at that point, charged from his goal to claim.

The game felt oddly stretched, as though Liverpool's early goal had caused the usual cagy overture to be bypassed. Lawrenson played the ball left to Whelan, who carried on his run after playing a pass infield to Dalglish and took the ball back from Rush, before attempting a low shot from thirty yards. Tancredi got down comfortably to save but the feel remained of a match nearing its final stages rather than one still in its first quarter.

Gradually, Roma began to dominate. Di Bartolomei dragged

a shot wide from twenty-five yards as a corner was half-cleared and then strode forward before sweeping a pass out to Conti on the left. He won a throw off Neal and took it quickly, allowing Graziani to charge into the box; Grobbelaar saved sharply at his near post. Liverpool, for the first time in the game, were under real pressure. A throw-in on the right was taken to Cerezo, who came infield and played the ball short to Conti in the centre-circle. He sent a long pass into the path of the left-back Bonetti on the overlap and when he crossed, Lawrenson got there ahead of Pruzzo to divert the ball behind for a corner. Hitting the space behind Neal, who was always keen to advance, seemed a concerted Roma tactic.

A minute later, Whelan went in hard on Falcão – perhaps in retaliation for a late challenge on him by the Brazilian a few minutes earlier that had gone unpunished. Whelan's offence, though, was seen, giving Roma a free-kick about twenty-five yards out in a central position. Conti, standing over the ball, nudged it right for Di Bartolomei and although he didn't catch his shot cleanly he won another corner as the ball was deflected wide. Liverpool at that stage seemed in danger of losing their discipline. Neal was booked for tripping Conti about thirty yards out to the left of centre. Falcão took an age preparing and then blasted his free-kick high over the bar and wide. Grobbelaar then came out to grab a Di Bartolomei throw-in above Pruzzo's head and Whelan charged down a long-range effort from the centre-forward.

For a moment, it seemed Liverpool had broken the siege as Nela gave the ball away to Rush, who bustled into the box before drawing a low save from Tancredi, but Roma's pressure eventually told three minutes before the break. Nela played the ball forward to Pruzzo who was bundled over by Lawrenson around forty yards out on the Liverpool right. Bonetti played the free-kick infield to Di Bartolomei then took the return. He went down the line for Conti, whose initial attempt at a cross was blocked by a combination of Neal and Lawrenson. The ball bounced back to him, though, and his second attempt was arced in to the near post, where Pruzzo got in front of Hansen and glanced a firm header past Grobbelaar.

The first half had been surprisingly open and, ominously, Roma had got better and better as it had gone on. The second half, though, began as if the first half hadn't happened, the game taking on the sort of wary aspect that had been expected from the start. Liverpool seemed intent on asserting control by holding possession, waiting again for the fury of the crowd to blow itself out but it was Roma who had the better of the few chances there were. As Cerezo led a break after forty-nine minutes, it took all Lawrenson's pace to get back and clear before his pass could reach Graziani. With Liverpool sitting deep when Roma had possession, they seemed to accept that Roma would attempt long-range shots and that they couldn't prevent crosses if Roma wanted to hit them from deep. Graziani fired over from five yards outside the box and then, after a neat move facilitated by a Conti volley, he shot weakly at Grobbelaar after Pruzzo had flicked on a Bonetti delivery from the left.

Liverpool seemed at their most vulnerable on the odd occasions when they did come forward, something that suggested the wisdom of the cautious approach. Ten minutes into the second period, for instance, a Whelan cross was just too high for Rush at the back post and Roma cleared. Lawrenson attempted to intercept but the ball struck Di Bartolomei who ran on until Neal held him up. He checked back then came inside switching the play to Nappi on the right. He laid it inside to Falcão just outside the box and the Brazilian turned away from Lawrenson only to shoot straight at Grobbelaar.

Liverpool remained patient, apparently unflustered – with the exception of Kennedy who, as he admitted in his autobiography, had a 'nightmare' spell in which he couldn't stop giving the ball away and had to ask Whelan to sit in and cover for him – but the only attempts on goal came from Roma. Just after the hour, Grobbelaar, flawless until then, missed a Falcão cross from deep on the right and was fortunate the ball fell for Lawrenson, who headed straight back to him. Undaunted by his error, Grobbelaar then charged from his box to cut out a Cerezo ball to Graziani. And then came a moment of luck that gave Liverpool hope as Pruzzo, having struggled for a few minutes, was forced off with a thigh injury. On came Odoacre Chierico, a wide forward, with Graziani switching to the centre; without the Graziani–Pruzzo partnership and their understanding, Roma's threat was diminished. Roma continued to boss possession but there was less sense that they might do something with it.

Liverpool made a substitution of their own eight minutes later, bringing on Steve Nicol for Craig Johnston, who had been suffering cramp. Neither the Australian nor Dalglish, flanking Rush but playing slightly deeper, had been able to make much impression on the game and Dalglish's frustration at that was perhaps the cause of a strange altercation with Di Bartolomei after a slightly clumsy challenge.

Still Roma offered the greater threat. A Chierico cross reached Falcão but, unable to get over the ball, he headed over. Then Graziani released Bonetti down the left only for Lawrenson, slightly fortuitously, to cut out the cross with three Roma players waiting in the box. Briefly, as the game entered the final ten minutes of normal time, it threatened to open up. Lee took a corner quickly, pulling it back to the edge of the box where Dalglish met the ball with a volley that dipped near Tancredi, forcing him into an awkward save tumbling to his right. Lawrenson, who had an outstanding second half, dispossessed Conti as he threatened to break and then, with three minutes remaining, came a glorious chance for Liverpool to win it. Lee switched play left to Whelan, he came inside and played the ball back to Dalglish, and he threaded the ball through for Nicol, whose shot across Tancredi forced the goalkeeper into another save.

It finished at 1–1, with the strange sense that the halves had been played the wrong way round, caution following the Roma equaliser after Liverpool's early goal had prompted an unexpectedly open first half. Tiredness didn't open things up much in extra-time, although it was fatigue that led to Dalglish being removed for Robinson after three minutes. By then, there'd already been another exhibition of Grobbelaar's willingness to come to meet play as he darted from his box to intercept Di Bartolomei's long pass, then wandered by Falcão before finally laying the ball off to Nicol. A couple of minutes later Grobbelaar was quickly off his line again to smother Falcão's attempted through-ball for Graziani.

Liverpool may not quite have been playing for penalties but neither did they offer much in the way of attacking threat. A cross still seemed the most likely source of a goal and when Di Bartolomei fouled Nicol on the left with 100 minutes played, they were given the ideal opportunity to pressure Tancredi. Kennedy's delivery was deep, sailing over everybody in the goalmouth but coming to Neal at the back of the box. He returned it to the centre and Whelan headed down, but Falcão was able to clear.

Nicol's freshness, his willingness to run in a game reduced to walking pace, made him a potential source of danger and when he was chopped down by Righetti on the corner of the box, Liverpool had another chance. Lee took it low to Rush but under pressure he lost his footing and Roma cleared.

And then came another moment of tetchiness as Robinson chased a ball into the box. Tancredi judged it well and gathered before clattering to the ground. A fracas developed with Roma defenders pushing Robinson, who looked bewildered and walked away as Rush got involved. Replays weren't definitive in showing whether Robinson had made contact with the keeper or not, but it was clear that if there had been, it had been a glancing blow and certainly hadn't been deliberate. Just as Dalglish's flare-up had suggested his frustration so this seemed to indicate that Roma were rattled, realising perhaps that as they tired their chances of forcing a winner were diminishing. Nicol, meanwhile, kept running and in the final minute of the half met a Kennedy cross with a highly ambitious diving header from the edge of the box. He made reasonable contact but the ball drifted well wide.

Half-time in extra-time brought the end of the Liverpool mini-surge. It wouldn't be fair to say they were hanging on for the remainder of the game but they certainly didn't look like scoring. Chierico and Graziani played a one-two down the right and, as Kennedy slipped, the substitute had time to measure his cross to the back post for Conti, but his volley was blocked. Then Nicol was dispossessed on the Liverpool right. Conti lifted the ball inside to Cerezo, who controlled it flamboyantly on his chest and played it right for Chierico. He crossed towards Falcão but Lawrenson headed clear. Di Bartolomei gathered and played the ball out to Conti on the left. He cut infield and shot but Grobbelaar got down well at his near post to save; his performance and that of Lawrenson had been key in keeping Roma out. Di Bartolomei, a splendidly elegant figure throughout, saw a shot deflected just over off Hansen's head a couple of minutes later, at which the certainty seemed to settle over everybody that the game would be drawn.

Cerezo, having already collapsed once with cramp, was stricken again and had to go off to be replaced by Mark Tullio Strukelj, who had been born in Dorking of an English mother and a Yugoslav father. He was a Liverpool fan, Brian Moore announced in commentary, and, having moved to Italy when he was two, still spent summer holidays with his grandparents in Horsham. He barely had time to make an impact, though, and, aside from Di Bartolomei being booked for a cynical trip on Lawrenson, the only other action of the game was a long free-kick aimed by Di Bartolomei at Graziani. As he had been all game, though, Grobbelaar was alert and quickly off his line to claim, and the game finished 1–1.

It was the first time the European Cup had gone to penalties, although Spurs had beaten Anderlecht in the Uefa Cup final on penalties the week before. Fagan congratulated his players at the end of extra-time and, privately, told Grobbelaar nobody expected a goalkeeper to save a penalty. As ever, his aim was to relax his players as much as possible.

Nicol strode forward, apparently boyishly unconcerned. Tancredi, Moore warned, had the best record of saving penalties of any goalkeeper in Serie A and kept notes on opposing penalty-takers. He didn't, though, need to save Nicol's effort as his kick flashed a foot or so over the bar. As Nicol turned back to the centre-circle, his right hand plucked at his throat. He looked, if not horrified then at least shocked, walking with an oddly disengaged air. It was, he said, 'a terrible moment'.

Graziani started to go forward but then switched with Di Bartolomei. The Roma captain took a short run and, as Grobbelaar dived to his right, lashed the ball straight down the centre. Neal, Liverpool's usual penalty taker, was up next. He wiped his palms on his shirt as though to steady himself and then slammed his penalty high into the right side of the goal as Tancredi went the other way. Then came Bruno Conti. Grobbelaar, irritated by the way the Italian was 'dancing around' gave the hint of a leg wobble. Conti went to his right, Grobbelaar went the right way and the ball went at least as high over the bar as Nicol's had done. After two penalties each, it was 1–1.

Souness was Liverpool's third taker. He had arguably been the man of the match, bristling with purpose throughout. He did not seem somebody to suffer unduly with nerves but showed just a hint of anxiety as he plucked at the back of his shorts. His penalty, though, was magnificent: Tancredi went the right way but the ball arrowed unstoppably into the top right corner. The pressure, suddenly, was on Roma. Righetti, though, was equal to it. He wiped the ball furiously on the spot and then sidefooted it to the right as Grobbelaar dived the other way: 2–2.

Rush, socks around ankles, calmly rolled the ball to the right as Tancredi went the other way to make it 3–2. Grobbelaar came forward and, objecting to the way Graziani put his arm around the referee, began staggering like a drunk. As he waited on the line, he swayed, 'doing the spaghetti legs' as he termed it, mimicking terror. He fell still as Graziani took the penalty. Whether his antics put the Italian off is impossible to say but, whatever the cause, the forward's shot clipped the top of the bar and went over. 'If he scores they win,' Brian Moore shouted off mic. 'Is that right?' Having received confirmation, Moore informed viewers, still unused to penalty shoot-outs, that if Kennedy could convert, Liverpool would be European champions.

Although the full-back had scored the winner in the 1981 final, he was far from an obvious player to take the last kick. He'd taken a penalty in pre-season and in the practice at Melwood. Both, by his own admission, had been 'shocking'. 'What he [Fagan] must have seen was something that maybe the other players didn't have,' he said. 'It definitely wasn't my ability because I was limited in that. I suppose it must have been my bottle.' He went left, the opposite way to his penalty at Melwood the previous week; Tancredi went right and Liverpool were champions.

It was deserved glory but that night now, through no fault of Liverpool's, cannot be recalled without reference to tragedy, one deeply personal, the other more general. Di Bartolomei left Rome that summer, moving with Liedholm to Milan. He never quite settled there and the arrival of Arrigo Sacchi to replace Liedholm saw him moved on, first to Cesena and then Salernitana. He retired in 1990, aged thirty-five. Di Bartolomei tried but failed to set up a football school and found himself struggling with debts and depression. A decade to the day after the final against Liverpool, he shot himself through the heart with a pistol. 'I can't see a way out,' he wrote in his suicide note.

As Liverpool celebrated their victory in their dressing-room, singing more Chris Rea, a section of the Roma ultras rioted. Bonfires were lit on the terraces, while gangs armed with knives roamed the streets looking for Liverpool fans and buses were attacked. On the Ponte Duca D'Aosta, pitched battles were fought as Liverpool fans – acting largely in self-defence – retaliated. Uefa, mystifyingly, decided both clubs were to blame and fined each £1,270, but the mayor of Rome, Ugo Vetere, issued an apology and the British Embassy had no doubt who was to blame. 'The message we have,' said a spokesman, 'is that the Liverpool supporters behaved as everybody expected them to and maintained their good reputation. It appears they were the subject of unprovoked attacks by a small minority of Roma fans.'

The British media, though, was more concerned by violence closer to home. On the day of the final, 3,000 striking miners had fought with 2,000 police at the coking works at Orgreave, South Yorkshire, leaving sixty-nine hurt. The full-on battle, which would become a byword for police heavy-handedness in dealing with the Miners' Strike, would come two and a half weeks later, but this preliminary skirmish was bad enough as buildings were set on fire, telegraph poles felled and tripwires set for horses as mounted police charged pickets. In total there were eighty-one arrests, including the miners' leader Arthur Scargill. With the sports pages understandably preferring to focus on Liverpool's achievement, a genuinely staggering Treble, only local papers on Merseyside reported the clashes in Rome in much detail and it was only the following year, in the most awful circumstances, that the seriousness of the attacks in Rome – and their potential consequences – would be understood.

CHAPTER 7

Football League Division One, Anfield, Liverpool, 13 April 1988

Liverpool	**5–0**	**Nottingham Forest**

Houghton 18
Aldridge 37, 88
Gillespie 58
Beardsley 79

Bruce Grobbelaar	Steve Sutton
Gary Gillespie	Steve Chettle
Gary Ablett	Stuart Pearce
Steve Nicol	Des Walker
	(Darren Wassall 46)
Nigel Spackman	Colin Foster
Alan Hansen	Terry Wilson
Peter Beardsley	Gary Crosby
John Aldridge	Neil Webb
Ray Houghton	Nigel Clough
(Craig Johnston 85)	
John Barnes	Lee Glover
Steve McMahon	Brian Rice
(Jan Mølby 78)	
Kenny Dalglish	Brian Clough

Ref: Roger Milford
Bkd:
Att: 39, 535

TOM FINNEY WAS IN NO doubt what he had just witnessed. 'Liverpool must be the best team of all time,' he said. 'It was the finest exhibition of football that I have seen during all my time playing and watching the game.' They had demolished Nottingham Forest, who would go on to finish third that season and were a very fine side in their own right, to all but guarantee the title, their seventeenth – eight ahead of their nearest challengers, Everton but that was only part of it. This was a performance of extraordinary verve and style, a display that seemed to embody the new, more progressive spirit of the team Kenny Dalglish had created. Under Shankly and Paisley, Liverpool had at times been accused of playing functional football; nobody would ever describe the side that won the championship in 1987–88 as doing that. They were attacking, vibrantly so, and, in the European wilderness after the tragedy of Heysel, there was something comforting in that.

Looking back now, knowing that there was another tragedy to come, there is a poignancy to that game, an innocence even: that was a time when you could watch Liverpool play Forest in the spring sunshine and think only of football, not of advertising hoardings being used as stretchers, and bodies lined up on the pitch and a cowardly establishment covering their tracks with a despicable conspiracy of lies.

And looking back now, there is a less visceral sadness, the thought that in that game Liverpool reached some kind of apogee, that that was the last time they could truly be described as great. Perhaps there is even a more general sense of nostalgia, a reminder that there was excellence before the glitz and the cosmopolitanism of the Premier League era.

In the weeks immediately after winning the 1984 European Cup final, Liverpool's success seemed part of a wider pattern. With Everton having ended a fourteen-year trophy drought by winning the FA Cup, the Garden Festival in full swing, *Brookside* beginning to find a foothold in the national consciousness and Frankie Goes to Hollywood in their pomp, that summer began with a sense of great Merseyside pride, of resistance to Thatcher and the hardships of Conservative economic policy. Even though Liverpool had won a Treble, and clinched the European Cup in the most testing circumstances, some frailty had been evident in 1983–84, something Fagan had acknowledged. His side had at times seemed to win by force of will, almost by habit, as much as by outclassing opponents. Graeme Souness, as he had proved in Rome, was the embodiment of that and so, when he left for Sampdoria for £650,000 in June 1984, it was a major blow. He was, Brian Glanville warned in the *Sunday Times*, the 'heart and mind' of the team. Fagan had wanted to keep him, but as Peter Robinson acknowledged, English teams simply couldn't cope financially with Italian sides at the time and there was little point begrudging a player who took the opportunity to set himself up for life.

Craig Johnston, meanwhile, was a further issue. He had gone home to Australia in the summer and decided to postpone his return until October, ostensibly waiting for his wife to give birth although he later admitted his bitterness towards Fagan over his substitution in the League Cup final and the signing of Wark may have affected his judgement.

Liverpool showed just two changes from Rome for the Charity Shield, Wark and Nicol replacing Souness and Johnston, but the European champions were 'shocking' according to Fagan in losing 1–0 to Everton through a Grobbelaar own goal. 'Without Souness, Liverpool are clearly lesser mortals,' Clive White wrote in *The Times*, 'and the opposition greater ones by this knowledge.' Jan Mølby, who'd been on trial at the club, was signed the following week but in the friendly against Home Farm in Dublin in which the Dane had proved he was worth bringing in on a permanent basis, Rush suffered a knee ligament injury.

Rush had already been linked with a move to Italy – which, given Liverpool's predilection for long-term planning, may have been behind the £700,000 signing of Paul Walsh from Luton that May – and it was reported that, before signing Diego Maradona, Napoli had offered £4.5m for him. That deal collapsed, leaving Rush aggrieved with the chairman John Smith. There was no one overwhelming problem but with niggles proliferating, Liverpool began the season poorly. They'd taken eight points from four games when they were beaten 3–1 away at Arsenal, prompting Fagan to note in his diary that Liverpool were lacking drive and strength in midfield – near enough an admission that they were missing Souness.

After two draws and a defeat to Sheffield Wednesday, Fagan took shocking action, dropping Dalglish for a Friday night televised game against Tottenham. Before Fagan could tell him, Dalglish read of the decision in the newspapers and was furious; with Rush only just returning and not fit enough to play it left Liverpool short of attacking options. They lost 1–0, the decision to omit Dalglish looking even more 'daft' – as Fagan later put it – when Walsh was injured midway through the second half and Liverpool finished the game with Gillespie playing at centre-forward. The following week, Rush and Dalglish were back in tandem for the Merseyside derby. Graeme Sharp's famous volley won the game and Liverpool slipped to seventeenth.

There wasn't even the familiar comfort of the League Cup. Having needed extra-time to beat Stockport over two legs, Liverpool were eliminated by Spurs, the winner scored by Clive Allen after Grobbelaar had spilled a shot from Tony Galvin. A distraught Grobbelaar asked to be dropped; Fagan told him to sort himself out.

Only Europe provided solace. Lech Poznań were comfortably beaten 5–0 over two legs – Wark scoring in the winner
in Poland and then a hat-trick at Anfield, following Fagan's
advice to sit a little deeper and so make his runs later. Rush
scored a hat-trick against Benfica at Anfield in the next round
as Johnston returned from Australia. In the league, Liverpool
were struggling along at just over a goal a game; in Europe,
goalscoring posed no such problems.

Finding a replacement for Souness, though, remained a
major issue. Lawrenson played in midfield against Benfica but
his composure was needed at the back and advancing him
was never regarded as a long-term solution. Accepting that
a like-for-like replacement for Souness simply didn't exist,
Fagan instead paid £400,000 to sign Kevin Macdonald from
Leicester. Wiry and a little ungainly, he was a very different
player from the Scot, but he restored steel to the centre and
provided some balance. Frustration, though, lingered. Johnston became increasingly disgruntled at his lack of first-team
opportunities when he felt he was 'playing outrageously well'
in the reserves and put in a transfer request, as did Gillespie.
Both were granted, although Fagan was keen not to lose Gillespie at that stage. Mølby was also frustrated at his lack of
playing time but he was persuaded to stay, while Robinson
was sold to QPR in the January and Thompson moved on to
Sheffield United.

As Dalglish returned to form, Liverpool slowly climbed the
table. He was unavailable for the European Cup quarter-final
against Austria Vienna, though, having been sent off away in
Lisbon. Walsh, recovering from knee surgery, came in to replace him as Nicol's late goal earned a 1–1 draw in Austria.
Walsh then scored twice at home in the 4–1 second-leg victory,
but missed a penalty that would have given him his hat-trick.

By April, Liverpool were up to fifth, although twelve points
adrift of the league leaders and eventual champions Everton, and had reached the semi-final of the FA Cup which
fell between the two legs of their European Cup semi-final.

Panathinaikos were beaten 4–0 at Anfield, Rush scoring twice while Jim Beglin on his first European start wrapped up the scoring. In Athens, a fortnight later, Lawrenson got the only goal as Liverpool reached their fifth European Cup final in nine seasons.

The FA Cup semi-final against Manchester United, though, showed the flaws of the early part of the season hadn't been eradicated. In a fearsome gale at Hillsborough, Liverpool were largely outplayed but twice struck back having gone behind to draw 2–2. Fagan was furious and – in his diary at least – accused the entire team with the exception of Grobbelaar and Dalglish of being bottlers. The replay was little better. Despite going ahead just before half-time through a Paul McGrath own goal, Liverpool lost 2–1 to goals from Hughes and Robson.

Fagan was highly critical of Macdonald, describing him as being 'slow as a carthorse'. He appreciated the stability he provided but worried his passing and movement weren't up to Liverpool standards. Rebuilding, he knew, was necessary and in the February, as he approached his sixty-fourth birthday, he had already decided to retire, telling Peter Robinson and John Smith of his decision. He went to Brussels for the European Cup final knowing it would be his last game in charge, hoping for a glorious finale. The news that he would stand down and be replaced by Dalglish as a player-manager was broken by John Keith in the *Express* on the morning of the final. Fagan confirmed the story before lunch. At the time it seemed news of huge significance; by the following morning it was barely a footnote.

Juventus, who had reached the final by beating Bordeaux 3–2 on aggregate, had had an even poorer domestic season than Liverpool, finishing sixth in Serie A. With such stars as Michel Platini, Zbigniew Boniek and Paolo Rossi, they remained a dangerous side and had beaten Liverpool to win the European Super Cup, although it says much about Liverpool's disregard for the competition that they agreed to play it over one leg in Turin, essentially to get it over with, Juve eventually winning 2–0 at a snowy Comunale in January. Fagan had not been overimpressed by Juve in that game and announced long before kick-off that he would start with both Walsh and Rush, with Dalglish tucked behind them.

Yet even to talk of line-ups and past form seems trivial. Of far more significance was the stadium, something of which both clubs were grimly aware long before match-day. Robinson had led a small delegation of Liverpool officials to Brussels to inspect the ground and had immediately flagged up concerns about the 'chicken-wire' fencing that was used for segregation. The Juve president Giampiero Boniperti was similarly scathing, describing the stadium as 'old, decrepit and looking like a scrap yard'.

Worse, a 'neutral' section, Sector Z – printed on tickets given to Liverpool fans but then crossed out with felt pen, had bafflingly been designated at the Liverpool end of the ground. Given the number of Italians living in Brussels, it seemed inevitable that the majority of them would be bought by Juve fans, creating an obvious potential flashpoint. With thousands of counterfeit tickets on sale, Neil Macfarlane, the Minister of Sport, acting on Smith's advice, sent a telex to Uefa and the relevant football bodies in Belgium outlining their concerns. They received no reply. In England, meanwhile, football reached its lowest ebb. Chelsea fans rioted at both legs of the League Cup semi-final against Sunderland, Millwall fans ripped up Kenilworth Road and attacked police at an FA Cup sixth-round tie against Luton Town and a teenager was killed amid fighting between Leeds and Birmingham fans on the final day of the league season. Even when fans weren't disgracing themselves there was tragedy, fifty-six spectators killed in a fire at Bradford City on May 11, eighteen days before the European Cup final.

As the players performed their usual walkabout on the pitch in the late afternoon, there seemed little untoward, although one Liverpool fan had been stabbed and there had been isolated instances of looting and violence. According to

Brian Reade in his memoir *43 Years with the Same Bird*, there had been 'no running battles' in the centre of Brussels, 'just little confrontations kicking off'. Still, the overall mood had been relatively cordial and the fans at the stadium were in good voice. A ball was thrown from the Liverpool section and the players kicked it about in the sunlight.

But all these things are relative. Liverpool fans had never previously been involved in the sort of mass violence and rioting that certain other British teams had but that did not mean their fans were without fault. In *Red Men*, John Williams spoke of the 'utterly poisonous atmosphere' at the Manchester United Cup semi-final. There had been clashes between Liverpool fans and police in Paris in 1981, while shoplifting was commonplace, sports stores being a particular target. In *Kicking and Screaming* the Liverpool fan Barry Fay said that before the 1981 European Cup final there had been thieving from shops that displayed produce outside while a lot of fans had indulged in 'a little bit of blow'. One, with a Union flag tied round his neck, jumped from a bridge believing he could fly. 'In preference to violence, the main thrill was shoplifting clothes, especially continental menswear and exclusive sports gear,' wrote David Goldblatt in *The Ball is Round*. 'By the late 1970s the coolest clobber on the terraces was foreign anoraks, training tops, cycling gear and, above all, the right trainers.'

Williams, an academic who followed Liverpool throughout that period, noted a gradual deterioration in behaviour. Employment in Liverpool fell by 33 per cent between 1972 and 1985 and, Williams wrote, 'as people's lives in the city were getting harder, with joblessness booming, things had noticeably been getting wilder, more desperate.' Add in the memories of what had happened after the game in Rome the previous year, a desire in some cases for revenge on Italian fans – or at the very least a sense that Italian fans were dangerous and it was best to get retaliation in first – and the result was a tinderbox. 'As the day wore on,' Reade added, 'the initial friendliness towards the Italians turned to suspicion, then animosity ... the longer the sun beat down, and the more lager that was being necked, the uglier central Brussels became.' With just over an hour till kick-off, the inadequacy of the stadium became clear. A flimsy wall beside the Liverpool turnstiles was kicked down, leaving a gap twenty feet wide through which fans could enter and leave at will.

As feared, Sector Z was populated almost entirely by Juventus fans, separated from the bulk of the Liverpool support by a thin wire fence and five Belgian policemen. Hansen recalled that as the players walked past that area before the game, missiles were thrown at them. When the players had returned to the dressing room, fans turned their attention to each other and, as two Belgian youth sides played out an exhibition match, missiles were exchanged between Liverpool fans in Sector Y and Juventus fans in Sector Z, the atmosphere worsened by memories of the violence in Rome the previous year.

Terry Wilson, who was then eighteen, was jailed for his part in what followed. He insisted he saw a boy in a Liverpool shirt, he guesses aged between eight and twelve, being set upon by Italians. He and others charged, tearing down the fence. 'It was the type of skirmish that you'd seen 100 times before, on grounds all round the country, over a fifteen-year period and you thought to yourself, "Well, that's a skirmish and within a couple of minutes there'll be a police line there and they'll force both lines of fans back ..."' said Peter Hooton, the vocalist of The Farm and the founder of the Liverpool fanzine *The End*. 'That didn't happen ... There was no one taking control.' Juventus supporters trying to escape found there was nowhere to go. A crush developed and the retaining wall collapsed under the pressure. As thousands fled, thirty-nine were crushed to death amid the rubble: thirty-two Italians, six Belgians and a Northern Irishman.

Players heard the wall crash down and then screams. Fagan hurried them to the dressing-room, which was only a matter of yards from the fateful wall, and locked them in. Still unaware of how serious the incident was, Fagan appealed for calm over the public address system and when that had little effect he went to confront rioting fans himself, taking off his dark jacket and white shirt to reveal a Liverpool top with the number thirteen on the back. Unable to make himself heard, he began to sob in frustration.

Fagan returned to the dressing-room and tried to focus his team on the game. The accounts of players are contradictory and quite who knew what when about the severity of the incident remains unclear. Outside, riot police sought to contain Juventus fans at the other end of the stadium, lining up a row of horses across the centre of the pitch. On television, Juventus fans could be seen ripping concrete posts out of the ground while one brandished a gun, later shown to be a starting pistol. Officials from both sides wanted the game called off, but Uefa and the Belgian authorities insisted it went ahead with the chief of the gendarmerie arguing that the time it would take for the game to be played would allow troops to be brought in to quell further violence when fans left the ground after the final whistle. Ninety minutes later than scheduled, two and a quarter hours after the wall had collapsed, the game began. It went ahead, the *Guardian* reported, 'alongside hideous scenes as corpses in green plastic shrouds were carried to a makeshift tented mortuary outside the main entrance'.

The match, for what it was worth, was settled by a fifty-seventh minute Michel Platini penalty, awarded after Gillespie had tripped Zbigniew Boniek just outside the box. Ronnie Whelan was then denied a penalty for a clear foul, leading Dalglish and Neal to claim in their autobiographies that Liverpool were never going to be allowed to win. Lawrenson and Walsh both suffered first-half injuries, reducing Liverpool's options from the bench, and Stefano Tacconi made a fine late save from Wark but Rush was surely not alone when he admitted he barely cared whether Liverpool won. Perhaps the chief of the gendarmerie was right and playing the game did prevent further casualties but on every level other than the bluntly practical it was hard to believe the game should have gone ahead. The Juventus midfielder Massimo Bonini certainly didn't think so. 'I don't feel like I won anything on that day,' he said. 'It was just senseless. I just couldn't celebrate. That stadium wasn't suitable to stage such an important final. It must have been because of football politics it was used.'

Fagan somehow composed himself for a dreadful post-match press conference. 'I won't be able to forget my last game of football for the rest of my life,' he said. 'It is tragic. It was really horrific. I broke down and cried. I felt I was part of the supporters and I was letting everybody else down in Liverpool and everyone in the football world. I felt really bad about it. There was nothing much I could really do. It's something when the game has come to this. It's not the way we would have hoped things would have worked out. My heart just wasn't in it. Tonight upset me very much but it wasn't over the result. What is a game of football when so many are dead? The match itself just fades into insignificance.' He may have seemed composed then, but as he disembarked from the plane at Speke Airport, Fagan broke down and he had to be helped across the tarmac by Roy Evans, an awful way for a great football man and servant of Liverpool to depart.

Fourteen Liverpool fans were found guilty of involuntary manslaughter. Half were sentenced to three years in jail, the other half given suspended sentences. Captain Johan Mahieu, the police officer in charge of security in Sector Z, and Albert Roosens, the secretary of the Belgian Football Union, were both convicted of criminal negligence. English clubs were banned from European competition for an indefinite period, with Liverpool to serve an additional year's suspension after they'd been readmitted.

And so, in the worst possible circumstances, for reasons that had little to do with football, the period of English domination of the European game, an era Liverpool had inaugurated with victory over Borussia Mönchengladbach in 1977, came to an end.

*

The league game against Nottingham Forest at Anfield, played on a sunny Wednesday evening, was the final part of a trilogy played out over the course of eleven days, following a league game at the City Ground and an FA Cup semi-final at Hillsborough. With Forest the only other side in the country playing with any level of consistency, these were the matches that shaped the season.

They began poorly for Liverpool. Dalglish opted for a five-man midfield in Nottingham, leaving out Beardsley and using Aldridge as a lone striker with Johnston and Barnes on the flanks. 'It is not my policy to discuss the reasons for my team selection in public and I do not intend to start now,' Dalglish wrote in his end-of-season diary – a weirdly portentous piece of phrasing for a decision that could easily have been explained in tactical terms. Or he could even have avoided the subject altogether – it was his diary, after all; by anticipating a question from an imagined interlocutor and then avoiding it, Dalglish hints at some dark secret or scandal.

Whatever the reason, Liverpool didn't play especially well and fell behind as a Neil Webb cross was deflected into his own net by Hansen. Grobbelaar saved a Nigel Clough penalty on forty-six minutes after Gillespie had fouled Gary Crosby but Clough did then make it 2–0, converting a Crosby cut-back shortly after Beardsley had come on for Mølby, making his first appearance of the season. Webb fouled Barnes to concede a penalty that Aldridge converted with twenty minutes remaining, but Forest held out for a 2–1 win – only Liverpool's second league defeat of the season. Their first had come just under a fortnight earlier, a scrappy 1–0 defeat at Everton that meant Liverpool had only tied Leeds United's then-record unbeaten run from the start of a season, set at twenty-nine matches in 1973–74.

A week later, Liverpool met Forest again, in an FA Cup semi-final at Hillsborough. Aldridge again struck from the penalty spot, this time after Steve Chettle had fouled Barnes. He added a second seven minutes after half-time after fine work from Barnes and Beardsley and, although Clough pulled one back, Liverpool took a step nearer the Double.

By kick-off against Forest in the league match at Anfield, Liverpool were eight points clear of second-placed Manchester United, with three games in hand. Forest were fourth, fourteen behind the leaders, having played the same number of games. With seven games remaining, there was little chance of Liverpool being caught but they did go into that match in comparatively poor form, having won only one of their previous five games, and some sense of anxiety was apparent in the opening minutes.

Having received the ball from Liverpool's first thrust, the Forest goalkeeper Steve Sutton sent a long punt downfield that was controlled just inside the Liverpool half by Clough. He played a short pass right to Lee Glover, who was still three weeks shy of his eighteenth birthday and hadn't played in either of the previous games. He knocked it back infield to Clough who had space but in trying to work the ball onto his left foot was closed down. The shake of the head he gave after his effort had been blocked suggested he felt he should have done better.

A couple of minutes later, Des Walker faltered under a high ball, missing his clearance – a rare error from one of the English game's most composed and reliable defenders, and a worrying sign. Peter Beardsley's cross came to nothing but as Walker was treated by the Forest physio Liam O'Kane he was clearly in some distress. He'd needed pain-killing injections in an ankle injury to play and the indications were that the problem was still troubling him.

Gradually Liverpool, after a slightly frantic opening, began to impose themselves. 'For twenty minutes the team wasn't performing as it should,' said Phil Thompson, by then the assistant manager. 'It was solid and we didn't lose a goal but we were far from the most complete side for that opening spell. We were battling with Forest who were biting, snarling and scrapping but once we imposed our superiority it was happy days. We wore them down with our passing and movement which was of the first order.'

The impact of Heysel on Liverpool was profound. 'Liverpudlians grieved for the loss of life, but they also grieved for the city's pride because football had been one of Liverpool's last remaining sources of pride,' wrote Andrew Ward and John Williams in *Football Nation*. Pickpocketing had been rife on the Kop and there had been incidents of misbehaviour at away games, of fans forcing their way into matches without paying, but generally Liverpool's support had been seen as one of its great assets: witty, passionate and knowledgeable. The vast majority still were, of course, but the image of the fans and of Liverpool itself was tainted by the disaster. During the 1985–86 season, Liverpool City Council conducted a study into the attitudes of young people to football. A fourteen-year-old girl seemed to sum it up best. 'It was disgusting the way the fans fought like that,' she said. 'It was degrading. It made me ashamed to be a Scouser ... Now if you go abroad, and you voice out where you come from, you can't say it with pride like you should be able to. You have to sort of mutter it because of the shame and guilt we carry.'

While many were so revolted they stopped going to games, others began to fight back. So many rallied to support the club, in fact, that attendances actually rose in 1985–86. A group of Liverpool fans, meanwhile, led by Rogan Taylor, founded the Football Supporters Association, the first national body to represent fans and a key step in the rehabilitation of the game.

The club had to respond and it did at remarkable speed. The day after Heysel, fretting because he hadn't been given time to change out of his tracksuit into a suit, Dalglish gave his first press conference as player-manager. Two days later, he had to persuade Bruce Grobbelaar, horrified by what had happened in Brussels, not to quit the game. It's hard to imagine more difficult circumstances in which to take over. Dalglish admits he probably would have found it difficult anyway, saying that taking the job 'entailed forgoing a lot of the pleasure I derived from playing football'. On his first full day, before the players had returned for pre-season training, Dalglish found himself sitting in an office watching a phone and waiting for it to ring, just to give him something to do. Bob Paisley, still a key part of the Boot Room, told him waiting was part of the job.

The job also meant he couldn't join in the dressing-room japes and that his relationship with players who had until a couple of months previously been his teammates changed. Only one, he said, was difficult: Neal, who had hoped to get the manager's job himself. By then, the right-back was thirty-four and Dalglish, doubting he would hold his place in the team ahead of Steve Nicol for much longer, stripped him of the captaincy, giving it instead to Alan Hansen, for no other reason he said, than that his fellow Scot was 'a very lucky person'. That, of course, only worsened Neal's mood further and he would insist on calling Dalglish 'Kenny' rather than 'Boss'. 'His reaction was obviously calculated,' Dalglish said, 'almost like he was not admitting I was his new manager.' A potentially disruptive situation was averted when Neal took the player-manager's job at Bolton.

There is a strange defensiveness about Dalglish's recollection of the period in his autobiography. 'More than a few people hoped I would fall on my face,' he says in the first paragraph of the chapter dealing with his time as manager. 'It gave me great pleasure to prove them wrong.' There were doubts, it's true – after all, nobody could remember the last player-manager to have achieved any kind of success – and it's understandable that Dalglish should have been irritated by the contradiction of being simultaneously accused of changing the team too much and of having done nothing other than inherit a winning team, but it still seems strange he should adopt such a self-justificatory tone. After all, in domestic terms, that season was the most successful in Liverpool's history, as they did the Double for the first time.

Yet Hansen admits he was sceptical about Dalglish's squad.

He wasn't alone in wondering whether Mølby, for all his elegance, had the energy to compete in the heart of an English midfield. The Dane was a key figure that season, though, and scored an iconic goal against Manchester United in the League Cup, one made all the more legendary by the fact that for twenty-four years after it was scored it was thought there was no television footage of it because of a dispute over rights. Dispossessing Norman Whiteside about twenty yards inside his own half on the right-hand touchline, Mølby surged forwards, went by Clayton Blackmore and, from just outside the box, crashed a drive of ferocious power just under the crossbar to equalise. A couple of minutes later, he converted a penalty and Liverpool had a win that had seemed wholly improbable given how the first two-thirds of the game had gone.

United had begun the season with a top-flight record ten straight league victories – matched stride for stride by Reading in the Third Division, with the Biscuitmen going on to break the Football League record by making it to thirteen – but even as they crumbled, it was Everton who took control. At the start of March, having just been comprehensively beaten by them at Anfield, Liverpool were eight points behind their city rivals and five behind United, who had a game in hand. But then came one of the great Liverpool charges, a late-season surge to rival the famous title-winning turnaround of 1981–82. Ian Rush snatched an injury-time winner in the snow at White Hart Lane, the first in a sequence of eleven wins in the final twelve games. Dalglish, who had been reluctant to play himself, started putting his own name down on the teamsheet and the title was sealed, appropriately, by the player-manager, as he chested down a through-ball and finished with characteristic calm away at Chelsea on the final day.

Everton were Liverpool's opponents in the first all-Merseyside FA Cup final and they took the lead before half-time as Gary Lineker outpaced Hansen. A second-half double by Ian Rush either side of a Craig Johnston goal, though, the comeback masterminded by Mølby, secured Liverpool's first FA Cup since 1974. Dalglish, following Liverpool tradition, reflected that it could have been better: they'd only lost to QPR in the League Cup semi-final after scoring two own goals and missing a penalty.

Ray Houghton, influential on the right, slipped a pass inside to Beardsley, who dragged the ball from Stuart Pearce's challenge, spun away from him, then darted inside Terry Wilson only to cuff his shot wide. Forest, like so many sides before them, began to find themselves under pressure, not facing too many specific threats as such, but slowly suffocated by the impossibility of relieving the siege. Crosby was tackled by Gary Ablett and the ball bounced to Barnes on halfway. He advanced and spread the ball to Beardsley on the left. As Chettle closed him down, he gave the ball back to Steve McMahon who carried the ball across field and then laid a pass outside to Nicol on the charge. His shot from an angle was pushed over by Sutton.

That was the early pattern: Forest tried to pass their way out from the back and Liverpool intercepted and came back at them. That was how the first goal came about, after seventeen minutes. Wilson's pass to Glover was intercepted by Hansen, who brought it over the halfway line. He played it right to Houghton who drifted infield, exchanged passes with Barnes on the edge of the box and slipped a neat finish past Sutton, the one-two effectively taking five Forest defenders out of the game.

Liverpool's method, in a sense, was to create counter-attacks wherever they could. Although they were certainly capable of holding possession, or playing with the patience of Shankly's and Paisley's teams, it was far more about rapid transitions, about winning the ball back and striking when the other team's defence wasn't set. And the problem that creates for opponents is that they, paradoxically, become most at risk when they are attacking. Two minutes after the goal, a Forest corner was cleared. Aldridge played it to Barnes who helped it on to Nigel Spackman. Beardsley was crowded out but Forest couldn't fully clear, the ball coming to Nicol, pushing forward from right-back as ever. His shot was slightly mishit but wasn't too far wide. 'Stevie Nicol was our secret weapon,' said Barnes of a full-back who'd scored seven goals in the season's first seven matches. The first had been a stunning long-range header to secure an opening-day win at Highbury, while he got a televised hat-trick at Newcastle, completed by a brilliant chip over the keeper from the edge of the box. 'He often played a major role in games without getting the headlines.'

Again and again curtailed Forest moves led to Liverpool efforts on goal. Midway through the half, a Sutton clearance came to Wilson. His touch was poor and he was dispossessed by Beardsley, who immediately looked to play in Aldridge. Walker held him up on the right side of the box and as Pearce closed in the ball broke loose for Wilson. Under pressure from Houghton, though, he misplaced his pass, presenting the ball to Aldridge. The forward gave it back to Spackman who cut infield and laid a pass along the top of the box for Barnes who hit the ball first time with the outside of his left foot as Chettle charged to close him down. He didn't perhaps catch it quite as keenly as he might have done but still forced Sutton into a decent save low to his right.

The waves of Liverpool pressure kept rolling. Nicol took a throw to Beardsley about twenty yards out on the Liverpool right. He played it back to Nicol, took the return as he advanced into the box and crossed. Aldridge flicked the ball on and Barnes, arriving at the back post, had his volley blocked by Chettle. Forest simply couldn't get the ball clear. Rice, deep on the left, aimed a pass forward for Clough but Hansen headed clear to Houghton, who rolled it outside to Barnes, operating on the right. He beat Rice almost casually and ran at Pearce, before slipping a ball through for a typical Beardsley spurt. From the right side of the box, he struck his shot powerfully, but Sutton, reacting superbly, got enough of a hand on the ball to tip it over the bar.

And then, at last, with half an hour gone, Forest had a chance – and like most of Liverpool's most dangerous moves it came from a counter-attack. Gillespie was held up by Pearce and then dispossessed by Rice, who played it inside to Clough. He helped it on to Webb, who kept from the flow of the move to the right, finding Crosby. He took on Ablett and then played it infield to Webb, who sent an angled pass behind Glover for Clough, whose shot from the edge of the box was saved low by Grobbelaar.

It was a rare moment of respite. The whole game has entered history as perhaps the greatest of all Liverpool performances, and within that the finest quarter-hour came at the end of the first half. Nicol took a throw deep in his own half, returning the ball to Grobbelaar. He rolled it out to Hansen, who laid it outside to Nicol who, unusually, struck it long. Walker got across to cover but the loose ball fell for Houghton. He cut infield and laid a square pass to McMahon. The ball ran away from him a little but he was able to regather by the left-hand touchline. Turning back infield, he played the ball square to Spackman, who angled the ball forward into the path of McMahon. From twenty-five yards out, he struck a fierce shot that Sutton did well to beat away, the ball coming to Barnes. It had bounced to mid-thigh height when it reached him, but he was able to guide the ball goalwards with the inside of his left foot. With Sutton beaten, the ball glanced the outside of the post and went wide.

McMahon, after taking another Spackman pass, drove just over but a second goal was coming and it arrived eight minutes before the break. As with so many of Liverpool's most dangerous moves, it began with a Forest attack. Chettle took a throw to Crosby but he was dispossessed by Barnes, the ball breaking for Beardsley just inside his own half. He hit a glorious sweeping ball between Walker and Pearce for Aldridge to run on to and lift the ball over the advancing Sutton. It was devastating and effective, a goal beautiful in its simplicity, but it did raise the question of what might have happened had

Forest sat back and sought to contain Liverpool rather than taking the game to them. Perhaps in the context of the championship, that was probably their only option – and given the European ban they had little to lose in terms of potentially dropping a place or two in the table – but their open approach made them vulnerable.

It's often thought that 4–4–2 is an unsophisticated formation, blockish and more concerned with restricting the space between defensive and midfield lines than with fluency or creativity. It can be, certainly, but the way Liverpool played it, it was thrillingly fluid. Numerical designations of formations are only ever crude guidelines and it could be argued that at times Liverpool tended more to a 4–2–3–1 than 4–4–2. Aldridge was clearly the leader of the line, but the wide men pushed high up the pitch – Barnes probably higher than Houghton – protected by Spackman sitting deep in front of the back four. Nicol was notably attacking from right-back, his overlapping runs providing balance as Houghton drifted infield. But the most mobile of all was Beardsley who covered vast amounts of ground with his stooping gait, always looking for space for a rapid shuffle goalwards or the possibility of a one-two. Running onto a diagonal pass from Nicol shortly after the second goal, he just kept running, beating Colin Foster and Wilson, only for his shot to be brilliantly pushed onto the bar by Sutton.

There was an extraordinary imagination to Beardsley. To witness him at his peak was surely to experience what the evolutionary biologist Stephen Jay Gould described as 'the universality of excellence'. 'I don't deny the differences in style and substance between athletic and conventional scholarly performance,' he wrote, 'but we surely err in regarding sports as a domain of brutish intuition … The greatest athletes cannot succeed by bodily gifts alone … One of the most intriguing, and undeniable, properties of great athletic performance lies in the impossibility of regulating certain central skills by overt mental deliberation: the required action simply doesn't grant sufficient time for the sequential processing of conscious decisions.' Beardsley had an astonishing ability to conceptualise the pitch, to absorb the positions of players and the spaces between them and act accordingly, something perhaps most famously illustrated by a goal he scored for Newcastle against Brighton and Hove Albion in 1984, hooking a ball from between two defenders in a tackle before springing up to lob the former England goalkeeper Joe Corrigan from twenty yards.

A Barnes free-kick was played low to him just inside the box and, with a first-time flick with the inside of his heel, he laid in Houghton, whose shot was saved by Sutton, Pearce making a sliding recovery challenge to nick the rebound away from McMahon. Liverpool's threat could come from anywhere. A minute before half-time, Hansen advanced from the back, played a one-two with Beardsley and was in his shooting stride when Chettle made a superbly timed sliding challenge. Pearce then had to make a similar immaculate tackle on Aldridge after McMahon had dummied a Barnes through-ball. Half-time came at 2–0 and with Forest relieved to get off the pitch only two behind. In that final fifteen minutes of the half Liverpool had played football not merely of extraordinary, relentless quality. 'It was like the Alamo,' said Sutton. 'I know how Davy Crockett felt now. The lads were looking for the cavalry to arrive. We felt like having a count up to make sure they only had eleven players on. Although I'd had a couple of saves to make I thought that after twenty minutes we were the better side and could have gone one up but once they got the first goal they absolutely destroyed us … I don't think there was much between us but on that night we were a million miles apart.'

Dalglish's second season, 1986–87, had been one of frustration. A run of nine wins in ten games carried them to the top of the league by mid-March, but three straight defeats allowed Everton in and they put together a run of seven straight wins to finish nine points clear of Liverpool. They went out of the FA Cup in the third round, beaten on the plastic pitch at Luton in a second replay, and, in the League Cup final, they lost 2–1 to Arsenal, the first game in which Ian Rush had scored and Liverpool had lost. It wasn't a dreadful season by any means, but those who suspected the Double had been won with the momentum of the Paisley and Fagan years found fresh ammunition.

Dalglish's response was to rebuild the team. With the sale of Rush to Juventus for £3.2 million in the summer of 1987 – a deal that had been agreed the year before, and had arguably given Liverpool's subsequent season a *fin de siècle* air – there were fears that Liverpool had taken an irrevocable step backwards. He was a symbol of an age of dominance, just as surely as Keegan had been when he moved to Hamburg in 1977 – and Keegan, at least, had left on a high. Dalglish, though, reinvested astutely, signing Beardsley from Newcastle and, more controversially, Barnes from Watford. Barnes was seen as an individualist, a player antithetical to the sort of team ethic that had characterised Liverpool's play for decades. He was also black: not the first black player to play for Liverpool – that was Howard Gayle, who had been born in Toxteth – but the first black player to be signed by them and there can be little doubt that there was a racist element to many of the doubts as to whether he would fit in. 'Some people seem surprised that a player of such obvious individual skill as John should come to a club like Liverpool whose successes have been based on teamwork but I think he will complement us and vice versa …' said Dalglish in *The Liverpool Year*, his diary of that season. 'We know he has the speed and ability to go past people and not only is he one of the best, if not *the* best crosser of a ball in British football but he will contribute a great deal to the team effort. He is never shy of going back to help out in defensive situations and, of course, at set pieces he can be a menace to the opposition.' As it turned out, Barnes would become the most effective and popular Liverpool winger since Billy Liddell.

That crossing ability was evident in Liverpool's opening match as he latched onto a Beardsley pass and crossed for Aldridge to head the first goal of the season, away against Arsenal. Liverpool went on to win 2–1 but their campaign got off to a stuttering start because of the collapse of a Victorian sewer under the Kop that forced the postponement of their first three home games. It hardly mattered. When they did play, Liverpool were imperious. By mid-October, when they faced the early leaders QPR at Anfield, they had taken twenty-six points from eight games and scored twenty-four goals. Johnston gave Liverpool the lead from a Barnes cut-back, an Aldridge penalty made it 2–0 before Barnes rounded off the win with two sumptuous goals: the first placed forcefully into the top corner after a one-two with Aldridge, the second following a languorous wander past two challenges after he'd dispossessed Kevin Brock on halfway. That took Liverpool top and, apart from a couple of weeks in November when they drew three in a row, they remained there for the rest of the season. 'Although it was a different Liverpool side from previous years it was guided by the same principles,' said Dalglish. 'The graft was as strong as ever. There was just more flair than before.'

Walker was withdrawn for the nineteen-year-old Darren Wassall at half-time and, for a brief time, there was a sense Forest might get back into the game. Brian Rice and Pearce combined on the left to create an opening for Glover, but as the seventeen-year-old drove the ball across the face of goal, nobody could get a touch. Then Webb chipped the ball over the top for Clough, who sliced wide under pressure from Houghton; replays confirmed it probably should have been a penalty. Liverpool had thrown away a two-goal advantage against Manchester United in their previous home game, on Easter Monday, and for a brief moment there was perhaps a thought that Liverpool were again wobbling in defence of a lead.

Forest's problem, though, was that the more they attacked,

the more Liverpool looked like scoring: there was always the potential for Beardsley or Barnes to exploit the space left by their forward movement. That was precisely what Barnes did to break Forest's momentum, surging from inside his own half, evading three challenges and laying the ball to Aldridge who touched it off to McMahon. His shot was straight at Sutton but the reminder of Liverpool's attacking potential had been issued and the momentum shifted back their way.

Gillespie caught Glover in possession and passed to Nicol who charged infield before sliding the ball outside him for Houghton. He crossed towards Aldridge and although the ball was cleared away from him, it fell for Beardsley. His footwork was characteristically quick as he opened space for a shot, which Sutton turned wide. The respite was brief. The corner was taken quickly, Barnes playing it to Houghton who advanced into the box and then cut a cross back for Gillespie to drive home. He reacted with a straight-arm horizontal finger point, one of the iconic celebrations of the age.

And that, really, was the end of the game as a contest. 'The lads produced such variation tonight,' Dalglish wrote in his diary. 'Movement, passing, finishing – it was all there in abundance. I think our lads were so good that the result does not reflect badly on any Forest player.' Pearce, with the chance to set up Glover, misplaced his cross and Webb fired over, but really it became just a matter of how many Liverpool would score. Hansen, as he had in the first half, came striding forward and played a one-two with Beardsley that took him into the box. With the opportunity to shoot and Sutton advancing, he attempted to square the ball to Aldridge, but hit a laughably bad pass that hurtled in front of the forward at waist height. Gillespie played a ball over Forest's back four for McMahon, who seemed to have outmuscled Foster, only for the defender to stretch out a leg and get a toe to the ball. Nicol then sliced wide from an indirect free-kick awarded for obstruction by Pearce on Beardsley.

But the fourth goal came soon enough. Chettle's pass to

Clough was poor and, as he miscontrolled, Spackman won possession. He laid the ball back to Gillespie, who played it right for Houghton, who returned it to Spackman. He advanced and knocked the ball left to Barnes who ran at Chettle. He nutmegged him, skipped by Crosby and pulled the ball back for Beardsley, who sidefooted the ball into the bottom corner – another goal from a cutback and another goal scored within a few seconds of Liverpool regaining the ball.

The fifth quickly followed, and again it stemmed from Forest giving the ball away. Chettle passed to Webb who was dispossessed by Spackman, the ball breaking for Beardsley. He played it through to Spackman, who had made a forward run after tackling Webb, and he squared it to Aldridge who had pulled off Wassall and Pearce and finished easily, his fifth goal in the three-match sequence against Forest. 'One way and another there were a few reasons to celebrate, and Liverpool are nowadays not in the habit of disappointing their customers,' wrote Stuart Jones in *The Times*. 'Yet no one could realistically have expected that the evening would embrace such sweeping beauty and five goals, all of them memorable, especially after a typically subdued opening. Liverpool were merely stoking their embers. Once they blazed, the sight was as breathtaking, as colourful, and as riveting as watching the most lavish firework display.'

Dalglish, following Liverpool tradition to the letter, ignored the beauty and praised his side's focus and work-rate. 'It would have been easy for them to become complacent after Saturday but it is to their credit that they put the amount of work in that they did and the amount of football that was played,' he said, before finally grudgingly acknowledging that the performance had been something special: 'Every goal was a great goal.'

Although Liverpool thrashed Sheffield Wednesday 5–1 at Hillsborough in their penultimate game – with the Wednesday boss Howard Wilkinson staying pitch-side after the final whistle to applaud Dalglish's players off the field – the victory over Forest represented the highpoint of the run. Liverpool drew four of their final six games, which was still enough to finish nine points clear of Manchester United and equal the record points tally of ninety set by Everton in 1985, despite playing two games fewer as the size of the top flight was reduced. Even greater anticlimax was to come in the FA Cup final.

Wimbledon's victory over Liverpool, achieved thanks to Lawrie Sanchez's thirty-seventh-minute looping header, is considered one of the great shocks in FA Cup history and in terms of the history and stature of the clubs it was. Wimbledon, though, had finished seventh that season and sixth the year before, their uncompromising style, summed up in Vinnie Jones's crunching challenge on Steve McMahon in the first minute of the final, unsettling a host of more illustrious opponents. John Aldridge became the first player to miss a penalty in a Wembley final, Dave Beasant saving low to his left after Clive Goodyear had been penalised for what was actually a clean challenge, but that aside Liverpool, as Dalglish put it in his diary, 'didn't get one bounce of the ball'. Beardsley had a goal ruled out because a free-kick had already been awarded for a foul on him as he wriggled away from Andy Thorn while Wimbledon survived a welter of pressure. Dalglish, meanwhile, noted that Spackman and Gillespie, having both required stitches following a clash of heads during a league game against Luton the previous Monday, were less able to deal with aerial balls than they might otherwise have been. There may have been an element of misfortune in the defeat but it was also true that Liverpool had been, as Peter Corrigan put it in the *Observer*, 'subdued'. In the *Guardian*, David Lacey wondered whether the league had perhaps been won too early and too easily for Liverpool to retain their hunger.

At the time, it seemed a blip, another Double missed by a tiny margin, and it was assumed Liverpool would simply carry on. They had been among the elite for a quarter of a century and pre-eminent for fifteen years. There was little reason to believe the process would not be re-enacted. When Len Capeling wrote in the *Post* that 'Liverpool are now so far ahead of most other challengers that to talk of them in the same breath is to compare iron pyrites with pure gold or cut glass with fine diamonds,' few disagreed with him. Twenty-five years later, though, that exhibition at Anfield, that demonstration of Liverpool's superiority over one of their closest rivals, stands as the high point of a dominance that may never be repeated.

CHAPTER 8

FA Cup, fifth round replay, Goodison Park, Liverpool, 20 February 1991

Everton   **4–4**   **Liverpool**
Sharp 48, 73   *Beardsley 37, 71*
Cottee 89, 113   *Rush 77*
                                   Barnes 103

Everton	Liverpool
Neville Southall	Bruce Grobbelaar
Ray Atteveld (Stuart McCall 46)	Glenn Hysén
Andy Hinchcliffe	David Burrows
Kevin Ratcliffe	Steve Nicol
Dave Watson	Jan Mølby
Martin Keown	Gary Ablett
Pat Nevin (Tony Cottee 86)	Peter Beardsley
Neil McDonald	Steve Staunton
Graeme Sharp	Ian Rush
Mike Newell	John Barnes
John Ebbrell	Barry Venison
Howard Kendall	Kenny Dalglish

Ref: N Midgley
Bkd:
Att: 37,766

THE SIMILARITIES BETWEEN KENNY DALGLISH'S resignation in 1991 and Bill Shankly's retirement seventeen years earlier are obvious and unavoidable. Both announcements came from nowhere, a shock both to the club and the wider game. Both men – both unquestionably club legends – had run themselves into the ground; emotionally drained, they felt they had nothing left to give. Both would, once recharged, come to regret their decision only to find the club had moved on without them. Even the aesthetics, the *mise-en-scène* of those fateful days, are practically facsimiles of each other: the protagonist with eyes fixed on a point approximately a thousand yards in the distance; a grim-faced chairman to the right of the frame reading sullenly from his script; the beige, sub-*Abigail's Party* decor which hinted, in the 1991 staging, that too little had moved on behind the scenes during the intervening period.

There was one crucial difference, though. Liverpool were able to take control of the situation when Shankly dropped his bombshell. For a start, Shankly had departed during the close season, affording the club time to consider their options. In Bob Paisley, they had a successor in waiting. Most importantly, Shankly was leaving a young team on an upward trajectory: they had won the league and Uefa Cup the year before, had just landed the FA Cup with a total-football flourish and on the morning of Shankly's departure, had unveiled a new star signing in Ray Kennedy.

Dalglish's abdication was another matter. It came in the middle of a season which, after a superb start, had begun to spiral out of control. There was no modern-day Paisley ready to take over from the Boot Room. And the team, astonishingly successful in the not-too-distant past, was ageing fast and beginning to betray signs of wear and tear, especially at the back. Dalglish's last signing – leaving aside the seventeen-year-old midfield prodigy from Bournemouth, Jamie Redknapp – was no Kennedy, but a thoroughly unremarkable winger from Millwall, Jimmy Carter, an eyebrow-raising choice even as the squad player he was surely meant to be. Liverpool as an organisation found itself in uncharted waters, the serenity with which it had navigated crises of various stripe and severity no longer in evidence. Sir John Smith had stood down as chairman the year before, ending a long-serving, low-profile partnership with the secretary Peter Robinson that had served the club well.

But Dalglish can hardly be blamed for his decision. He was exhausted. The Liverpool job has always been highly pressurised at the best of times, but in fewer than six years, Dalglish had to deal with four monumental, and singular, problems. He had to repair the club's reputation in the wake of the Heysel disaster, which he managed with good grace and humility during a season that ended with the Double. He was charged with keeping the most prominent side in England at the top of the tree, a feat he achieved with slightly more intermittent but occasionally spectacular success, the 1987–88 side in particular one of English football's most revered. He had to rally his players after arguably the most painful defeat suffered by any club in league history, as Arsenal snatched the 1988–89 title in the very last minute of the season, a Herculean effort which culminated in Liverpool regaining the title the following year. And, on a wholly different scale, he bravely and selflessly led the club through its, and the city of Liverpool's, darkest days after Hillsborough.

'This is the first time since I came to the club that I take the interest of Kenny Dalglish over Liverpool Football Club,' he announced. 'This is not a sudden decision. The worst I could have done was not to decide. One could argue that this decision hadn't come at a good time but there is no good time in cases like this. The main problem is the pressure I put on myself because of my strong desire to succeed. The stress that comes right before and after games has got the better of me. Some might have difficulty understanding my decision but this decision stands. I would be betraying everyone if I wouldn't let them know there is something wrong. I have been involved with football since I was seventeen. Twenty years with the two most successful teams in Britain, Celtic and Liverpool. I've been at the front all these years and it is time to end it.'

Those who witnessed Dalglish attempting to hold back the tears, not with total success, knew that the man had reached the end of the road. The last straw had been a tumultuous FA Cup replay against Everton during which, although nobody was looking for them, the signs that Dalglish was nearing the end had been clear. Liverpool lost the lead four times, but with the famous old stadium bouncing around him, not once did Dalglish respond. The figure he cut on the touchline seemed, at the time, to be his usual undemonstrative self: one hand in pocket, the other draped across the roof of the dugout. With the benefit of hindsight, it was a picture of a man drained of all energy. This game, and the decision it precipitated, was a blow from which Liverpool have arguably never recovered. Many still wish Dalglish had never left but, looking back, it's an achievement that he'd managed to make it that far.

Having been beaten by Wimbledon in the 1988 FA Cup final, Liverpool enjoyed at least partial catharsis at Wembley in the Charity Shield at the start of the following season. They beat Wimbledon 2–1 in the midst of a tempest, a cheap and cheerful metaphor for a cheap and cheerful spiritual cleansing: a Charity Shield would not calm the dull throb of another lost Double. But it did allow Liverpool to turn the page. John Aldridge, who had missed the crucial penalty during that painful defeat back in May, scored both goals. Steve McMahon, who had been unceremoniously clattered in the opening seconds of the FA Cup final by Vinnie Jones, went some way to repairing his reputation with a series of thumping tackles, the high (or low) point being a hilariously unnecessary follow-through on the Wimbledon keeper Simon Tracey (Dave Beasant having upped sticks for an unsuccessful sojourn at Newcastle). Wimbledon had proved themselves awkward opponents again – they'd taken the lead early on through John Fashanu – but while Liverpool's passing wasn't quite up to their highest standards, the natural order had been reasserted.

There were a couple of worrying harbingers, though. Liverpool's back-line had a distinctly rickety look to it. Alan Hansen was injured – and in any case past his best by then – recovering from knee surgery, his second time under the knife that year. Poor Mark Lawrenson had been forced to retire towards the end of the 1987–88 season as a result of a recalcitrant Achilles tendon, taking on an impossible job at Oxford United, where he was tasked with managing a club being sabotaged from the inside by the Derby chairman Robert Maxwell, who was effectively running Oxford through the proxy of his son, Kevin. Shorn of two genuinely world-class talents, Liverpool's central defensive pairing for the season's curtain-raiser was Gary Gillespie – a talented centre-back in his own right but ultimately Hansen-lite – and Alex Watson, the brother of the Everton stalwart Dave, who was destined for a handful of appearances for the club before embarking on a career in the lower leagues at Bournemouth, Torquay United and Exeter City. The pair struggled under Wimbledon's aerial bombardment and although that hardly made them unique, it wasn't the rock upon which title-winning sides are built.

But while Liverpool's defensive worries were abundantly clear at the time, the more troubling development of the day only snaps into focus with hindsight. The crowd at Wembley that day was only 54,887, and while much of that could be attributed to Wimbledon's small support base, many seats remained empty for another reason. Tickets had been on general sale that day for £8, but many who turned up in plenty of time to pay on the door simply couldn't get in: the Wembley turn-stiles were so slow that many fans only made it to their seats for the half-time whistle. This for a showpiece match at the country's premier stadium. It was clear to anyone bothering to look that English football was an organisational shambles from the top down, the interests of fans barely a considera-tion. But as would be gut-wrenchingly proven by events in Sheffield seven months later, those running the sport were complacent and myopic.

Defensively suspect they may have been, but Liverpool had no such worries up front – or so it seemed. Aldridge's double was timely, because waiting on the sidelines to return to the side was Ian Rush. The striker had just been re-signed for a British-record £2.8m fee by Dalglish after a season at Juven-tus which was less of an outright failure than is often now assumed. Rush had only scored seven league goals in his time at the Stadio Comunale, but that was enough to make him the leading league scorer for a Juve side that had a dismal season and it was seven goals more than the normally superlative Michael Laudrup had managed in his twenty-seven league appearances that campaign. To put Rush's supposedly meagre haul into further context, the main strike pairing that season for the champions Milan, a team preparing to dominate Europe, was Pietro Paolo Virdis and Ruud Gullit. Virdis scored eleven goals, Gullit nine. Even the league's leading scorer that season, Diego Maradona, a player emphatically on a plane of his own, could only manage fifteen and he was taking penal-ties for Napoli as well.

In fact, Juventus – with that era's restrictive two foreign-ers rule in mind – had decided to move Laudrup on and stick with Rush. But the Welsh striker was homesick and wanted to return to Britain. Liverpool offered to repay most of the money they had taken for him twelve months earlier, and the Italian club's plans were hastily rearranged.

But at what cost to Liverpool's all-conquering class of

1987–88? Dalglish's side stuttered through the first half of the new season, the team displaying some very strange form over the opening four-and-a-half months. By the end of 1988, they had won only two and drawn five of nine games at Anfield, scoring only nine times and just twenty-two in eighteen games overall. By contrast, the league pacesetters Arsenal, nine points ahead of Liverpool, had scored forty times.

Rush, signally, had not hit the ground running. Waylaid first by a virus, and then by injury, he didn't score his first post-Juve goal until October, in the League Cup against Walsall, and failed to find the net in the league until later that month, during an otherwise miserable defeat at Nottingham Forest. Although few would be foolhardy enough to question a manager who had won two titles in his first three seasons in charge, there was a nagging feeling that Dalglish had needlessly tampered with a winning recipe, that reputation was conquering reality. Aldridge was blessed with a more basic talent than Rush, yet had proved a relentless goalscorer since joining from Oxford in early 1987 and boasted a string to his bow that Rush was without: he could play the role of target man. Rush, by comparison, was more about pace and stealth, hardly a combination of talents worthy of criticism, but that skillset – or, more specifically, the lack of that offered by Aldridge – did nullify much of the threat posed by John Barnes and his crossing (although Rush's heading would improve dramatically, and very quickly).

Off-field shenanigans, meanwhile, had deprived the team of the steadying and artistic influence of Mølby. The Denmark international was over the limit when he was spotted by police driving on the wrong side of the road. In a panic, he jumped red lights, then drove straight at a police car to avoid capture. He was finally arrested the following day and sentenced to three months in jail, although he had served only six weeks when he was released early for good behaviour, whereupon he left prison in the boot of a car to avoid a gaggle of waiting journalists. (Mølby was later offered £8,000 by the *News of the*

World to restage this escape for the paper's photographers, but wisely thought better of the shoot.)

Liverpool would be extremely thankful that Mølby had kept his nose clean while incarcerated, for he was required to settle the nerves of an increasingly shaky team. Their title challenge looked as good as over as early as New Year's Day, when they were felled by an astonishing burst of activity from Russell Beardsmore at Old Trafford, the Manchester United youngster responding to John Barnes's seventieth-minute goal by setting up two and scoring a third within six minutes. United at that time were a mid-table shambles, priced at 16–1 for the title – and yet suddenly only a point behind the underachieving reigning champions. A day later, Arsenal had beaten Tottenham at Highbury to move twelve points clear of Liverpool.

But in the immediate wake of Beardsmore's blitz, Mølby had been reintroduced to first-team football, coming on for the last few minutes of the Old Trafford humiliation. Liverpool had won only four of the twelve games since he was jailed, the United defeat coming as the third in that spell. He would subsequently feature in only a handful of matches before succumbing to injury but his return proved essential to Liverpool regaining their equilibrium. After Old Trafford, they would lose only one more game all season.

A resolute 1–0 win at home to Aston Villa, Mølby's first full game on his return, spread calmness through the team from the back, Steve Nicol in particular taking advantage of a renewed licence to roam forward. It was Liverpool's first victory at Anfield since November. After an uneventful 3–0 win in the FA Cup at Carlisle United and a draw at Sheffield Wednesday, another crucial player returned: Bruce Grobbelaar, who had been out injured for four months, his stand-in Mike Hooper dependable enough but hardly inspiring. 'The Kop have missed him,' reported the *Guardian* as he came back against Southampton at Anfield, although most plaudits continued to be reserved for Mølby, who had set up a still-out-of-sorts Rush with 'the kind of through-ball that Dalglish used to feed him all the time'. Rush's goal, the second in a 2–0 victory, meant Liverpool had scored more than one goal in a home match for the first time since the beginning of November. That statistic, along with the upturn in Liverpool's fortunes, was welcome, although the wiser seers in the Kop were becoming slightly concerned at just how dependent the side – especially the defence – was becoming on the remaining members of the old guard. With Lawrenson gone and Hansen's knees in ribbons, it was clear something had to be done to address the problem before too long.

But there was no point worrying about that quite yet. Pragmatism was still the order of the day for Dalglish, who was continuing to reignite Liverpool's season by getting the defensive basics right first. Beardsley was left on the bench for an FA Cup game at Millwall, the manager concerned by the aerial threat posed by Teddy Sheringham and, especially, Tony Cascarino. Alex Watson was drafted in as an extra centre-back, allowing Mølby to sweep up around him and pull strings. Liverpool muzzled the Lions effortlessly, winning 2–0, prompting David Lacey in the *Guardian* to suggest the performance 'recalled many an occasion when the teams of Bill Shankly and later Bob Paisley would take a long hard look at a situation boiling with dark possibilities, reduce the temperature from the start, wait patiently for scoring chances, and take them cleanly when they arrived'. The reputation of Dalglish the manager today rests mainly on his team-building expertise in the late eighties at Liverpool then at Blackburn Rovers in the early 1990s; here is evidence of tactical prowess, too.

Confidence restored, Beardsley edged his way back into the team midway through a draw at Newcastle, whereafter Liverpool took things up a gear. Hull were dispatched 3–2 in the FA Cup, the first of eleven consecutive wins. Mølby hobbled off in the next game, a simple 2–0 victory over Charlton Athletic at Anfield at the beginning of March and wouldn't be seen again all season. No matter, because his job had been done and Beardsley was preparing to pick up the baton for the re-invigorated side. He starred and scored in consecutive wins over Middlesbrough (4–0) and Luton Town (5–0) and twice in the sixth round of the FA Cup against Brentford (4–0).

Barnes, who had been quiet for a while but was beginning to rekindle his old spark with Beardsley and Aldridge in the side rather than the injured Rush, was superb in a 3–1 win at Coventry. Liverpool were suddenly only six behind a worried Arsenal – a young team arguably running ahead of George Graham's rebuilding schedule – and had two games in hand.

Beardsley boosted his personal tally to six in six with another goal in a 2–1 win at Tottenham. Derby County and Norwich City were dispatched by single goals, and then on 8 April, the morning of the Grand National, Beardsley scored another two as Sheffield Wednesday were battered 5–1 at Anfield. Arsenal weren't quite giving it the full Devon Loch – they won that day too, at home to Everton, and were still top – but it was only their third victory in their previous nine games.

Liverpool made it nine league wins on the bounce with a 2–1 win at Millwall three days later, nudging Arsenal off the top on goal difference. Ten weeks earlier, Dalglish had pragmatically played five at the back to counter Millwall's aerial threat, leaving Ray Houghton alongside Beardsley on the bench. Now his team were flying forward from all angles; Barnes and Aldridge were the scorers, but it was another Beardsley masterclass, the player combining English football's trademark eighties bother and bustle with a subtle, wily, time-bending craft. Eleven wins on the spin, seventeen unbeaten since being overturned on New Year's Day: all the title momentum was with Liverpool, having put together one of *the* great title-chasing sequences, a run of results surely to be remembered through the ages.

Alas each result, and every point, would soon be forgotten, reduced to a bittersweet footnote. Having reached the top, Liverpool – both the football club and the city – would suffer a sickening plummet. Beardsley, the man of the moment, would find that his next notable act on a football pitch would become notoriously and heartbreakingly symbolic.

After four minutes of Liverpool's FA Cup semi-final against Nottingham Forest at Hillsborough, Beardsley clattered a spectacular shot off the crossbar. 'Naturally, at the time I was disappointed,' he said years later. 'In hindsight, it was good that I didn't score, because people outside the ground heard the roar when I hit the bar and tried even harder to get into the terraces. They were just excited; they didn't know what was happening at the front. If I had scored, the fans would've been even more excited and more people could have been crushed. But as soon as I hit the bar I turned round, and from even way up the pitch I could see there was trouble behind the goal. There were people climbing over the fences. We didn't have a clue what was going on.'

The facts are now, thankfully, a matter of public record and widely acknowledged: gross mismanagement of the crowd by the South Yorkshire Police, followed by a gross misrepresentation of events by police, government and a shockingly compliant media.

Dalglish and the players and staff of the football club reacted heroically to help a broken city grieve. The wise veteran sportswriter Peter Corrigan, in the *Observer*, noted that 'it was Dalglish, ironically much criticised for his lack of public relations acumen, who set the tone of sincere and respectful concern for those most affected and it was taken up by his players, who appeared at services, hospitals, funerals and among the crowds at Anfield – not regimented as a team, but spontaneously, in ones and twos, blending into the background of the mourning.

'And as they threw open the doors of Anfield as a shrine to comfort and unite the grieving, Liverpool found time to indicate unflinchingly what must be done to avoid future catastrophes. Since it involves adding the name of their

beloved Kop to the list of casualties, it was a profoundly difficult gesture to have to make.'

It would be a further five years before the grand old terrace was demolished to make way for seats, but arguably
the Kop's last great stand – and there's a case for it being its
greatest ever – came just over a month after the disaster. Liverpool resumed the business of football eighteen days after
Hillsborough, aptly, with a goalless draw in a league fixture at
Goodison. Nottingham Forest were overcome in the replayed
FA Cup semi at Old Trafford and Everton were beaten in an
emotional final at Wembley. In between the cup ties, Liverpool won league matches against Forest, Wimbledon and QPR,
then trounced West Ham 5–1 at Anfield in their penultimate
fixture. With Arsenal taking a single point from their final
two home games against Derby and Wimbledon, the title –
and the Double – was within Liverpool's grasp. They would be
champions even if they lost their final home fixture against
Arsenal by one goal. Of course, they famously lost it by two,
Liverpool's front line, physically and emotionally shattered,
unable to work their way through Arsenal's extra centre-back,
Michael Thomas dealing the decisive blow in slow motion as
the sands of time ran out on the season.

Heartbroken in more ways than one, the Kop warmly ap-
plauded and cheered their conquerors, staying late into the
evening to watch Tony Adams joyously lift the trophy, a gesture to the eternal credit of Liverpool's support. Down in the
tunnel, Dalglish paid tribute to his team in a statesmanlike
fashion nothing short of astonishing, given all that had gone
before. 'Of course we are all proud of them,' he said. 'But at the
end of the day, Arsenal deserved it.'

The Herculean efforts of comforting the city had yet to take
their toll on Dalglish and in the summer the manager addressed the side's main problem – the rickety, superannuated
defence – by snatching the Fiorentina defender Glenn Hysén
from under the nose of the Manchester United boss Alex

Ferguson, who had been 'confident that Hysén would sign' in early July. A battle won rather than the war – United would re-direct their attention towards an altogether more dependable target in Middlesbrough's Gary Pallister – but at least Liver-pool would get a few months of decent form from the Sweden international before anxiety set in. Liverpool might have been better going after Pallister as well, as although Hansen would feature for most of the 1989–90 season, he was clearly run-ning out of time. Dalglish elected to keep money in the bank, although that didn't stop him making a late, cheeky but ul-timately unsuccessful attempt to steal the Barcelona striker (and erstwhile Evertonian) Gary Lineker from the grasp of Tottenham.

The difficulties Dalglish had been facing in keeping Liv-erpool at the summit were amply illustrated by the new champions Arsenal, who started the new season by getting hammered 4–1 at Manchester United – seemingly inspired by the prospect of being taken over by Michael Knighton, who juggled the ball on the pitch before kick-off – and then by the early leaders Coventry City who having reached the top for the first time in their 106-year history, could only stay there for forty-four seconds, the time it took for Teddy Sheringham to set Millwall on their way to victory in City's next game.

Liverpool served early notice with their biggest-ever league victory, a 9–0 win over Crystal Palace in which eight mem-bers of their team scored, a Football League record. One of the goalscorers was Aldridge, brought on in an uncharacteristic show of sentimentality from the Anfield dugout to convert a penalty in what would be his final game before being prema-turely sold to Real Sociedad to make way for Rush. Revenge, meanwhile, was dished up to Arsenal at Anfield in a 2–1 win, McMahon driving home from twenty-five yards and Barnes, to the left of the D, sending an out-curler into the top-right corner, an exquisite free-kick which went a little way to repay-ing the careless loss of possession which had led to Michael Thomas's title-winning goal, six months to the day earlier.

ROME 1984 Phil Neal scores the opening goal (PA).

Ian Rush leaps above Ubaldo Righetti to head the ball (Getty).

ROME 1984: *continued.* Bruce Grobbleaar catches a cross, watched by Mark Lawrenson and Phil Neal.

Alan Kennedy fires home the winning penalty past Franco Tancredi (both PA)

LIVERPOOL 1988 *Clockwise from top left* Peter Beardsley, John Barnes and Ray Houghton, and Bruce Grobbelaar joking with fans (all Getty).

LIVERPOOL 1991
Above left Kenny Dalglish (Action Images).

Above right Gary Ablett and Graeme Sharp battle for the ball (PA).

Left Ian Rush celebrates his goal with Peter Beardsley (PA).

ROME 2001 Nick Barmby pulls away from Damiano Tommasi.

Robbie Fowler takes on Damiano Tommasi and Walter Samuel (both Getty).

ROME 2001: *continued.* Michael Owen skips Damiano Tommasi's tackle (Getty).

Gérard Houllier leaves the Stadio Olympico with Michael Owen (PA).

ISTANBUL 2005 *Above* Jerzy Dudek makes a brilliant save from Andriy Shevchenko in the final minute of extra time (Getty).

Left Dietmar Hamann powers forward (Getty).

Below Rafael Benítez (AFP/Getty).

ISTANBUL 2005: *continued*. Steven Gerrard begins the comeback and heads the first goal (Bob Thomas/Getty).

Vladimír Šmicer scores during the subsequent penalty shootout (PA).

There was a third signature match of their title-winning campaign: a 4–0 win at Charlton Athletic, during which the new signing Ronny Rosenthal scored a perfect hat-trick: right foot, left foot and header, the run of goals unbroken by any other scorer. The Israel international, on loan from Anderlecht, scored eight times in his eight late-season appearances, and earned himself a permanent move (at twice the cost to the club that had initially been agreed). Another successful season, by most measures.

However, for the third year in a row, the result that would come to define their season to most fans, and certainly most outside observers, was an abject defeat in a crunch fixture. First came the Wimbledon Cup final – which neutrals are always likely to cite ahead of the Forest exhibition – then the Michael Thomas smash-and-grab and then Crystal Palace. As well as the nine-goal shellacking, newly promoted Palace had been ruthlessly dispatched 2 0 in the reverse league fixture at Selhurst Park. The two were drawn together in the last four of the Cup, with the *Guardian* claiming that a Palace win would 'be the biggest shock in an FA Cup semi-final since 1949 when Leicester City, struggling to stay in the Second Division, defeated Portsmouth, who were on their way to the championship and a possible Double, by 3–1 at Highbury'.

The comparison was slightly hyperbolic: Palace were on their way to fairly comfortably consolidating their new top-flight status, and since their battering at Anfield had signed the dependable central defender Andy Thorn from Newcastle, plus a £1.65m goalkeeper in Nigel Martyn. Even so, Liverpool were hot favourites and should have won the tie easily enough, but a backline containing a reticent Hysén and a fading Hansen bent almost at every corner or free-kick, and the South London side made it to Wembley with a 4–3 win after extra-time. Liverpool's defence was becoming so vulnerable that even a free-scoring front line of Rush, Beardsley and Barnes was no longer enough to guarantee victory. As if to emphasise Liverpool's decline, the Palace manager Steve Coppell

– perhaps mindful that Dalglish, after the 9–0, had on request helped the Palace manager lift his recently promoted players by sending a letter insisting that 'the scoreline didn't reflect your performance' – went out to bat for them in the post-match press conference. 'I don't think Liverpool are weak at set pieces,' he said, 'but teams know that these are the only occasions when they can be sure of getting in crosses with five or six men in the box.'

Few were buying it. Dalglish certainly wasn't; he'd simply been of the opinion that his team had defended appallingly. The bottom line was that Liverpool had been embarrassed in front of a huge lunchtime TV audience. A nation wondered whether English football's dominant club might finally be, almost unthinkably after fifteen years, showing signs of terminal decline. The following season served up ultimate proof.

When he made the step-up from player to manager in the summer of 1985, Dalglish had promised his wife Marina that he would take the job for 'probably … only five years'. That time had elapsed, although those five years must have seemed far longer. Physically and mentally spent by the summer of 1990, Dalglish 'wanted a break, there and then'. But despite having gone way beyond the call of duty in his response to Hillsborough, he still felt he owed the club a debt. 'Liverpool had been so good to me and my family,' he would reflect later. 'I felt obliged to carry on.'

A selfless act, especially given Liverpool's refusal to meet Dalglish's request for shares in lieu of cash payment for his services. Dalglish was already perhaps unconsciously recalibrating his relationship with the club. The shares, he reasoned, 'would give me some sort of continued attachment to Liverpool if I felt forced to leave. I felt that if I couldn't sustain the job and had to resign, at least I would have some shares in the club I love, some permanent connection.' Dalglish explicitly told the board that, with enough on his plate as manager anyway, he wanted no say in running the club away from the football side. However, Liverpool claimed, rather dubiously, that there were simply no shares available. Dalglish could have been forgiven for feeling the sort of frustration Shankly had in 1974. Not only did the Liverpool board have form for keeping their managerial talent at arm's length but their counterparts at Dalglish's *alma mater*, Celtic, had shamefully refused his mentor Jock Stein a place on the board, infamously offering their European Cup-winning manager an insulting role at the helm of the club's pools operation. The maximum wage and retain-and-transfer system might have been abolished in the early 1960s, but the subservience of British football's top talents lasted much longer.

Already feeling the strain, Dalglish later admitted to becoming irritable at home, requiring a couple of glasses of wine to relax and coming out in red blotches which necessitated the constant attention of the club doctor. During the summer, absent-mindedly pottering in his garden, he was nearly killed by a badly wired garden strimmer. But in front of the curtain, all was well. Liverpool started the 1990–91 season at a ferocious pace. They won twelve and drew one of their first thirteen games to establish an eight-point lead over Arsenal, with Tottenham four points further back in third.

That run included a comprehensive 3–1 win at Spurs, Mølby pulling the strings with Barcelona representatives in the stands considering signing him as a replacement for the injured Ronald Koeman, as well as a 3–2 win at Everton and a 4–0 rout of Manchester United at Anfield, an in-form Peter Beardsley the star of both, scoring a hat-trick against United. The United victory was Liverpool's biggest in the fixture since a 5–0 win at Anfield in 1925, some achievement as United were by then beginning to display ominous signs of resurgence under Alex Ferguson. 'It will take something cataclysmic to knock Liverpool off the top,' suggested Cynthia Bateman in the *Guardian*.

It took something cataclysmic all right. Liverpool's first defeat of the season came at the end of October, United paying back Dalglish's side at Old Trafford in the League Cup with a comprehensive 3–1 win. Then, in the league, Manchester City came to town and planted further seeds of doubt: three ex-Evertonians – Peter Reid, Neil Pointon and Adrian Heath – promised to, in the words of Reid, 'get at Liverpool up front and in their midfield'. City were much the better side in a 2–2 draw, Liverpool's first goal on 82 minutes by Rush constituting only their second shot of the match. 'You should be happy leaving Anfield with a point,' said Reid, 'but we are disappointed, I think we deserved three.' Dalglish did not disagree: 'They deserved what they got. We can consider ourselves fortunate to have got even a point.'

Dalglish's reaction was to retreat into his shell, picking a ludicrously defensive team for the next match, at Highbury, a game that had the feel of a title-decider despite being played in December. Liverpool stood six clear of George Graham's team, who had been docked a couple of points by the FA after a twenty-one-man brawl at Old Trafford, and were coming straight off the back of a humiliating 6–2 home loss at the hands of a Lee Sharpe-inspired Manchester United in the League Cup. Arsenal were down and it seemed an opportunity to finish off their title aspirations. But in the wake of the debacle at home to City, Dalglish immediately relinquished the initiative, replacing Ray Houghton, Beardsley and McMahon with Nicol, Mølby and Barry Venison. The line-up contained six defenders. Beardsley was not even on the bench. Arsenal went two up early in the second half and, with Rush isolated up front and Barnes stranded on the left, Liverpool had no chance of turning the match round and ended up losing 3–0.

Their aura had been punctured. On the final Sunday of the calendar year, Liverpool went to Crystal Palace, by then supremely confident at their new level, fourth in the table at the halfway mark and only six points behind their visitors. Dalglish again opted for caution, deploying Mølby as sweeper alongside Gillespie and Hysén. It did them little good: Mark

Bright won the majority of aerial battles, Ian Wright's pace was a menace and Palace won 1–0.

Liverpool's defence – exposed with Hansen gone – was beginning to look its age. The team would bounce back against high-flying Leeds on New Year's Day but it would be one of only two league wins between then and March, by which time Jimmy Carter and David Speedie had been signed and Barnes and Beardsley were being linked with moves to Marseille and Celtic respectively. The Speedie signing, especially, provoked consternation, partly because he was thirty-one and partly because he just didn't seem good enough (and if Liverpool needed a striker, why sell Aldridge?). It was, Derek Hodgson wrote in the *Independent*, 'a stroke-of-midnight move that thwarted Everton and Aston Villa but one that smacked of panic and poor decision making, the act of a man who senses the iron dice of destiny were rolling against him'. Speedie ended up playing just twelve league games. By the March, Arsenal had knocked Liverpool off of their perch – for all Alex Ferguson may lay claim to that feat, George Graham got there first – and Dalglish had smacked the football world off its axis.

Liverpool's 3–1 win in the Merseyside derby at Anfield on 9 February was only their second league victory of 1991. They were still unbeaten but had stuttered in the league with three draws on the bounce (at Aston Villa and Manchester United and at home to Wimbledon), although they still led the table as Arsenal had been beaten at Chelsea in what would turn out to be their only defeat of the campaign.

The Reds were not much more convincing in the FA Cup. Seconds from defeat in the third round at Second Division Blackburn Rovers, they were saved by a moment of panic from Rovers's young left-back Mark Atkins, who poked an equaliser for Liverpool past his own keeper during an eminently containable penalty-box brouhaha. On the BBC, the ever-dependable Jimmy Hill tacked a surreal coda onto the game by blaming Blackburn's failure to close out the win on an unfortunate ball-girl who had quickly shuttled the ball back into the arms of Liverpool before they took the desperate last throw-in that led to Atkins's own goal.

Having made a meal of dispatching Rovers via a replay, Liverpool then struggled past Brighton and Hove Albion, also of the second tier, in the fourth round. First they gave away a two-goal lead at Anfield, then fell behind during extra-time in the replay at the Goldstone Ground, before Beardsley – only just returned from an eight-match absence with an ankle problem – came off the bench to be the catalyst for another escape act.

On, then, to the fifth round, and the cataclysm which the *Guardian* had a few months earlier identified as a prerequisite for any Liverpudlian decline. Liverpool would face Everton at Anfield, although first up, directly before it in a quirk of the fixture list, came the very same fixture in the league. Everton by this time were a shadow of the side they had been in the mid-eighties, when Howard Kendall had managed the club to two league titles, an FA Cup and the European Cup-Winners' Cup before leaving in the summer of 1987 on an ill-fated mission to further himself in Bilbao. Kendall's successor, his assistant Colin Harvey, went on an underwhelming shopping spree – Tony Cottee, Pat Nevin, Peter Beagrie and Stuart McCall were promising talents, but off the shelf were not at the level of the recently departed Gary Lineker, Trevor Steven or Peter Reid – and was eventually asked to step back in line behind Kendall, who returned in the autumn of 1990. Kendall would fail to rescale the heights of his first period in charge – Everton's few remaining big names, Neville Southall, Kevin Ratcliffe, Graeme Sharp and Kevin Sheedy, were all ageing and past their best – but he did at least lift Everton out of the relegation bother he found them in on his return. When his team travelled to Anfield in the league, they might have been twenty-one points adrift of their neighbours, but they were at least safely ensconced in mid-table, a first relegation since 1951 no longer a threat.

Dalglish's team for that league encounter was far from popular with fans. Beardsley was on the bench, standing down for
the new signing Speedie (who had scored on his debut for the
club in the draw at Old Trafford). Dalglish's lack of faith in
Beardsley was a mystifying niggle throughout the later days
of his reign, something even the loyal Barnes questioned in
the *Mirror*. The manager would be vindicated on that occasion, with Speedie scoring a quickfire double in the second
half to ease Liverpool to a 3–1 win. In the midfield, Mølby had
little problem dealing with Mike Milligan and a gulf in class
between the two sides was apparent despite Dalglish's idiosyncratic selection. The victory came at a cost, however, with
Ronnie Whelan carted off with a cracked shin. He would play
no further part in the campaign. (Whelan, incidentally, was
replaced by Jimmy Carter, the crowd having bayed for Beardsley, who had to make do with an eight-minute cameo at the
end of the game.) Everton, desperate to salvage some succour
with the following week's FA Cup tie in mind, looked to the
busy Nevin's troublesome contribution and the fact that Liverpool's back-line continued to buckle alarmingly, Graeme
Sharp at one point winning a totally unchallenged header in
the Liverpool area which forced Steve Nicol to hack off the
line.

Everton did indeed take heart and should have won the FA
Cup tie the following weekend. Pre-empting the robust style of
Joe Royle's Dogs of War by several years, they lined up with an
extra man in defence, Martin Keown coming in to supplement
Dave Watson and Kevin Ratcliffe, with Ray Atteveld deployed
to quell Barnes. Within fifteen high-octane minutes, McMahon
came off worse after making a two-footed lunge towards John
Ebbrell and departed with damaged tendons in his knee, like
Whelan before him out for the season. 'Ebbrell's shinpad has
gone to hospital for treatment,' deadpanned Kendall after the
game. Thereafter Liverpool looked the most likely to concede,
Sharp once again causing all manner of bother under the
high ball, Nevin troubling a creaking back-line to the point

at which Gary Ablett tripped up the Scottish winger as he ghosted past him in the area. Ridiculously, Nevin was booked for diving – an incident that prompted a wag to drape a red scarf around the referee Neil Midgeley's neck at the pre-match photos before the replay. Grobbelaar was later forced into a double save from Sharp and Nevin. Liverpool, having again started with Speedie, offered little. Beardsley came on for the striker after seventy minutes to huge cheers, then shaved the post. Anfield's unease was palpable and the crowd weren't the only ones suddenly questioning Dalglish's ability to make the big calls.

Forty-eight hours after the FA Cup tie at Anfield, the night before the replay at Goodison, Kenny Dalglish lay on his hotel bed, staring at the ceiling and made the biggest call of all. In his first four years as manager of Liverpool, he had always prided himself on his firm decision-making, but as everything closed in on him, he was starting to second-guess himself. Falling back on old principles, he came down on one side of a problem that had been bugging him and having reached a conclusion, decided to stick with it.

'I had to get out,' he wrote in his autobiography. 'The alternative was going mad. I promised myself that I would inform [the Liverpool chairman] Noel White and [the chief executive] Peter Robinson of my decision at our usual meeting the following morning. Irrespective of the outcome against Liverpool's oldest rivals, I was going to tell them that I was resigning. If we had won 4–0 I would still have resigned the next day. I could either keep my job or my sanity. I had to go.'

Both managers made changes for the replay at a thunderous Goodison for a match which had the air, despite the paths of the two sides having diverged since Merseyside's mid-eighties pomp, of a real clash of giants. Dalglish, certain that Everton would be as aggressive as ever, but missing the combative Mc-Mahon, picked the tough-tackling David Burrows in midfield to add bite. It was a logical choice – the former West Bromwich

Albion full-back had marked Paul Gascoigne out of the game at Spurs earlier in the season – and he would clean out Nevin soon enough, causing much Evertonian ire and in one moment justifying his selection. More to the point, though, was the return of Beardsley for Speedie. As calls go, this would prove a pretty good one, showing that even when sinking, Dalglish was still a smart tactician.

As for the home side, Kevin Sheedy was missing through injury, Andy Hinchcliffe coming in, though Kendall's master gambit was to throw Mike Newell up alongside Sharp, a blatant attempt to unsettle Liverpool in the air and at set pieces. The harum-scarum nonsense that was to follow – a match which would immediately be crowned Game of the Decade, a bold claim fewer than fourteen months into the 1990s – has subsequently been painted as a typically robust side, schooled in the no nonsense English style, tenderising a shower of brittle artisans who had pretensions to a more expansive continental approach. This is to a large extent true, with Everton unabashed in testing Liverpool under high balls, while Dalglish's side attempted on the whole to keep play moving on the floor, in pretty triangles if at all possible (although on a ploughed pitch and in the midst of a raging storm, this was at times easier said than done). But Dalglish's side were not afraid to mix it themselves, possession very much a secondary consideration to pressing, winning the ball back and getting forward at pace, the match being played at *prestissimo* tempo to the overall detriment of quality. Just as the fifties, in cultural terms, lasted in reality long into the sixties, and what is commonly thought of as the sixties didn't happen across most of the country until well into the seventies, the more excitable aspects of British football in the 1980s took a bit longer to die out than we now care to remember.

The teams wasted no time taking swings at each other. Everton flew out of the traps, John Ebbrell cutting in from the right within the first couple of minutes and dragging a shot across the face of the goal as Nevin lurked with intent. Two minutes later, Liverpool, kicking towards the Gwladys Street End with the iconic church of St Luke's poking its nose in at the corner, went close themselves through the recalled Beardsley, who sent a low shot buzzing goalwards after gliding in from the left. Southall parried, then made a point-blank second save from Rush, six yards out.

Liverpool began to take a semblance of early control, Steve Staunton nearly finding Nicol at the far post with a long cross from the left; Mølby sending a dangerous free-kick in from the same wing which forced Ratcliffe to head clear from deep; the clearly pent-up Beardsley nearly opening Everton up down the left with a cheeky backheel; Barnes releasing Staunton along the same flank for a leggy run and shot. Liverpool had clearly targeted Atteveld, who was already looking out of his depth. 'I didn't play in the second replay,' the Dutch right-back acknowledged, 'because I was quite awful.'

On ten minutes, Burrows made his intervention on Nevin, scissoring the winger's standing leg. Here, Liverpool's luck was in: the challenge could easily have resulted in serious injury, yet the young full-back-cum-midfielder wasn't even booked. Nevin stayed down for lengthy treatment. 'I don't think it went unnoticed in the Liverpool camp how well Nevin played on Sunday,' noted the co-commentator Andy Gray drily, the match going out live to a minuscule audience on The Sports Channel, part of the five-channel package offered by Sky's doomed precursor, British Satellite Broadcasting.

(This game is arguably one of only three things anyone in Britain remembers BSB for, the other two being the company's tasteful Squarial satellite dishes, half the size of Sky's huge white plastic bowls, and the company's not-so-tasteful sitcom *Heil Honey, I'm Home!*, a parody of *I Love Lucy* which detailed the carefree capers of Adolf Hitler and Eva Braun, and the easy-going Jewish couple who lived next door. It was cancelled after the airing of its first episode, which had featured Neville Chamberlain popping round for a drinks do.)

Everton, establishing the back-and-forth nature of the

contest pretty much from the start, responded by teasing several high balls into the Liverpool area for Sharp and Newell
to attack. On eleven minutes, the latter was barged to the
turf in the box by Hysén as the two came together; it would
have been a soft decision but penalties have been given for far
less. Even Atteveld, lumbering upfield along the inside-right
channel, was proving a nuisance, simply by loitering under
hanging balls. The burst of pressure nearly broke Liverpool's
dam, Sharp heading down at the right-hand post for Ebbrell,
who dragged another shot wide left of the target. Less than a
quarter of an hour had been played and it was goalless, but it
could quite easily have been two apiece.

The game settled into a strange sort of pattern, each team
occasionally breaking out of a high-speed pressing maelstrom
to repeat their pre-planned party pieces. Liverpool concen-
trated the bulk of their efforts down the left, Barnes sticking
tight to the touchline, Beardsley buzzing around in the hole,
Staunton quick to come upfield and join them wherever possible on the overlap. Everton meanwhile kept posing Liverpool
problems with the long ball, a tactic that proved in practice
slightly less agricultural than it sounds in theory: these were
long high passes delivered with precision, Sharp and Newell
winning the majority of them, Nevin, Ebbrell and McDonald
picking up the bulk of second-phase ball in midfield. If anything, Everton began to take the upper hand, with Venison,
Hysén, Grobbelaar and Staunton all taking turns to flap under
Everton's tactical bombardment.

The centre of the field was becoming an almighty skirmish,
the football equivalent of a cartoon cloud with fists and boots
sticking out of it. Liverpool, gradually, worked out that there
might be benefits in spreading the play. First Nicol looked to
break down the right. Barnes then sashayed down the left,
reaching the byline, before over-elaborating to concede possession with teammates screaming in the middle. Beardsley,
having dropped deeper to probe between the lines, nearly
sprang Rush clear with a through pass only for the striker to

mistime his run. Another measured Beardsley ball was denied the rampaging Nicol by a magnificent tackle from Andy Hinchcliffe. Barnes skated along the byline from the left and fired a ball to the near post, where Rush saw his cute flick blocked, then billowed the side netting after taking a high ball down athletically (still an adjective worthy of note in 1991) and looking for the bottom-left corner.

Slowly Liverpool had established an ascendancy and they took the lead after thirty-three minutes. Yet they did so as a result of one of Everton's increasingly rare excursions into enemy territory: as numerous teams had found over the preceding three decades, you attacked Liverpool at your peril. While Liverpool had spent the previous ten to fifteen minutes working the channels at the other end, Everton were still minded to test the visitors under the high ball whenever the opportunity arose. On the half-hour, Nevin took advantage of another Sharp victory in the air by sending a low rasper towards the bottom corner from the right of the D. Grobbelaar was behind it all the way, and held on well, but it was a decent effort from the inventive Nevin and more evidence of the Liverpool defence's flakiness under any sort of strongarm pressure.

Three minutes later, emboldened, Everton sent a free-kick into the Liverpool area from the right. Burrows struggled to head clear and Hinchcliffe returned the ball to Newell on the edge of the box. For once, though, the Everton striker hesitated, allowing Staunton to jump in and rake clear with a long ball down the left. Ratcliffe made it across to the ball before Rush but, in attempting to clip the ball past the stampeding striker, only succeeded in clanking it straight into his path. Rush entered the area, shimmied, dropped a shoulder to put Southall on the ground and sent the ball whistling into the heart of the goal. Hinchcliffe, chasing back, acrobatically hooked the ball off the line, but Beardsley was standing on the penalty spot to skelp home into the unguarded net. It was his first goal since 12 November, vindication for those who had been pleading with Dalglish to put him straight back into the team ever since his return from injury.

On the touchline, as Liverpool's gleeful fans responded by detailing in song their travel plans for May, Dalglish cut a relaxed figure. And yet within a minute of the restart, he was out from the dugout to hoof the ball back into play in a fit of anger, a disproportionate response to a wholly insignificant skirmish in the middle of the park. That the red mist came down seemed all the stranger as Liverpool played out the rest of the half in almost total control, the wind suddenly out of Everton's sails, their heads momentarily gone. 'Liverpool, uncharacteristically diffident on their own ground last Sunday, were momentarily swaggering and in complete control,' wrote Stuart Jones in *The Times*.

Atteveld overhit a backpass that nearly beat Southall as he rushed out of his area to collect; the keeper was forced to dangle out his right leg to block and clear. Nicol whipped a cross in from the right that Venison flicked on to Barnes, who smacked the ball straight at Southall from close range. (He had been flagged offside, relieving his embarrassment, although Ebbrell had been playing him on.) Atteveld, repeatedly giving the ball away to the crowd's frustration, allowed Barnes another run down the left. Nicol, with Liverpool looking to hug the touchlines and stretch the play, nearly made progress again down the other flank. Liverpool reached the interval in the lead, and in control, though hardly playing well. Dalglish had watched the half peter out with his arm insouciantly draped over the roof of the dugout, a misleading picture of tranquillity.

He wore a more anxious expression at the beginning of the second half, perhaps as a result of Kendall having sent on McCall to replace Atteveld, whose right-back role was taken by the more dependable McDonald. Within two minutes of the restart, a newly energised Everton had levelled, Sharp rising over the static Ablett and Staunton to meet a left-wing cross and head through Grobbelaar's flailing hands for his sixth goal in a Merseyside derby. Liverpool responded immediately, Mølby sending in a rising drive from twenty-five yards that Southall did well to palm away, then looking to release Rush with a couple of long balls of their own, their artistic equilibrium having been shaken by Sharp's goal.

The response may have been brave at the front, but the defence was repeatedly failing: Everton, coming straight back at Liverpool, went close twice within a minute, first as Nevin was set one-on-one with Grobbelaar, after Hysén and Ablett had performed a silent-movie skit on the edge of the area, but lifted over the bar, and then as Venison inexplicably ducked under a right-wing cross, deflecting it towards Newell whose first-time volley fizzed just wide. McCall, meanwhile, was at the heart of everything, his energy and commitment highlighting the absence of Whelan and especially McMahon in the Liverpool engine room.

On BSB, Andy Gray suggested that 'there's as much action on the benches as on the pitch,' though in truth he appeared to be projecting the heady tumult in the stands onto the dugouts. Dalglish in particular was practically motionless. Everton's deployment of McCall in the middle was stifling Mølby, who had dominated the game during the latter stages of the first half. McDonald, meanwhile, was offering Everton a bit of much-needed width down the right, from where his crosses troubled Liverpool.

Dalglish's players evidently attempted to mix it up themselves, Beardsley and Barnes exchanging roles, the former dropping to left midfield, the latter pushing up alongside Rush. It was a late-era example of the fluid game that Liverpool had practised for years and which Barnes explained to Pete Davies in *All Played Out*. 'I can play for Liverpool,' he said, 'and it's like the continentals – they'll have someone in that zone, but not necessarily the same person. So Alan Hansen can go past me, and I'll take his position.'

With England's 1990 World Cup squad, he said, it was different: 'But here, if Chris [Waddle] comes off the line, or I come off the line, and no one goes into that position, if the full-back doesn't come, then the marker's free. With the sweeper [system], the full-back can go, and the sweeper can cover; or the marker can cover and the sweeper can mark – you're not caught short anywhere. In England, they place too much importance on position.' *All Played Out* also includes an inadvertently prescient observation from the England manager Bobby Robson. As Davies pressed him on whether 4–4–2 had had its day, Robson spoke 'with his mouth tight and angry': 'Is Liverpool Football Club outdated?' he asked. 'In Europe next season, how would they play? Some clever concoction? When people talk to me [and say] it's outdated – are they talking about Liverpool?' They probably weren't but, unthinkably, if they had been they would have been right.

Beardsley – and indeed the whole Liverpool team – would soon illustrate the importance of the fluidity that Barnes had described. Having made little headway in Barnes's position, he took himself across to the other wing. Liverpool, with sixty-nine minutes played, had just fashioned their first real chance of the half, Barnes meeting a long ball down the inside-left channel and heading inside to Rush, who nearly recreated the finish of his first goal in the 1989 FA Cup final, turning and steering his shot towards the bottom-right corner, only for Keown's telescopic leg to deflect the effort away. Then Beardsley sprang into life with a goal that was a masterclass in patience and the importance of possession.

Burrows – suddenly cast in the role of touchline-hugging winger – had found himself in space on the right near the Everton area, but hesitated and opted to turn back up the flank until a pass could be picked. He eventually shuttled the ball to Mølby who, retreating towards the halfway line, suddenly spun and played a delicious reverse ball back down the flank to Nicol. Facing away from goal and under pressure from behind, Nicol nudged the ball towards the right-hand touchline, where Burrows had remained since finding Mølby. Burrows clipped a first-time ball inside for the wandering

Beardsley who, running from a deep position along the inside-right channel, dropped a shoulder, dragged the ball to the left past Keown, and launched a rising shot into the top-left corner.

It was an exquisite goal, and one which should by rights have been a game-changer. Rush's chance apart, Everton had been enjoying the better of the ten minutes leading up to Beardsley's strike, Newell and Sharp repeatedly winning their aerial battles, Ebbrell snatching at a lovely chance from twelve yards created by a majestic Sharp knock-down. But Liverpool were almost immediately undone by their defensive uncertainties. Two minutes later, as the rain continued to batter down, the pitch cutting up, Southall launched a long kick downfield. Newell beat Ablett to the first ball, heading on towards the D. There should have been no trouble for Liverpool: Hysén had the situation covered patrolling the Everton inside-right channel ahead of Sharp, Nicol was coming in from the other side and Grobbelaar had raced off his line, in position either to gather or hack clear should an emergency arise. But Hysén slipped, Nicol stuck out a leg in a panic and nudged the ball past the onrushing keeper; Sharp had a head start on everyone to chase after the loose ball and bundle it into the goal. As the home crowd staged a minor pitch invasion, Dalglish was pictured staring into the middle distance, pensive, his arm on his knee, his hand supporting his chin.

Liverpool's frustrations momentarily got the better of them, a wild Mølby hoof at a breakdown in play nearly clattering into McDonald's head and McDonald fluffing a half-decent chance to get a shot away in the Liverpool area not long after. But Barnes released the pressure with a run down the left, forcing a corner with a cross-cum-shot that was palmed out by Southall. The corner was worked out to Mølby on the right-hand edge of the area, the Dane swung a languid leg to curl a cross right onto Rush's eyebrows and the striker guided Liverpool's third into the top-left corner. It was his twenty-fourth goal in twenty-eight games against Everton and his thirty-fourth

in the FA Cup. (He had one more to come in Merseyside derbies and another five in the FA Cup altogether, his next in
the 1992 final.) In the Liverpool dugout, Dalglish stood agape,
almost gasping for air, now nothing more than an exhilarated
spectator.

Given the parlous state of Liverpool's back-line, it would be
ludicrous to argue that they should have closed the game out
from their third winning position of the game. But apart from
one incident in which Staunton, attempting to clear an Everton corner, nearly flicked into his own net at the near post,
Grobbelaar being forced into desperate action to save the defender's embarrassment, it did appear that Liverpool finally
had the situation in hand. For the majority of the ten minutes
after their third goal, Liverpool managed to control the game
in a manner they had only achieved in the final minutes of
the first half. Rush sent Burrows scampering into acres down
the inside left, but the young midfielder, a defender at heart,
couldn't get a shot away. Beardsley, ever flitting around, sent
a weak effort towards the bottom left corner after cutting in
from the left wing, then reached the byline on the left only
for the opportunity to be lost through lack of support. Staunton indulged himself with a couple of quickfire hoofs from
the edge of the box, to no avail. Barnes hit a low fizzing ball
through the six-yard area from the left, Ratcliffe adroitly
managing to avoid contact and the very real danger of divert-
ing the ball into his own net. There was even a rare moment
of quality at the back, Hinchcliffe having burned down the
left past Nicol and pulled a low centre into the Liverpool area:
Mølby stepped in to intercept, then swanned past the sliding
McCall and out of the danger zone with the pomp and arrogance of a Beckenbauer.

But a third equaliser awaited. With four minutes to go, Tony
Cottee replaced Nevin, whose influence on the game had been
marginal, certainly compared to his performance at Anfield.
Two minutes later, he was cavorting in front of the Gwladys
Street End.

McDonald, to the right of the centre circle, helped the ball forward. Via a deflection, it reached McCall, facing back up-field, just to the left of the D. McCall instantly turned the ball on down the middle and into the area behind Ablett, stationed far too deep and playing Cottee onside. The substitute raced past him and flicked a shot into the bottom-left corner. Dalglish, hand to mouth, looked less stunned than numb. There was no reaction at all.

With just a couple of minutes remaining, there was only time for McDonald to plant his studs on Barnes's back – other than Burrows's early reducer on Nevin, the only rash challenge of an intense match that had been played in a highly sporting fashion – and for Rush to spin for a second time in attempted homage to his first 1989 FA Cup final goal; it finished 3–3.

Everton, with three strikers on the field, kept attacking and almost took the lead early in extra-time. McCall hit a looping crossfield ball into the Liverpool box from deep on the right. Newell beat Nicol to the header, guiding the ball down into a gap eight yards in front of goal. Cottee, rushing in, ballooned a first-time shot miles over the bar. Not the easiest of chances – the ball had fallen just behind the ideal spot for Cottee to strike it – but nevertheless good enough to go down as a flagrant miss, thirty-one seconds into the half.

It was not a harbinger for the rest of the first period of extra-time. Liverpool were simply dominant, Barnes finally exerting a significant influence. Four minutes in, he glided off the left flank, dismissing McDonald, before firing a low ball towards the near post. Southall gathered well with Rush lurking. Another run two minutes later forced Keown to slash behind for a corner, from which the ball was worked to Mølby on the left edge of the area. Mølby – 'a colossus of composure and finesse in his role as midfield leader in the absence of McMahon and Whelan', according to Stuart Jones – lifted the ball into the middle of the box, without pace, where Rush somehow generated the power to send a dangerous header towards the bottom-left corner. Southall turned the effort away with an outstanding reaction save that recalled Gordon Banks in Mexico in 1970.

The constant threat of Barnes on the left afforded Staunton some space to swing in a cross for Venison (who had switched positions with Nicol, another example of Liverpool's ability to interchange). The former Sunderland full-back planted a header towards the bottom-right corner, Southall's save again echoing Banks. The resulting corner was dispatched upfield by Everton without too much fuss, but there wasn't a blue shirt outside the home side's final third, a measure of how the game had turned into attack versus defence.

Liverpool were totally in control, Everton were hardly getting a touch and Barnes eventually rewarded the away side for their excellence since the restart with his side's fourth on 102 minutes. Bombing down the left, he cut inside only to be illegally checked by McDonald. From the resulting tapped free-kick, Barnes cut inside, smoothly drifted past Ebbrell, and with his right foot curled a wonderful shot into the top-right corner from the left edge of the box. He leapt towards Mølby and was held aloft in a bear hug, one of the iconic Barnes celebrations. Just reward for a relentless period of wing-play, it was one of the great FA Cup goals, hit with his weaker foot over a crowded penalty box and into the far corner; Southall – after all those magnificent saves – had been given no chance. The helplessness of Everton's defence was illustrated by Ebbrell's reaction, the midfielder's shoulders slumping conspicuously as the shot bent through the air, its destination clear long before the ball had crossed the line.

It was a moment that deserved to win any match but football doesn't work like that. Liverpool eased to the turnaround, but the brief break in play did their nerves no favours. As the second period of extra-time developed, all the doubts emerged again. Cottee was nearly scooped free down the inside-left channel by McCall, but Nicol managed to intercept. Grobbelaar cleaned out Staunton to punch clear amid a defensive shambles. Newell again caused mayhem in the box, Hysén heading out nervously, McCall nearly sending a rising drive whistling home. On the touchline, Dalglish surveyed the turmoil, seemingly unperturbed. His demeanour belied his inner torment. 'At 4–3 I was going to make a positional change,' he recalled. 'Because Everton and particularly Cottee were causing us problems, I wanted to push somebody back into defence. Turning to Ronnie Moran, I said: "We'll move Jan back to sweeper." Ronnie replied: "Hold on." So I left it. I still blame myself now for not doing it, for being weak-willed when normally I was so decisive. It was my fault that Liverpool did not win that game. If I had been 100 per cent right in my own mind, I would have made the decision. We needed to get a hold of Cottee. But I failed to take command. All my old decisiveness drained from me.'

Despite the turning tide and Dalglish's inertia, Liverpool still managed to put together perhaps the best moment of the entire match. Beardsley, down the left, slid the ball inside to Barnes, who tapped back for Mølby, the Dane hitting an instant rolled pass to release the still-scampering Beardsley on the left. It was a move of geometric brilliance but Beardsley uncharacteristically hesitated, allowing Keown time to move in to hustle, and under pressure shot weakly at Southall. A tie-settling fifth goal, and a move for the ages, was lost to the ether.

That miss with eight minutes remaining – and a mistake two minutes later by Mølby – would prove much more costly than any indecision by Dalglish. In an attempt to stop Hinchcliffe meandering down the left, Mølby stuck out a lazy leg to prod the ball away from the Evertonian and back to his keeper. Weak and directionless, all the intervention achieved was to release Cottee into the area. The striker poked the ball through Grobbelaar's legs and home for a fourth equaliser. 'I haven't played in a game like that since I was at school,' said Ablett. 'When you score four goals away from home you expect to win, but we got sloppy at the back and were punished for it.'

At the side of the pitch, Dalglish bit his lip in frustration, although seeing the final mistake of the night had been made by his preferred choice to shore up Liverpool's creaky back-line, it's difficult categorically to pin Everton's fourth on his inaction. Self-flagellation is understandable under the circum-stances, but there's a sense that Dalglish has always been too hard on himself about this. Would Beardsley, on form and on a hat-trick, usually muck up such a presentable goalscoring opportunity? Was that really the normally unflappable Mølby who set Cottee away?

Both teams made half-hearted efforts to look for a winner, but it quickly became clear that, all twenty-two players spent physically and drained emotionally, everyone was happy to settle for a draw and a second replay. On the whistle, Dalglish shook hands with Kendall, serenely and with the thinnest of smiles. He trudged off to the dressing room, where, accord-ing to Barnes, the Liverpool squad – their substitutes signally unused – embarked on a full and frank debrief which involved 'a lot of screaming'. In public, the tone was one of ruefulness. 'If there has ever been a better [derby] I wish someone would send me a video of it,' Dalglish said. 'We gave three great ex-amples of how to score goals and three bad examples of how to defend.'

And then, two days later, stunned silence, as Dalglish opted out. In the *Guardian*, David Lacey observed that this had been 'the first time in forty years that Liverpool have been caught on the hop'. An unnamed club insider noted, with no little prescience, that 'the system Bill Shankly brought to Liver-pool has been crumbling for years because it relied on certain people being there. Kenny Dalglish was the last bastion of that order. This could prove the most important time in the club's history.'

Uncertainty abounded. Ronnie Moran would take over as assistant, while a series of big names were mooted as the next Liverpool manager: the Rangers boss Graeme Souness; Alan

Hansen, with Moran as adviser, replicating the Dalglish–Paisley dynamic of a few years earlier; Phil Thompson, on the coaching staff at Anfield; the former Swansea and Real Madrid boss John Toshack, then at Real Sociedad; Phil Neal, managing in the third tier at Bolton having been passed over for the job when Dalglish was offered it in 1985; and a few more eyebrow-raising suggestions in the Tottenham boss Terry Venables, the then-long-retired Kevin Keegan (still a year from his managerial debut at Newcastle), Ronnie Whelan, Emlyn Hughes and Jack Charlton.

Dalglish, who spent the afternoon after he had resigned playing golf with Ron Yeats, was forced to deny rumours that he was planning to take the USA job ahead of the 1994 World Cup, before being allowed to slip quietly away from the game. Leaving aside his undoubted and unparalleled contribution as a player, Dalglish (in his first period at the helm) also left behind a magnificent legacy as a manager. Off the field, his selfless actions in the wake of Hillsborough were both exceptional and exemplary. On it, he had put together arguably the most aesthetically pleasing side in the club's history, the class of 1987–88, although Paisley's swashbucklers of 1978–79 also have a claim to that title. Three titles and two FA Cups in just under six years was a superlative return. In addition, Dalglish had introduced a more fluid tactical approach, one in which players were not afraid to interchange positions on the hoof. Had English clubs not been banned from Europe, there is no reason why the Barnes-and-Beardsley side at its peak could not have at least challenged Arrigo Sacchi's AC Milan.

On the debit side, the Double of 1986 had been a startling smash-and-grab of property which probably should have belonged to Everton, a triumph which was arguably more down to Dalglish's Indian summer as a player, reinstating himself during the run-in, than his managerial performance. The Barnes–Beardsley team had been allowed to grow old and became frayed during the latter stages of Dalglish's reign: there was an over-reliance on old names, the faultlines running through a crumbling defence were not addressed and no new big-name players, the re-signing of Rush apart, were purchased after the arrival of Beardsley and Barnes in 1987. The team had also developed the unfortunate habit of losing crunch games, with the 1988 FA Cup, 1989 league championship and 1990 FA Cup all slipping through their fingers after inexplicable collapses. (Not that they brooded too much on these failures: after sealing their 1990 title triumph, three weeks after crashing in the FA Cup semi-final against Palace, Hansen, floating into the Anfield changing room on a cloud of champagne bubbles, struck up a chorus of 'We're Forever Blowing Doubles'.)

Perhaps most contentiously, Dalglish's biggest error might have been the reintroduction of Rush. During his second spell at the club, the Welsh striker won the league, two FA Cups (scoring three times in two finals) and a League Cup, his ninety goals during that eight-year period firing him to the top of the club's all-time scoring chart, but Rush, unquestionably at his peak when Dalglish was himself in his pomp during the early eighties, never quite slotted into the multi-dimensional Barnes-and-Beardsley side in the way John Aldridge had. Aldridge was far less naturally talented, but he was a poacher too and was arguably more adept at bringing others into play. Aldridge, unhappy at being benched so often upon Rush's return, was always bound to lose the face-off: he was three years older than Rush and often painted as a bad cover version. Yet their stats were as similar as their moustachioed looks: Rush had scored 139 times in 224 games during his first spell at the club, a rate of 0.62 goals per game. Aldridge notched 50 times in 83 matches, a rate of 0.60 goals per game. The older man, while leaving his heart on Merseyside, traipsed off to Spain, where he would score goals at the rate of just over a goal every two games in La Liga for Real Sociedad, before returning to rattle them home in the second tier for Tranmere Rovers. Rush meanwhile would hardly let Liverpool down – look at his achievements upon his return – but with the side never again reaching the heights of 1987–88, it's at least legitimate to debate what would have happened had Dalglish stuck with Aldridge instead.

But much of this is nitpicking. Dalglish's first stint as manager at Anfield brought critical acclaim and objective success, thanks to a tactical sophistication with which he strangely seemed to lose faith during his mixed post–1991 career (save for a couple of free-flowing months in 2011, starring Luís Suárez and Maxi Rodríguez, in the wake of Roy Hodgson's departure). He raked in the trophies at a rate that bore comparison with Shankly, Paisley and Fagan. But most importantly, he righted a listing ship after Heysel, and gently shepherded it through the unspeakable bleakness of Hillsborough. To guide a club through one tragedy is difficult enough; to guide it through two truly extraordinary. The Liverpool support – Dalglish's people – loved and trusted him unequivocally. Dalglish had ensured that, through the storm, nobody ever walked alone. Liverpool, the club and the city, will be forever grateful.

But the show had to go on. Liverpool kept fighting to retain their league title, but with Whelan and McMahon out for the season and Dalglish having taken his leave, a hopeless funk hung over the club. Liverpool got back on the horse a day after the King's abdication – and quickly fell off it again, losing 3–1 at Luton despite going ahead. In one sense it was hardly a surprise, being their fourth loss on the unloved Kenilworth Road plastic in six visits. But on the other hand, Luton hadn't won a league game since the turn of the year. Iain Dowie, scoring twice, bossed the continually beleaguered Ablett and Hysén. The defeat meant Arsenal deposed them at the top on goal difference.

Then it was time to face Everton for the third time in the Cup and the second time at Goodison Park. The Toffees won thanks to an early Dave Watson goal, though Liverpool were at least sprightly, Southall producing another outstanding display to deny Rush, Nicol and Barnes. But it seemed telling that in their previous two games – the 4–4 and the defeat at Luton – Liverpool had given up a winning position for the sixth and seventh times that season. Asked to claw a lead back themselves, falling behind for the first time in an epic Cup tie, they simply couldn't manage it.

Arsenal then came to Anfield and won, Paul Merson scoring the only goal, which meant Liverpool had lost three on the bounce since the departure of Dalglish under the yoke of Ronnie Moran, the first time they had done so in five years. Liverpool would later regain the lead of the division after a 3–0 win at Manchester City, aided by two soft penalty decisions; scrape an awful 2–1 home win against relegation-bound Sunderland, who would have gone 3–0 up had the nineteen-year-old David Rush not missed two one-on-ones; and then beat Derby, another side destined for the drop, 7–1 in a surreal match at the Baseball Ground, in which Dean Saunders repeatedly cut through the Liverpool back-line to prove the defence was still a huge concern.

Saunders having jangled defensive nerves loudly enough for others to notice, Liverpool were then worked over 3–1 by QPR at Anfield, the home side being booed off at half-time after Les Ferdinand and Roy Wegerle had put the away side two up, and they lost at Southampton, where Matthew Le Tissier scored and Alan Shearer put himself about much to the displeasure of an ageing defence unable to cope with such a combative youngster.

Micky Gynn's equaliser at Anfield for Coventry City a week later pretty much meant the jig was up, though there was still time for one last, late, desperate run for glory. And time for one last statement from the stand-in manager Moran. Liverpool went to Leeds and won a ludicrous match 5–4. They had been 4–0 up after twenty-six minutes, Barnes and Beardsley having performed all sorts of elaborate pincer movements from the wings. 'It was a little bit of a system we'd been working on, something I remembered from our days in Europe,'

Moran said, a bittersweet comment that warmed the hearts of Liverpool fans while reminding them that the better days were increasingly far behind them.

After the match at Maine Road, there had been rumours of a Dalglish comeback. 'Kenny's return is feasible,' Peter Robinson had confirmed. 'The door is open.' But just over a month later, the Rangers boss and former Liverpool captain Graeme Souness was appointed as manager. The early signs were good; Souness dropped Hysén and played Mølby as a sweeper alongside Ablett and Gillespie, Liverpool cruising to a 3–0 win over Norwich at Anfield. The Reds then dispatched Crystal Palace in another 3–0 home win.

But early signs can be deceptive and Liverpool relinquished their title after suffering two defeats in quick succession. Kerry Dixon, Dennis Wise and Gordon Durie ripped Liverpool apart as Chelsea spanked them 4–2 at Stamford Bridge. (It would not be the last time a 4–2 result at Chelsea would stop a Liverpool manager's gallop, as Roy Evans would find out to his cost in the FA Cup in 1997.) Liverpool were then totally outplayed at Nottingham Forest, Ian Woan's long-distance pearler sending the title back to Highbury.

In retrospect, the series of games against Everton had derailed Liverpool's campaign in more subtle ways than simply precipitating Dalglish's walkout. Whelan had been injured in the league game, McMahon the following week in the first Cup match. Liverpool had maintained a serious challenge up until that point, an experienced engine room doing half of the defence's legwork. But without them, the loss of Hansen – who had been injured all season and retired soon after Dalglish left – soon became glaringly obvious.

Souness was, nevertheless, bullish about Liverpool's prospects, suggesting that Liverpool were strong enough that a nineteenth title would soon arrive. 'I would say that without a doubt over the whole season Liverpool have lost the championship rather than Arsenal have won it,' he insisted. 'Anyone who plays for me takes defeat badly. Second may be a healthy place for some clubs, but not us. That's the burden I have to carry.'

It was not a burden he carried particularly comfortably. Dalglish would later admit that, had Liverpool shown patience until the summer, he would have come back, strong enough to take the load once again.

CHAPTER 9

Uefa Cup fourth round, first leg, Stadio Olimpico, Rome, 15 February 2001

Roma	**0–2**	**Liverpool**
		Owen 46, 71

Francesco Antonioli	Sander Westerveld
Cafú	Markus Babbel
Hidetoshi Nakata	Sami Hyypiä
(Marcos Assunção 51)	
Vincenzo Montella	Stéphane Henchoz
Emerson	Jamie Carragher
Damiano Tommasi	Nick Barmby
(Gabriel Batistuta 66)	
Walter Samuel	Dietmar Hamann
Alessandro Rinaldi	Gary McAllister
Marco Delvecchio (Guigou 82)	Robbie Fowler
Amedeo Mangone	Michael Owen
	(Jari Litmanen 79)
Vincent Candela	Christian Ziege
	(Vladimír Šmicer 74)
Fabio Capello	Gérard Houllier

Ref: M Merk
Bkd: Mangone
Att: 59,781

LIVERPOOL'S CROWNING ACHIEVEMENT DURING THE Premier League era is obvious: the 2005 Champions League victory in Istanbul under Rafael Benítez. But just as Bill Shankly would have been forced to dig his own foundations had George Kay's side not kept the club's flame flickering with a league championship and FA Cup final appearance in the immediate post-war years, and the three-time European Cup winner Bob Paisley would always owe a debt to Shankly for all his preparatory work, Benítez and the class of 2005 have Gérard Houllier to thank for rebuilding the continental reputation of a club whose status had been seriously downgraded during a decade of alarming post-Boot Room decline.

Houllier these days tends to be respected but not loved, partly because his philosophy placed function ahead of aesthetics and partly because this approach, along with his autocratic manner, led to the marginalisation and eventual ostracising of crowd-pleasers such as Jari Litmanen, Nicolas Anelka and especially Robbie Fowler. History, though, will surely be kinder to him. Liverpool were a meandering shambles when he joined the club as joint manager in the summer of 1998, assisting then quickly replacing Roy Evans who seemed to have lost his drive. Within three years they had won the club's second Treble, a clean sweep of all three cup competitions they had entered that season, a unique feat for an English club. Along the way, they rode their luck, outrageously so at times, but Liverpool's 2001 vintage were impressive enough to have earned much of the good fortune that came their way.

Houllier would also take two abortive tilts at the Premiership title, before ill health begat ill judgement and the project went awry. But by the time of his enforced resignation in 2004, Houllier had rebuilt the club's foundations and re-established Liverpool's confidence to the extent that the team was able consistently to challenge for the game's top prizes at home and in Europe. His replacement was afforded the opportunity to take things to the next level.

Houllier to Benítez wasn't such a leap. Liverpool were as good a side as any in Europe during 2001 and 2002, taking a serious challenge for the Champions League in the latter year, and winning the Uefa Cup in the former, a success which involved seeing off the Serie A champions-elect Roma, a Porto side on the brink of European triumph themselves, Llorenç Serra Ferrer's Barcelona and an exciting and dangerous Alaves side for whom the stars had briefly aligned.

The 2001 Uefa Cup final win over Alaves should, by rights, stand as Houllier's signature achievement: an unprecedented rollercoaster ride for a major European final, a 5–4 win in golden-goal extra-time which won contemporary plaudits as 'the greatest European final', no small claim in an era when Manchester United's ludicrous comeback in the 1999 Champions League final was still fresh in the memory and widely considered untouchable in terms of sheer drama.

But while that game set the seal on his legacy – Houllier will always be synonymous with the 2001 Treble – it's completely anomalous to his oeuvre. Houllier, for better or worse, was all about control. That final, a heady, manic nine-goal rush, could hardly have been less representative of Houllier's grinding genius. His was an approach which sometimes – often – produced dire spectacles. But it got results, and getting results was a habit Liverpool had fallen out of during the 1990s. And, on the occasions when Houllier's micromanaged plans came perfectly together, Liverpool's performances could be a delight.

The pinnacle of his reign came – as so many Liverpudlian pinnacles had – in Rome, with the dismissal of Roma in the first leg of the fourth round of that successful Uefa Cup run. The Italians were on their way to their first *scudetto* since 1983 and had been strong favourites to progress in the tie. Houllier's side made them look thoroughly ordinary at the Stadio Olimpico with a smash-and-grab performance that showcased control, poise and, by the end, no little swagger. 'To come to the home of the Serie A leaders and win so well, so convincingly, is absolutely wonderful,' said Houllier, beaming like a proud parent. He had every right. It was, Oliver Kay wrote in *The Times*, 'their most significant result for more than a decade': 'If the eleven years since their last championship have been exacting, [the win in Rome] offered yet more compelling evidence that the next ten will prove worth the wait.' Europe, which had understandably forgotten about Liverpool since the team's 1980s pomp, had been issued with a reminder. Liverpool were back.

The Uefa Cup was always strangely unloved and undervalued in England – strange, because while by definition the tournament was understandably considered second-best in terms of status to the European Cup and its latter-day equivalent the Champions League, the difference in quality between the two tournaments was not always particularly apparent. In the years when only champions could enter the European Cup, the Uefa Cup was often stuffed with notable forces from each major footballing nation, populated by up-and-coming teams and those in the process of winning their domestic league, young sides budding or coming into full bloom. (It is no coincidence that Liverpool's two Uefa Cup triumphs in the 1970s coincided with league titles, the latter in 1976 also being a portent of dominance in Europe's premier competition.)

By the time of their round-of-sixteen tie in the 2001 Uefa Cup, Houllier's Liverpool were certainly developing. However, their opponents, Fabio Capello's Roma, were nearing their peak. En route to the Serie A title, the *giallorossi* boasted a stellar squad from back to front – the Brazil captain Cafú and Argentina's Walter Samuel in defence, Gabriel Batistuta and Marco Delvecchio in attack, the *trequartista* Francesco Totti their star turn – and were second-favourites for the Uefa Cup behind a Barcelona side that had tumbled from the early stages of the Champions League but looked dangerous with a cast including Rivaldo, Patrick Kluivert, Marc Overmars and Pep Guardiola (as well as a young Pepe Reina in goal). To il-lustrate the perceived gap between the two teams, Liverpool were 16–1 shots to lift the trophy ahead of the tie. Roma were 9–2, tucked in behind the 4–1 favourites Barça but ahead in the reckoning of other European heavyweights such as Inter-nazionale (15–2) and Parma (9–1).

That pecking order is worth revisiting, purely because Liverpool's subsequent victory in the tournament, and their defeat of Roma on the way, is seriously undervalued as an achievement. This was an incredibly strong competition – and Roma were a highly dangerous foe, six points clear in Serie A of a Juventus side containing Zinédine Zidane. It's true that Capello's men would go into the first leg of the Liverpool tie at the Stadio Olimpico without Totti, who had a minor groin strain and was being rested ahead of a Serie A match with Lecce but they were still a seriously good side. 'The league remains the priority of my club and I must act accordingly,' insisted Capello before the game. Batistuta, the top-scorer in Italy at that point, was left on the bench, too, slightly injured and only to be brought on in the event of panic. But Roma could still call on Delvecchio and Vincenzo Montella, while Liverpool were left short by injuries as well, Steven Gerrard, Emile Heskey and Danny Murphy missing out.

Houllier was aware of the match's importance in his side's development. 'People say that our ties with Roma will show how far we have progressed,' he said ahead of the first leg. 'That is unfair because you cannot really judge a young side, which is only now starting to develop and blossom, against a team like Roma. They are a great side and at the moment there is simply no comparison.' Houllier was correct in terms of quality – Roma were significantly stronger on paper, and further down the track in terms of both development and success, than his side – although one part of his analysis was slightly disingenuous: the average age of Roma's starting eleven was 27.4 years; Liverpool were hardly toddling behind them at 27.1.

Liverpool, in depressingly dull Reebok yellow, kicked off as underdogs. But they were buoyed by three factors: the last match the Reds had played against Roma, in this same sta-dium, had been the 1984 European Cup final; Roma had been knocked out of the previous season's Uefa Cup at the same stage by English opposition in Leeds United; and Liverpool were going into the game in decent form, having won eight of their previous twelve games, drawing three of the others, and conceding a mere four goals while doing so.

Houllier's plan was apparent from the outset and did not deviate from the norm: two banks of four, the team shape kept compact in the middle, relentless pressing all over the pitch, the match approached almost as a defensive drill with the strikers available to relieve pressure on the break. It would be executed almost to the letter.

Totti looked on from the stands, peering out from under-neath the rim of a baseball hat, a red-and-white scarf coiled around his neck. His guile would be missed, although as things panned out, it's hard to see exactly what space he would have been afforded to work in anyway. The Japan in-ternational Hidetoshi Nakata, taking up the creative reins in his stead, was hardly a slouch, but he endured an hour of frus-tration, harried beyond reason by Dietmar Hamann, before finally being withdrawn.

Liverpool gave an early indication of their intentions as Christian Ziege came straight through the back of Cafú, play-ing high upfield on the right. Ziege really should have been booked for clattering into the Brazil captain's standing leg but Liverpool got lucky. To say Roma were rattled would be an overstatement, but it quickly became clear that Liverpool had the defensive nous to create an extremely oppressive atmosphere. From the resulting free-kick, Nakata shaped to shoot on the edge of the D, but was hurried into mishitting his effort, sending it rolling miserably into the arms of Sander Westerveld.

Delvecchio attempted to release Montella with a backheel, but Jamie Carragher was immediately on hand, coming inside to hack clear. Delvecchio then trundled down the left, his low cross cut out by Stéphane Henchoz and, after a fashion, Westerveld, and the Italy forward was then upended by Henchoz down the same flank. Having had time to reorganise in the middle, Liverpool dealt with Nakata's free-kick, effectively a corner, first through a firm Westerveld punch, then by crowding in on Cafú, who from distance could only send the ball well wide.

For Liverpool, it had been a long trek back towards the summit of European football. The beginning of their decline – from the top of English football at least – is usually regarded as having begun in 1991 with Dalglish's resignation and the appointment of Souness, breaking with the comfortable certainties of the Boot Room, but the seeds were sown at least a couple of years previously, at the indeterminable juncture where Dalglish had, in the wake of the spectacular Beardsley–Barnes splurge, stopped reinvigorating the team with fresh talent. The received wisdom of Bob Paisley's maxim, that one or two players should be replaced each year with 'better models', was neglected. Nobody could argue that Glenn Hysén was an improvement on Alan Hansen, that Ronny Rosenthal represented a step up on John Aldridge or that Jimmy Carter was ever going to be able to fill Beardsley's shoes. The mess, although there was no comparable trophy drought, was not dissimilar to the one Bill Shankly had made for himself by 1970: members of a magnificent team had been shown too much loyalty and had been allowed to grow old together. Liverpool were in need of a major overhaul.

It's through this contextual prism – a massive and unavoidable rebuilding programme at a time when Arsenal were in the ascendency, Leeds were enjoying a brief renaissance, and Manchester United were finally and ominously getting their act together – that the reign of Souness should be viewed. The few shafts of daylight first: he identified the need to revamp a creaking defence by signing a ball-playing central defender in Mark Wright and the superlative but injury-dogged attacking right-back Rob Jones; gave youth its head by fast-tracking Steve McManaman, Jamie Redknapp and Robbie Fowler into the first XI; and won one FA Cup – slim pickings compared to his predecessors, but the last time Liverpool would win one of England's two classic prizes for nearly a decade.

Sadly for Souness, the over-excitable way he otherwise went about his business has obscured all that, his time in the Anfield dugout seen now as nothing short of a fiasco. The pack certainly needed reshuffling, but the way he split the cards seemed wantonly perverse. Peter Beardsley, Ray Houghton, Steve Staunton and Steve McMahon were all jettisoned before their time, and the replacements – Dean Saunders, Nigel Clough, Paul Stewart – were woefully below par. Some other transfers were irredeemably, and notoriously, appalling: Dunfermline's Hungary international midfielder István Kozma, the occasional Denmark centre-back Torben Piechnik and West Ham's overly robust left-back Julian Dicks probably representing the worst of the bunch.

Souness kept Liverpool on the periphery of the title race in his first full season, 1991–92. A run of thirteen unbeaten league games from November to the end of January, culminating in a 2–0 defeat of the reigning champions Arsenal at Anfield, tucked them nicely in third place behind the Uniteds of Manchester and Leeds. But there would only be four more league wins that season. The FA Cup final victory over second-tier Sunderland partially made up for Liverpool's lowest league placing since 1965 – sixth – but by then Souness had queered his own pitch by selling the story of his heart-bypass operation to the *Sun*, reviled on Merseyside for its heartless and inaccurate coverage of Hillsborough. Souness initially pleaded ignorance of local sensitivities, which added insult to injury – it later transpired he had written to a supporter explaining how he had banned his players from speaking to the newspaper – and although he has since apologised, the incident added to an atmosphere of discontent and distrust.

Liverpool spiralled downward. In the eighteen seasons before Souness had taken charge, the club had finished outside the top two in the First Division only once. Eighteen months after he took over, the Reds found themselves sixteenth in the league after a quarter of the campaign, two points off the relegation zone. They had already been held to a scarcely believable 4–4 draw at home in the League Cup by Chesterfield of the third tier. (They had been put out of the previous season's League Cup by Peterborough United of the same division.) On their return to European competition for the first time since Heysel, Liverpool were humiliated 6–2 on aggregate in the second round of the Cup-Winners' Cup by Spartak Moscow. They ended the season in sixth place again, having suffered an unprecedented number of heavy defeats on their travels: 4–2 at Aston Villa, 4–1 at Blackburn Rovers, 5–1 at Coventry City. The FA Cup, meanwhile, was quickly relinquished after a home defeat to Bolton Wanderers, another humiliation at the hands of third-tier opposition. An article in the *Independent* quoted an unnamed fan who compared Souness with the floundering Conservative prime minister John Major: 'A man presiding over a long-term decline that is beyond anyone, but making all sorts of unhelpful short-term decisions.'

Liverpool's plight was, to audiences of the time, unprecedented and the club were expected to fire Souness at the end of that season but, after a surreal 6–2 home win over Spurs on the final day, they opted to retain their manager, with one proviso from the board: the promotion of the first-team coach Roy Evans to assistant manager, an imposition which would later have echoes in Evans's Anfield career. There was a brief glimmer of hope at the start of the following campaign, when the new signing Nigel Clough scored twice as Liverpool saw off a highly proficient Sheffield Wednesday side at Anfield, then won at QPR and Swindon, routing the latter 5–0. They topped the table, but few were convinced and Liverpool quickly slipped down the standings. Fans had little to cheer for the rest of the season, other than a comeback at Anfield from 3–0 down against Manchester United, a 3–3 draw which at the whistle felt like a victory, albeit one that served merely to emphasise the growing gulf between Alex Ferguson's champions and Souness's side. Souness resigned, the final blow coming with another lame FA Cup capitulation to lower-league opposition at home, this time against Bristol City. Alan Hansen, by then establishing himself as an insightful pundit on the BBC's *Match of the Day*, was linked with the job, but the smart money was on a Roy Evans ascension.

And so it was that Evans was installed as Souness's successor. It was a conscious return to the Boot Room, which had been physically and spiritually demolished during Souness's reign. A full-back who had been purchased by Bill Shankly, Evans was moved on to the backroom staff when it was clear he would fail to make the grade as a player. 'I've been privileged to work with some great people, like Shanks, Bob Paisley and Kenny,' said the shy Evans on his unveiling. 'I can't help but to have learned from all of them. My aim is to restore this club to its rightful place.'

After their early burst, Roma fell quiet, Hamann and Henchoz tireless in closing them down, while Liverpool began to show the occasional glimpse of menace. Carragher fed a low pass down the inside-left channel for Owen, the striker collecting a deflection off Alessandro Rinaldi before making for the Roma box, the ball eventually reaching Nick Barmby who shot poorly with Robbie Fowler in space, having peeled off down the right. Fowler chased a long Ziege ball along the same flank, but was muscled out of it by Samuel. Gary McAllister with a low diagonal pass from the left then almost managed to spring Michael Owen free down the right, but Vincent Candela was on hand to mop up when the striker failed to control properly. Roma's back three of Rinaldi, Samuel and Amedeo Mangone were coping with Liverpool's threat, even if they were a little stretched across the pitch at times, with the wing-backs Cafú and Candela called on to shuttle back from attacking positions more than they would have wished. Still, on the Roma bench, Capello looked relaxed enough during the opening exchanges, slumped back in his seat, resting casually on one elbow.

He was jolted upright on eighteen minutes when Fowler, picking up a Markus Babbel ball down the right, took one touch inside to go past Samuel and fizzed a low shot inches wide of the right-hand post, but for the remainder of the half, Roma reasserted a semblance of authority, at least in terms of possession. Nakata scooped a pass over the Liverpool defence from the right touchline which only just evaded Montella to the right of the D, although Henchoz was in close attendance. Delvecchio chased after a punt down the left only for Westerveld to come out to claim. Montella looked to slide Liverpool open down the left but his clever through-ball was pilfered by Sami Hyypiä, stepping across calmly and without fuss. Candela resorted to shooting wildly from distance. From Houllier's point of view, it was all very encouraging, even if his side were achieving little of note higher up the field – their few sorties were centred around McAllister, triangulating well with Ziege and Barmby on the left, although Owen and Fowler were tightly marshalled by Samuel – but their resistance had been staunch. Westerveld had yet to be forced into meaningful action, an increasingly frustrated home side being slowly, almost imperceptibly, pushed back into midfield, out of harm's way.

Arguably resigned to the fact that Roma, blessed with Cafú and Candela, were an irresistible force down either wing, Liverpool appeared happy enough to allow the home side a little space down the flanks, concentrating instead on keeping it tight and compact in the middle, where it really mattered. A good example of how that worked in their favour came on thirty-three minutes, when Emerson burst down the right, then guided a ball inside for Montella. With his back to goal on the edge of the area, the forward laid a pass off to Nakata, who shaped to shoot. But with Liverpool offering little daylight in front of the target, Nakata was forced to let the ball roll on to Candela, racing into the frame from the left in a manner that recalled Carlos Alberto in 1970. The result was less spectacular: Candela was quickly closed down by Babbel, Nakata then shot wastefully straight into a thicket of defenders, Cafú attempted to keep the move going by clipping in the rebound from the right and the move came to a limp end when Montella, hackles rising, shoved Henchoz while attempting, but failing, to fight his way into position at the far post for a header. Liverpool were perfectly happy to sit back, soak up pressure, and rely on their high-intensity but controlled pressing – a half-court press, really, waiting until their opponents crossed halfway before closing them down – to knock Roma off their stride.

The knife-edge risks of such a strategy were apparent three minutes before the break, Rinaldi beating Ziege and McAllister down the right, then whipping a ball to the near post, where Delvecchio slapped a header wide right from eight yards out. The close-range miss – which would prove to be Roma's sole clear chance of the evening – was not the only blemish on the striker's first half; ten minutes earlier, with Liverpool making a rare expedition down the other end, Ziege had curved in a free-kick from the right which Delvecchio, retreating, had nearly planted into the top-right corner of his own net with a misplaced defensive header.

One last dance by Cafú down the right, leading to a long-distance Emerson shot being easily deflected away from danger, and the half was over. It had been mainly Roma and Delvecchio really should have opened the scoring. But then again, Westerveld still hadn't had a serious save to make, so by any measure Houllier's scheme was working, a fact amply illustrated by the Liverpool fans, who were making far more noise than those in the home end.

Evans's quest was to restore Liverpool to the glories of the decade before. In that he failed, and his four-year reign has already been relegated to footnote status. And yet the Evans era is one of the great nearly stories in English football history. Liverpool scored at a prodigious rate at the start of his first full season, 1994–95, winning 6–1 on the opening day at Crystal Palace, then flattening Arsenal 3–0 at Anfield before polishing off Southampton 2–0 at the Dell. Robbie Fowler's hat-trick against the Gunners – four minutes and thirty-five blistering seconds fuelled by the unshakeable certainty of youth – was the highlight of the opening salvo. Fowler, still only nineteen, was beginning to stake his claim as the star of the team, a Toxteth hero beloved of the Kop, although Steve McManaman – at twenty-two a relative veteran – was almost equally electrifying on the wing, where he had displaced John Barnes. Barnes, having lost his pace after hamstring problems, was converted into a central-midfield playmaker in the style of Jan Mølby (right down to the increasingly generous waistline).

At that point Evans made the double signing of Phil Babb from Coventry City and John Scales from Wimbledon with a view to implementing a 3–5–2 system that had become increasingly fashionable since Carlos Bilardo's Argentina had won the 1986 World Cup using it. Despite England's dabble with the formation in 1990, the idea was still regarded with suspicion in the Premier League and would never really take root, arguably as a result of Liverpool's experiences. The system – Scales and Babb in the centre, Neil Ruddock sweeping, Jones and Stig Inge Bjørnebye attacking full-backs-cum-wingers – seemed jinxed from the off. Scales made his debut in a miserable goalless home draw with West Ham, then Babb made his first appearance at Manchester United,

coming on as a seventieth-minute substitute with the score
0–0. Four minutes later, Liverpool had shipped two goals and
the game was lost. While it would be harsh to blame Babb for
that particular capitulation – he had replaced the immobile
Mølby who, having bossed the early exchanges was in the process of being over-run by the United substitute Brian McClair,
and in any case it was Scales whose weak back header let in
Andrei Kanchelskis for the opener – his introduction represented the first time the new centrally defensive threesome
had appeared on the pitch together. The emblematic nature
of the subsequent 240 seconds would not be forgotten quickly
or easily.

A month on, Liverpool suffered their second league defeat
of the season, at Blackburn Rovers, by then managed by Kenny
Dalglish. 'The system's fine,' snapped Evans after a 3–2 defeat,
Rovers scoring all three of their goals while Liverpool's full-
backs were missing, presumed marauding. 'But if you make
mistakes, you are going to get punished for them.'

Evans and Liverpool would never get the balance right. The
Reds won the 1995 League Cup, McManaman a wispy two-goal
hero who wreaked havoc along the diagonal as well as straight
down the touchline in the final against Bolton, but that would
be the sum of the Evans haul. The defence never quite got their
act together, for various reasons: Scales was pretty but brittle;
Ruddock was often patently out of condition; Babb, who shone
at the 1994 World Cup for the Republic of Ireland, soon revealed himself to be a one-tournament wonder; Jones would
be blighted by injury; Bjørnebye, whose crossing was erratic,
simply didn't possess the requisite class or consistency.

The flakiness of Evans's sides is often overplayed. Few teams
have shown as much professional pride and character as the
one which beat Dalglish's Blackburn on the last day of the
1994–95 season, after falling behind and in full knowledge
that a supine defeat would have guaranteed a title for the Anfield faithful's hero and, perhaps more importantly, denied the
reviled Manchester United. (As it was, to everyone at Anfield's

relief that day, Blackburn's loss didn't matter.) But rather than lacking in character, the team from back to front fell short of the quality and concentration required for title-winning consistency. By far and away the most famous match of the Evans era was the see-saw 4–3 victory over Newcastle United in early April 1996, Stan Collymore's late goal keeping Liverpool on the edge of that year's title hunt. Three days after a win that should have provided impetus and succour, they meekly succumbed to a 1–0 defeat at Coventry City.

The pivotal match of Evans's reign was an FA Cup tie at Chelsea in January 1997. Liverpool were in the process of mounting their first serious title challenge since the Dalglish era, and were leaders of the Premier League as they headed to Stamford Bridge. Two up at half-time and coasting, their defence – especially the centre-back Bjørn Tore Kvarme, recently signed from Rosenborg – was battered around by Mark Hughes and Gianluca Vialli, and Chelsea won 4–2. By the time Liverpool engaged in league action again, they had been leap-frogged in the table by both Manchester United and Arsenal. Confidence shot, Liverpool's form for the rest of the season disintegrated. They were eventually undone by consecutive home defeats in April, the first a dismal slump from a winning position against Coventry, who were making a habit of dashing Evans's hopes, the second a depressing 3–1 thrashing by arguably the worst Manchester United vintage to win a title under Alex Ferguson (but yet still demonstrably in a different class to their arch-rivals).

When Liverpool began to stutter during the second half of the 1996–97 season, one newspaper came up with the headline: 'Give them an Ince and they'll win by a mile', a none-too-cryptic allusion to the suggestion that Evans's side was overly obsessed with aesthetic excellence and might benefit from the sort of bite and snap the former Manchester United midfielder, then at Internazionale, could provide. Pleasingly, if only for the sub-editor who came up with that particular line, Ince did arrive at Anfield – although, as it panned out, to little effect. Although Liverpool finished third in 1997–98, an improvement of one place on the previous campaign, there had been no coherent challenge and it paradoxically felt as though the team were going backwards.

The £2.5m signing of Sean Dundee from Karlsruhe did not look quite so preposterous then as it does with hindsight – he had been the Bundesliga's top scorer in 1996–97, after all – though it still was clearly far from enough to turn Liverpool into potential title winners. Liverpool's biggest capture that summer in any case was not a player at all, but Houllier, who had been manager of France for their failed campaign to qualify for the 1994 World Cup and had stayed on behind the scenes as his country won their home World Cup in the summer of '98. He had been expected to take over at Sheffield Wednesday, then at Celtic, only to end up in a curious joint managerial set up with Evans. 'I took the job on the condition that Roy stay on as joint manager,' said Houllier. 'I believe with our mutual respect and expertise we can fulfil the expectations surrounding this club.' Evans was quick to express his support for the arrangement, although like Souness five years earlier, he had little option but to go along with it. 'The titles of joint manager will cause concern for some and we know there will be problems we have to iron out,' he said, 'but I am looking forward to the challenge and I don't think we have anything to fear.'

Evans was gone by November, having resigned after a miserable run of form in the league and a pathetic League Cup defeat at home to Tottenham. He left a broken man. 'I have done this job with honesty and integrity and seeing the club suffer does affect me badly,' was his weary valediction. The players, unsurprisingly, had been unsure who was in charge, the emotional, friendly and popular Evans, or Houllier, an equally pleasant soul but someone more prepared to play the hard man when required.

Ultimately, by the exacting standards of Liverpool, Evans had been a failure. Certainly now he is seen mainly as a transitional figure, albeit one who spent nearly £40m on players. Yet his sides were, at best, beautiful to watch, Shankly's apostle preaching a traditional pass-and-move mantra which would not be embraced totally at Anfield again until Brendan Rodgers took over fourteen years later. He also made two half-decent stabs at the title and arguably was only a dependable goalkeeper away from major success in 1997 (the hopelessly freestyle David James was to blame for the crucial home defeats by Coventry and Manchester United that year and single-handedly put a Cup-Winners' Cup semi-final against Paris Saint-Germain beyond Liverpool, part of a quickfire nightmare triptych that defined his entire Anfield career).

But really Evans was undone by his own niceness. With no Fergusonian whip being cracked, his squad never seemed totally committed to the cause in the way Manchester United had been after their manager had stamped out the booze culture at Old Trafford, or as Arsenal would upon going through a similar detoxification process under Arsène Wenger. The Spice Boys – a nebulous umbrella monicker for the entire squad, with the emphasis on Fowler, McManaman, James, Babb, Ruddock, McAteer, Redknapp and Collymore – were only too happy to embrace the decadent spirit of the Britpop era.

The Spice Boys are probably best remembered for their cream Armani suits, paraded at the ill-fated 1996 FA Cup final; for Fowler and McManaman posing for *Loaded*; and for Neil Ruddock's pound coin game, which involved players passing a nugget to each other during every match, the person holding the coin at the full-time whistle saddled with that evening's bar bill. Not much thought, it can safely be assumed, was given to those paying pound coins at the turnstiles to watch a team that never seemed fully committed. (A less irritating example of the freewheeling spirit of the times can be found in a 1997 edition of *The Kop* newspaper, which featured the normally well-behaved and thoroughly unspicy Stig Inge Bjørnebye opening a health club on the Wirral – and toasting it with a bottle of champagne in one hand, a fully charged glass in the other.)

Liverpool's top talent had taken their eye off the ball and Evans was ill-equipped to respond. The more autocratic Houllier would be rather less willing to put up with such a carry-on and his decisiveness and attention to detail would soon whip Liverpool into shape.

At the interval, many assumed Houllier would respond to Roma's dominance of possession and its accompanying threat of danger with a typically conservative substitution, neither Fowler nor Owen having made much of a mark. But this was a classic broken-team approach; pack eight men behind the ball to frustrate the opposition and leave two up to forage for chances. Owen and Fowler were far from a natural fit as a partnership but in this situation it didn't matter. Houllier left both on with instructions to poke and harry Roma's three-man back-line which, while hardly fraying, had looked stretched on the few occasions Liverpool had been brave enough to push forward. The gamble paid off almost instantly.

If Montella's shot straight from the restart was designed to unnerve the visiting team, it was a gambit that failed. The ball having been dispatched to the other end, Alessandro Rinaldi played a loose, blind pass inside from Roma's right-hand touchline. Owen snaffled it gleefully, taking one touch with his right foot to kill the ball in mid-air on the left edge of the D, bringing it to the right of the spinning Amedeo Mangone and whipping a confident shot into the bottom-left corner. Liverpool had the lead within thirty-eight seconds of the kick-off. One obvious corner excepted, the stadium fell silent as Owen cavorted with the Liverpool staff on the touchline, Houllier a picture of boyish delight.

Rinaldi searched for instant redemption by taking an elaborate swing at the ball from distance, but the shot sailed miles to the right of goal. The effort had come after a brief period of Roma possession in front of and around the Liverpool box;

once again Hyypiä and Henchoz holding firm in the middle, forcing the home team into frustrated and improbable efforts. Capello responded by removing the increasingly ineffectual Nakata for Marcos Assunção, a defensive change on the face of it, but one designed with the later arrival from the bench of Batistuta in mind.

Roma threw bodies forward, Delvecchio the spearhead, but to little effect. As in the first half, Liverpool were content to soak it all up, but this time Owen and Fowler, the pair constantly on the move, pulling Rinaldi and Mangone first one way then the other, were a nagging threat. Mangone, stuttering, nearly let Owen in with a loose ball across the face of his own area. Babbel looked to release Fowler down the right, but the striker was caught miles offside. Ziege, from the inside-left channel, curled a pass towards the inside-right for Owen and Fowler, but both were flagged offside, by millimetres this time.

Uncertainty spread through the Roma ranks. Fowler and Owen, by now hunting as a pair, flustered Mangone who, under pressure from Owen on the edge of the Roma area, tried to flick a far-too-clever ball over the striker's head. Making an awful rick, he sliced high into the air. Fowler swarmed in quickly to complicate matters and Owen came close to latching on to the loose ball. A couple of minutes later, Fowler dropped back from the right touchline and sprayed a diagonal ball towards the left for Ziege, whose instant pass inside was flicked well wide of goal by Barmby from a very promising position.

Which is not to say Liverpool were piling forward recklessly. By the time twenty minutes of the second half had elapsed, Roma's only threat had been a weak near-post header by Cafú from a free-kick on the left by Assunção. The shape of play was very much to Houllier's liking, if not necessarily to that of neutrals watching on television: Roma were throwing aimless punts into the Liverpool box, which were being regularly hoofed clear with neither ceremony nor fuss. On the touchline, the Liverpool manager sat hunched forward but with a palpable air of contentment, not quite the picture of relaxation, but notably calm for a manager often prone to showing signs of irritation and tension. Meanwhile his opposite number Capello was doing exactly that, removing his heavy coat, screaming, then punching the air in frustration. With Liverpool sitting back, the equally agitated crowd soundtracked Capello's ostentatious irritation with dissatisfied whistles.

It was then that Roma roused themselves, taking their first serious shot at goal of the half, and arguably, given the woefulness of Delvecchio's earlier miss, the evening. Assunção took a rangy stride down the inside-right channel and fired a low shot straight at Westerveld, who parried, Henchoz hacking upfield. The home side's tail was suddenly up. Emerson dinked a ball down the inside-right channel – not wholly dissimilar to Graeme Souness's delicious flick to set up Kenny Dalglish in the 1978 European Cup final – releasing Cafú. The Brazilian lifted a cross into the centre, but his delivery evaded Delvecchio and Candela, coming in from the other side, was pestered away from the ball by the hard-working Barmby. Batistuta then replaced the midfielder Tommasi: Assunção could sit back, allowing Roma to throw three up front in Batistuta, Montella and Delvecchio.

It is to Liverpool's – and Houllier's – credit that this burst of energy from the Italian side proved to be brief, despite the introduction of the big Argentinian, and that in fact it was they who made the next (and ultimately decisive) intervention. Cafú tormented Carragher down the right – an early sign that the defender didn't quite have it at the very top level as a full-back, a message that would be amplified in the final by Cosmin Contra of Alaves – but otherwise Roma did very little with their possession. Liverpool broke up the play well, their pressing as strong and relentless as ever and they began to draw free-kicks from the home players as they again showed signs of irritation.

That frustration would be costly. Candela betrayed his

impatience as Liverpool faffed at a throw down the right. From it, Mangone, picking up the mood, needlessly shoved Owen in the back: a free-kick, thirty yards out. Ziege hammered a low curler into the box which Francesco Antonioli was forced to parry. The ball, cleared only to the edge of the area, was picked up by Ziege, who exchanged rat-a-tat passes with McAllister and made for the byline, from where the German dinked a ball to the near post. Roma's back-line in chaos, Owen nipped in ahead of the static Assunção to eyebrow a glancing header across the flapping Antonioli and into the left-hand side of the goal. It was a brilliantly opportunistic finish, one reminiscent of his strike partner Fowler. Owen, all sparkly teeth, sprinted off with both arms in the air and palms flat open to the front, a celebration of childlike abandon.

At the start of the 1998–99 season, Evans and Houllier had thought about bolstering the centre of Liverpool's problem defence with the Borussia Dortmund veteran Jürgen Kohler. The transfer didn't come off but the interest was instructive of Liverpool's ambition at the time: the thirty-three-year-old Kohler, although a driving force behind Dortmund's recent Champions League win, would have been nothing more than a stopgap signing. But Liverpool required something more than a short-term measure. The defence was crying out for major surgery.

Houllier set about the task with gusto when flying solo the following summer. He purchased a new keeper in occasional Dutch international Sander Westerveld, the defensive midfielder Dietmar Hamann from Newcastle (having got Middlesbrough to take Paul Ince, fingered as a disruptive influence), and two new central defenders in Stéphane Henchoz from Blackburn Rovers and Sami Hyypiä, a virtual unknown who had helped the unheralded Willem II to an unprecedented second-place finish in the Dutch Eredivisie. Houllier was focused and sure he could match the club's ambitions, a fact ascertained by Hyypiä almost immediately upon meeting the Liverpool manager before signing. 'He explained that he was going to build a new, successful Liverpool side and he needed someone at my position,' recalled the Finn. 'I really started to believe that they meant business.'

Liverpool began the season slowly. Hyypiä's debut at Anfield was a dismal 1–0 defeat by newly promoted Watford, but Henchoz was injured and would not line up alongside him for the first couple of months. Dominic Matteo, Rigobert Song and a still-raw Carragher all proved below-par partners. Henchoz's belated arrival coincided with a major upturn in form as Liverpool began to grind out wins, Houllier building from the back with two banks of four and utilising the pace of Michael Owen and the one-season flash-in-the-pan Titi Camara up front. Hyypiä and Henchoz struck up an understanding quickly, the former positionally aware and aerially dominant, the latter almost acting as full-time sweeper round the giant Hyypiä, adept at scuttling about to block, tackle or shuttle attackers out towards the flanks while Hyppiä and everyone else regrouped.

Liverpool were never quite in the title race – which was rendered a formality anyway by a runaway Manchester United – but they were moving in the right direction. Perhaps the signature performance during a run which took them from twelfth place in October to second in April had been a 1–0 victory at Highbury in February, Camara scoring an early breakaway goal, a prize staunchly defended by his teammates as Arsenal subjected them to intense pressure. In the *Guardian*, David Lacey suggested that Liverpool's 'dedicated, disciplined defending … recalled the era of Bill Shankly when nothing, absolutely nothing, was given away'. By the middle of April, at the business end of a feel-good season which had seen Steven Gerrard announce himself as a goalscoring midfielder of rare talent and the equally promising (though less well-fated) Emile Heskey had been signed from Leicester for a club-record £12m, Liverpool were clear favourites to end the season as runners-up and qualify for the Champions League for the first time. A gleeful Houllier, upon leaving Highbury after the Camara game with his swag, had announced that Liverpool were 'mentally tougher than we were a year ago'. Famous last words. His side failed to win any of their last five matches, losing three, the last to a Bradford City side who would have gone down had they not battled to a thoroughly merited 1–0 win. Liverpool missed out on the Champions League by one point, in fourth place.

Although there were early signs that Houllier's approach might cause trouble down the line – he had already fallen out with Robbie Fowler, benched for most of the run-in and finally dropped after responding to a demand that he attend a post-match team-talk with a curt 'fuck off' – it was clearly paying dividends already. And although the team's sorry late-season capitulation was extremely painful at the time, it stood them in good stead mentally. It also, such are the vagaries of history, set them up for an unforgettable campaign.

Two attempts on goal, two goals. There were still eighteen minutes of the leg remaining, but Owen's finish had effectively ended the game. Batistuta put himself about in the immediate aftermath of Liverpool's second, but it quickly became clear that the visiting defence was in no mood to buckle. The Argentinian spun past a flat-footed Henchoz in the area, only for the defender to recover his poise quickly enough to harry the striker into a misdirected scoop at goal. Batistuta then attempted to hoick the ball down the middle, but only succeeded in booting it smack into the face of Hyypiä, who didn't flinch. 'We shall not be moved,' hollered the away support, fans schooled in the English league always ready to show their appreciation of meat-and-potatoes determination, no matter what sophistication they have been served up over the years.

Roma spent the dying moments of the match losing their cool. Vladimír Šmicer, who had replaced Ziege with a quarter of an hour to go, took down Emerson, who sprang up to demand the referee show a yellow. It was a fit of pique out of keeping with an even-tempered match, an incongruous response to a common-or-garden foul. Mangone came through the back of Barmby and that was a booking, the first caution of the evening. (Roma's frustration here at least was understandable, given Ziege's early escape.) Cafú executed a preposterous belly flop over Carragher's leg in a risible attempt to win a penalty kick. Liverpool meanwhile calmly locked it down; Owen made way for Litmanen with ten minutes to go, the Finn taking much of the sting from the game, always blessed with an extra couple of seconds on the ball.

Houllier made his way to the touchline, holding up five fingers, a human timepiece exhorting his players to keep it together for as many minutes. For the first time in the evening, his face betrayed a smidgen of concern – before giving way to a small, contented smile. There would be no need for worry, anyway. Batistuta looked to get a jump on Hyypiä on the edge of the Liverpool box, but despite being slightly under the ball, the defender still managed to hang and head clear. It was a symbolic end to an overall display of stunning aerial domination. Liverpool should have scored a third, Litmanen looking to release Fowler down the right, Mangone's poor clearance only finding Barmby, who clipped forward past the final defender and latched onto his own ball before hitting a poor shot straight at Antonioli.

Roma still had time for only their second shot of real menace during the entire match, Candela seeing his effort deflected over from the left of the D by the extended leg of Henchoz, then Batistuta finally won an aerial duel – but only because he'd been fouling Henchoz. There was no way through for the hosts. Houllier's side had registered a win against one of the best sides in Europe which two hours previously had seemed rather unlikely – and done so comprehensively. To put the result into some context, Roma had only previously lost three matches all season, one in the Coppa Italia, two in Serie A. They were leading the league, in the middle of a seven-game winning run domestically, and had been unbeaten in all competitions at home. 'We were poor, very poor,' said Capello after the game, which may have been true to an extent, though they were only as good as a ruthlessly drilled Liverpool had allowed them to be. And Liverpool hadn't conceded an inch. Tactically, Houllier had got it spot on: it was, Harry Harris wrote in the *Mirror*, 'his finest moment as Liverpool boss'.

Houllier, well aware that his project was on the right tracks and that there was no longer need for refit or revolution, refrained from indulging in any over-elaborate transfer dealings during the summer of 2000. The signing of Nick Barmby caused a minor media brouhaha; as well as coming from Everton, the first player to move from Goodison to Anfield since Dave Hickson in 1959, he had been a target for Manchester United, and therefore represented a double coup for Liverpool. 'You are talking as if he has changed religion or political label,' spluttered the manager when quizzed on the magnitude of the transfer, confirming (should anyone not have been paying attention) that he didn't quite possess the hyperbolic skills of a Shankly. But on his own terms, Barmby was a fuss-free purchase, a hard-working midfielder capable of the odd goal or two, an easy clip-on addition to Houllier's system. Ditto Markus Babbel, a free transfer from Bayern Munich who offered an instant upgrade at right-back.

Perhaps the least heralded arrival was that of the thirty-five-year-old Coventry City midfielder Gary McAllister. The transfer seemed puzzling at the time, but Houllier was vindicated by a signing that combined prescience with a good deal of self-awareness, the manager accepting that Liverpool's occasionally one-dimensional power game needed a touch of craft and savvy to take the team to the next level. McAllister was tasked with adding a splash of colour to a midfield built around the hard-working Hamann and passing on a few tips to upcoming talent such as Gerrard, Murphy and Carragher. 'The manager explained there was a need for some experience around the squad, an old head in the side,' said McAllister on his arrival. 'It's too early to say just how many games I will play. Maybe people will be surprised.' They certainly would be: from the start of October, McAllister took part in all but six of the season's remaining forty-nine matches.

Liverpool actually started Houllier's *annus mirabilis* poorly. In the third game of the league, at Southampton, the team somehow managed to blow a 3–0 lead with seventeen minutes to play, the substitute Matthew Le Tissier waddling on to orchestrate an unlikely draw for the home side. If nothing else, the farce showed Liverpool the importance of a calming influence amid the tumult of the high-octane Premiership. A challenge for the title was already improbable by the end of November, Liverpool having lost three of their four league games that month, two from winning positions (2–1 at Spurs, 4–3 at a Mark Viduka-inspired Leeds).

The side was, however, grinding out performances home and away in the Uefa Cup, stifling Rapid Bucharest, Slovan Liberec and Olympiakos in the early phases, and that obduracy soon transferred to the domestic stage. Having cleared out their pipes after the travails of November with an 8–0 win at Stoke in the League Cup, Liverpool embarked on a run that saw them concede just four league goals between December and February, reach the League Cup final, and register back-to-back victories over Manchester United (1–0) and Arsenal (a flattering 4–0), two results that stood as testament to the efficiency of Houllier's counter-attacking gameplan.

Liverpool were slowly becoming a serious proposition, capable of consistently going toe-to-toe with the top teams in a manner rarely seen since the tail end of the glory era under Dalglish. The trade-off was an aesthetic one – Houllier's was a functional team – and partly one which cost a little pride, too, as it necessitated Liverpool responding to 'better' footballing sides, negating and stifling their talent, then hitting them with a sucker punch. After years of decline, though, it was worth it, as the victories over Manchester United and Arsenal proved.

Houllier was no crazed ideologue and moved to secure the services of Jari Litmanen, who had been underused at Barcelona. 'He gives us different qualities, different options,' the manager explained on signing the Finn. 'He is an experienced on-and-off striker.' Litmanen would also eventually find himself equally undervalued by Houllier, a strange outcome that felt like an opportunity missed. But on arrival he was welcomed and he hit the ground running (even if, in the manner of the schemer of stereotype, he seemed less inclined to run around than hover above it all).

Litmanen's grace immediately became apparent. Coming on for his debut as a substitute against Crystal Palace in the League Cup semi-final, he floated down the right and rolled a cutback from the byline to lay on a goal for Šmicer. In his first start for the club, at Aston Villa in the league, his slide-rule pass from the centre-circle down the inside-left channel sprang Murphy into space, Murphy flicked inside for the on-rushing Gerrard to bash home from twenty-five yards, a mix of the exquisite and the direct which encapsulated the Houllier style at its best. Liverpool suddenly had options up front: a foursome of Litmanen, Owen, Heskey (who in his first season had yet to suffer the self-doubt that ravaged him and was scoring regularly enough) and Fowler (who had yet to fall out with Houllier completely) promised a less one-dimensional future, especially with Gerrard, Murphy and McAllister chipping in from midfield.

Even so, it would be overstating it to claim that Liverpool were on the verge of turning into a free-flowing attacking side. Houllier's methodology was still concerned first and foremost with locking things down at the back – the time-honoured two banks of four – and springing forward on the break. It wasn't always pretty, but at its best the theory was unplayable – and Liverpool were about to go to Rome and deliver a textbook example of its potency, Houllierisme *in excelsis*.

If anybody doubted how good that Roma side was – and by

extrapolation how impressive Liverpool's performance in the Stadio Olimpico had been – they were disabused in the second leg. Roma had never in their history won in England, but did so at Anfield, although their 1–0 victory was not enough to turn the tie around. Liverpool rode their luck in that match: after Gianni Guigou had scored from long range on seventy minutes, Montella then forced Babbel into a clear handball in the area, the referee José María García-Aranda correctly pointing to the spot before bafflingly changing his decision in Liverpool's favour, seemingly influenced by Batistuta – unaware that the referee had initially awarded the penalty – racing off to take a corner. Then again, Liverpool should have been out of sight early in the second half, Owen having spurned a glorious close-range chance before missing a penalty.

Roma's misfortune was the first instance of the bread regularly falling jam-side up for Houllier's Liverpool during the business end of the season. Three days after squeaking past the Italian side, Liverpool faced Birmingham City in the League Cup final. They outplayed the Blues for the majority of the game, as they should have done against second-tier opposition, and looked to have done enough, Fowler walloping home one of the great cup-final goals, sending a ball which had dropped over his shoulder looping in at pace from thirty yards. But a clumsy last-minute lunge in the penalty area by Henchoz had allowed Darren Purse to take the game to extra-time and Henchoz was extremely fortunate not to concede a second spot kick during the added thirty minutes after sliding in haplessly on Andy Johnson. Liverpool prevailed on penalties to win their first trophy in six seasons.

The dam broke. The second stage of Liverpool's Treble was completed in the FA Cup, but only after scraping past third-tier Wycombe Wanderers in the semi-final, then surviving an onslaught against Arsenal in the final, Thierry Henry repeatedly (and rather uncharacteristically) procrastinating in front of goal. Twice he was denied by Henchoz, who was really testing his luck with an egregiously blatant handball to make a near-post save on the goalline, then another while sliding across the face of the area in the second half with Liverpool losing and Arsenal looking to close the game out. Owen's close-range equaliser with eight minutes to go, followed by his superlative last-gasp winner across David Seaman having latched onto a raking length-of-field Patrik Berger pass along the inside-left channel, represented one of the great larcenies in FA Cup final history. That the victory might not have been entirely deserved was hinted at in the song that commemorated the winner – 'One-nil down, two-one up,/Michael Owen won the cup,/When a top-class Paddy pass/Gave the lad the ball,/Poor old Arsenal won fuck all.' Not that anybody from Anfield cared too much as Liverpool lifted their first FA Cup since 1992.

Liverpool would also finally make it into the following season's Champions League, a closing run of six wins and a draw from the last seven games set in motion by Gary McAllister's astounding long-range injury-time free-kick in a 3–2 victory at Goodison Park, an effort which even the most myopic Red would admit was only made possible by McAllister stealing a good ten yards when the referee's back was turned. (The unsung hero of that match, incidentally, was young Gregory Vignal, who had made a bustling run from deep inside his own half before being fouled to set up McAllister's free-kick.)

Luck was less of a feature in Europe, where Houllier's side cruised past Porto before annoying Barcelona at Camp Nou in the Uefa Cup semi-final, partly by kitting themselves in provocative Madrid-white shirts, but mainly by playing out another defensive masterclass. 'I'm not going to apologise for becoming only the third team to come here and stop Barcelona from scoring,' said Houllier after a dour goalless draw. 'If I'd gone out and attacked and lost by three goals, you would be calling me naive. What's the point in being naive? That would be a betrayal to our supporters.' A McAllister penalty in the second-leg was enough to send a deserving Liverpool to their first European final in sixteen years. Not that the arch-aesthete and former Barça manager Johan Cruyff agreed. 'In my opinion a team is horrible if they are incapable of stringing three passes together,' he harrumphed, to widespread amusement on Merseyside.

Liverpool triumphed over Alaves in the Dortmund final, a 5–4 victory after golden-goal extra-time. For the second time in the season, Fowler was denied the honour of the winning goal, Jordi Cruyff heading past a flapping Westerveld in the dying minutes of normal time, Fowler having earlier scored what had seemed to be the decisive goal in seven with a gorgeous left-to-right drift and fierce snapshot. As it panned out, McAllister would (perhaps deservedly, given his overall contribution to the season) deliver the golden blow, his free-kick diverted into his own net by Delfí Geli. 'These players made their own history tonight,' smiled Houllier as he hugged the giant trophy. 'They were playing for immortality. People remember finals.'

McAllister meanwhile purred in anticipation of a great future for Houllier's side. 'This is an amazing game for all the young guys at the club to be playing in so early in their career,' he said. 'Hopefully they will go and make Liverpool great again.' The club were indeed destined to revisit the pinnacle of European football, and it was assumed that, having turned Liverpool into a trophy-winning proposition again, and been hailed in some quarters as a modern-day Shankly, it would be Houllier who would lead the way. But the journey would not pan out as expected.

CHAPTER 10

Champions League final, Atatürk Stadium, Istanbul, 25 May 2005

AC Milan	**3–3**	**Liverpool**
Maldini 1		Gerrard 54
Crespo 39, 44		Šmicer 56
		Alonso 59

(Liverpool won 3–2 on penalties)

Serginho missed	Hamann scored
Pirlo saved	Cissé scored
Tomasson scored	Riise saved
Kaká scored	Šmicer scored
Shevchenko saved	

Dida	Jerzy Dudek
Cafú	Steve Finnan
	(Dietmar Hamann 46)
Jaap Stam	Sami Hyypiä
Alessandro Nesta	Jamie Carragher
Paolo Maldini	Djimi Traoré
Andrea Pirlo	Harry Kewell
	(Vladimír Šmicer 23)
Gennaro Gattuso (Rui Costa 112)	Steven Gerrard
Clarence Seedorf (Serginho 86)	Xabi Alonso
Kaká	Luis García
Hernán Crespo	Milan Baroš
(Jon Dahl Tomasson 85)	(Djibril Cissé 85)
Andriy Shevchenko	John Arne Riise
Carlo Ancelotti	Rafael Benítez

Ref: Manuel Enrique Mejuto González
Bkd: Baroš, Carragher
Att: 72,059

IN THE SHOWERS, DIDI HAMANN and David Moores lit up conspiratorial cigarettes. In the dressing-room, the defender Mauricio Pellegrino, who had missed out on the European campaign through being cup-tied, distributed among the victorious coaching staff the runners-up medals Milan's players had discarded. Outside, Liverpool fans began the arduous process of making their way back to central Istanbul. A sense of disbelief was universal: the inconceivable had happened. Liverpool's passage to the Champions League final had been improbable, but what they had done in the final, coming from 3–0 down to win on penalties, was impossible: no wonder it became known as the Miracle of Istanbul.

It took three seasons for Houllier to relinquish his grip on the top job at Anfield, though a slow descent began almost immediately in the wake of his greatest triumph.

Liverpool, after the cup Treble, went into the 2001–02 season as the team most fancied to depose Manchester United, who had just become only the fourth English club – after Huddersfield Town, Arsenal and Liverpool themselves – to win three league titles in succession. Liverpool had by that stage a relatively settled and dependable team, Houllier having completed his overhaul of the flaky Roy Evans side, turning them into a staunch proposition: difficult to beat, with enough goals in them to expect to win most matches and an increasingly trustworthy big-game mentality.

They had won nine of their final ten games in 2000–01 and, perhaps more significantly, they had done the league double over United for the first time since 1978–79 and made it three in a row at the start of the new campaign with a deserved (if ultimately dogged) win over Sir Alex Ferguson's side in the Charity Shield at the Millennium Stadium, goals in the first sixteen minutes from Gary McAllister and Michael Owen enough to see out a confidence-boosting 2–1 win.

'I still think United's team is better than mine, although that doesn't mean we won't improve and reach their level,' admitted Houllier, who at his wiliest was a master of passive aggression. United had spent over £50m in bringing Ruud van Nistelrooy and Juan Sebastián Verón to Old Trafford and looked formidable, although some wondered whether Verón might disrupt the delicate ecosystem of the Giggs-Scholes-Keane-Beckham midfield. Verón at Lazio, noted Simon Kuper in the *Observer* before the start of the season, often played at '75 per cent', had 'off days', and 'consistently played below his best … Verón has made a leap of faith, moving to a country he barely knows to join a club he had never visited before his medical, but Ferguson, in signing a footballer who has consistently played below his best, is making the bigger leap.' And so it would prove, with United out of sorts for much of the season. For Liverpool, the opportunity was there.

Houllier saw no need for major changes. The only pre-season signing was John Arne Riise, brought in to bolster a left-hand side previously populated by the right-footed and erratic Jamie Carragher – yet to find his true home at centre-back – and an uninterested Christian Ziege.

Liverpool opened with five wins: two Champions League qualifiers against FC Haka of Finland, the Charity Shield, a Premier League game against West Ham United and the Uefa Super Cup in which they beat the new European champions Bayern Munich 3–2 in a mildly distracting thriller in Monaco. Houllier was ecstatic, claiming – accurately if misleadingly – that his side had bagged five trophies in the calendar year of 2001. 'It is six months to the day since we won the Worthington Cup and I said the first trophy would be the most difficult to win,' he said. 'Looking back it probably was. But I thought that would be the catalyst for our development.'

In that there were shades of Brian Clough, who always claimed that the most important trophy he won at Nottingham Forest was the 1977 Anglo-Scottish Cup, which instilled belief and acted as a springboard for the greater glories that lay ahead. Houllier understood that and, although he was derided by many, his claim of 'five trophies' was a self-conscious trumpeting of Liverpool's intent. The club had competed only erratically for the major honours during the 1990s, and he was determined to assert that Liverpool were back and ready to compete again at the very highest level.

Understandable the gambit may have been, but the sense of positivity did not last long. In fact, much momentum was lost before the 2001–02 season had even begun with the outbreak of a power struggle between Houllier and Robbie Fowler. During training ahead of the Charity Shield, the latter had pelted a ball in the general direction of the assistant manager Phil Thompson, triggering an astonishingly childish spat. Thompson believed Fowler was aiming for him on purpose and demanded an apology; the player refused, pointing out the ball had struck a goal net between him and the captain of the 1981 European Cup winners. 'Thompson claimed I had tried to hit him deliberately,' Fowler recalled, 'the big fucking girl.'

As these two professionals (total major medals between them: twenty-eight) bickered, Houllier unexpectedly dropped Fowler a couple of hours before the Charity Shield against United. It would turn out he had made a long-term strategic decision which did not include Fowler, having decided to build the team around the strike-force of Michael Owen and Emile Heskey, and saw an opportunity to drive a wedge between the fans and a player they adored. 'I've been bombed,' Fowler told journalists gruffly. He also missed the season opener against West Ham, forced to sit in the stands as Owen scored twice in a laboured 2–1 win.

At the time, it seemed Houllier was fighting from a position of strength, but it didn't last long as Liverpool's form disintegrated. First they lost, live on Sky's *Monday Night Football*, at Bolton Wanderers, Sander Westerveld failing to get his body behind a speculative last-minute effort from Dean Holdsworth. 'The Liverpool keeper has made a mistake that will haunt him for many days to come,' cried the Sky commentator Alan Parry, a line of eerie prescience. By the end of the week, Houllier had conducted an astonishing piece of transfer business, signing Coventry's young keeper Chris Kirkland for £10m after a move for his preferred choice, Feyenoord's Jerzy Dudek, fell through – then bringing Dudek to the club as well as the deal was resurrected just before the transfer window closed. It was an unnecessary humiliation for Westerveld, a solid if not quite top-class performer. More worryingly for Liverpool, the double signing reeked of panic, Houllier for once reacting to events rather than shaping them with the measured sense of calm that had characterised his approach since his arrival in 1998.

Dudek was thrown straight into the team against Aston Villa at Anfield but was helpless as three goals whistled past him, Liverpool losing their second game in a row and this time being thoroughly outplayed. After only three matches, Houllier's side were already five points behind Manchester United and Leeds, and four behind Arsenal. Much of the pre-season optimism had evaporated, not least because, geared to playing for Owen, Liverpool were looking very narrow, especially on the left where Carragher and Danny Murphy were often deployed, cutting inside onto their favoured right feet. Even Riise, brought in at least in part for his attacking qualities from left-back, favoured drifting infield with a view to unleashing long-range shots.

It was then that Liverpool's season took a surreal turn. Their Champions League debut – the club's first match since 1985 in Europe's premier tournament– had been keenly anticipated, but 11 September 2001 would be remembered for events of far greater significance. The game against the surprise Portuguese champions Boavista – only the second club outside Portugal's big three of Benfica, Sporting and Porto to win the title – kicked off exactly six hours and one immaculately observed minute of silence after the first plane hit the twin towers, lending an air of thorough futility and distressing perspective to the evening's proceedings.

The Brazilian striker Silva gave Boavista a second-minute lead and although Owen equalised midway through the first half with a cutely taken curler into the top corner, Liverpool spent the majority of the evening on the back foot, offering little up front and looking extremely nervous defensively. A draw away to Borussia Dortmund and successive wins over Dynamo Kyiv put Liverpool on the brink of the second group phase, but by then their season had taken another unexpected twist, one as unpredictable as it was unpleasant.

Houllier's side had regrouped following the defeats to Bolton and Villa. They fell behind early in the Merseyside derby, but eventually overpowered Walter Smith's Everton, Owen scoring his twenty-second goal in fifteen outings, justifying the manager's preference up front as Fowler spent the match on the bench. After narrow wins over Tottenham Hotspur and Newcastle, Liverpool were suddenly only five points off the early pacesetters Leeds with a game in hand. David O'Leary's young side were next up but for the second time in just over a month, a hugely anticipated Anfield occasion was a sideshow to distressing events off the pitch.

At half-time, with Liverpool second best and trailing to a Harry Kewell goal, Houllier delivered an untypically short speech to his team and, sweating profusely but hiding his discomfort from the players, left the room with the club doctor Mark Waller. Much improved, Liverpool salvaged a draw through Murphy. But Houllier had not come out with them: instead he was rushed to Broadgreen Hospital with chest pains caused by an acute dissection of the aorta, the main artery taking the blood to the heart.

Broadgreen, older fans recalled pensively, was the hospital where Shankly suffered his second and fatal heart attack in 1981. Houllier survived but only after an eleven-hour operation. Remarkably he was receiving visitors and, with Thompson taking temporary control, Liverpool exhaled with relief and found themselves inspired by the thought of their stricken manager.

They won six of their next seven league games, establishing a six-point lead over Arsenal with just over a third of the season gone. Fowler did his bit, scoring a hat-trick away at Leicester in the first Premiership game after Houllier had been taken ill. But all was not well. By that stage, Fowler claimed, Houllier's recuperation had reached a stage at which he could telephone messages of support and congratulation to his team. 'I never got a phone call after I scored a hat-trick for him,' he said. 'All I got was the axe.' Fowler would only start three more games for the club, his final appearance, against Sunderland, aborted at half-time as Thompson reshuffled after Didi Hamann had been sent off. At Houllier's behest, Fowler was packed off to Leeds for £12m. The departure of the club's fifth-greatest all-time goalscorer – only Ian Rush, Roger Hunt, Gordon Hodgson and Billy Liddell had found the net more often – was commemorated in a small article in the middle of the next Anfield programme. 'I know there are a lot of disappointed fans,' wrote Thompson, 'but I hope they will have belief … When you look at how the club has developed under Gerard's leadership, I don't think anybody can complain.'

While the manner of Fowler's exit felt inconsiderate – he was a player, after all, who had kept Anfield's spirits buoyant for the best part of a decade while the club stumbled across the barren (by standards set during the previous two decades) post-Dalglish terrain – it's hard to argue that Houllier was acting irrationally. Fowler, despite a late blossoming the previous season when his spectacular goals in the Worthington and Uefa Cup finals would have been winners but for rudimentary defensive errors, was by that stage some way off the impish force he had been before suffering a medial ligament injury against Everton in 1998. There were still fine performances but there were many more sluggish ones and Fowler's subsequent career stats suggest Houllier cashed in at the right time – even if the more romantic wished it were not so.

It was certainly difficult to argue against Houllier and Thompson's stance as Middlesbrough were swatted aside in the first match at Anfield after Fowler's departure to leave them six clear of Arsenal and eleven ahead of Manchester United. 'They are the team to beat this season. Liverpool's side has emerged over the last couple of seasons and they don't give anything away and can score goals out of nothing,' said the Boro defender Gareth Southgate, dismissing the accusation that Liverpool were little more than grinders. 'As for boring, it depends on how you like your football. I couldn't accuse them of not passing the ball or not scoring spectacular goals. Sure, they are solid defensively, but as a centre-half I'm bound to say that.'

But there had been warning signs that Liverpool's occasionally one-dimensional approach – soak up pressure at the back before springing Owen and Heskey clear down the channels – might not be foolproof. In the second phase of the Champions League, Barcelona came to Anfield and highlighted the major flaw in Houllier's reactive tactics. This match is now remembered as a one-sided embarrassment for Liverpool – which to a large extent it was, Barcelona spending the last half an hour hogging possession as the home side vainly scuttled around in search of the ball – but the plotline was slightly more complicated. Barça won 3–1, easily in the end, but they went behind to an Owen goal and cleared a Heskey shot off the line before Patrick Kluivert equalised from an offside position. Owen then missed an open goal on the hour before Fabio Rochemback hammered home from twenty yards, after which Barça – conducted by a twenty-one-year-old Xavi – took control. And even then Marc Overmars's late third was steered home after an offside burst. Liverpool had shown they had the tools to trouble the best – Barça were one of the favourites for the competition and would make it to the semis before being outclassed by Real Madrid – but it was also plain that any team capable of keeping hold of the ball and boasting any sort of schemer in their ranks could cause Liverpool serious discomfort.

The Middlesbrough game proved a watershed. (Boro would serve as major staging posts in the narratives of each of Liverpool's three serious title tilts during the 2000s. Defeat at the Riverside undermined Liverpool's good start in 2002–03 and it was after a 2–0 defeat there in 2008–09 that they cast off the defensive shackles and almost reeled in a United side that at one point had led by seven points with a game in hand.) Fulham, having won promotion the previous season, came to Anfield, hustled, bustled and came away with a comfortable goalless draw. 'We adapted our game,' explained the Fulham manager Jean Tigana. 'We usually play a very offensive style, but we knew Liverpool are strong on the counter, so I made the team slow down the tempo.' Liverpool then went to Chelsea, where they were denied the ball, battered by Jimmy Floyd Hasselbaink and Eiður Guðjohnsen, and thrashed 4–0. Arsenal were next at Anfield and, despite losing Giovanni van Bronckhorst to an early red card, won there for the first time in nine years.

In the *Guardian*, David Lacey's report was damning. Liverpool did not possess 'the subtlety or precision needed to break down determined defending,' he wrote, their football becoming 'laboured and predictable'. An injury to Heskey at half-time had disrupted Liverpool's equilibrium up front, reducing Owen's usefulness; Litmanen came on and scored a consolation, but his clever promptings were rarely read by a team that knew only one way to play. Top of the table at the start of December, Liverpool were down to third before Christmas. Houllier and Thompson responded by bringing in

Nicolas Anelka on loan from Paris Saint-Germain, a cunning signing, but one that would eventually highlight the fault-lines running through the Houllier philosophy.

After stuttering through December and January, Liverpool negotiated the second half of the season with confidence, losing only once more in the league. They completed the double over Manchester United at Old Trafford, notched back-to-back 4–0 and 6–0 victories at Leeds and Ipswich, and won nine of their last ten games. They even topped the table again during March, but the draws and defeats of the winter months meant they were never totally in control of their own destiny, and although they finished second – ahead of Manchester United for the first time since 1991 – Houllier's side was seven points adrift of the champions Arsenal.

Houllier had personally given Liverpool's campaign impetus by returning unannounced to the Anfield touchline for the Champions League fixture against the Serie A champions Roma, a game his team had to win by at least two goals if they were to qualify for the quarter-finals. On a tumultuous night, and with Owen injured, Liverpool threw three up front: Heskey, Litmanen and Šmicer. All three played with verve and panache, as Litmanen and then Heskey scored the goals to seal a famous victory. At the final whistle, the Anfield announcer George Sephton urged the crowd to cherish the memory of the evening forever. 'I have never seen Liverpool play like this,' said the Roma coach Fabio Capello. And then, before the Reds faced Bayer Leverkusen in the quarters, and with his side still in the title hunt domestically, Houllier chimed in with an ill-fated soundbite of his own: 'We are ten games from greatness.'

His very presence had given his men a boost against Roma, but Houllier undid much of the good work with a notorious substitution against Leverkusen. With Liverpool leading 2–1 on aggregate with half an hour of the second leg remaining, Houllier replaced his midfield linchpin Hamann with the lightweight Šmicer. Liverpool ceded control to Michael Ballack, Yıldıray Baştürk and Dimitar Berbatov, let in two goals within seven minutes of Hamann's departure and, although Litmanen looked to have salvaged a semi-final place late on with a drop of the shoulder and threaded shot, Lucio delivered a killer blow with six minutes to go. It was an inexplicable tactical blunder – although on another day Owen would not have wasted three golden chances to put the tie beyond Leverkusen.

Perhaps the greater fault, though, had lain in the home leg, as Houllier sent his team out in an overly cautious manner, the compelling arguments for positivity offered by the Roma game – Liverpool's only victory in six second-stage group matches – ignored. Liverpool bumbled their way to a 1–0 win, but only after being pushed back for the majority of the second half. As a result, Houllier's side lost momentum in their European development as well as priceless confidence ahead of the away leg, the chance to face Manchester United in an all-English semi-final passed up. Liverpool's gallop towards greatness had been halted with nine fences still to jump.

It got worse. In the summer of 2002, Houllier splurged £18.7m on El Hadji Diouf, Salif Diao and Bruno Cheyrou. In retrospect it came to be regarded as a disaster, but at the time the three signings stimulated a sense of excitement. Diouf and Diao had both shone for Senegal at the World Cup in South Korea and Japan, the former ripping the holders France to shreds in the opening game, the latter scoring one of the goals of the tournament, a lung-busting box-to-box effort against Denmark that brought comparisons with Patrick Vieira. Cheyrou, meanwhile, was hailed by Houllier as the new Zidane. He also brought in the French youngsters Anthony Le Tallec and Florent Sinama-Pongolle, both of whom would go on to make small but vital contributions to the Champions League campaign that culminated in Istanbul.

More culpable was Houllier's refusal to make Nicolas Anelka's loan deal from Paris Saint-Germain permanent. On the face of it, his pace may have seemed to offer little not already provided by the Owen–Heskey partnership but there was a greater subtlety to his play, allied to superior touch and technique. In the closing months of the previous season, Liverpool's most impressive display had come in the 3–0 home win over Newcastle as Anelka repeatedly scorched down the inside-right channel, making space for himself and bringing others into the game.

Houllier preferred the limited if willing Heskey, Boxer from *Animal Farm* chosen ahead of a more temperamental thoroughbred. The decision suggested Houllier's authoritarian approach, beneficial in the early days of his reign to offset the damage caused by the laissez-faire managerial style of Roy Evans, was beginning to go too far. It had done for Fowler and it sent Anelka to Manchester City instead, apparently because Houllier didn't care for the pushy way in which the player's brothers conducted his business affairs. The implied message was that Anelka was more trouble than he was worth. As Anelka went on to score regularly at City, Fenerbahçe, Bolton and Chelsea, Diouf made little impact on the pitch while causing all manner of bad feeling off it.

If the decision to snub Anelka seemed odd – almost as though Houllier could not bear to admit that the £11m spent on Heskey might have been a mistake – the jettisoning of Litmanen bordered on the absurd. At thirty-one, the Finn had left his best years behind him at Ajax and Barcelona and yet was still a world-class operator, a fact illustrated by his performances in the Champions League the previous season. But after signing Litmanen from Barça in January 2001, Houllier had granted him only twelve league starts in a season and a half, a frustrating spell that remains one of the club's great lost opportunities and indicative of the increasingly prosaic nature of Houllier's philosophy. (Berger too would soon be on his way out, though to be fair to the manager, injury would be the Czech's nemesis.)

The Anelka affair notwithstanding, it seemed for a time that Houllier was, on the whole, getting it right. Despite conceding late equalisers three times in their first four games of the 2002–03 season, Liverpool went twelve unbeaten from the off and were top of the table at the start of November. Another challenge for the title looked on the cards, although there were warning signs that Houllier's side, without the fluidity offered by Litmanen and Anelka, was coagulating into something altogether more stodgy and predictable.

The alarms began sounding in the middle of that good league run, away to Valencia in the Champions League. Liverpool were eviscerated. 'I can't remember a European tie when we've been so much on the back foot,' admitted Houllier after the Spanish side had won 2–0. 'We looked shaky in defence, we didn't look bright in midfield and we should have done better up front.'

It was a thrashing in every sense other than the scoreline, the effervescent Pablo Aimar and Rubén Baraja harrying the visitors from start to finish. Valencia, Spanish champions for the first time in thirty seasons, had conceded only twenty-seven goals in their title-winning season, a template Houllier would have approved of. But Valencia boasted a dash of wonder in attack, too. 'People accuse me of playing defensive football,' said their coach Rafael Benítez. 'I think we made our point out there.'

If the Liverpool hierarchy's interest had not been piqued by that display, it certainly was a month later, when Valencia came to Anfield and won 1–0, another comprehensive humiliation not totally reflected on the scoreboard. Aimar was once again Valencia's playmaker and Liverpool's tormentor, with Baraja and David Albelda neutering Didi Hamann and Steven Gerrard in the centre, especially during a tetchy second half when the visitors showed they were just as adept at the physical as the technical side of the game.

In terms of getting results, if not quite on stylistic grounds, Liverpool had looked as good as any team in Europe in their Treble season of 2000–01 and had arguably been just as good when reaching the quarter-final of the Champions League the season after. But this was a severe blow, evidence that a gap was emerging again between Liverpool and the European elite.

The Valencia humiliations derailed the season. Liverpool managed workmanlike home victories over West Ham in the league and Southampton in the League Cup but they relinquished their unbeaten league record at Middlesbrough. Needing a win away to Basel to stay in the Champions League, they conceded three times in the first twenty-nine minutes. Liverpool did fight back in the second half to force a draw but, other than offering a glimpse of glory to come, that changed little and they slipped into the Uefa Cup.

Liverpool failed to win again in the league until the middle of January, by which time a seven-point lead at the top of the table had been turned into an eleven-point deficit, Houllier's side slipping to sixth place. The League Cup was won at the expense of a slightly uninterested Manchester United in March – whatever criticisms can be made of the Houllier reign, he at least kept the roll of honour ticking over – but the feelgood factor lasted less than three weeks, by which time Celtic had thoroughly outplayed Liverpool home and away in the quarter-final of the Uefa Cup. Henrik Larsson was far too wily for a defence with Djimi Traoré in its centre, while Liverpool lacked the creative tools to respond. 'If Houllier thought Gary McAllister [who had departed to manage Coventry] had passed on enough of his wisdom to the younger men before leaving Anfield,' wrote Richard Williams in the *Guardian*, 'he was mistaken. None of the players available to the Liverpool manager has that particular kind of footballing intelligence.' A damning but accurate indictment of Steven Gerrard, Dietmar Hamann and Danny Murphy, players who boasted many positive qualities but couldn't dictate the flow of matches on their own terms. Heskey, meanwhile, was becoming exposed as a striker lacking the tools to flourish at the top level. A lumbering performance against the Scottish champions was the latest stumble in a career increasingly defined by moments of unfortunate slapstick; recent mishaps had included a seventy-yard free run at second-tier Crystal Palace in the FA Cup which culminated in a cushioned chip into the keeper's arms and a fresh-air swipe at Wembley against Manchester United which nearly sent a divot of earth, rather than the ball, sailing goalwards.

'Making a Champions League place will make up for this,' said Houllier, but they didn't. Liverpool finished fifth, three points off their target, after a run in which three embarrassments stand out: a 4–0 gubbing at Old Trafford, a home defeat to Manchester City, the jettisoned Anelka scoring in the last minute, and a final-day reverse at Chelsea in a winner-takes-all showdown for that final Champions League spot.

Houllier attempted to liven up his increasingly predictable team with the Leeds forward Harry Kewell, a progressive idea in theory, but of limited use in practice: it was fine to ask the Australian to operate in the hole behind Owen and Heskey, but his influence was always going to be limited in a team conditioned to battering long balls down the channels, much of the play bypassing Kewell altogether. Kewell cut a hopelessly isolated figure as Liverpool lost the opening game of the 2003–04 season 2–1 to Chelsea and their season never got started: by the time Patrik Berger, sold by Liverpool in 2003, struck a winner against them for Portsmouth in mid-October, they were already twelve points behind the leaders Arsenal. Bolton ended their defence of the League Cup at Anfield, another defeat at Portsmouth ended FA Cup hopes and Marseille, with Didier Drogba in fine form, knocked them out of the Uefa Cup with little fuss.

Liverpool managed to scrape into fourth spot, ahead of Newcastle and into the following season's Champions League. By then, a sizeable proportion of supporters, playing the long game, would have been happy enough to see Newcastle pip them, fed up as they were with Houllier's increasingly scratchy football and hopeful of managerial change. As it panned out, events turned their way anyway. Houllier, desperate to remain in charge, spent £14m on Djibril Cissé and bundled Emile Heskey, who had become almost a symbol of what was wrong with the manager's reign, off to Birmingham. But it was too late. Houllier was bundled out of the door himself, the club having lined up the man whose Valencia team had arguably done the most to nudge his Liverpool off the tracks in the first place.

Rafael Benítez arrived at Anfield with a reputation as one of the brightest young managerial talents in the world game, perhaps second in rank only to José Mourinho, who had just won the Champions League with Porto before moving to Chelsea. Liverpool had reportedly considered Mourinho themselves only to have dismissed him as gauche, his famous touchline celebration at Old Trafford during Porto's successful Champions League run troubling a board that still fancied itself as the upholder of old-school sporting values. Whether Liverpool were, in truth, capable of attracting a property as hot as Mourinho when a club backed by a billionaire was also in the market for a new manager is debatable. The other names commonly reported as Liverpool targets at the time – Martin O'Neill of Celtic, Charlton's Alan Curbishley and Gordon Strachan, freshly cashiered from Southampton – suggest an appointment of Mourinho's stature might have been beyond them.

Benítez was certainly a step up from Curbishley or Strachan, though. In fact his record was pretty much the equal of Mourinho's, even if his international profile was not. After an unexceptional start to his managerial career at Valladolid, Osasuna, Extremadura and Tenerife, he succeeded Héctor Cúper as manager of a Valencia team which had made the 2000 and 2001 Champions League finals. Benítez had been fourth choice for the job, but soon proved his worth, turning the nearly men into winners. His methodical, hard-working and sometimes comically intense approach didn't go down well initially with either players or fans. The players were irked by the banning of ice cream, olives and paella (which, as a dish that had its origins in Valencia, had a symbolic power: Benítez, the Madridista, overturning local custom). Nobody was impressed by early results: just before Christmas Valencia lay in mid-table, having drawn nine and lost two of their opening fourteen games. Benítez, booed regularly by his own fans, was close to the sack.

After a spectacular 3–2 win at Espanyol in a game in which Valencia had trailed 2–0, Benítez's side began to click. He had instigated a slightly more direct style of play than Cúper, the ball being funnelled quickly up the channels towards Mista, who would bring goalscoring midfielders such as Ruben Baraja, Pablo Aimar and winger Kily González into play. The side were tight and assertive at the back, the defence bolstered by the aggressive defensive midfielder David Albelda. While the goals-for column at the end of the campaign showed a modest fifty-one from thirty-eight matches, the goals-against total was a mere twenty-seven. The mix worked. After the turnaround at Espanyol, Valencia won fifteen of their remaining twenty-one matches, claiming the league by seven points from Deportivo La Coruña.

It was an epochal achievement, although Valencia failed to put up much of a defence of their title the following season despite their performances against Liverpool in the Champions League. In 2003–04, though, Benítez inspired their greatest season. They won La Liga again; with Aimar still pulling the strings and Mista pushed further up the field, they scored twenty more goals in this title-winning campaign than their first, while keeping it equally tight at the back. In addition, Benítez inspired the team to the Uefa Cup, their first European trophy since defeating Arsenal in the Cup-Winners' Cup final of 1980.

This was unprecedented achievement, yet the club seemed strangely cool towards their manager. Benítez considered his 'ideal scenario' to be a long and fruitful relationship with Valencia, but the feelings were not reciprocated. The managing director Manuel Llorente refused to offer him an improved contract – 'If I give you two more years,' reasoned Llorente, 'and then you lose three matches, it's going to be my problem' – while the director of football Jesús García Pitarch became infamously intransigent during a stand-off over transfers. Benítez had suggested signing the wing-back Cafú from Roma, only to be presented with Uruguayan forward Fabián Canobbio, prompting the oft-repeated line, 'I asked the club for a sofa and they bought me a lampshade, and that can't be right.' Benítez accused Llorente of being 'a man with no friends who stays in the shadows waiting to stab you in the back'. Valencia later changed their minds and offered their title-winning boss more money, but by then they were informed it was too late. Benítez was in tears as he announced his resignation to the press, then set off for Merseyside.

He arrived at Anfield in June 2004 with Liverpool if not in crisis exactly, then at least deep in gloom, the giddy promise offered by the Treble season of 2001 already a distant memory. But Houllier had at least left a legacy: the club had restored its habit, forgotten in the 1990s, of picking up trophies, and while the team was far from perfect, it was at least reasonably dependable, with good defensive habits ingrained. Just like Cúper at Valencia, Houllier had left Benítez solid foundations on which to build.

Benítez's approach was not vastly different to that of Houllier: a methodical and staunch defence, balls hit into spaces behind the full-backs for pacy strikers to chase down, midfield runners supporting the attack. Benítez would place more emphasis on his midfield schemer, a strange blind spot of Houllier's given Liverpool's positive experiences with McAllister, and to that end, Benítez spent the bulk of a limited transfer purse on the young Real Sociedad midfielder Xabi Alonso, whose metronomic short passing, coupled with an ability to rake the occasional spectacular long one, would instantly dictate Liverpool's tempo. The addition of Alonso allowed Benítez to move Gerrard away from the centre, where his impatient style too often ceded possession for any side with genuine aspirations to be title-winners.

Despite his wariness about Gerrard's occasional wastefulness in possession, Benítez was in no doubt that he was crucial to Liverpool's future as an attacking force, and told him as much during a flying visit to England's Euro 2004 camp, a desperate attempt to convince him to turn down a move to Chelsea. Houllier may have left behind a team with a solid work ethic that was ripe for development, but there were few stars and Benítez couldn't afford to lose talent like Gerrard – especially as Owen had opted to move to Real Madrid and his replacement, the skitteringly erratic Djibril Cissé, was most certainly not a man Benítez would have spent £14m on himself. Gerrard opted to stay.

Benítez made two other crucial decisions in his first summer at Liverpool. One was to purchase a touch of wonder in the Barcelona creator Luis García, a player with a tendency to hover down the inside-left channel, not quite a winger, midfielder or number 10, but a mercurial ball player with a habit of scoring spectacular and important goals whom he had signed on loan while coach of Tenerife. The other was to shift Jamie Carragher, a workaday full-back at best, into central defence, where he would find his calling as an unpretentious but highly effective stopper.

There were early struggles. Liverpool were as good as out of the title race by mid-October, twelve points behind the leaders Arsenal and ten shy of the eventual champions Chelsea. They would never really gain any serious momentum in the league. The Champions League campaign, meanwhile, was very nearly over before the group stage, Liverpool scraping through the qualifier despite an abject 1–0 home defeat by Grazer AK. Lame defeats in the group stage at Olympiakos and Monaco suggested Europe would be little more than an exercise in experience for a side in transition.

And then, as November became December, two successive home games changed the mood. Benítez's side had already

shown signs of resilience at Fulham in October, having won
4–2 after being two goals down at the break, the first time
Liverpool had come back to win from a half-time deficit since
– astonishingly – 1991 against Notts County. Then they hosted
the reigning champions Arsenal, a team that had lost just one
of its previous fifty-five league matches. The match is remembered for Neil Mellor's preposterous stoppage-time winner, a
long-range precision missile at the end of a route-one move, a
one-in-a-million surgical strike. But what was really notable
was Liverpool's resilience: with five in midfield, arranged in
two banks, they kept the champions at arm's length for large
chunks of the game, while displaying the patience to snap
forward when the opportunity arose. As well as Mellor's explo-
sive strike, Liverpool opened the scoring with a picture-book
team goal: Robert Pires, looking to break down the inside-left
channel, was robbed by Hamann; Steve Finnan raked a diagonal pass to Kewell on the left wing; Kewell nodded inside
first-time to Gerrard, who laid the ball off for the onrushing
Alonso to batter a shot into the top-left corner, Mellor having
made room by dragging Arsenal's central defenders to the left
with a decoy run. On the touchline, Benítez gave a small wink
and thumbs up, arguably his most demonstrative display of
emotion during his six years at Anfield.

Then came Olympiakos in the final match of the Champions League group stage, a game Liverpool had to win if they
wanted to progress, and by two goals if the Greeks managed
to get on the scoresheet – which they did, midway through
the first half, Rivaldo rattling home a free-kick after Antonio Núñez went walkabout from guard duty on the post. The
second half was almost certainly the pivotal act in Liverpool's
modern history, although there is little Benítez can claim
as a tactical victory. Having set up initially by packing the
midfield and waiting patiently for the goal they required, Liverpool had no option but to go hell for leather, as they sought
the three goals they needed to progress. Florent Sinama-
Pongolle came on for Djimi Traoré, whereupon a freshly styled

front three – Sinama-Pongolle, Kewell and the first half's lone striker Milan Baroš – repeatedly ran at the visitors. There was an instant reward, Kewell dispossessing Anastasios Pantos down the left before rolling one across the face of the goal for the substitute to poke home.

Liverpool spent the next half hour huffing and puffing, before Benítez swapped Baroš with Mellor. The young striker, who had scored hatfuls of goals in the reserves, but didn't quite have the delicacy to make it in the first team, nevertheless earned himself a small sidebar in the club's history with his thirteen-minute contribution. Within a minute of coming on he had equalised, driving home from close range after Sinama-Pongolle and Núñez had caused a minor scramble in the box. Then, with four minutes to go, came the second-most famous goal to be scored in front of the Kop (David Fairclough's strike against St Etienne in 1977 surely still untouchable). Carragher, probing down the left before checking back, dinked a ball inside towards Mellor, who from the edge of the area cushioned a header back into the centre towards the feet of Gerrard, twenty-five yards out. With glorious inevitability, Liverpool's captain thrashed a first-time drive just inside the right-hand post. As Anfield cavorted, Benítez was prevented from passing on tactical instructions by a steward grabbing him in a bear-hug. 'Everyone at the club wants to stay in the Champions League and we don't want to be thinking about the Uefa Cup draw at the end of the week,' Gerrard had said before the game, which many took as a coded reference that he would be likely to leave for Chelsea, possibly in the January transfer window, if Liverpool failed to progress. He had ensured he would be staying at Anfield for at least the rest of the season.

Liverpool were beaten at Anfield by Chelsea on New Year's Day, a game in which Frank Lampard clattered ineptly into Xabi Alonso, breaking the ankle of the home side's most influential player. The miserable result presaged what was in many respects an indifferent five months: Liverpool won only thirteen of their remaining twenty-seven matches, and crashed out of the FA Cup at Burnley as a result of a ludicrous own goal, the increasingly hapless Traoré attempting a drag back and turn in his own six-yard box but instead planting the ball baroquely into his own net. The suggestion, there and then, that Traoré would have a heroic contribution to make in a European Cup final, just over four months down the line, would have seemed ridiculous. But Liverpool, with Traoré part of the set-up, were about to make a habit of winning – or at least coming through – the big games that really mattered.

The exception to that rule would be the League Cup final, lost in extra-time to Chelsea. Liverpool were eleven minutes from victory but were undone by another ludicrous own goal, Gerrard somehow managing to guide a backwards header into the top-right corner of the net from twelve yards. As José Mourinho, playing the pantomime villain as ever, shushed Liverpool fans by holding a finger to his lips, Chelsea made off with the silverware. But as he'd later find out to his cost, Liverpool were saving all of their luck – and their best performances – for Europe.

Liverpool took up in the knockout stages of the Champions League where they had left off in 2002, against Bayer Leverkusen. Benítez fielded three centre-backs in Carragher, Hyypiä and Traoré, played García and Baroš high to prevent Leverkusen passing out from the back and patiently waited for opportunities to arise. Leverkusen were no longer the side they had been three years previously and chances came along soon enough. Igor Bišćan – a much-maligned figure during his time at Anfield, unsuccessfully hawked to Crystal Palace, but about to become a dependable midfield presence during Liverpool's run to the final – sucked in the Leverkusen defence with an intricate run down the middle. Sashaying past Paul Freier and Carsten Ramelow, he slipped a ball through for Luis García, curving his run from the right, to notch an early goal. Liverpool's control was not total – Dimitar Berbatov should have equalised when sent clear by Steve Finnan's lazy defensive header – but it was good enough. Milan Baroš missed a one-on-one too, while Riise and Hamann added to a comprehensive win with goals from free-kicks.

The performance was sullied, though, in the dying seconds. Berbatov lashed a shot from distance that should easily have been fielded by Dudek, but the keeper – who had made several high-profile errors since taking over from Westerveld, most notably against United – spilled the shot, allowing França to sweep the loose ball into the net for a crucial away goal.

Given the breakdown Liverpool had suffered in Germany three years earlier under Houllier, Benítez and his side had reason to worry about the lifeline thrown to Leverkusen. Their response, though, was magnificent, and the next two games went a long way to turning outsiders for the Champions League into serious contenders.

First came the Leverkusen away leg. As at Anfield, Benítez played five at the back, with a lone striker. That forward, Baroš, was hardly a target man in the grand English tradition, but he was prepared to chase down long passes fired behind the full-backs. It was he who set the tone, charging into the area from the right and being hacked down by Jan-Ingwer Callsen-Bracker – the penalty wasn't given – before teeing up Gerrard for a shot which led to the corner that yielded Liverpool's first goal, flicked home by Luis García. The increasingly confident García soon doubled Liverpool's lead, effectively putting the tie beyond the Germans, redirecting Bišćan's downward header into the net from close range. Baroš plundered a reward for himself in the second half, the match ending 3–1 as Jacek Kryznówek struck late on. Leverkusen had been thrashed 6–2 on aggregate, a result all the more impressive for the resolute manner in which Liverpool had ignored the ghosts of 2002. 'The other teams in the competition will watch our game tonight and will start to say, be careful, they won't be easy opponents,' noted Benítez.

Having established their solidity and bolstered their

confidence, Liverpool grew yet further in their quarter-final against Juventus. Before the first leg, at Anfield, home fans displayed a necessary but heartfelt humility, offering an apology to Juve and their followers for the events of Heysel, this being the first time the two teams had met since the tragic day in Brussels nearly twenty years previously. A mosaic, which covered the Kop, read '*AMICIZIA*' – the Italian for 'friendship'.

Finnan played narrower than usual, picking up Pavel Nedved, while two defenders were employed against Zlatan Ibrahimović, one to challenge and one to screen in front of him. But startlingly, Liverpool began at a blistering pace. Fabio Capello's side was on its way to the Serie A title (albeit one they would later be relieved of in the wake of the Calciopoli match-fixing scandal) and had been installed as favourites to become European champions too. Most assumed Benítez, who excelled at taking the heat out of a game, would play it cagey throughout. Instead, he had instructed his team to tear into Juve with a view to establishing a lead and locking it down later. It was a bold gambit and one that paid off, just.

Gerrard introduced himself on Emerson with a thunderous challenge in the opening few seconds of the match and effectively set Juve mentally spinning. It wasn't quite Vinnie Jones on Steve McMahon in the 1988 FA Cup final, but it fulfilled a similar function, asserting intent and control. After ten minutes, Gerrard sent a corner flashing through the Juve six-yard box from the right. Luis García – better in the air than he had any right to be at 5ft 7ins – flicked on for Hyypiä, whose sidefoot from ten yards, aimed firmly through a gap, flew into the unguarded left-hand side of the net.

Anthony Le Tallec, who never delivered on promise he had shown as a prolific youth international for France, then stepped up to make his minor, but crucial, contribution to Liverpool's history. First a trial run: he flicked a ball down the right for García, who checked back and sent a dipping ball across the Juve goal at pace, Baroš millimetres away from sliding in to poke home. Then came what is arguably the greatest goal ever scored at the Anfield Road end, Terry McDermott's powerful header against Spurs in 1977 perhaps the only rival. Bišćan – again quietly asserting himself – guided the ball to the right touchline near the centre-circle, where Finnan smartly kept the ball in play, then fed it slightly inside to Le Tallec, who guided a first-time looping pass further inside, over Baroš and into the path of García. The Spaniard, in order to meet the dropping ball just so, shortened the length of his stride to a rat-a-tat pace, before stroking an arcing screamer with the outside of his left foot and into the top-left corner of the net. In goal, Gianluigi Buffon bent his body back in desperation, but could do nothing to divert the shot. As the ball whipped its way around the inside of the net then rolled back out over the line, Buffon was already sat on the turf, legs splayed, looking back up the field in queasy bemusement. This was the moment Liverpool's dreams crystallised: the moment at which they believed they really did have enough quality to win the competition.

And yet still there was a wobble. As they had against Leverkusen, Liverpool let their opponents back into the tie via a goalkeeping howler, poor Scott Carson – who had in the first half come out on top in a one-on-one duel with Alessandro Del Piero – letting Fabio Cannavaro's downward header straight through the gates. The away goal meant Juventus were still favourites to progress. What followed was a performance in Italy to rank alongside Houllier's greatest caper at Roma back in 2001.

Liverpool were boosted by the return of Xabi Alonso, playing for the first time since suffering his ankle injury four months earlier. That he was mended, and mended well, was proved early as he crashed into Del Piero to the home crowd's displeasure. Alonso – with Bišćan and Antonio Núñez on either shoulder, 'almost as bodyguards', as Benítez put it – bossed a flooded midfield. Juventus carved out only one clear opportunity in open play, Ibrahimović sidefooting a Gianluca Zambrotta cross from the left recklessly over the bar from ten yards. Liverpool confidently absorbed what little Juventus had to offer, the midfield sitting tightly in front of the back three (although they started in a 4–2–3–1, switching after a couple of minutes to confuse Juve). But they weren't entirely negative, breaking with sufficient frequency and menace to prevent Juve ever just pouring men forwards. Alonso swept one delicious pass down the left to spring Baroš into the box, only for the profligate striker to lose his nerve as Buffon closed down the angle and poke weakly wide right.

There was one scare, Del Piero sending a free-kick from the left to the far post, where Cannavaro was inches from repeating his goal at Anfield. Instead, the ball ballooned off the upright, clattered onto the knee of Traoré, scrambling back, and nearly over the line, only for the ball to be scooped out at the last by the hand of Dudek. It was the first of three key moments in Liverpool's campaign where time seemed to slow down as all the stars aligned for them. Eiður Guðjohnsen and Andriy Shevchenko also fated in the future to feel the same impotent pain as Cannavaro.

Juventus had conceded only two goals in their Champions League campaign until they met Liverpool. Now another two had put them out. Suddenly Liverpool's defensive record began to attract notice: en route to a semi-final against Chelsea, they had let in only six themselves (seven if you count the Grazer AK debacle at Anfield in the qualifiers). Chelsea, running away with the Premier League, were favourites to progress, but Liverpool had shown great resilience in Europe.

It was a chance they took. Chelsea, despite hogging the ball for most of the two legs, would carve out only two clear chances in the entire tie – and this a team who had, on their run to the semis, scored five times against Barcelona and six against Bayern Munich. At Stamford Bridge, Liverpool's defending was near perfect, Didier Drogba losing heart early on after a powerful run into the box had been checked by Hyypiä, Carragher covering to shuttle him down a blind alley. It was Lampard who missed the one overt chance, blazing over from six yards. Dudek was nearly beaten by a comical leg-break bowled from the right by Joe Cole, an aimless long hoof which bit into the turf and jagged off to the left, but otherwise there were few scares for the visiting side as they secured a 0–0 draw.

They completed the job at a tumultuous Anfield six days later. Benítez, as he had done in the quarter-final, ordered his men to make use of the incendiary atmosphere and go full pelt at Chelsea from the off. The plan worked again, albeit not quite as spectacularly, and they had to rely on a large slice of fortune to gain the advantage. With only four minutes played, Riise, on the left, fed the ball inside to Gerrard, who artfully scooped a pass through the Chelsea rearguard. Baroš looked to hook it home, but was upended by the outrushing Petr Čech. The ball, knocked past the keeper, clattered off the lunging John Terry and was helped on, weakly, by García. What happened next has never been categorically proven, but the Slovakian referee Luboš Michel believed that, despite William Gallas's efforts to hack it away, the ball crossed the line. Goal. The replays are inconclusive but it seems unlikely that the whole of the ball had gone in; had it not been a goal, though, Michel would have had to give a penalty and send Čech off. José Mourinho's subsequent complaints about the injustice of what he called the 'ghost goal' were never convincing.

However, unlike the Juve match, the Liverpool charge pretty much ended there. Now they had something tangible to lose – a place in their first European Cup final for twenty years – the fear set in. The game developed, without too much exaggeration, into attack versus defence. Chelsea – as the domestic league was proving, the better team – were always likely to dominate proceedings anyway, but Liverpool retreated into their shell. That wasn't necessarily the wisest move. While the goalless draw in Turin, followed by another at Stamford Bridge, had proved they could hold off Europe's best, now they were doing it without Alonso, who had picked up a yellow card in the first leg and was suspended. Gerrard, for all his qualities, could not offer the same sort of control. Bišćan put in another staunch performance alongside Hamann and for the most part Chelsea were reduced to long-range efforts from Drogba and Lampard, well resisted by Dudek. As they resorted to long balls, Benítez described their approach as being 'a little crude', as relying on 'a lottery'.

But the ball kept coming back and something had to give. It eventually did deep in injury time, Dudek failing to meet a cross from the left, the ball landing at the feet of Guðjohnsen, on the right-hand corner of the six-yard box. The goal gaping, the Icelandic striker faltered, shanking his shot straight across the face of goal as Carragher contorted heroically to ensure he didn't bundle it in himself. As Anfield erupted and Liverpool fans cavorted – and, to their eternal credit, the Chelsea players and their manager stayed on the field to watch grimly as their conquerors celebrated a win for the ages   the only fear was that Liverpool's luck might run out in the final.

The Atatürk Olympic Stadium received some poor notices for its hosting of the 2005 Champions League final. Never mind that there were piles of rubble around the outside of the stadium and on the roads leading up to it, or that sourcing a bottle of water and a programme before the match was practically impossible. The main problem was that of accessibility. The Atatürk had seemingly been plonked in the middle of nowhere, a good 20km outside of Istanbul city centre, with transport links that were poor to non-existent. Many fans, having taken six or seven hours to travel from the centre of town or the airport, ended up abandoning their buses and taxis and completing the final few kilometres through the moonscape on foot.

In the end it didn't matter; if anything, it contributes to the legend. Wholly impractical the Atatürk might have been, but its geography lent the event an epic feel from the start. Fans were embarking on a trek into the unknown, reminiscent of the trip to Rome back in 1977, when air travel was less common and the world, vast tranches of it still undiscovered and foreign to the average fan, seemed a far bigger place. Istanbul's location, on the edge of the continent, added a whiff of the exotic anyway; the lunacy of the stadium's position took things into another, almost other-worldly, dimension.

But the match would have had an old-school classic ambience even without the pan-European odyssey. This was one of Europe's great clubs returning to the top table after a twenty-year absence, facing one of the dominant forces of the previous two decades, and the heady atmosphere was commensurate with the event.

Liverpool went into the match as underdogs. Milan had easily dispatched Manchester United in the round of sixteen, before thrashing Internazionale 5–0 on aggregate in the quarters, then edging past a spirited PSV Eindhoven in the semis with a late Massimo Ambrosini header. Seven of their starting line-up had won the tournament in 2003 and they had another two of that year's victors on the bench. The team had spent the year with the *scudetto* on their shirts as reigning Serie A champions, and had just finished second behind a Juventus side later to be stripped of their title.

Benítez's side, by contrast, had finished fifth in the Premier League, having won only two of their final seven league matches, albeit in a period when they were focusing on Europe. It is fashionable now – as indeed it was fashionable then – to write off this Liverpool team as one of the worst to reach a European Cup final. And certainly their late-season domestic form, epitomised by a dismal defeat at relegation-haunted Crystal Palace in April, offers little to counter that view. But there is no question that the team, for all their deficiencies, had sussed out how to get the job done on the continent: on their way to Istanbul, they had been asked to dispose of the 2004 finalists and the champions elect of Italy and England. 'I am thinking in a European way,' shrugged Benítez after the Palace defeat, making no effort to disguise his priority. 'Everything is very different in the Champions League.'

The omens were good. As he waited for the lift in the hotel before final, Benítez noted there were four. If the one on the far left came first, he told himself, Liverpool would lose. If the second one came first they would win. If the third one came first they would draw and lose on penalties. If the fourth one came first, they would draw and win on penalties. The fourth one, needless to say, arrived first. Benítez also – and it seems bizarre for a manager so meticulous, so obsessed by facts – had his lucky underpants on: red ones bearing the picture of the Tasmanian Devil cartoon character. They'd been bought for him by his daughter Claudia and he'd worn them at key moments in Valencia's league and Uefa Cup campaigns, as well as in every round of the Champions League with Liverpool. He also had a lucky Mont Blanc pen that he protected so closely that he refused to get on the plane after the 2006 FA Cup final having been told he couldn't take it in hand-luggage. Eventually the pilot agreed to take it for him.

For the final push against Carlo Ancelotti's *rossoneri* (who would in fact be sporting their white change strip, considered lucky because they'd won all of the European Cup finals they had previously played in it), Benítez sprang a huge selection surprise, leaving the solid and dependable Hamann on the bench, ditching the usual 4-5-1 formation in favour of a 4–4–2 with Harry Kewell playing just off Baroš. Hamann only learned of his omission an hour before kick-off, having taken his place in the team for granted to the extent that, when Benítez announced the starting eleven, he assumed Alonso had been left out rather than him. 'I didn't expect not to be in the team,' he said. 'It was hard to take, but I had to keep focus.'

Jamie Carragher was equally shocked. 'We had reached the final because of our defensive strength, and didn't think it was going to be any different against Milan. We had been playing with Hamann in front of the centre-backs and Stevie [Gerrard] in an advanced role between midfield and the striker, and it was a big surprise to everyone that the boss changed it. He felt he had to go and win the game, that we couldn't sit back, that we had to be a bit bolder.'

Benítez insisted he'd wanted Kewell to close down Pirlo but it's possible that his judgement might also have been clouded by his own professional pride. While solidity was paramount, he occasionally betrayed a thin skin in response to criticism that his teams were overly defensive; witness his satisfaction in Valencia's performance at Anfield in 2004, an attacking masterclass which he gleefully used as a riposte to his naysayers in Spain. But in the end, Benítez is Benítez and there was cold logic to the gamble: Liverpool had won the ties against both Juventus and Chelsea by flying out of the traps to establish a lead to which they would later cling.

The gamble, it's fair to say, didn't pay off. Going into the final, Liverpool had gone 297 minutes in the Champions League without conceding a goal. The totaliser would not tick round to 298. Liverpool kicked off, whereupon Traoré, at left-back, suffered the most traumatic fifty seconds of his career. He rolled a long ball down the left, which was easily cut out, then clumsily clattered into Kaká as Milan came straight for Liverpool down their right. Andrea Pirlo swung in the free-kick towards Paolo Maldini on the edge of the area. The covering midfielder Xabi Alonso, sitting far too deep, was unable to make up the ground to close down the Milan captain, and Maldini had time to hook a volley into the net. Fifty seconds had elapsed, the fastest goal in European Cup final history.

Liverpool responded immediately – and well. Kewell made tracks down the right, before running out of space. Carragher – rarely commended for his perfectly serviceable passing ability, the price of spending the bulk of his career under two managers who demanded he dispatch the ball down the channels from defence at speed – very nearly released Traoré along the left with a low crossfield ball. Baroš won a corner from which Riise hit a powerful and spectacular volley straight at

Jaap Stam, before Hyypiä sent a header from Gerrard's right-wing cross into Dida's hands.

But slowly it became apparent that Benítez had, in his selection, ceded control of the midfield to Milan. Gerrard is many things, but a central midfielder capable of dictating the tempo of his own team's play while disrupting another's? No, or at least not against a midfield containing talents as sublime as Kaká and Pirlo and as ruthless and relentless as Gennaro Gattuso.

The opening goal having arrived before the game had a chance to take any sort of shape, the first sign that Liverpool were struggling in the centre came after six minutes. Pirlo was nominally positioned to patrol in front of his own back four, but with Alonso sitting deep, Riise and Luis García on either flank and Gerrard alone in the middle, the Italian playmaker had plenty of time and room to advance and spread the ball down the flanks as he chose. He released Shevchenko down the right, Finnan having been caught too deep on the other side. With the striker eating up the yards and Liverpool thin in the middle, Hyypiä slid across in the nick of time to block for a corner. The resulting kick betrayed Liverpool's nerves; usually so solid at set pieces, a quick blast of penalty-area pinball ended with Hyypiä slicing a clearance off his shin into the air, and backwards into the hands of Dudek.

Liverpool's defensive line held up better when sitting deeper. Pirlo sent Shevchenko away down the left to set up a session of tippy-tappy triangular passing also involving Maldini, Gattuso and Clarence Seedorf. But there was no way through a narrow, tightly packed back four and Milan's possession was broken up by Gerrard, who raked a pass upfield towards Baroš, the striker nearly racing away from Stam down the inside-right channel. It seemed a throwback to the Houllier years, soaking up pressure then scuttling upfield at pace, and it was a tactic that at times had also borne fruit during the run to the final.

Liverpool, though, seemed unwilling to show such patience and the defence became increasingly caught between staying back at least to gain a foothold in the game and pressing forward looking for a quick and spectacular fix. As a result, Milan prospered. Gattuso teased a high ball into the middle from the right for Shevchenko to chase. The striker bustled his way ahead of a hastily retreating Carragher, only for a flag to be raised for handball. Hernán Crespo battled down the right and won another corner off Hyypiä; from Seedorf's set piece, the Argentinian striker flicked a near-post header goalwards, Luis García stopping the ball on the line with a timely spasm of the shoulder. 'There is no way they can afford to go 2–0 down in this game,' gasped the ITV co-commentator Andy Townsend, prescient as ever.

The probing continued. Kaká nutmegged Alonso in centre-field and Milan flooded forward, Cafú ranging down the right and crossing for Kaká, who guided a poor header left of goal from a promising position. Seedorf, to the left of the centre-circle, stroked a long pass towards Shevchenko who, having romped ahead of the flat-footed Carragher and Hyypiä and blindsided Traoré, narrowly failed to bring the ball down with only Dudek to beat.

Liverpool's disorganisation was illustrated on twenty-three minutes when Kewell, Benítez's great gamble, was forced off with a groin injury, the latest item on a season-long list of niggles that also included calf and ankle problems. Having limped off in the Carling Cup final against Chelsea, after which he found himself arguing with Benítez through the press over the severity of his injury, Kewell departed to boos from the Liverpool end, the assumption of many being that he was crying off when the going got tough. 'I knew after the problems I'd had that everyone would be thinking, "Oh yes, look at this,"' recalled Kewell. 'But what was I supposed to do? Play on?' While the Liverpool fans can be forgiven for siding with Benítez in a snap judgement made during the heat of battle, it's equally understandable that Kewell – not only genuinely injured in this game, but also forbidden from undergoing corrective surgery earlier in the campaign by his manager

– harboured some bitterness as he trudged off, head hung low. It doesn't take much to crack the code of Kewell's statement, issued not long after he left England for the Turkish league in 2008, that 'Liverpool fans don't compare to Galatasaray fans'.

The disappointed Kewell nevertheless had the good grace to wish his replacement, Vladimir Šmicer, all the best. Šmicer's entry – delayed for a couple of minutes as he had forgotten to put his boots on – sent a signal that Benítez was even at that stage unwilling to change his pre-match game-plan. He could have brought on Hamann or even Bišćan and his stubbornness nearly cost Liverpool everything.

For a few minutes, Liverpool seemed to have stemmed the tide, Luis García coming in from the right, where Maldini had hardly afforded him a touch, to play in the hole behind Baroš. A little flick sent the Czech striker off down the left, but Stam held strong to snuff out the attack. Luis García's industry, coupled with some rare upfield support from Gerrard and Alonso, offered brief respite. But Milan were nevertheless holding Liverpool at arm's length and on twenty-eight minutes they seemed to have doubled their advantage. A period of sterile Liverpool possession in the Milan half was broken up when García attempted to trick his way past Seedorf. The ball was quickly shuttled upfield to Kaká, who advanced rapidly on the Liverpool area and poked a pass down the inside-left channel towards Shevchenko, ahead of the Liverpool back-line. The Ukrainian opened up his body and sidefooted gorgeously into the bottom-right corner, only to see the linesman's flag whip up to save Liverpool. It was an incredibly fortunate call for the Reds: Shevchenko had indeed been half a yard offside past Carragher, but it hadn't been Kaká who poked the ball through to him; it had been Gerrard, sliding back and sticking out a desperate leg. The goal should have stood.

Liverpool were beginning to look frantic and increasingly shambolic. On the half hour, Finnan sent a ball into the Milan area from the right, only for Luis García and Riise to get in each other's way. The confusion allowed Gattuso to clear, somewhat unconvincingly, but even then Liverpool betrayed their lack of composure, Baroš hacking wildly in the vague direction of the goal, taking the ball away from the onrushing Alonso.

At least those moments of anxiety were being played out away from danger. A couple of minutes later, Pirlo, operating like a quarterback, once again set Shevchenko away with a pass from the halfway line. The appallingly positioned Traoré, having played the striker onside after failing to push up with Hyypiä and Carragher, made up for his mistake by staying just about strong enough to remain goalside, forcing an off-balance Shevchenko to take a weak swipe at the ball as he fell. Dudek came out to claim, but Liverpool were living dangerously. Crespo twice came close, haring down the left only to find Hyypiä and Finnan closing ranks, then battering the ball straight at Dudek after being sent clear (albeit marginally offside) by Kaká, who was again relaxing in an unacceptably large pocket of space.

Liverpool's few sorties upfield came through Luis García, who had a wild crack at a dropping ball from twenty-five yards – the chance coming from a weak hook cleared by Cafú headed back by Gerrard, a small signal that Milan were far from impregnable at the back themselves – and screwed a shot wide to the right from the left-hand edge of the D with his weaker foot. Then, on thirty-eight minutes, he was sent dancing towards the Milan box down the right by Šmicer, cut inside to enter the area and dinked the ball onto the tip of the right elbow of Alessandro Nesta, sliding across the turf from the centre to snuff out the danger. The award of a penalty would have been extremely harsh on Nesta and Milan – there was no intent – though García and Liverpool were within their rights at least to make the claim.

What momentarily looked like turning the game back in Liverpool's direction took it further the other way. In the wake of the penalty claim, Milan hit Liverpool with an elegant counter. With Alonso, Gerrard and Šmicer all caught in attack, having chased after Luis García in support, Pirlo took them out of play with one pass upfield to Kaká, who immediately shuttled the ball further forward to Shevchenko, free down the right. Carragher, Hyypiä and Traoré, already caught on the hop by the quick break, bunched in the centre as they all followed Crespo, making a diagonal run from right to left. Shevchenko, with the right-hand side of Liverpool's area to himself, slid a ball across the middle, past Traoré and behind the desperately lunging Carragher, for Crespo to sidefoot home at the back post. All the tumblers had fallen into place at once for Milan, Liverpool's once impregnable safe cracked with a flourish.

No team had come from two goals down to win a European Cup final since 1962, when Benfica, inspired by Eusébio, beat Real Madrid 5–3. On the bench, using his lucky Mont Blanc pen, Benítez made a note to bring on Hamann and go to a back three to stiffen the midfield. Liverpool hauled themselves up and, just as they had done upon conceding at the start, responded with vigour, Šmicer meeting a poor Stam clearance from a Riise cross with a low fizzing shot straight at Dida, who fumbled but eventually gathered. But a minute before half-time came another Milan goal, and a fine one at that. Gerrard, considering a probe down the left, was dispossessed by Pirlo, who played a one-two with Cafú deep inside the Milan half. Enter Kaká, who turned Gerrard, and fed Pirlo in the centre. His immediate right-foot flick down the middle sent Crespo ahead of what was left of Liverpool's tattered back-line, Carragher's lunge a mix of the heroic and pathetic. Crespo disdainfully clipped a first-time finish past Dudek to make it 3–0. Liverpool's defensive and midfield performance had teetered between the hopelessly naive and tactically negligent and the game, it seemed, was over.

Liverpool's half-time shenanigans have become the stuff of (rather confused and conflicting) legend. To introduce Hamann, Benítez sacrificed Traoré and switched to three at the back. The hapless full-back took off his boots and trotted to the shower, only to be recalled when it was discovered that Finnan was injured and could not continue (although the Ireland international did not agree and spent the best part of the interval screaming at Benítez to demand reinstatement, only for the physio, Dave Galley, to make the decision he could not last forty-five minutes). The manager then further toyed with his formation on the whiteboard, adding Cissé then removing him, then scrubbing out Luis García's name with a view to redeploying him elsewhere, only to forget to do so. As Liverpool prepared to go out for the second half, there were at various times either twelve or ten names in Benítez's line-up.

Fortunately, the manager had already dealt with the majority of his tactical rejig by giving Hamann his orders, before sending him out to warm up as the bedlam continued in the dressing room. 'One of our major offensive problems in the first half had been the fact that we weren't threatening in and around their penalty box,' explained Benítez. 'So our idea was to change that pattern by using two players in the hole between midfield and Baroš, who was in the centre-forward role on his own. The vital task for these two support strikers was to produce terrific movement, which would help us creatively, but would also put massive pressure on Milan building the play out of defence, through Pirlo in particular. If we could do that then we guessed it would slam the brakes on the damaging work which Gattuso and Seedorf, but most of all Kaká, were doing further up the pitch. The next point was that using three centre-halves would make us much more secure at the back by staying tight on the runs of their twin strikers. Meanwhile Hamann also had the role of making Kaká's life much tougher for him.'

Eleven men were eventually sent back out looking initially simply to save face. Traoré had convinced himself that several of the Milan players were celebrating victory at half-time, an accusation later denied by the Italians, and was accordingly in a righteous funk. Carragher was preoccupied by the thought of receiving mocking texts from Evertonian friends.

Xabi Alonso was aware that 'some of the guys were in pieces', although he himself was more sanguine. 'I knew the importance of still having forty-five minutes left,' he told himself, 'and so I reckoned, "why not?" There was still hope.'

Faith, rather than hope, was the order of the day among the Liverpool support, who during half-time belted out a defiant rendition of 'You'll Never Walk Alone' at a steady, hymn-like, slightly eerie tempo, far closer to Gerry Marsden and the Pacemakers than Craig Johnston and his Anfield Rap. Modern Liverpool crowds have a habit of belting out their anthem at a rapid lick, but this was a touching, dignified moment straight out of the old school.

Did this haunting – or perhaps haunted – version of Liverpool's signature song contribute to the slightly surreal atmosphere which permeated the Atatürk during the opening exchanges of the second half? Possibly, although more prosaically, the almost complete absence of crackle in the air was a simple reaction to the fact that, realistically, the game was as good as over. No team had ever come from three down in a European Cup final to win, and Liverpool, confused and abject in the first half, looked extremely unlikely to buck that trend.

Accompanied by little more than a murmur, the game kicked off again. Liverpool had set themselves up with three central defenders in Hyypiä, Carragher and Traoré, with Riise and Šmicer as attacking wing-backs, Xabi Alonso and Hamann sitting behind Gerrard and Luis García in midfield, and Baroš alone up front. The team did show a couple of signs of recovery in the first few minutes of the half – Hamann had clearly locked onto Kaká and was winning his fair share of loose balls, while Alonso sent a low shot from twenty-five yards just wide of the left-hand post – but they could easily have conceded a couple more during the early exchanges. This match has gone down in the collective memory as the archetypal game of two halves, but Milan's first-half dominance continued nearly nine minutes into the second.

Almost straight from the kick-off, Liverpool's back

three were nearly caught out when Kaká attempted to set Shevchenko free, a ricochet nearly falling at the striker's feet before springing off upfield too quickly for the Milan star to react. A low, hovering Cafú cross from the right wavered in the air, forcing Dudek to save in unorthodox fashion with his knees and palms at the near post. The ball ballooned out to Crespo, who instead of shooting teed up Cafú again, Hyypiä this time lunging in to deflect the ball away from danger.

Then, the turning point. Milan were failing to chase and harry with the intensity they had displayed during the first period, although with the team still in the ascendancy, few watching at the time would have considered that much of a problem. It did, however, betray a certain lack of killer instinct for which they would pay a severe price.

On fifty-two minutes, Traoré clumsily let a simple pass roll under his foot while standing in the centre-circle. Crespo gleefully made off with the ball and knocked it to Kaká, who hared off down the inside-left channel. Sashaying past Hyypiä, about to break clear into the area, he was sent crashing to the ground by the big Finn. This was a red card offence and had the score been 0–0, the referee Manuel Mejuto González would surely have sent Hyypiä off. As it was, he shirked the decision, perhaps taking pity on a Liverpool side surely already defeated. But if the referee was at fault, then Milan were professionally negligent too. Hyypiä, fearing the worst, held Kaká's shoulders and begged 'Please, please'. The long hours spent by the God-fearing Brazilian studying the Bible might have done Liverpool some favours here; Kaká forgave the sinner and turned the other cheek, opting not to harangue the referee but quietly walk away instead. The referee, feeling no pressure to act, merely pointed goalwards for Milan to take their free-kick. Hyypiä was not even booked.

And even then – even then – it should not have mattered, for from the resulting set-piece Shevchenko hit a ferocious shot that arrowed towards the bottom-right corner. Dudek, emerging at this point as a hero merely in face-saving terms, stuck out a strong left arm to turn the ball round for a corner. Milan – not that they could possibly have known it – had just spurned their chance to put Liverpool away. Within a minute, the game was back on.

The corner was cleared. Alonso attempted to shuttle the ball up the right, but was robbed by Maldini, who then shanked an out-of-character pass straight across the face of the Liverpool area. The mistake allowed Liverpool to surge upfield. Riise intercepted the ball, exchanged passes with Gerrard, then made off down the left. His gallop stopped by Gattuso, Riise turned back and left the ball for Gerrard. Liverpool suddenly felt the benefit of their extra man in midfield. Gerrard, Alonso and Hamann nudged the ball inside and back out to the left, where Riise had moved to the touchline. The wing-back's first cross was blocked by Cafú, but his second attempt to get the ball into the box found the head of Gerrard, ten yards out. The Liverpool captain, neck as periscope, guided a clever header into the top-right corner, though Dida's attempt to scuttle over and stop the ball going in was thoroughly half-hearted, his lack of vim compounded by what appeared to be a misjudgement of the flight. The Liverpool fans erupted, the air alive again, the match suddenly back on, even if the odds on a full recovery were still outlandish.

Milan, shamefully, dismally, failed to respond. Liverpool and their supporters were too caught up in the excitement of renewed hope to realise it, but demons, consciously or subconsciously, had suddenly surrounded the Italian team. In the quarter-final of the previous year's Champions League, they had, as reigning champions, taken a 4–1 lead to Deportivo La Coruña, only to capitulate abysmally at the Riazor, losing 4–0. No team had previously given up such a comprehensive first-leg lead in Champions League history. The first three goals in that game had come in the opening forty-five minutes; Milan were perfectly capable of serving up a half as bad as their first half in Istanbul had been good.

Perhaps more pertinently, they had shown appalling

late-season form in Serie A, failing to win a single game in May as they collapsed during the title run-in to gift the *scudetto* to Juventus. Their championship hopes had been extinguished in the penultimate round of matches; requiring a win at home to Palermo to keep their faint flame aflicker, they were 3–1 up with thirteen minutes to play but conceded two goals in quick succession and were held to a 3–3 draw. Liverpool's task might still have seemed unlikely, but they were not playing a team well-disposed to coping with pressure.

Milan froze. Even with over half an hour to play, Gerrard's goal should really have been nothing more than a consolation for previously battered opponents, but instead a strange inevitability settled over the Atatürk. Milan let Liverpool straight back into the game, resisting the regenerated team's pressure for no more than two minutes. Baroš was caught offside down the left and was flagged accordingly, but González waved play on. It was another questionable decision by the official, with no discernible advantage to Milan. Still, there's no excuse for the slipshod and somnolent way in which the *rossoneri* responded. Gattuso gifted the ball to Traoré, who immediately won a throw down the left. It was at this point that Kaká's shinpad slipped out. Disgracefully, with Liverpool on the front foot and on the attack, the Brazilian opted to readjust his sock while the game went on. Alonso, on his shoulder, was therefore given time and space to roll the ball inside to Hamann, who moved it on further right for Šmicer, coming in from the right. Šmicer took a touch and zipped a magnificent low shot that crept into the bottom-left corner, Baroš twisting himself into a C-shape to avoid taking the sting out of the shot. Dida once again failed to do his job properly, his hand weakly meeting the shot and flapping back, the ball bowling on through.

Consolation had turned into catalyst. Suddenly a preposterous recovery *really was on*. And even then, Milan failed to rise from their second-half slumber. It was old-school English pressure: Luis García, Gerrard and Hamann all took turns to lump or head balls straight down the middle, Milan's centre-back pairing of Stam and Nesta looking worryingly shaky under every one. Their midfield, meanwhile, so dominant for the first fifty-three minutes, was finding it almost impossible to string two passes together. And again an inexplicable lack of energy was to be their final undoing. Their players failed to press in the centre of the field, wandering around aimlessly like sprites in a carelessly programmed computer game; Carragher, of all people, was invited to bomb forward down the right. He presented the ball to Baroš, who looked to release Gerrard with a back flick. Gattuso, lightly but nonetheless clumsily, sent Liverpool's captain crashing to the floor from behind. Penalty.

Alonso equalised, roofing the equaliser off the rebound, Dida finally doing the decent thing and saving the penalty well to his right. But the unsung hero during Liverpool's march to parity had arguably been Baroš. Having already adroitly avoided getting in the way of Šmicer's goal, then setting up Gerrard in the move which led to the penalty, he completed a personal trifecta by cynically grappling with Nesta on the edge of the area as Alonso ran up to take his penalty. His final tug on the Italian defender was crucial, giving Alonso extra time to get across to the rebound, a millisecond or two ahead of Nesta's despairing lunge.

The magnitude of what had happened in those six minutes seemed to slap both teams back into reality. A couple of minutes after the equaliser, Riise sent a rising effort goalwards from the edge of the Milan area, Gerrard having cushioned a ball inside from the left touchline, but Dida parried into the air and collected. Five more minutes had elapsed when Milan finally responded, Dudek awkwardly shovelling a Kaká cross from the left into the air, Shevchenko spinning to send a shot towards the bottom-right corner, Traoré enjoying a moment of redemption as he cleared off the line. But that was the sum of the whirlwind in the regulation ninety minutes as the game morphed into the defensive chess match everyone had assumed it would be from the start, nobody willing to gamble.

Liverpool's recovery had revived confidence in their own ability. They had a nose-to-nose, toe-to-toe presence in the midfield now; if they didn't win the first tackle, they were more often than not picking up the second-phase ball. Luis García began to float dangerously in the hole, on one occasion beating Seedorf and making it to the touchline, where he shot against Dida's shins at the near post, on another nearly taking down Gerrard's crossfield rake down the same channel, the ball hitting his chest hard as he edged ahead of Maldini.

But it was Milan who finished stronger. Shevchenko raced after a Pirlo floater down the right, but was crowded out by a pincer movement from Hyypiä and Traoré. Crespo declined to shoot from a tight angle on the right and laid off for Kaká, whose concentration was snapped by the increasingly influential Carragher. Serginho came on for Seedorf and, with a splash more trickery and pace, began to trouble the makeshift wing-back Šmicer.

For the few minutes that remained of normal time – and indeed, as it would transpire, for the entirety of extra-time – Benítez and his side opted to sit back and keep what they had, an understandable decision given their efforts to drag themselves back into contention, and yet it was hard to avoid the thought that, with the momentum, they might have kept going and seen if Milan would yield again.

After his recalibration, Milan moved forward with more pace and purpose whenever they had the ball, but even so did not throw too many men forward. When they finally did, they nearly won the trophy in the dying moments of normal time: Shevchenko burst through only to be denied by Carragher's last-ditch tackle, Stam sent a penalty-spot header left of the goal from the corner that resulted and then Kaká came close to turning it in at the far post. Not for the first time, or the last, Liverpool could consider themselves very fortunate still to be standing.

Yet they had made it to extra-time. It was a position they could scarcely have dreamt of at half-time, but there were concerns that control of the game, violently wrested from Milan in the early stages of the second half, was slipping back to their opponents. Cissé's late introduction for Baroš had not helped; in shades of the Chelsea semi-final at Anfield, the ball was not sticking to the French striker and kept coming back at Liverpool – another illustration of the underrated Baroš's subtle but important contribution.

Benítez stuck with three at the back during extra-time, though Liverpool played deeper, and Gerrard took over from Šmicer as the right wing-back to cope with the new threat of Serginho, specifically his pace. Gerrard's success in the role, one he had gained experience of during the Houllier era, was mixed – he was constantly nagging at the Brazilian but the Milan player still proved a major irritant. In the first period, Serginho swung a ball in from the left that caught Traoré, out on the other side, on the back foot; Jon Dahl Tomasson, cutting in from the right, was inches from connecting at close range. In the second period, he engaged in a memorable duel with Carragher, putting in two consecutive crosses from the left, each one deflected acrobatically, each time the block resulting in agonising cramps for the defender.

Carragher's travails were astonishingly brave, but proof that Liverpool were beginning to run on empty. A third Serginho cross was headed clear by Hyypiä. Pirlo, checked on the left-hand edge of the area by a desperate Hamann, saw his whipped, flat free-kick deflected over by the staunch Luis García. Hyypiä cleared with his head again, from Serginho, this time from the right.

It had become attack versus defence. Cissé was by then almost totally incapable of holding it up; even when he managed to waste a few seconds and lay the ball off to a teammate, the striker would fail to offer himself in space for the return. At both ends of the pitch, this was the Chelsea match all over again. And there would be a similar Guðjohnsen-style denouement, Liverpool getting away with it once more as time again seemed to slow.

Serginho swung the ball in from the left, this time over Hyypiä. Shevchenko, at the near post, headed goalwards. Dudek parried, but only straight back to the Ukraine striker. With less than two minutes of extra-time remaining, Liverpool's comeback appeared to be in vain. Shevchenko lined up a right-footed strike as the ball dropped and hammered a shot at goal. Somehow, the ball struck Dudek, ballooned into the air and looped miraculously over the bar. The luckiest escape.

Or was it? 'Dudek positioned himself even before Shevchenko made contact with that great header,' the Liverpool goalkeeping coach José Manuel Ochotorena told Guillem Ballagué in *A Season on the Brink*. 'And he had his arms positioned correctly ... It was about technical ability as well as pure instinct. But what you have to do next in that situation is concentrate on the rebound. You have to get back in the game immediately ... The body instinctively tends to go to ground even more when the save is near the goal-line. If your body position is hunched low when the ball is struck, then the likelihood is that the ball will continue on its trajectory towards the back of the net. But if the keeper gets up and stands tall, then he's like a wall. We worked really, really hard on these concepts with Dudek in training ... In that precise moment, psychology was important because Dudek was more calculating than Shevchenko.'

In real time, Dudek appeared to have done nothing more – nothing more! – than get in the way. There was, however, a camera squinting at the play from far down the other end of the ground, straight at the Liverpool goal. From that perspective, it's possible to spot Dudek's left arm go up to block the shot. It was an instinctive point-blank save of sheer brilliance. This was the moment when Milan must surely have decided it simply wasn't going to happen for them. The assault on the Liverpool goal, practically relentless throughout extra-time, was over. Milanese faces, to a man, suddenly had a glazed, washed-out look.

Dudek's hand-waving, star-jumping and spaghetti-legged antics are understandably the most memorable element of the keeper's heroics during the subsequent penalty shootout. (Carragher had demanded that he perform a Bruce Grobbelaar tribute act on the line. 'He's a really nice fella,' Carragher said. 'I thought he'd just stand in the goal being dead polite and nice.') But the Shevchenko save was the moment that broke Milan's spirit.

Serginho, so brilliant in extra-time, set the tone for the penalties by launching his kick into orbit, before walking off wearing a pained expression. Dudek, it should be noted, had guessed the direction of the kick correctly. Or perhaps it wasn't a guess. The goalkeeping coach Ochotorena had studied Milan's takers and signalled to Dudek which way to dive.

Hamann scored, a nervous stutter with a broken toe. Pirlo, shoulders drooping, took the ball off Dudek, who had decided personally to deliver it to each Milan player in order to make himself seem larger. (Dudek also enticed them a step past the spot for the handover, ensuring the goal looked that little bit further away when they shuttled back to twelve yards.) Pirlo, a broken genius, hit a weak effort to Dudek's right. The keeper – having taken three outrageous steps off his line – parried easily. The kick should have been retaken, but once more fortune favoured Liverpool. 'Kick the ball away and get booked if you like,' Carragher had advised Dudek. 'Just do anything to gain an advantage. Fuck it.'

Cissé, who had scored from the penalty spot against Aston Villa in the last league game of the season, sidefooted confidently into the right-hand side of the goal, a positive contribution at long last. Tomasson put his kick into the bottom left. As the ball sailed in that direction, an ambulance, presumably containing some poor Milan fan unable to cope with the drama, zipped off round the track behind the goal.

Then, for the only time since Gerrard had headed what looked like a consolation goal for Liverpool, the tide turned Milan's way. Riise, who should have put his foot through the ball in trademark fashion, attempted to steer one into the bottom-left corner, but Dida kept it out with a strong hand. Kaká, following, was never going to miss, something Dudek almost seemed to realise from the off, his spaghetti legs routine half-hearted; the Brazilian roofed it to the left.

It was 2–2, and suddenly the pressure was on Šmicer. Benítez had been worried that he was exhausted and indeed he was, cramping severely, but the Czech insisted he had enough energy to take a penalty. He probably took the best one of all, a firm sidefoot high into the right-hand side of the net. Šmicer kissed the badge; not a bad last kick in a club career which had promised more than had been delivered.

And then Andriy Shevchenko stepped up. He had scored the winning kick when Milan had beaten Juve on penalties in the 2003 final and, needing to score to force Gerrard into converting Liverpool's fifth, he sent his kick straight down the middle. Dudek had set off to his right, but alert in the moment, readjusted himself at the last and stuck out his left leg.

Steven Gerrard – captain, local hero, star player, driving force, scorer of Liverpool's first goal, the player who earned the equalising penalty, the man who played in three different positions during the match, forever subservient to the team's cause – is commonly cited as the man of the 2005 Champions League final. Jamie Carragher is also often mentioned in dispatches, the bleakly comic image of him holding his cramped thighs in extra-time after desperately throwing himself in front of incessant Milan attacks – 'He's done both groins,' as Andy Townsend memorably noted – the perfect illustration of a heroic performance.

But it is Dudek who should surely go down as Liverpool's true hero of their greatest match. The Pole, despite a career at Anfield which could most generously be described as inconsistent, was popular with fans – his working-class mining background chimed with the down-to-earth ethos of the club and the city – although most knew his time was running out, with the signing of Villarreal's José Reina an open secret. Certainly, few would have bet much before the match on Dudek being their prospective star turn.

Indeed for the majority of the game, his performance was as erratic as many worried Liverpool supporters had suspected it might be. Although he couldn't be blamed for any of Milan's goals in the first half and made a pivotal save from Shevchenko's free-kick just before Liverpool launched their comeback, he also made a couple of trademark handling errors in the second period which could easily have cost Liverpool the match.

But nobody in Liverpool red put in a fault-free performance, so it would be unfair to criticise Dudek too much for those. And it was the keeper when Liverpool, despite 118 minutes of burning effort, looked to be fizzling out who stepped up, seized the game and became the author of its denouement. From the double save from Shevchenko to the penalty shoot-out, this was a one-man show. No other player so decisively seized his moment.

In any case, it's a very modern habit of fans to insist the big names get the most credit. So many of Liverpool's greatest achievements have been shaped by unlikely heroes: Jackie Balmer in 1946–47, Gerry Byrne in 1965, Tommy Smith in 1977, Alan Kennedy in 1981 and 1984. Steven Gerrard, steeped in Liverpool tradition, would, you suspect, understand that too. Dudek it is, then.

As the players celebrated in the dressing room at the Atatürk, their former manager Gérard Houllier popped his head round the door. A few players, such as Xabi Alonso, thought it 'a bit strange', while Houllier's former assistant Phil Thompson later said that, despite feeling a tinge of jealousy at no longer being involved, he would have certainly not gone down to encroach on 'Rafa's day'. (In any case, he was busy making a magnificent show of himself on Sky Sports, where he was nominally a pundit but essentially became the everyman Red, gloriously losing himself in the moment, thumping on the glass separating studio and pitch with delirious glee.)

Houllier has received a bad press for his dressing-room visit, though he has never tried to claim any credit for Liverpool's glory. 'I was feeling a bit apprehensive because, after all, it was they and Rafael Benítez who had won the trophy,' he said, although old habits die hard and he couldn't quite help himself from pointing out that, 'The only thing I had contributed was the fourth-place finish the previous season that got them into the competition.'

Still, he deserved to share a few hugs with players he had worked with for several years – 'I was so proud of their performance ... I never fell out of love with Liverpool ... I'm a fan for life' – and he also deserves a little credit for the Champions League win. Unquestionably it was Benítez's achievement, but it was one which could never have been were it not for the triumphs and tribulations of the Houllier era. Those years gave the team's beating-heart triumvirate of Carragher, Hyypiä and Gerrard the big-match experience that proved vital to the Milan turnaround, not to mention the solid team shape upon which Benítez could build a more expansive Liverpool by slotting in the likes of Alonso and Luis García. Just as Paisley had conquered Europe after embellishing Shankly's blueprint, so Benítez had relied on Houllier's foundation work to reach the top.

The managerial achievements of Houllier and Benítez, while genuinely from the top drawer and strangely underappreciated in the wider football world, cannot of course be compared to those of Shankly and Paisley. Benítez, having set himself an almost impossible task of matching his early achievement at Anfield, never quite made it. He gave it a good try, though, winning the FA Cup final the following year – Gerrard can certainly have the man-of-the-match award for *that* one – and taking his team to a second Champions League final in 2007.

Again they played Milan, this time in Athens, and this time

they were much the better side. Football being football, Milan ran out 2–1 winners. For the first time, some fans questioned Benítez's team selection. Craig Bellamy and Peter Crouch seemed the pair most likely to cause Milan's superannuated back-line trouble. Bellamy remained benched, while Crouch came on for the last twelve minutes, causing the bedlam which led to Dirk Kuyt's goal, but by then Pippo Inzaghi had scored twice and the game was – really – over. Benítez used his post-match press conferences to criticise the spending plans of the club's new owners, Tom Hicks and George Gillett; the ensuing battle would define the rest of his period in charge, shades of Valencia, albeit a fight which, with the very survival of the club suddenly in question, needed to be fought.

Benítez's bravery in defending Liverpool's honour off the field was not quite matched on the pitch and the 2008–09 season stands as the most heartbreaking league challenge since the long drought began in 1990. Liverpool led the table for half of the season, having got into their stride after chancing a couple of close early-season victories. A 5–1 romp at Newcastle during the Christmas break sent out a message that this might be the year. But draws proved to be their undoing, careless ones (the 2–2 at home to Hull, having gone two down in twenty-two minutes) causing less damage than overly cautious ones (goalless at home against Stoke, Fulham, West Ham, late equalisers conceded from comfortable positions against Everton and Wigan). After a miserable 2–0 defeat towards the end of February at Middlesbrough – Boro again – Benítez took the shackles off. Too late: despite one of the most spectacular weeks in Liverpool's entire history – a 4–0 Champions League shellacking of Real Madrid, a 4–1 win at Manchester United and a 5–0 rout of a decent Aston Villa side – they could never rein back United. Liverpool came in second, four points adrift and with a painful sense of a chance gone begging. Adding insult to injury, it was United's eighteenth title. A nineteenth would come two years later, finally surpassing Liverpool's record.

It was Liverpool's last hurrah. Since then, Benítez has departed, Roy Hodgson never seemed to have a feel for the job and Kenny Dalglish returned for a semi-successful stint, winning a League Cup while never producing consistently in the league. Then Brendan Rodgers was appointed to bring a smidgen of pass-and-move entertainment back to Liverpool for the first time since the Roy Evans era.

Where next? Liverpool have found themselves drifting through fallow periods before – the 1910s, the 1930s, the 1950s and the 1990s – each time bouncing back to the top, each period with a different, distinct flavour. Given the fanbase, it is surely only a matter of time. But even if better days aren't coming back any time soon, Liverpool fans can take succour in an unparalleled history, as glorious and gilded as that of any club in the world.

BIBLIOGRAPHY

Balague, Guillem, *A Season on the Brink: Rafael Benítez, Liverpool and the Path to Glory* (Orion, 2005)

Benítez, Rafa, *Champions League Dreams* (Headline, 2012)

Bowler, Dave, *Shanks: The Authorised Biography of Bill Shankly* (Orion, 1996)

Carragher, Jamie with Chris Bascombe, *Carra: My Autobiography* (Corgi, 2009)

Dalglish, Kenny with Henry Winter, *Kenny Dalglish: My Autobiography* (Stodder, 1997)

with John Keith, *The Liverpool Year* (Willow, 1988)

Darby, Tom, *Talking Shankly: the Man, the Genius, the Legend* (Mainstream, 1998)

Du Noyer, Paul, *Liverpool: Wondrous Place, Music from the Cavern to the Coral* (Virgin, 2004)

Fagan, Andrew and Mark Platt, *Joe Fagan: Reluctant Champion* (Aurum, 2011)

Fowler, Robbie with David Maddock, *Fowler: My Autobiography* (Macmillan, 2007)

Gerrard, Steven with Henry Winter, *Gerrard: My Autobiography* (Bantam, 2006)

Glanville, Brian, *Champions of Europe: The History, Romance and Intrigue of the European Cup* (Guinness, 1991)

Goldblatt, David, *The Ball is Round: A Global History of Football* (Viking, 2006)

Graham, Matthew, *Liverpool* (Hamlyn, 1984)

Green, Geoffrey, *The Official History of the FA Cup* (Naldrett, 1949, rev. ed. Heinemann, 1960)

Hale, Steve and Ivan Ponting, *Liverpool in Europe* (Guinness, 1992)

Hamann, Dietmar, *The Didi Man: My Love Affair with Liverpool* (Headline, 2012)

Hansen, Alan, with Jason Tomas, *A Matter of Opinion* (Partridge, 1999)

Hey, Stan, *A Golden Sky: The Liverpool Dream Team* (Mainstream, 1997)

Hill, Dave, *Out of His Skin: The John Barnes Phenomenon* (WSC, 2001)

Hopkins, Stephen, 'The Modern Origins and Development of the Liverpool Way' in John Williams, Stephen Hopkins and Cathy Long (eds), *Passing Rhythms: Liverpool FC and the Transformation of Football* (Berg, 2001)

Hyypiä, Sami with Okki Halala, *From Voikka to the Premiership* (Mainstream, 2003)

Inglis, Simon (ed.), *Charles Buchan's Liverpool Gift Book: Selections from Football Monthly 1951–1973* (Malavan, 2008)
　Football Grounds of Britain (Collins Willow, 1996)
Keith, John, *Billy Liddell: The Legend who Carried the Kop* (Robson, 2003)
　Bob Paisley: Manager of the Millennium (Robson, 2000)
　The Essential Shankly (Robson, 2001)
　Liverpool: Champions of Europe (Duckworth, 1977)
　(ed.), *Liverpool Supreme* (Cockerel, 1986)
Kelly, Stephen, *Bill Shankly: It's Much More Important than That* (Virgin, 1996)
　The Boot Room Boys (Collins Willow, 1996)
　The Liverpool Encyclopedia: An A-Z of Liverpool (Mainstream, 2001)
Kennedy, Alan with John Williams, *Kennedy's Way: Inside Bob Paisley's Liverpool* (Mainstream, 2005)
Lane, Tony, *Liverpool: City of the Sea* (Liverpool University Press, 1997)
LLoret, Paco, *Rafa Benítez* (Dewi Lewis, 2005)
Lloyd, Larry, *Hard Man, Hard Game* (John Blake, 2009)
Motson, John and John Rowlinson, *The European Cup 1955–1980* (Queen Anne, 1980)
Parkinson, Michael, *Liverpool on the Brink* (Hermitage, 1985)
Phillips, Darren, *Better than the Brazilians: Liverpool's 1987–88 Season* (Carnegie, 1999)
Platt, Mark, *Cup Kings: Liverpool 1965* (Bluecoat, 2000)
　Cup Kings: Liverpool 1977 (Bluecoat, 2003)
Ponting, Ivan, *Red and Raw: A Post-War History of Manchester United v Liverpool* (Andre Deutsch, 1999)
　The Book of Football Obituaries (Know the Score, 2012)
Reade, Brian, *43 Years with the Same Bird: A Liverpudlian Love Affair* (Macmillan, 2008)
　An Epic Swindle: 44 months with a Pair of Cowboys (Quercus, 2010)
Scraton, Phil, *Hillsborough: The Truth* (Mainstream, 2009)
Shankly, Bill with John Roberts, *Bill Shankly: My Story* (Trinity Mirror, 2013)
　The Lost Diary (Sport Media, 2013)
Shaw, Gary and Mark Platt, *At the End of the Storm: The Remarkable Story of Liverpool FC's Greatest Ever League Title Triumph* (Gary Shaw, 2009)
St John, Ian, *Liverpool: The Glory Decade 1980–1990* (Sidgwick & Jackson, 1990)
Taylor, Rogan and Andrew Ward, *Kicking and Screaming: An Oral History of Football in England* (Robson, 1998)
　Three Sides of the Mersey: An Oral History of Everton, Liverpool and Tranmere Rovers (Robson, 1998)
Thompson, Phil, *Liverpool in the Eighties* (Tempus, 2006)
　Liverpool in the Seventies (Tempus, 2005)
Wagg, Stephen, *The Football World* (Harvester, 1984)
Wangerin, David, *Soccer in a Football World: The Story of America's Forgotten Game* (WSC, 2006)
Ward, Andrew with John Williams, 'Bill Shankly and Liverpool' in John

Williams, Stephen Hopkins and Cathy Long (eds), *Passing Rhythms: Liverpool FC and the Transformation of Football* (Berg, 2001)

Williams, John, *Red Men: Liverpool Football Club – The Biography* (Mainstream, 2011)

'Kopies, Scallies and Liverpool Fan Cultures: Tales of Triumph and Disasters' in John Williams, Stephen Hopkins and Cathy Long (eds), *Passing Rhythms: Liverpool FC and the Transformation of Football* (Berg, 2001)

Williams, John, Stephen Hopkins and Cathy Long (eds), *Passing Rhythms: Liverpool FC and the Transformation of Football* (Berg, 2001)

Wilson, Alan, *The Team of All the Macs* (Vertical, 2011)

Wilson, Jonathan, *Inverting the Pyramid: A History of Football Tactics* (Orion, 2008)

The Outsider: A History of the Goalkeeper (Orion, 2012)

Websites
guardian.co.uk
kjellhanssen.com
lfchistory.net
soccerbase.com
statto.com

Magazines
Liverpool 87–88 Uncut (Sport)

Newspapers
Daily Express
Daily Mirror
Guardian
Independent
Independent on Sunday
Liverpool Echo
Liverpool Mercury
Liverpool Post
Manchester Guardian
Observer
Sporting Life
Sunday Times
The Times

INDEX